1993

John E. Hanke
Arthur G. Reitsch

Eastern Washington University

Fundamentals of
Business Statistics

Charles E. Merrill Publishing Company
A Bell & Howell Company
Columbus   Toronto   London   Sydney

Published by Charles E. Merrill Publishing Co.
A Bell & Howell Company
Columbus, Ohio 43216

This book was set in Century Schoolbook and Frutiger
Cover Design: Cathy Watterson
Text Design and Production Coordination: Mary Harlan

Chapter 11 Case Study, "Brown Bottling Company" (pp. 225–28; adapted) and Exercise 29 (pp. 232–33), Chapter 12 Figure 12–5 (p. 245), Figure 12–7 (p. 253), and Exercises 25 and 26 (pp. 268–72) from John E. Hanke, Arthur G. Reitsch, and John Dickson, *Statistical Decision Models for Management,* © 1984. Reprinted by permission of Allyn & Bacon, Inc., Boston.

Library of Congress Catalog Card Number: 85–62478
International Standard Book Number: 0–675–20333–3
Printed in the United States of America
1 2 3 4 5 6 7 8 9—91 90 89 88 87 86

PREFACE

In our consulting work we find that many mid-level and senior executives do not understand the most elementary statistical concepts. At the same time, we are encouraged that younger business people are being exposed to statistics and quantitative methods in their business degree programs and are becoming more aware of the usefulness of statistics. A person entering the world of business today without some awareness of statistical tools and their applications is at the mercy of colleagues and competitors whose knowledge of statistics is superior.

Our purpose in writing this textbook is to enhance the learning of statistics on the part of business students and others whose future careers require knowledge of ways to convert data into useful information. The text is designed to accommodate both the quarter system and the semester system. In the former case, we suggest study of the material through hypothesis testing, which is the usual stopping place for a one-quarter course in statistics. For programs on the semester system, additional material on regression analysis, index numbers, and time-series analysis has been included to provide students with a complete introductory exposure to a wide range of statistical applications.

The prerequisite for study of this text is a basic mathematical ability, specifically the ability to perform and understand simple arithmetic. No calculus or advanced mathematical ability is assumed. In our own teaching we have found that almost any mathematics course beyond algebra is adequate for a successful mastery of skills necessary to understand statistics. We find that a specific mathematics course is not as important as an exposure to the orderly and logical thinking required for a passing grade in almost any mathematics course.

It is our hope that this text will provide an understandable approach to a subject that students often fear and postpone in their degree programs. Over the course of several years of teaching, consulting, and textbook writing, we have found a few keys to explaining concepts that can easily become buried in formulas and inadequate examples. We have devoted a majority of our effort to the subjects through hypothesis testing, because those subjects make up the essential content of a first statistics course. This leaves the professor with a wide range of fine choices for a more advanced text in subsequent quantitative courses. We hope students will appreciate not having to pay for several hundred pages of text that will never be used in their first course.

Students and professors will find two unique features of this text useful. First, the data base in Appendix I includes a population of data values covering nine variables on the 200 employees of a fictitious company. A number of chapter-end problems throughout the text refer to this data base.

Secondly, a Student Questionnaire appears following this Preface. We find it useful to have students fill out this questionnaire during the first class period. The numerical responses in raw form are then given to each student to use in working several of the homework problems. Since the questionnaire involves both numerical and non-numerical responses, we find it helpful in demonstrating several statistical techniques using actual classroom data. Questions involving the use of questionnaire data appear at the end of several text chapters when appropriate; the data for these questions are the data values collected from the student questionnaire and are referred to in the problems as the class data base.

We are grateful to hundreds of our students over several years who have helped us develop understandable explanations for the concepts in this text. We also thank our faculty colleagues who contributed ideas, problems, and examples for our use. We appreciate the many helpful comments and suggestions made by Stewart Fliege, Pepperdine University; J. J. Kustura, Saint Louis University; Robert Leekley, Illinois Wesleyan University; Pat Maddox, Lubbock Christian College; Robert E. Meier, Eastern Illinois University; Jeff Mock, Diablo Valley College; Joseph Monks, Gonzaga University; William E. Pinney, University of Texas at Arlington; George Q. Strong, University of Alabama; and E. J. Willies, Virginia Beach, Virginia.

Finally, we are eternally grateful to the developers of microcomputers and word-processing software; without their efforts we would still be writing this book.

STUDENT QUESTIONNAIRE
FOR CLASS DATA BASE

1. Class standing:

_____ Freshman _____ Sophomore _____ Junior

_____ Senior _____ Graduate _____ Other

2. Sex: _____ Male _____ Female

3. High school grade point average: _____

4. Current cumulative college grade point average (all colleges attended): _____

5. Age: _____

6. Average number of hours worked per week during current school term: _____

Place one of the following numbers beside statements seven through ten to indicate your level of agreement:

    1   Strongly agree

    2   Agree

    3   Neutral or no opinion

    4   Disagree

    5   Strongly disagree

_____ **7.** Statistics will be an important part of my work-life after I leave college.

_____ **8.** The business administration program should be less structured and allow more electives.

_____ **9.** It would be a good idea to impose more difficult admission requirements for entry into the business administration program.

_____ **10.** Given the nature of statistics, I would prefer to have a quiz each week.

CONTENTS

9   ESTIMATION   159

10   GENERAL CONCEPTS OF HYPOTHESIS TESTING   183

1

Introduction to Statistics

**Where You
Have Been**
Unlike other business or social science courses, statistics is a subject you probably know little about. At first, you may find it difficult to achieve the analytical state of mind necessary to understand and apply the concepts used in statistical investigations. However, as your understanding of the basic ideas begins to grow, you will find that statistics will become easier and that your past experiences will become more relevant.

**Where You
Are Going**
This chapter lays the foundation for the study of specific statistical techniques that are widely used in the management of all organizations and introduces a few important terms and general concepts.

DECISION MAKING UNDER UNCERTAINTY

Decision making under uncertainty might stand as an accurate definition of the entire business administration or management process. Indeed, the main function of managers in all organizations is to make decisions about customers, competitors, government actions, weather, unions, and many other factors in the face of uncertainty. Persons who demonstrate their skill at making such decisions over a period of time tend to become executives, assume considerable responsibility, and draw large salaries. Those who are unskilled at making such decisions assume jobs with lower pay and skill requirements.

Many years ago it was possible to compete in the decision-making arena without possessing quantitative or statistical skills because not many people had these skills. The best decision makers had the best intuitive feeling for a situation and could make decisions on this basis better than their competitors. But it is no longer possible to compete as a decision maker without analytical as well as intuitive skills.

The emphasis throughout this book is on the analytical or quantitative elements of decision making. These factors are not the only elements of good decision making or even the most important in every case. Rather, studying the statistical skills necessary for good decision making is the task at hand; other texts and courses deal with the qualitative features of organizational problems.

Also, the quantitative factors discussed in this text are vital for proper understanding of effective decision making because these factors are so difficult to assimilate informally or intuitively. In our consulting work, we are often amazed that managers who are responsible for important organizational decisions have little understanding of vital statistical concepts. It always takes some adjustment for prospective young managers to leave a classroom where they are deeply involved in rather sophisticated analyses of data to meet with mid-level and upper-level managers who have little understanding of the most basic elements of statistics.

But this is changing. In five or ten years these managers will be retiring, and the students who grappled with statistical concepts in their college classrooms will replace them. As the level of statistical sophistication is raised, it becomes more important to have a solid understanding of the quantitative elements of decision making.

Data to Information

The first step in the effective decision-making process in any organization is to convert data into useful information. Data are composed of countless numbers that are generated in any organization to describe transactions. Unless there are only a few pieces of data in a situation, the collected data elements exhibit little or no useful information; that is, there are so many numbers that data cannot be assimilated and used in the decision-making process.

In contrast, we use the word information to mean data that have been processed or summarized so that their essential features become evident and can be used in decision making. Decision makers need information to help them guide the company—the more information the better. Decision makers do not need vast quantities of untreated data; modern organizations equipped with electronic computers can generate rooms full of data. But it takes a skillful manager to convert data into information that will be helpful in the decisions that must be made.

Information to Action

The second step in the decision-making process is to use the information extracted from the data in a meaningful way. Decision makers must understand how the data were converted to information so that they can place the proper amount of credence on the results. Putting an inappropriate amount of trust in statistical results, especially if information has been generated by an "error-free" computer, is very dangerous. A lack of understanding of statistical concepts not only leaves managers in a weak position for effective decision making but also puts them at the mercy of others whose understanding of the quantitative aspects of a situation are superior.

The steps involved in converting data to information to action are performed by decision makers in every type of organization. Persons who do not understand basic statistical concepts are not able to use pieces of information effectively after data have been processed. Those who have such skills tend to make effective decisions that benefit their organizations and themselves.

DESCRIPTIVE STATISTICS

One of the major ways of describing large data collections is through the use of *descriptive statistics*. The next two chapters will teach you to convert data into information. You will learn various ways of describing and summarizing the essential features of data sets; these descriptions will enable users of data to assimilate and use numerical values to guide the organization.

> Descriptive statistics involves various methods of describing data collections so the information they contain can be used by decision makers.

STATISTICAL INFERENCE

The second major area of statistical study is *statistical inference,* which involves drawing conclusions about all the items of interest after examining only a few of them.

> Statistical inference involves sampling items from the population of interest and inferring that this population has the same attributes as those measured in the sample.

In statistics, the word *population* is used to designate the complete set of items that are of interest in any investigation. The term *sample* is used to designate a subset of items that are chosen from the population and measured.

> The population consists of all the items of interest in a statistical study; the sample consists of those items chosen from the population and measured.

When a sample of data is taken from a population, one or more specific measurements are made. These measurements on the sample produce what are known as *statistics;* the population counterparts of these measurements are known as *parameters.*

> Numerical attributes of populations are called parameters; numerical attributes of samples are called statistics.

Thus, in statistical inference a sample is selected from the population and certain measurements are made on the sampled items. These statistical values are then inferred to the population. That is, it is inferred that the sample statistics have the same values as the population parameters. As you can imagine, there is a distinct possibility of error in this estimation process. In a later chapter the probability and magnitude of this error will be measured so that the appropriate amount of confidence can be placed in the inferential process.

PITFALLS OF USING STATISTICS

Throughout this text you will learn about proper methods of conducting statistical investigations, describing data collections, and making statistical inferences. Because of the widespread ignorance of proper statistical methods in organizations, these methods are often misused. A secondary purpose of your study of statistics is to alert you to the possible misuses of statistics, either through ignorance or by design. Although you may or may not be actively engaged in using statistical techniques during your career, you will certainly be a consumer of statistical investigations on almost a daily basis. This is why a basic understanding of proper statistical methods is so important; as a consumer of statistics, you must be able to assign the proper amount of credence to each piece of information before it is used in the decision-making process.

A common problem in statistics is reaching conclusions based on a sample size that is too small. For example, consider the statement, "Three out of four doctors prefer Pill A to relieve pain." How large was the sample? Four doctors or four thousand doctors? If a sample of four was used, the result should be of no interest to anyone. If four thousand doctors were asked, the results might be significant.

A second problem in statistics often occurs when the sampled objects are people. Depending on how questions are asked of them, their responses can become biased or misleading. For example, suppose the management of a company wanted to know the extent of union support among its unionized employees. The local union representatives also wish to measure this support. Each group comes up with a question that is asked of a sample of employees. The questions are as follows:

- Since inflation has gone up faster than your wages in recent years, do you really think your union officials are acting in your best interests?
- Do you think it is necessary for the working person to be represented by a strong union so that the arbitrary whims of management cannot be shoved down your throat without a fight?

Which question will produce an accurate measure of union support among company employees? Neither, of course. They are both extremely biased questions and will produce radically different estimates of union support among the population of company employees. Each side, union and management, may enter negotiations armed with the results of its investigation, but neither will have an accurate estimate of the population parameter of interest—the percent of company employees that support the union. If an accurate estimate of this parameter is really desired, an unbiased question needs to be asked of company employees.

Another common mistake made in statistics is drawing a biased sample. In statistics a *random sample* reduces the possibility of bias; this means that each population item has the same chance of being selected for the sample. For example, it might be a mistake to take a sample of logs from a lumber mill's log yard by selecting only those logs on top of the log piles. Although this method of sampling would be easier and faster than removing logs on top of the pile to get at the logs underneath, it could very well result in biased results because the logs on top of the pile are probably different than the ones underneath; they have a higher moisture content, for example. The key point is, whenever a sample has been used you should know how the sampled items were selected before accepting the results of the investigation.

In general, consumers of statistical investigations should be prepared to ask the following questions whenever they are confronted with the results of a statistical study:

- Who conducted the study?
- What data were collected?
- What analysis was conducted on the data?
- What was the sample size?
- Is there a chance of unintentional bias?
- Would the investigator benefit from an intentional biasing?

- Are the data and analysis really relevant to the problem at hand?
- Would some other data or analysis be even more beneficial to solving the problem?

OVERVIEW

The next two chapters in this text deal with descriptive statistical procedures that involve methods of describing data collections so that their essential features become apparent and useful in decision making. Next, the subject of probability is examined. Before the inferential process is studied, it is necessary to understand a few basic notions about the likelihood, or probability, of various outcomes in situations. Although probability is useful by itself, its primary value is as background material for the study of statistical inference.

Specific statistical distributions are examined next. These distributions are of great interest in business because many real-life situations can be modeled by these theoretical formulations. The important ideas of estimation and hypothesis (claim) testing are examined next; these comprise some of the most important procedures in statistics. Many quarter-long statistics classes will finish with these two topics.

Finally, the two most widely used statistical procedures, regression analysis and time-series analysis, are examined in the last three chapters along with an introduction to index numbers. These subjects are sometimes studied in a second statistics course or can be studied on your own.

SUPPLEMENT: SUMMATION NOTATION

Throughout statistics and other mathematical studies, the capital Greek letter sigma is used to indicate that several designated items are to be added. Sigma is represented by the following symbol: Σ. As an example, suppose there were 35 employees in an office, and it was necessary to compute their average age. The average age can be obtained by adding the ages together and dividing the sum by the number of employees, 35. Using the symbol X to represent the variable age, the average age of the office employees could be represented by the following notation:

TABLE 1–1
Data summation

X	X²	X – 3	(X – 3)²
1	1	−2	4
2	4	−1	1
3	9	0	0
4	16	1	1
5	25	2	4
Sum 15	55	0	10

$$\frac{\Sigma\, X}{35}$$

The numerator of this notation means to sum all the X's (variables). This sum is then divided by 35 to get the average.

Table 1–1 displays five values of a variable X. Also shown are the values of each X when the variable is squared, when three is subtracted from each X, and when this latter value is squared. From the sums of the four columns shown in Table 1–1, the following summation notation is possible:

$$\Sigma\, X = 15 \qquad \Sigma\, X^2 = 55$$
$$\Sigma\, (X - 3) = 0 \qquad \Sigma\, (X - 3)^2 = 10$$

A common mistake made in using summation notation in statistics is to confuse the following two sums, which are different:

$$(\Sigma\, X)^2 \neq \Sigma\, X^2$$

The data values from Table 1–1 can be used to illustrate the difference between these two sums, as follows:

$$(\Sigma\, X)^2 = 15^2 = 225$$
$$\Sigma\, X^2 = 55$$

The key point when evaluating a summation expression is to compute all the quantities following the summation sign before adding them. Thus, the notation $\Sigma\, X^2$ means to first square all the X's, *then* add them.

Finally, it should be noted that some writers use a different version of summation notation. The method already described is the simpler way, but some writers prefer a more detailed and more precise method of expressing summation. The following are two summation notations.

$$\Sigma\, X \qquad \sum_{i=1}^{10} X_i$$

On the left is the method used in this text that states that several X values are to be summed. On the right is a notation that is read as follows: add ten X values together beginning with X_1, then X_2, then X_3, and so on through X_{10}. The subscript i on the X's is defined by the values at the top and bottom of the summation sign. The first desired subscript appears at the bottom of the summation sign; the subscript increases by one for each term in the sum with the final value being equal to the value that appears at the top of the summation sign.

EXERCISES

1. What is the difference between a sample and a population?

2. What is the difference between a statistic and a parameter?

3. Describe the conditions under which each of the following collections of items could be a sample. Then describe the conditions under which each could be a population.
   a. Fifty electronic parts.
   b. One hundred automobile tires.
   c. Five company employees.

4. Define descriptive statistics and inferential statistics.

5. Briefly describe the process of decision making in a modern organization.

6. What is the difference between data and information?

7. Indicate whether each of the following would be data or information.
   a. The ages of ten thousand company employees.
   b. "The average age of our employees is 34."
   c. A computer printout of the account balances of all checking account customers of our bank.
   d. "Fifty percent of our checking account customer balances are below $300."

8. Describe the conditions under which each of the following statements could be misleading. Then describe the conditions under which each could represent significant and useful information.
   a. "I took a sample of your employees and found that over half have a poor opinion of company management."
   b. "The night shift is demonstrating a below average quality level."
   c. "It seems as though we're working more overtime around here than we used to."

2

Descriptive Statistics: Data Description

Where You Have Been
In Chapter 1 the basic framework for the study of statistics was presented. The importance of extracting useful decision-making information from the data of everyday organizational life was stressed.

Where You Are Going
The basic methods of displaying data of interest are presented in this chapter. These methods are the easiest and most common techniques used throughout the business world in assessing important data collections.

VARIABLES VERSUS CONSTANTS

Two types of numerical quantities are of interest when studying the data collections of organizations. A numerical quantity that always takes on the same value in each situation is known as a *constant*.

> A constant is a numerical quantity that does not vary in a given situation.

Examples of constants are the number of ounces printed on a food container, the number of salespeople assigned to a sales territory each month, and the price per pound of a raw material under contract with a supplier.

In contrast, some numerical quantities assume different values each time a different case is examined. Such quantities are known as *variables*.

> A variable is a numerical quantity that assumes different values in different situations.

Examples of variables are the actual number of ounces of food placed in a container by a filling machine, the number of persons placing orders with a firm during a month, and the market price of a raw material from week to week. In each of these cases, the quantity of interest usually assumes a different value from one event to the next. As discussed in Chapter 5, when the actual value assumed by such variables is randomly determined, the variable is known as a *random variable* and is the subject of much interest in statistics.

FREQUENCY DISTRIBUTIONS

Suppose the president of a large company asks the data-processing manager for information on the ages of company employees. The president is concerned that not enough young people are being hired. The data-processing manager returns a few days later with a large stack of computer paper and indicates that all 100,000 employees in the company have their ages recorded on this listing. Since a complete listing, rather than a sample, was produced in a brief time, the data-processing manager is rather proud of this accomplishment. But the president frowns and says, "I don't have time to read through this huge stack of paper. Even if I did, by the time I got done I wouldn't know what I had read and couldn't make any decisions about hiring more young people. Bring me something I can understand."

A useful technique in such a situation is to form a *frequency distribution* of the data collection; such a distribution summarizes the large number of data values by placing them in categories.

> A frequency distribution summarizes a data collection by forming categories of values and indicating the number of occurrences in each.

Suppose the data-processing manager remembers the usefulness of frequency distributions from college days and decides to construct such a display using the 100,000 ages assembled earlier. The result of this effort might look like Table 2–1.

Table 2–1 contains the essential features of every frequency distribution. First, the groupings, or classes, are displayed. Notice that the class intervals do not overlap; that is, a person could not possibly

TABLE 2–1
Frequency distribution

Age (X)	Frequency (f)
≤20	500
21–30	25,450
31–40	21,785
41–50	23,604
51–60	16,783
61 +	11,878
	100,000 = Total

belong to more than one category. Next, the counts, or frequencies, in each class are shown. Since the frequencies add up to 100,000 in this example, all company employees have been included.

Notice that there are six categories in Table 2–1. Analysts usually choose between four and ten classes when constructing a frequency distribution. If there are only a few categories, the detail contained in the data is lost because the classes are too large. For example, if the frequency distribution of employee ages indicated that 500 people were under 21 and 99,500 people were 21 or older, most of the information in the age distribution of Table 2–1 would be lost. However, it is possible to have too many classes. If, for example, the frequency of each separate age from 19 to 68 were shown for the company, there would be so many classes that it would be difficult to use the distribution for any decision-making purpose. The objective of forming the frequency distribution is to summarize the 100,000 ages so that the essential qualities of each category can be used.

Finally, notice that the last category in Table 2–1 could contain any age above 60; that is, this category has no theoretical upper limit. This category is called an open-ended class and is often used in frequency distributions. The disadvantage of such a class is that it is difficult to calculate the average value of the distribution since the composition of values in the open-ended class is obscured.

Suppose that an accounting department is interested in examining the current outstanding balance of its receivable accounts. Since there are several hundred accounts in the company, it would be unwise to obtain a listing of all account balances even though this would be possible because all accounting records are on a computer file. Instead, the accounting department decides to construct a frequency distribution using some important dollar values as class limits. The frequency distribution shown in Table 2–2 results.

The distribution in Table 2–2 indicates that the accounts receivables are concentrated in the lower amounts with fewer and fewer accounts as the amounts get larger. As a result of this distribution,

TABLE 2–2
Frequency distribution

Accounts Receivable Balance (Dollars) (X)	Frequency (f)
0–1000	552
1001–5000	378
5001–10,000	27
10,001–50,000	10
Over 50,000	2

accounting management may wish to collect on a few large accounts rather than bother with smaller ones. The key point is that the frequency distribution summarizes a large volume of data values, dollar amounts in this case, and extracts useful decision-making information from the data. This information can then be used to direct management's attention to areas important to the company.

In summary, the following points are important features of good frequency distributions:

1. Class intervals do not overlap.
2. Class intervals are of equal width (except for open-ended classes).
3. Between four and ten classes are normally used.
4. The number of data values falling into each class are indicated.

An alternative method of indicating the frequencies in a distribution is sometimes used when the frequencies are very large. Instead of using the actual number of data values in each class, the frequency distribution shows the percentage of the total in each class. In Table 2–1, this would involve dividing each frequency in the table by 100,000, the total number of company employees, and then moving the decimal point two places to the right to obtain percentages. The result is shown in Table 2–3.

The *cumulative frequency distribution* reflects the number of data items that are less than or equal to, or greater than or equal to, certain values. For example, the president of the company may wish to know how many company employees are over 50 years of age or how many are 30 years old or less. These values can be displayed in a cumulative frequency distribution. The data shown in Table 2–1 can be used to form either the less-than-or-equal-to or the greater-than-or-equal-to distribution. The former appears in Table 2–4.

TABLE 2–3
Frequency
distribution

Age (X)	Percentage
≤20	0.5
21–30	25.4
31–40	21.8
41–50	23.6
51–60	16.8
61 +	11.9
	100.0 (100%)

TABLE 2-4
Cumulative frequency
distribution (less than
or equal to)

Age (X)	Cumulative Frequency (f)
20	500
30	25,950
40	47,735
50	71,339
60	88,122
61 +	100,000

In Table 2–4, each number in the f column answers the question, "How many items are less than or equal to the value of X in this row?" There are, for example, 47,735 people less than or equal to 40 years of age in the company. This value is the sum of the first three values in Table 2–1. The last row of Table 2–4 shows that the ages of all 100,000 company employees are less than or equal to the age 61 +.

Table 2–5 shows another type of cumulative frequency distribution, where the numbers of items greater than or equal to the row value are presented. For example, the fourth row of this table shows that 28,661 employees are greater than 50 years old. Notice that the table begins with the frequency 99,500. This is the total number of company employees who are older than 20.

In summary, frequency distributions are good descriptive techniques for presenting large data collections. They may either show the exact number of data values in each class or may accumulate these values to show the number less than or equal to, or greater than or equal to, the category values. Either actual frequency counts or percentages can be used. In all these cases, frequency distributions allow management to assess data collections and use them for decision-making purposes.

TABLE 2-5
Cumulative frequency
distribution (greater
than or equal to)

Age (X)	Cumulative Frequency (f)
21	99,500
31	74,050
41	52,265
51	28,661
61	11,878

CHARTS AND GRAPHS

Although frequency distributions are very helpful in displaying data collections, managers may wish to have a more visual summary of data. Charts and graphs present pictures of data collections that enable their users to quickly grasp the fundamental features of the original data values, without studying the original data or numerical summaries such as frequency distributions. Because charts and graphs are so useful, it is difficult to pick up a business report, news magazine, or newspaper without seeing them. Their purpose is to quickly and accurately convey the important features of data collections even if such collections contain thousands or millions of values.

Although the frequency distribution in Table 2-1 is easier to read and assimilate than the original data values for 100,000 company employees, this table can be graphed to present an even easier method of assessing data. One method of constructing such a graph is shown in Figure 2-1; statisticians refer to this type of graph as a *histogram*.

Figure 2-1 plots the data values or categories on the horizontal axis and the frequency on the vertical axis. It presents the essential features of the original 100,000 numbers in an easy-to-understand fashion. The histogram is one of the most common types of graph and can be found throughout the literature of business and many other areas.

If the centers of the bar tops in the histogram of Figure 2-1 are connected by straight lines, a *line graph* results. This type of graph is called a *frequency polygon* and appears in Figure 2-2. As shown in the next section of this chapter, it is very important to label the axes in such a graph carefully to avoid misleading the reader. In fact, two

FIGURE 2-1
Histogram

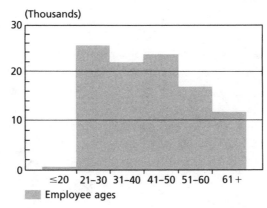

Employee ages

FIGURE 2–2
Frequency polygon

FIGURE 2–2
Frequency polygon

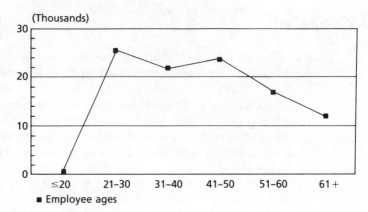

graphs that seem to suggest very different conclusions can be created from the same data.

Another common type of chart is shown in Figure 2–3 for the ages of the fictitious company discussed earlier. This is called a *pie chart* and is often used to show the sources and expenditures of funds. As Figure 2–3 suggests, the area of each slice of the pie is proportional to the percentage of the data items falling into that category. To construct a pie chart, it is necessary to divide up the area in the circle to reflect these percentages. This can be done by computing the circumference of the circle and measuring the outside of each slice so that each represents the correct proportion of the total circumference; the circumference of any circle is approximately equal to the diameter times 3.14.

The cumulative frequency distribution shown earlier in this chapter can be graphed as well. For the company ages, these graphs are shown in Figure 2–4 for the less-than case and in Figure 2–5 for the greater-than case.

FIGURE 2–3
Pie chart

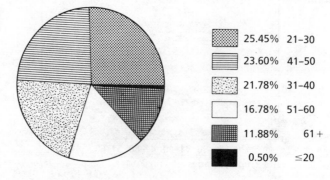

FIGURE 2–4
Cumulative frequency
distribution (less than
or equal to)

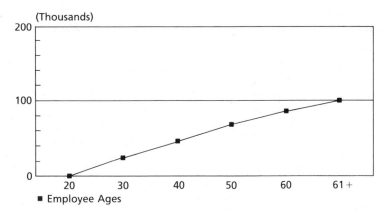

In summary, charts and graphs are descriptive methods used to display large data collections so that their essential features become obvious and can be used for managerial purposes. The basic principle in creating effective charts and graphs is the same as for making frequency distributions: graphs and charts give observers quick and accurate summaries of original data collections. All rules of thumb regarding the number of classes, class sizes, scaling of axes, and so forth are derived from this basic commonsense notion.

Data Distortion with Graphs

Whenever a chart or graph is used to represent a large data collection or to illustrate the movement of numerical values over time, it is important that the final result truly represents the original data. By manipulating the graphing techniques it is possible to present a pic-

FIGURE 2–5
Cumulative frequency
distribution (greater
than or equal to)

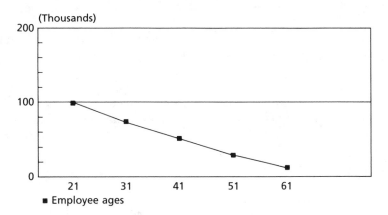

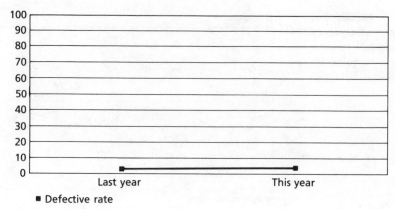

FIGURE 2-6
Defective rate

ture that is far removed from what can be supported by the data. In fact, two very different pictures of the same data values can be presented, as shown in Figures 2-6 and 2-7. A delightful book called *How To Lie With Statistics*[1] explains many of the manipulative techniques used by politicians, advertisers, and others to present distortions of data collections.

Suppose that a large corporation has experienced a mild increase in the defective rate of its major manufacturing process during the past year. The vice-president of manufacturing, who must present the quality control picture for the year at the annual meeting of the board of directors, notes that the defective percentage has risen from 3% to 4% during the year. To minimize the impact of this increase on his job performance, he prepares the graph shown in Figure 2-6. When he presents his report to the board of directors he shows the graph presented in Figure 2-6 and casually refers to the mild increase in the defective rate and then mentions that this rate is somewhat variable from year to year and will probably come down during the current year.

The company's finance manager believes that the manufacturing manager's job would be a good next step on the road to the presidency and attempts to discredit him by displaying the "deterioration" of the company's quality during the past year. She prepares the graph shown in Figure 2-7 to illustrate her point. During her presentation she indicates that the company's current financial strain is to some extent due to the lower quality control on the factory floor. After referring to Figure 2-7, she expresses doubts about the future if this trend continues.

[1] Darrell Huff, *How To Lie With Statistics* (New York: W. W. Norton & Company, 1954).

FIGURE 2–7
Defective rate

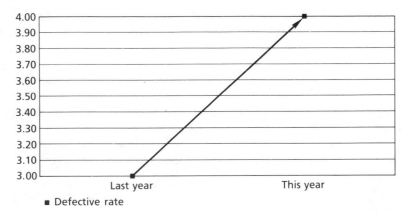

■ Defective rate

Although both Figures 2–6 and 2–7 are based on a 3% to 4% defective rate increase, these graphs appear to make the opposite point. One graph shows a relatively stable defective rate, whereas the other graph shows a sharp increase. Both managers have distorted the original data in an attempt to mislead the viewers. To present the defective rate increase correctly, it would be necessary to determine the seriousness with which an increase of this magnitude is viewed in this company. The slope of the graph could then be designed to reflect the appropriate amount of concern.

Now suppose the same company has been concerned with the quantity of oil purchases from foreign suppliers used in its operations. A year ago the vice-president of purchasing was instructed to shift to domestic sources and to report to the board at the next annual meeting. During the year he was able to cut the volume of overseas oil in half but became overly enthusiastic in preparing for the board meeting. The chart of Figure 2–8 was the result.

FIGURE 2–8
Use of foreign oil

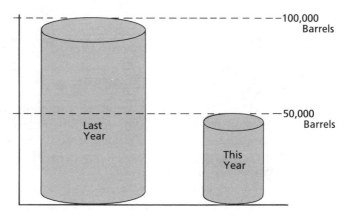

The vertical axis of Figure 2–8 is a fair treatment of the original data since it is scaled from zero to a value representing the maximum quantity of foreign oil used in the past two years. However, the use of three-dimensional barrels to represent the data values has resulted in a distortion. Although the heights of the barrels show a 50 percent decrease in accordance with the original data values, the viewers' attention is directed to the *volumes* of the barrels, which imply a dramatic decrease in oil imports. This impression is not supported by the data values. The purchasing manager should have used a simple line graph or histogram to make his point.

SUMMARY

When making charts and graphs it is important to choose a graphing method that will convey an accurate impression of the data being summarized. As consumers of visual data representations, managers must be on guard against the kind of distortions possible with manipulations in graphing techniques. If you look for such distortions in magazines, newspapers, and reports, you will find an abundance of examples to illustrate this point.

This chapter has presented the more common methods of describing data collections so that their essential features may be understood and used by managers in the decision-making process. Many other methods are used to summarize large data collections. Books on descriptive statistics can be consulted if the analyst wishes to use more elaborate methods of constructing graphs or summary tables. Numerical measurements used to describe data arrays are the subject of the next chapter.

CASE STUDY: ABC CIVIC THEATRE

The ABC Civic Theatre is interested in applying to a large corporate foundation for the funds necessary to upgrade its theatre lighting system. As a member of the theatre's Board of Trustees you have been assigned the task of writing a proposal that will have the greatest chance of receiving the grant.

You begin working with the theatre's technical director by outlining the problems with the current lighting system and specifying several alternatives for new lighting equipment that would meet the theatre's needs for the next several years. The technical director is more artistically inclined than business oriented, but finally, both of you agree on the following alternatives:

A. The ultimate system would involve replacing all lighting equipment and controls with the latest computer-controlled system. This system would meet all possible artistic requirements for the next fifty years. Cost is estimated at $55,000.

B. A mid-range system would involve using some of the current lighting instruments but would replace those which are constantly breaking down and for which it is difficult to obtain replacement parts. This system would do almost everything a production might require, and although it is manually controlled, the system has the capability of having a computer control added at a later date. Cost is estimated at $28,000.

C. A low-cost system would involve simply replacing those components that are currently unreliable. No additional capabilities are included in this system, and replacement within a few years is inevitable. The technical director is not happy with this option, which would cost about $7000.

After discussing these three options with both the technical director and the theatre's executive producer, it is decided that alternative B meets the theatre's needs and would appear reasonable to the granting corporation. With the technical director's help, you write a description of this system along with supplier's names, delivery dates, and installation procedures.

After the grant is completed you wonder about the possibility of making a graph to show the costs of the three alternatives. Such a graph might illustrate that the threatre is not asking for an amount of money anywhere near the cost of an ultimate system. At the same time you do not want to overemphasize a point that may be obvious. You finally decide to make two graphs that show the three amounts of money; one will make the point in fairly direct fashion whereas the other will understate it. You can then show these to the executive producer and discuss the possibility of including one of them in the final grant application. As you sit down to prepare the two graphs you try to remember what you have learned about making graphs and wonder how they should look.

Questions
1. How would you prepare the two graphs discussed in the case?
2. Which of the two graphs do you think would make the most effective presentation?

EXERCISES

1. What is the advantage of using a frequency distribution or a graph to describe a data collection?

2. How many categories should be used in constructing a frequency distribution?

3. Consider the following numbers that represent the number of accounts assigned to the account executives in a stock brokerage firm:

3	2	5	6	3	5	2	1	4	5	2	1	2	3
6	5	3	5	3	2	1	2	4	2	3	5	4	5
1	2	4	5	6	5	3	2	1	5	4	2	4	6
3	5	2	1	4	5	2	3	5	4	2	4	5	4
5	6	5	2	3	2	5	4	5	2	6	5	3	4
5	4	5	6	2	5	4	5	2	4	6	5	3	5
4													

     a. Construct a frequency distribution of these data.
     b. Plot the distribution formed above using a histogram.
     c. Plot the distribution using a frequency polygon.
     d. Plot the distribution using a pie chart.

4. Using the data base in Appendix I, take the first 25 values of variable $X4$, number of company courses completed, and construct a frequency distribution and a histogram.

5. Refer to the data base in Appendix I. Describe the first 30 data values for $X5$, the number of sick days taken during the past six months, by constructing a frequency distribution and a frequency polygon.

6. The annual salary of company employees appears as variable $X8$ in the data base found in Appendix I. Describe the first fifty values of this variable using cumulative frequency distributions. Construct both a less-than-or-equal and a more-than-or-equal distribution using an appropriate number of classes. Plot both these distributions.

7. The average hourly wage of the employees in a company has increased from $5.35 two years ago to $6.75. Union representatives are scheduled to meet with company management to discuss the possibility of unionizing the company's employees. Prepare two graphs of the company's hourly wage increase: one to reflect the union's view, and the other to reflect management's view.

8. In preparing a frequency distribution, what is the disadvantage of having only a few classes? What is the disadvantage of having too many?

9. Construct a histogram to summarize the following data values:

4	6	5	8	0	1	2	4
7	6	3	4	3	1	2	6
5	6	7	9	4	5	7	5
8	9	6	7	3	5	4	2

5	6	4	5	1	3	2	4
7	6	8	7	5	6	7	3
5	7	6	4	2	4	5	5
1	2	1	3	7	6	4	3
2	4	8	9	1	2	1	4

10. Display the following frequency distribution using a histogram and a frequency polygon.

X	f
10	5
11	8
12	12
13	15
14	9
15	7

11. A small business collects the following data that reflect the percentage of orders received from various sources during the past six months. Summarize this information using a pie chart.

Mail order	28%
Store	53%
Telephone	19%

12. Construct a greater-than cumulative frequency distribution for the following summary of company employee ages:

under 25	127
25 to 35	714
36 to 45	947
46 to 55	519
over 55	468

13. Construct a less-than cumulative frequency distribution for the following summary of checking account balances at a small branch bank:

under $300	486
$300 to $999	836
$1000 to $1999	378
$2000 or more	93

14. Comment on the adequacy of the following frequency distribution:

X	f
0 to 5	7
5 to 100	743
100 and up	2

15. Explain why a company might want to summarize the lifetimes of the electric components it manufactures using a less-than cumulative frequency distribution rather than a regular frequency distribution.

148,499

The following questions refer to the data base generated from the student questionnaire following the Preface.

16. Refer to Question 5 on ages of students in the class. Describe these ages using a frequency distribution.

17. Suppose it is of interest to know the distribution of class standing in your class. Use the answers to Question 1 on the student questionnaire to form a frequency distribution. Display this information using an appropriate graph.

18. Suppose the business school is considering making it more difficult for students to declare a business major. The business school is interested in students' reactions to this possibility and would like to know the results of Question 9 on the student questionnaire. Tabulate these answers using a frequency distribution and a histogram to assist the administration in assessing students' reactions.

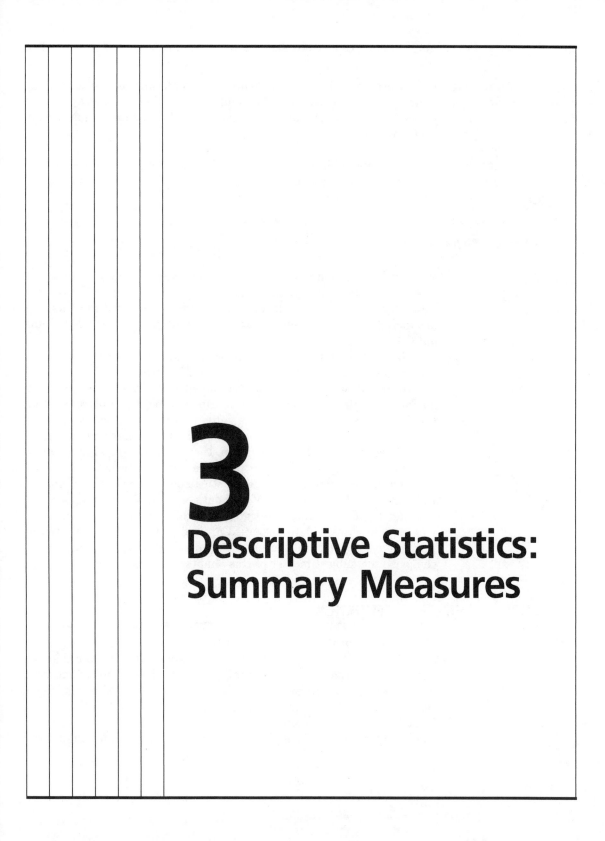

3
Descriptive Statistics: Summary Measures

**Where You
Have Been**   In the previous chapter you looked at simple methods of describing data collections. Frequency distributions and charts and graphs were introduced as useful ways of summarizing the essential qualities of such collections.

**Where You
Are Going**   In this chapter additional methods of summarizing data collections are examined. Numerical measurements of the two most important qualities of data values are presented.

DESCRIPTIVE STATISTICS

A major branch of statistics is called *descriptive statistics*. In this area of study, methods of representing the essential features of large data collections are examined. In fact, the methods described in Chapter 2 are included in this category because they are also ways of describing data.

In this chapter numerical measurements of the two most important characteristics of data collections will be examined. The first is a measurement of a centrally located data value. This value, called an *average,* is a single numerical value that will be used to represent all the data values. Since this single value will represent many pieces of data, it is important to choose one value that will represent the entire data collection well. As will be seen, there are several kinds of averages and only one may be appropriate in any specific case.

The other important characteristic to be measured with a numerical value is the dispersion of the data values. Ways of measuring whether the data values are tightly packed around their average or whether they are widely dispersed around this central value will be presented. These two measurements, central tendency and dispersion, comprise the subject matter of this chapter.

MEASURES OF CENTRAL TENDENCY

Measures of central tendency, usually called averages, produce a single value that is in the center of the larger data collection and that can be taken as a summary value for all the data. Three kinds of averages will be examined. In any particular case, one way of computing a centrally located value may be more appropriate than the others. That is, one kind of average may be more representative of the larger data collection and may be more descriptive of the data values than other averaging methods.

Mean

The most common type of average is the *mean,* or *arithmetic mean.* It is what is commonly known as the average and is found by adding data values together and dividing the sum by the number of items in the data collection.

> The mean is a measure of central tendency that is found by adding the values in the data collection and dividing the sum by the number of items in the data collection.

Consider the data collection shown in Table 3–1. Although this collection is small and might not need a summary value so it can be assimilated, a much larger array of data can be imagined that cannot be understood and used in decision making until a summary value is computed. The mean of the data shown in Table 3–1 can be computed by adding the values and dividing by 24, the number of data in the collection. Their sum is 83, and 83 divided by 24 is 3.46. Thus, the mean of the data values shown in Table 3–1 is 3.46, and this represents a central value that can be used to summarize the entire data array.

This calculation can be represented with symbols as soon as it is known whether the data in Table 3–1 represent all the values of interest in the population or whether they represent only some of the values of interest (a sample). Samples and populations were discussed in Chapter 1, and the distinction between these two groups will become increasingly important throughout this text.

If the data collection in Table 3–1 is known to be a population, the symbol for the mean is the Greek letter μ, pronounced *mu*. If the data collection is known to be a sample from a larger population, the mean will be represented by the symbol $\overline{X}$, known as X-bar. In either case, calculation of μ and $\overline{X}$ results in the same mean, 3.46. The following are the equations for computing either the population or sample mean.

TABLE 3–1
Data collection

2	3	2
4	3	2
1	5	3
2	1	7
6	2	3
5	7	6
3	5	3
4	3	1

$$\text{for a population: } \mu = \frac{\Sigma X}{N} \tag{3-1}$$

where N = population size

$$\text{for a sample: } \overline{X} = \frac{\Sigma X}{n} \tag{3-2}$$

where n = sample size

If the data values in Table 3–1 are known to be a population, their mean is computed as follows:

$$\mu = \frac{\Sigma X}{N} = \frac{83}{24} = 3.46$$

If Table 3–1 represents a sample of data values, the calculation of their mean is

$$\overline{X} = \frac{\Sigma X}{n} = \frac{83}{24} = 3.46$$

The mean is the most widely used type of average because it is easily understood and easy to calculate. In addition, the mean has mathematical properties that make it useful in inferential statistics, which will be discussed in later chapters. The disadvantage of the mean is that extremely high values or extremely low values in the data array pull the mean away from the central location of the data collection. For example, if an extremely wealthy person moved into a small town, the mean income of that town would suddenly jump to a very high value. This "average" income might be $100,000 per year, which is not a good central value for the incomes of that town. In such cases, there is a better way of describing the central value in a data collection.

Median

When the mean of a data collection is pulled away from the center of the set, it does not provide a good single-value description of the data. The *median* is often a more desirable average in these cases because it is located in the exact center of the data array.

> The median is an average that lies in the center of the data collection such that half the data values are greater than or equal to it and half are less than or equal to it.

To find the median or central value of the data array in Table 3–1, it is first necessary to arrange the values from high to low or from low to high. Table 3–2 provides such an array.

Once the data values are arrayed from low to high, the value in the middle can be found and that will be the median. If there are an odd number of data values, the one in the middle is the median. If there are an even number of data values, as there are in Table 3–2, the two values in the middle are averaged to find the median. As shown in Table 3–2, the values in positions 12 and 13 are circled. The average of these values is the median, and since they are both equal to three, the median is computed to be three. It can now be said that half the values in the data collection are less than or equal to three and half are greater than or equal to three.

The value of the median can be seen more easily when there are extreme values in the data. For example, the following data values might represent the number of units purchased by five different company customers during the past month:

$$99 \qquad 90 \qquad 85 \qquad 80 \qquad 78$$

The median number of units purchased is 85, the data value in the center of the collection. Now suppose that the purchasing manager made an error in reporting sales for the month. The lowest number of units sold was not 78 but was actually 21. The median is still 85 because that value is in the center; half the number of units sold are still more than 85 and half are less. On the other hand, if the mean had been used to report number of units sold, the mean has now dropped to 75 (the sum of the values divided by 5). If this is taken to be the average number of units sold, then all but one account are above average. Thus, the mean is pulled away from the central location of the data values when very high or very low values are present. Under these conditions, the median is a better measure of central tendency.

The disadvantage of using the median is that it does not have the mathematical properties needed for use beyond descriptive statistics.

TABLE 3–2
Data collection, low to high

1	3	4
1	3	5
1	3	5
2	③	5
2	③	6
2	3	6
2	3	7
2	4	7

Although the median is often the best describer of data arrays, its further use in more advanced statistical applications is limited.

Mode

A final type of average is sometimes used when the most typical value in a data collection is desired. The *mode* represents the data value that occurs most often.

> The mode is the value in a data collection that occurs most often.

In the data collection shown in Tables 3–1 and 3–2, the mode value is three because there are more threes in the data collection than any other value.

The mode has limited applications but might be used when the most popular value is desired. For instance, a retailer might wish to know the modal number of children per family in a shopping area or the modal number of cars per family. Values that occur most frequently are often of interest in designing a product line or an advertising campaign.

As has been seen, there are both advantages and disadvantages in the use of any of the three popular types of averages. Table 3–3 summarizes these qualities and can be used in any situation when a way of summarizing data values with a single statistic must be chosen.

TABLE 3–3
Summary of averages

	Definition	Advantages	Disadvantages
Mean	Sum of values divided by number of value items	Easy to compute and understand	Distorted by extreme values
		Has mathematical properties useful in other applications	
Median	Half the values are equal to or greater, half are equal to or less	Not distorted by extreme values	Additional mathematical analysis not possible
Mode	Value that occurs most often	Is a typical value	Additional mathematical analysis not possible
			In some data sets, can be misleading or nonexistent

MEASURES OF DISPERSION

The measures of cental tendency of a data collection summarize many data values with a single summary value. This is especially true when the data collection is so large that it is difficult or impossible to assimilate and use the data values in the decision-making process. A second important measurement is used in conjunction with central tendency to describe data values: a measurement of the extent to which the values are scattered around their central value. This section is concerned with ways of measuring such dispersion.

Range

The simplest way to measure the dispersion of data values is to specify their highest and lowest values or the difference between them. This is called the *range*.

> The range of a data collection consists of specifying its highest and lowest values or the difference between them.

Thus, the range of the data values shown in Table 3–1 and 3–2 is 1 to 7 (or 6). These two extreme values, along with an average, give an indication of what the data look like. For Table 3–1, the mean is 3.46 and the range is 1 to 7. Even if there were thousands of data values instead of 24, these two summary measurements would provide a quick picture of these values.

The obvious disadvantage of the range is that it can be misleading if extreme values exist. For example, if the value 200 is added to the data list of Table 3–1, the range becomes 1 to 200. The range no longer gives an accurate measurement of the dispersion of the data collection. For this reason, when the range is used to describe a data collection, some other measurement of dispersion is usually specified also.

Average Deviation

It is possible to compute the average amount by which a set of data values differ from their central value. Since the mean is the mathematical center of the data values, the *average deviation* usually uses the mean in its calculation.

> The average deviation is the average amount by which the values in a data collection differ from their mean.

TABLE 3–4
Data collection

X	$|X - \mu|$	
2	4	
4	2	
$\mu = 6$	0	$\dfrac{12}{5} = 2.4$
8	2	
$\dfrac{10}{30}$	$\dfrac{4}{12}$	

The mean of the data in Table 3–4 can be calculated by adding all the values together (summing the X column) and dividing the sum by five. If these five values constitute a population rather than a sample, the symbol μ can be used to denote the mean. Next, the amount by which each of the five data values differs from the mean of six can be calculated. These values are shown in the second column of Table 3–4; notice that the absolute values are shown, that is, if the subtraction $X - \mu$ produces a minus sign, it is ignored. This must be done so that when these differences are averaged, they do not add up to zero.

As shown in the second column of Table 3–4, the five absolute differences add up to 12; their average value is thus 2.4. The following statement about the original data collection can now be made: the mean of the data values is 6 and the average deviation is 2.4. The average difference between each of the five original data values and their mean is 2.4. The average deviation provides a measure of the dispersion or variability of the data values. Along with the mean, it provides an accurate summary of the larger data collection.

In a data collection as small as the one in Table 3–4, it might not be necessary to summarize the data at all. But suppose a bank had several thousand savings account customers. In this case, the account balances of these customers would constitute a very large data collection, too large to assimilate without summary values. If the mean account balance was $2573 and the average deviation was $525, a very accurate and understandable summary of these thousands of account balances would exist. This is the purpose of central tendency and dispersion measurements.

Although the concept of average deviation is easy to understand, it is not usually the first choice when a measure of dispersion is desired. Standard deviation is a more popular and useful measure of dispersion.

Standard Deviation

The data collection shown in Table 3–4 can be used to calculate the standard deviation, which is the most widely used measurement of

TABLE 3-5
Population standard
deviation calculation

X	X − μ	(X − μ)²
2	−4	16
4	−2	4
μ = 6	0	0
8	2	4
10	4	16
Sum: 30	0	40

$$\sigma^2 = \frac{40}{5} = 8$$

$$\sigma = \sqrt{8} = 2.83$$

dispersion. Note that these original population data values also appear in Table 3–5 along with the differences between each of these values and their mean of 6. This time, however, the absolute values are not needed because each of these five differences are squared, as shown in the last column of Table 3–5. Next, these squared differences are added. Since the mean is the mathematical center of the data collection, this sum of squares is a minimum value. That is, any other number that is compared against the data values would produce a larger sum of squared differences. Finally, these five squared differences are averaged by dividing their sum by five. Since they add up to 40, their average is 8. The square root of 8 is called the *standard deviation:* it is close to, but not quite equal to, the average deviation. Nevertheless, it is a measure of the dispersion of the data collection.

> The standard deviation measures the typical or standard amount by which the values in a data collection differ from their mean.

We can now say that the standard deviation of the data collection is 2.83 units. This is not quite equal to the average deviation previously calculated as 2.4, but it is close in value and represents the same concept. The typical or *standard* difference between the data values and their mean has been calculated. The symbol for the standard deviation of the population is the Greek letter σ, sigma. The formula for the population standard deviation appears in Equation 3–3. Equation 3–4 is equivalent to Equation 3–3 but is easier to use if the population standard deviation is calculated by hand.

$$\sigma = \sqrt{\frac{\Sigma (X - \mu)^2}{N}}$$ (3-3)

$$\sigma = \sqrt{\frac{\Sigma X^2 - \frac{(\Sigma X)^2}{N}}{N}}$$ (3-4)

If the data collection represents a sample rather than a population, the calculation for standard deviation is slightly different. When a sample is used to calculate standard deviation, the sum of squared differences is divided not by the number of data values in the sample but by the sample size minus one. Thus, the equation for the sample standard deviation is shown in Equation 3-5, which is followed by the computational version in Equation 3-6.

$$s = \sqrt{\frac{\Sigma (X - \overline{X})^2}{n - 1}}$$ (3-5)

$$s = \sqrt{\frac{\Sigma X^2 - \frac{(\Sigma X)^2}{n}}{n - 1}}$$ (3-6)

Notice from Equation 3-5 that the symbol for the sample standard deviation is s. Also notice that the differences between each sample value and their mean, the sample mean $\overline{X}$, are measured. Because the variability of sample values is measured around their own mean rather than around the population mean (which is unknown because only a sample is available), the numerator in Equation 3-5 is biased on the small side. That is, these sample values would show more variability around the true population mean than around their own sample mean. This bias is removed by reducing the denominator in the calculation as well. Specifically, an unbiased estimate of the population standard deviation results if the numerator of Equation 3-5 is divided by $n - 1$ rather than n.

The value $n - 1$ in Equation 3-5 represents the *degrees of freedom*. It represents the number of data items that are free to vary, given that their total must be maintained. In this case, one degree of freedom is lost because, although five of the X's can vary, the sixth variable is determined so that the sum of all X's produces a total of 30. Whenever data values are tied up in maintaining totals or other values, fewer of them are free to vary and there is somewhat less information in the sample than the sample size suggests. As will be seen later, this loss occurs whenever sample statistics are used as estimates of population parameters; in any particular case this may result in the loss of one, two, or even more degrees of freedom.

> The degrees of freedom in a situation involving a sample represents the number of items in the sample that are free to vary and, thus, represents the number of variables that carry useful information.

To illustrate the calculation of sample standard deviation, assume that the data values shown in Table 3–6 constitute a sample from a much larger population. When these data values are added and divided by 6, the sample mean is 30.8 ($\overline{X}$ = 30.8). Next, the differences between each of the six data values and this mean are squared. The sum of these squared values is 296.84. As mentioned above, if the squared differences between the six data values and the population mean were calculated, this sum would probably be greater than 296.84. The fact that the dispersion of the sample values around their own mean is being used creates a bias that can only be overcome by lowering the denominator as well. Thus, the sum of squared differences is divided by $n - 1$, which is 5. When the square root of the result is taken, the sample standard deviation results.

The mean and standard deviation are widely used as the two measures of data collections that accurately summarize essential data characteristics. Unlike the average deviation which involves the elimination of minus signs or the median which involves counting, the mean and standard deviation are useful in statistical applications other than descriptive statistics because they are computed mathematically.

TABLE 3–6
Sample standard
deviation calculation

X	$X - \overline{X}$	$(X - \overline{X})^2$
23	−7.8	60.84
35	4.2	17.64
21	−9.8	96.04
39	8.2	67.24
38	7.2	51.84
29	−1.8	3.24
Sum: 185		296.84

$$\overline{X} = \frac{185}{6} = 30.8$$

$$s^2 = \frac{296.84}{5} = 59.4$$

$$s = \sqrt{59.4} = 7.7$$

However, the mean and standard deviation are widely used to describe data collections as well. For example, the number of ounces placed in soft drink cans may have a mean of 11.93 ounces with a standard deviation of .1 ounce. Or the average number of overtime hours worked by a factory work force may be 3.8 hours per week with a standard deviation of .5 hours. In both cases, these two summary values provide an accurate description of the data collection even though the number of data values being summarized may be quite large.

In summary, the standard deviation measures the extent to which the values in a data collection are scattered around their mean. The standard deviation can be found for both a population of data values and for a sample taken from a larger population. The equations introduced in this section are used to calculate these values. Along with the mean, the standard deviation provides an accurate summary of many data values.

Variance

The *variance* is another method of measuring the variability of a data collection. It is simply the value that results when the standard deviation is squared.

> The variance is the square of the standard deviation.

The variance is calculated and appears for the data collections in Tables 3–5 and 3–6. The population variance, symbol σ^2, is shown in Table 3–5 and is equal to 8. In Table 3–6 the sample variance, symbol s^2, is calculated to be 59.4.

The variance is of little use in describing data collections. For this purpose the standard deviation is a better measurement because it reflects the typical difference between the data values and their mean. However, the variance has other uses in statistics, and for this reason, it is identified as another method of measuring dispersion. The use of variance will be discussed in later chapters.

Coefficient of Variation

A statistic that is sometimes useful when comparing two data sets is the *coefficient of variation*. It is the ratio of the standard deviation of the data set divided by the mean.

> The coefficient of variation for a data set is its standard deviation divided by its mean.

Thus, the following equations represent the coefficient of variation of a population and a sample, respectively.

$$cv = \frac{\sigma}{\mu} \text{ for a population} \qquad \textbf{(3–7)}$$

$$cv = \frac{s}{\overline{X}} \text{ for a sample} \qquad \textbf{(3–8)}$$

For the population of data values shown in Table 3–5, the coefficient of variation is calculated as follows:

$$cv = \frac{2.83}{6} = .47$$

For the sample data set shown in Table 3–6 the calculations are similar, producing the coefficient of variation as follows:

$$cv = \frac{7.7}{30.8} = .25$$

As indicated, the coefficient of variation represents the standard deviation as a percentage of the mean. The coefficient of variation is useful when comparing two populations or two samples that are measured in different units. Although both the means and standard deviations of the two groups appear to be quite different because of measurement differences, the coefficients of variation can be compared because each is expressed in percentage units rather than in the units of original measurement.

For example, suppose two work forces need to be compared with regard to their variability of output. The first work force produces electronic parts measured in units produced per day whereas the second produces cement measured in tons per day. Thus, it is difficult to compare the two groups using the mean and standard deviation because they are measured in different units. Suppose the first group averages 25 units per day with a standard deviation of 2.5 units per day; the cement crew averages 2850 tons per day with a standard deviation of 228 tons per day. At first glance, the cement crew is more variable because its standard deviation is much larger. But the two groups are measured in such different units that this conclusion may not be valid. The coefficient of variation for each group is calculated as follows:

$$\text{Electronics crew: } cv = \frac{s}{\overline{X}} = \frac{2.5}{25} = .10$$

$$\text{Cement crew: } cv = \frac{s}{\overline{X}} = \frac{228}{2850} = .08$$

Thus, the cement crew is less variable in its daily output than the electronics crew as measured by the coefficient of variation.

SUMMARIZING GROUPED DATA

Chapter 2 discussed the frequency distribution as a way of describing a large data collection. Although the frequency distribution is an improvement over the original raw data collection, it is sometimes desired to further describe the data with the mean and standard deviation. When a frequency distribution is used to prepare these summary values, it is said that *grouped data* are being used.

Consider the frequency distribution, or grouped data array, in Table 3-7; assume these values constitute a population rather than a sample. These same values appear in Table 2-2 of the previous chapter. Notice from Table 3-7 that the midpoint of each class has been added to the frequency distribution. To calculate the mean and standard deviation of the data array, a specific value must be chosen for each of the 969 original data values. Because these values are not precisely known if only the frequency distribution is available, the midpoint of each class is taken as the typical value of the class and is used in calculating descriptive statistics.

Table 3-7 demonstrates the problem with using an open-ended class in a frequency distribution. The midpoint of the last class cannot be determined with any accuracy. It is not known whether the two values in this class are slightly above 50,000, or if they are quite large. Although this class summarizes the data, it is difficult to compute

TABLE 3-7
Frequency distribution (grouped data)

Accounts Receivable Balance (dollars) X	Frequency f	Midpoint of class
0–1000	552	500
1001–5000	378	3000
5001–10,000	27	7500
10,001–50,000	10	30,000
Over 50,000	2	?
Sum:	969	

descriptive statistics after the data have been placed in the last frequency distribution category.

To compute the mean and standard deviation of the frequency distribution in Table 3–7, a midpoint value of 75,000 is chosen for the last class. The mean is then computed by adding together 552 values of 500, 378 values of 3000, and so on; this sum is then divided by 969 to compute the estimated mean of the data. These calculations are as follows:

$$\mu = \frac{500(552) + 3000(378) + 7500(27) + 30,000(10) + 75,000(2)}{969}$$

$$\mu = 2128.48$$

Likewise, the standard deviation of the data is estimated from the frequency distribution by assuming that there are 552 values of 500, 378 values of 3000, and so on. The calculations are as follows:

$$\sigma^2 = \frac{\begin{array}{c} 552(500 - 2128.48)^2 + 378(3000 - 2128.48)^2 + \\ 27(7500 - 2128.48)^2 + 10(30,000 - 2128.48)^2 + \\ 2(75,000 - 2128.48)^2 \end{array}}{969}$$

$$\sigma^2 = 21,588,493$$
$$\sigma = \sqrt{21,588,493} = 4646.34$$

Based on the frequency distribution, the mean of the original data is estimated to be $2128.48 and the standard deviation, $4646.34. These values are called estimates of the original data because the actual data values were obscured when the frequency distribution was formed. For this reason, it is better to compute the mean and standard deviation from the original data values rather than from the frequency distribution. Although the distortions of working from the frequency distribution may be minor, having exact summary statistics is better than estimating them.

The following formulas are used in calculating the mean and standard deviation from a frequency distribution. Notice that these formulas are the same for ungrouped data presented earlier except that the value for each class midpoint is multiplied by the frequency for that class.

$$\mu = \frac{\Sigma fm}{N} \qquad \text{(3–9)}$$

$$\sigma = \sqrt{\frac{\Sigma f(m - \mu)^2}{N}} \qquad \text{(3–10)}$$

where m represents the midpoint of each class.

The following formulas for calculating the mean and standard deviation from grouped sample data are the same except that the denominators are n and $n - 1$ instead of N.

$$\overline{X} = \frac{\sum fm}{n} \tag{3-11}$$

$$s = \sqrt{\frac{\sum f(m - \overline{X})^2}{n - 1}} \tag{3-12}$$

where m represents the midpoint of each class.

CASE STUDY: JUDY'S BOTTLING COMPANY

Judy's Bottling Company was a small town supplier of soft drinks. The machine that filled the bottles with fluid had been used for several years and had to be stopped several times during each week's run for repairs. On these occasions, several gallons of soda were usually lost.

Judy thought she could afford the payments on a new filling machine. She asked her assistant, Ralph Rich, to look at several machines that might bottle the volume of soda required to meet business demand.

After surveying the industry and calling several similar companies in neighboring cities, Ralph settled on two machines that seemed capable of handling their fill volume requirements without having excess capacity that would never be used. Judy told him to talk to the two suppliers to determine specifications, cost, down payment terms, and so forth.

A month later Ralph sat down with Judy to discuss the possibility of buying one of the two machines. He reported that although one machine was slightly less expensive, its usable lifetime seemed to be somewhat shorter. The cost of both machines seemed to be about equal. Judy indicated that either machine could be paid for on the terms outlined to her from the bank.

Ralph then indicated that in terms of service, reliability, and speed, the machines again appeared to be about equal. This was confirmed by several other bottling companies who used the two machines.

"Well," Judy finally said, "we might as well just flip a coin to decide."

"I had an idea we might try out," Ralph replied. "I'd like to visit two plants in the state that use the two machines. I've already cleared it with the plant managers. I'll take a sample of the fill volume of several bottles coming off each line, and we can use these values to determine if one machine is better than the other."

"How long will that take?" asked Judy.

"About two days," he replied.

"Go ahead," Judy said.

Ralph returned with 100 measurements on each of the two machines under consideration. He decided to calculate the two fill volume averages to see if they were comparable. The sample average from Machine A was 12.05 ounces whereas the average volume from Machine B was 11.98 ounces. When he reported this to Judy she didn't seem to feel that his two days away from the plant had been worthwhile.

"Can't you get anything else out of that data?" she asked.

"Well, I noticed that the numbers from Machine B seemed to be more variable than those from Machine A," Ralph replied. "Maybe I'll find a way of measuring the variability of the two."

"Do that," Judy said.

That night Ralph dug out his college statistics book and read part of a chapter on measurement of dispersion. He recognized that the sample standard deviation would provide a good measure of the variability of the two data sets. He computed these two values on his calculator. To his surprise, he found that the standard deviation of Machine A was .05 ounce whereas the standard deviation of Machine B was .5 ounce.

When he reported this information to Judy the next day it was obvious to both of them that Machine B would create serious problems because of the extreme variability of its fill volumes. By contrast, the fill volumes of Machine A were essentially constant. After discussing this situation for several minutes they decided to purchase Machine A.

"Good work," Judy said.

Questions
1. How would you summarize Ralph's calculations using the notation presented in this chapter?
2. What factors other than those presented in this case might be considered before making a purchase decision?

EXERCISES

1. Give an example of a situation where a data collection would be well described by computing the mean. Give examples where the median and mode would be more useful.

2. What is the major disadvantage of using the mean as a measure of central tendency?

3. The following data set represents the number of large customer accounts assigned to company salespersons:

2	3	5	3	2	1	2	4	2	4
5	1	2	3	5	6	5	3	2	1
2	3	5	3	5	6	2	1	2	5
3	2	5	1	2	4	5	4	1	2

a. Assume that these values constitute a population and compute the mean, variance, standard deviation, and coefficient of variation.
b. Assume that these values represent a sample from a larger population and compute the mean, variance, standard deviation, and coefficient of variation.

4. Two branches of a bank each have several hundred checking account customers. Based on the following sample statistics, what can be said about the account balances of these two groups?

$$\text{Branch 1: } \overline{X} = \$548, \ s = \$53$$
$$\text{Branch 2: } \overline{X} = \$564, \ s = \$389$$

5. The following measurements were taken on the length of cables randomly sampled from a cable production line. Use the mean and standard deviation to summarize the data values.

50.3 51.0 49.8 49.9 50.5 49.3 51.3
48.9 49.5 50.7 49.4 49.7 50.6 50.2

6. If you were asked to calculate the mean of a data collection, you would not need to know whether the data values constituted a population or a sample. But if you were then asked to calculate the standard deviation, why would you need to know whether the data values were taken from a population or sample?

7. A collection of data values has a mean of 1250 and a standard deviation of 54. What is its variance? What is its coefficient of variation?

8. A data set has a mean of 55 and a variance of 9. What is its standard deviation? What is its coefficient of variation?

9. The following data values represent the number of sick days taken by a sample of company employees last year. Describe these values by computing the mean and standard deviation.

5	6	5	4	2	6	5	6	9
8	9	8	5	5	6	4	5	6
4	10	5	9	8	7	8	9	

10. Variable $X4$ of the data base found in Appendix I represents the number of company courses taken. Use the first 15 values as a sample of all employees, and calculate statistics that will describe these values.

11. Variable $X9$ of the data base found in Appendix I represents employee ages. Use the last 20 values for this variable as a sample of all employees, and compute the mean and standard deviation.

12. Why would the median be better than the mean in describing the average performance of a large class on a 100-point mid-term examination?

13. Consider the following data collection and assume these values were drawn from a large population.

2	4	5	7	5	6	8	7
9	8	4	5	6	7	8	4
5	3	6	4	5	7	5	6
3	5	4	6	7	8	9	2
1	4	3	6	4	7	5	6
7	9	7	8	5	6	4	5
3	6	4	5	7	5	6	8
7	9	7	8	4	6	5	3
4	3	5	6	7	2	4	2

Describe these data values by computing the sample mean and standard deviation.

14. The following scores were achieved on the final exam in a small class:

    53   68   74   81   87   92

    a. Compute the mean and median for these scores.
    b. Suppose the first score, 53, was calculated incorrectly. The correct value is actually 21. Now compute the mean and median for the class.

15. The ages of people in an office are as follows:

    23   25   34   35   35   41   42   56   59

    a. Assume that this data set represents the ages of all the employees in the office. Compute the mean, median, variance, standard deviation, and coefficient of variation for these data.
    b. Using the above calculations, give a brief description of the office ages.

The following questions refer to the class data base generated from the student questionnaire following the Preface.

16. To determine the relationship between high school and college grade point averages, use Questions 3 and 4 to compute the mean GPAs of the class.

17. Use Question 4 to compute the mean, standard deviation, and variance of college grade point average for your class.

18. Suppose the president of a student organization in the business school wants to know student reaction to a recent proposal involving less structure in the business curriculum. The answers to Question 8 on the student questionnaire would be of interest in formulating a position on this question. What is the median answer to this question?

4
Probability

Where You Have Been   In Chapter 3 you learned how to calculate and analyze numerical characteristics of data. You also learned how to describe the central tendency of data using the mean, median, or mode and how to determine the variability of data using the range, average deviation, or standard deviation.

Where You Are Going   Many situations in business and government require that people predict whether some future event will occur. Forecasting sales, predicting production costs, estimating demand for new products, preparing budgets, judging the impact of tax increases on inflation, all contain an element of chance.

Chapter 4 will present many decision-making situations where it is possible to evaluate the probability of possible outcomes. You will learn that forming policies and making decisions under conditions of uncertainty is important at all levels of management. Since uncertainties are present in most decision-making situations, an understanding of profitability can be a useful tool to a manager or administrator.

PROBABILITY

Probability Definition

Probability refers to the likelihood of the occurrence of an event.

> Probability expresses the likelihood that an event will occur.

The *event* could be a successful sale, defective part, 7 percent profit, stock increase, or a successful bid. The probability that event A will occur is denoted $P(A)$ and ranges from a value of 0 to 1 $(0 \leq P(A) \leq 1)$. An event that *cannot* occur has a probability of 0 whereas an event that is certain to occur has a probability of 1.

> The probability that an event will occur ranges from a value of 0 to 1.

Table 4–1 lists three probabilities that customers will buy unleaded gasoline. For example, suppose a gas station attendant determines the probability that the next customer will buy unleaded gasoline is .5 or 50 percent. The interpretation of this probability is that if a large number of customers arrive at the station during the day, 50 percent would purchase unleaded gasoline.

TABLE 4-1	Probability of Unleaded	Interpretation
Interpretation of probability	.0	No possibility
	.5	Just as likely to buy unleaded as not
	1.0	Absolute certainty

Probability computations take into consideration various events of interest and their relationships to one another. The terms mutually exclusive and complement are used to describe some of these relationships.

Complement

The *complement* of event A contains all outcomes other than those in A, or, simply stated, "not A." Symbolically, the expression "not A" is written A′ and the probability of "not A" is

$$P(A') = 1 - P(A) \qquad \textbf{(4-1)}$$

> The complement of event A involves all outcomes not in A.

Figure 4-1 illustrates the complement of event A with a Venn diagram. Some examples of complements are

Event A	**Event A′**
Sale	No sale
Defective part	Good part
Win the bid	Lose the bid

Mutually Exclusive

Two events A and B are mutually exclusive if they cannot occur at the same time. This concept is demonstrated in the Venn diagram shown in Figure 4-2. The area designated A represents the possibility that

FIGURE 4-1
Event A′ is the complement of event A

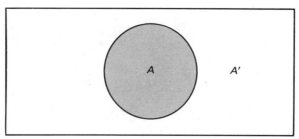

FIGURE 4–2
Events A and B are
mutually exclusive

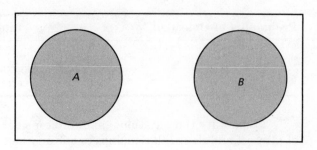

event A will occur, whereas the area labeled B represents the possibility that event B will occur. The area outside the labeled circles includes the possibility that neither A nor B will occur. There is no area showing the possibility that events A and B can occur at the same time so these events are mutually exclusive. Some examples of mutually exclusive events are

Event A	Event B
Buy the car	Sell the car
Project on time	Project late
Product A purchased	Product A not purchased

In each example event A could not occur at the same time event B occurred.

> Events are mutually exclusive if they cannot occur at the same time.

Figure 4–3 illustrates two events that are *not* mutually exclusive. Some examples of events that are *not* mutually exclusive are

Event A	Event B
Male	Worked at the plant today
Purchased stock X	Purchased stock Y
Have a checking account	Have a savings account

FIGURE 4–3
Events A and B are
not mutually
exclusive

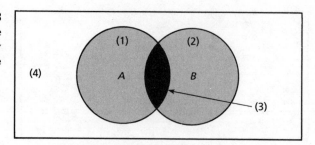

These outcomes can occur at the same time and can be contained in both events A and B. A person can be male and have worked at the plant today. A person can purchase both stock X and stock Y. A person can have both a checking and a savings account. Figure 4–3 identifies each of the following types of outcomes:

1. People who have only checking accounts
2. People who have only savings accounts
3. People who have both checking and savings accounts
4. People who have neither

PROBABILITY SOURCES

There are two types of probability: subjective and objective. Objective probability is determined through experimentation. Subjective probability is an estimate made by people.

Objective Probability

The classical approach to probability involves events with equally likely outcomes.

Example 4–1   Suppose a firm wishes to test the effectiveness of four television commercials. Before the testing begins, the firm assumes that a viewer is equally likely to choose any of the commercials as the most effective. The probability that a viewer will choose commercial one as the most effective can accurately be estimated.

Solution
$$P(\text{outcome}) = \frac{1}{\text{number of possible outcomes}} \qquad \textbf{(4–2)}$$

Since there are four possible outcomes and each is equally likely,

$$P(\text{four}) = \frac{1}{4}$$

The following equation shows the use of this approach with events involving two or more outcomes.

$$P(A) = \frac{\text{number of outcomes for Event } A}{\text{total number of possible outcomes}} \qquad \textbf{(4–3)}$$

The probability that a viewer will choose either commercial one or commercial two is

$$P(1 \text{ or } 2) = \frac{2}{4} = \frac{1}{2}$$

If the events do not have equally likely outcomes, the relative frequency approach is used. Historical data are collected or an experiment is conducted in an attempt to estimate the probabilities. The following equation illustrates the relative frequency approach:

$$P(A) = \frac{\text{number of times } A \text{ occurred}}{\text{total number of observations}} \qquad \text{(4–4)}$$

Example 4–2 An automobile dealer wishes to estimate the probability of selling three cars tomorrow. Records have been kept of sales for the past 100 days and the resulting historical data are shown in Table 4–2.

Solution The probability of selling three cars is

$$P(3) = \frac{15}{100} = .15$$

The following three factors need to be considered when the relative frequency approach is used:

1. A probability value is only an estimate. If only 50 days of historical data are observed, different probabilities might result.
2. The probability estimate is more accurate if a large number of observations is used.
3. The probability estimate should be applied only to situations that are similar to the one under which the data were acquired. Unfortunately, analysts are unable to control all the variables involved in most business situations. For example, the weather might have an effect on automobile sales. Therefore, the estimate .15 must account for any differences between

TABLE 4–2
Distribution
of car sales

Daily Car Sales	Number of Days Sold	Probability
0	2	.02
1	5	.05
2	7	.07
3	15	.15
4	20	.20
5	25	.25
6	10	.10
7	10	.10
8 or more	6	.06
	100	1.00

the conditions tomorrow and when the historical data were gathered.

> Probability is objective if the likelihood of an event's occurrence can be determined through experimentation.

Subjective Probability

There are numerous situations when historical data are not readily available. What happens if the decision makers of a firm are interested in estimating the probability of the success of a new product and an objective probability estimate is not available? The marketing manager may be asked to make a subjective estimate. A subjective probability estimate is a person's estimate of the likelihood that an event will occur. The marketing manager can estimate the probability of different sales levels of the new product by using sound judgment, past experience, and available historical information.

Once a subjective probability is determined, its use is similar to the application of an objective probability estimate. There are two disadvantages to using subjective probabilities. They are difficult to defend when questioned and can easily be biased.

> Subjective probability is a person's estimate of the likelihood of an event's occurrence.

Odds

An alternative method of expressing probabilities is through the use of odds. Odds express the ratio of favorable outcomes of an event to unfavorable ones and differ from probabilities, which express the number of favorable outcomes to the total number possible. Compare Equation 4–3, which shows the formula for computing probabilities, with the following equation:

$$\text{Odds} = \frac{\text{Number of outcomes in an event}}{\text{Number of outcomes not in an event}} \qquad \textbf{(4–5)}$$

Example 4–3   When the odds are 4 to 1 (4:1) that the Sonics will beat the Lakers, the Sonics will win four times and the Lakers once if these two teams play five games under identical conditions.

$$\text{Odds} = \frac{4}{1}$$

The probability that the Sonics will beat the Lakers is .8.

$$P(\text{Sonics}) = \frac{4}{(4 + 1)} = \frac{4}{5} = .8 \text{ or } 80\%$$

Odds are the number of successes or favorable outcomes compared to the number of failures or unfavorable outcomes.

RULES OF PROBABILITY

Business decisions are often concerned with the likelihood that a combination of events will occur. The relationships among events determine the approach for handling probability computations. When two or more events are considered, individual event probabilities are either multiplied or added, depending on the type of relationship. Suppose two events are of interest, A and B. Sometimes it will be necessary to determine the probability that both events will occur, $P(A \text{ and } B)$. At other times, it will be necessary to determine the probability that either A or B occurs, $P(A \text{ or } B)$. It is extremely important to recognize which of these situations is present.

Independent and Dependent Events

A *joint probability* is the chance that two events will occur simultaneously. This computation differs depending on whether the events are independent or dependent.

A joint probability is the chance that two events will occur together or simultaneously.

Two events are *independent* if the occurrence of one is unrelated to the occurrence of the other. Knowing that one customer will make a purchase does not aid in predicting whether another customer will make a purchase. Two events are dependent if the occurrence of one is related to the occurrence of the other. A product usually needs to be advertised in order to sell. If a large amount of advertising has taken place, then sales should increase.

> Two events are independent if the occurrence of one is unrelated to the occurrence of the other. In some cases independence is not easily assumed.

Consider the events "a person has a checking account at a bank" and "a person has a savings account at the same bank." The fact that a person has a checking account at a particular bank may increase the probability that she has a savings account at the same bank. If so, it would make sense to advertise savings accounts to checking account customers because this group of people is more likely to open a savings account than people who are not customers of the bank.

One approach to determining the relationship between two events is to assume independence and compare calculated probabilities with actual frequencies of outcomes. This situation will be discussed in the section on Chi square.

Addition Rule

The equation for the probability that either event A or B (or both A and B) will occur takes the following form:

$$P(A \text{ or } B) = P(A) + P(B) - P(A \text{ and } B) \qquad \textbf{(4–6)}$$

The probability that A or B or both will occur is found by adding simple probabilities and subtracting the joint probability of both occurring.

The Venn diagram in Figure 4–3 shows an example of non-mutually exclusive events. If event A represents persons who have checking accounts and event B savings accounts, then the shaded area represents people who have both savings and checking accounts. Notice that these people are not counted twice because the equation subtracts them out.

Example 4–4 Table 4–3 shows the results of a survey conducted in the lobby of a local bank. What is the probability that a person has either a checking or a savings account or both?

TABLE 4–3
Contingency table for checking and savings accounts[1]

	Savings	**No Savings**	**Total**
Checking	20 (3)	40 (1)	60
No Checking	30 (2)	10 (4)	40
Total	50	50	100

[1] The numbers in parentheses indicate the equivalent areas in Figure 4–3.

Solution The probability that a person has either a checking or a savings account or both is

$$P(C \text{ or } S) = P(C) + P(S) - P(C \text{ and } S)$$

$$P(C \text{ or } S) = \frac{60}{100} + \frac{50}{100} - \frac{20}{100}$$

$$P(C \text{ or } S) = .6 + .5 - .2$$

$$P(C \text{ or } S) = .9$$

When the probability of a person having a savings account was considered, the people who had both savings and checking accounts were included. Likewise, when the probability of a person having a checking account was considered, the people who had both were included. The 20 people who had both were counted twice. Equation 4–6 compensates by subtracting the number of people in this group. The probability that a person had either a checking account or a savings account or both equals $P(C \text{ or } S) = .9$. Furthermore, the probability of a person having neither a checking nor a savings account $P(NC \text{ or } NS)$ equals $(1 - .9) = .1$. However, a special case of the addition rule is used when events A and B are mutually exclusive. This involves the addition of simple marginal probabilities for either a row or a column.

$$P(A \text{ or } B) = P(A) + P(B) \tag{4–7}$$

The Venn diagram in Figure 4–2 shows mutually exclusive events. Recall that two events are mutually exclusive when they cannot occur at the same time or when $P(A \text{ and } B) = 0$.

Addition Rules

For nonmutually exclusive events

$$P(A \text{ or } B) = P(A) + P(B) - P(A \text{ and } B)$$

For mutually exclusive events

$$P(A \text{ or } B) = P(A) + P(B)$$

Conditional Probability

The likelihood that an event will occur given that another event has already taken place is called *conditional probability*. It is based on prior knowledge and is the likelihood or probability that an event will occur given that a certain condition exists.

> Conditional probability is the likelihood that an event will occur given that a certain condition exists.

Example 4–5 Refer to Table 4–3. If it is known that a person has a savings account, what is the probability that this person has a checking account?

Solution The column headed savings can be analyzed separately. Twenty out of the 50 people who had savings accounts also had checking accounts; therefore, the likelihood that a person has a checking account given that this individual has a savings account is 20/50 or .4. Likewise, given that a person has a savings account, the probability that this individual does not have a checking account is 30/50 or .6.

The term "given" is expressed with a vertical line. Thus, $P(C|S)$ means the probability that a person has a checking account given that this individual has a savings account. The conditional probability computation is shown in Equation 4–8.

$$P(A|B) = \frac{P(A \text{ and } B)}{P(B)} \qquad \textbf{(4–8)}$$

The conditional probability that a person has a checking account given that this individual has a savings account is

$$P(C|S) = \frac{P(C \text{ and } S)}{P(S)} = \frac{.2}{.5} = .4$$

Multiplication Rules

The multiplication rule for joint probabilities shown in Equation 4–9 is applied to determine the probability that events A and B will occur simultaneously.

$$P(A \text{ and } B) = P(A|B) \times P(B) \qquad \textbf{(4–9)}$$

Equation 4–9 can be derived from the conditional probability Equation 4–8.

$$P(A|B) = \frac{P(A \text{ and } B)}{P(B)}$$

If both sides of Equation 4–8 are multiplied by $P(B)$, then

$$P(A|B) \times P(B) = P(A \text{ and } B)$$

or

$$P(A \text{ and } B) = P(A|B) \times P(B)$$

Example 4–6   What is the probability that a customer has both a checking and a savings account?

Solution   Table 4–3 shows that the joint probability of a person having a checking and a savings account is

$$P(C \text{ and } S) = P(C|S) \times P(S)$$

$$P(C \text{ and } S) = \frac{.2}{.5} \times .5$$

$$P(C \text{ and } S) = .4 \times .5$$

$$P(C \text{ and } S) = .2$$

Solving for $P(S \text{ and } C)$, the result is identical:

$$P(S \text{ and } C) = P(S|C) \times P(C)$$

$$P(S \text{ and } C) = \frac{.2}{.6} \times .6$$

$$P(S \text{ and } C) = .33 \times .6$$

$$P(S \text{ and } C) = .2$$

A special case of the multiplication rule is used when events A and B are independent. This involves the simple multiplication of marginal probabilities.

$$P(A \text{ and } B) = P(A) \times P(B) \qquad \text{(4–10)}$$

When events are independent, $P(A|B) = P(A)$. Therefore, if $P(A)$ is substituted for $P(A|B)$ in Equation 4–9, Equation 4–10 results:

$$P(A \text{ and } B) = P(A|B) \times P(B)$$

If $P(A|B) = P(A)$,

then $P(A \text{ and } B) = P(A) \times P(B)$

Multiplication Rules

For dependent events

$$P(A \text{ and } B) = P(A|B) \times P(B)$$

For independent events

$$P(A \text{ and } B) = P(A) \times P(B)$$

Tree Diagrams

Counting techniques determine the total number of possible outcomes for an event or combination of events. The total number of outcomes can be simply listed. A more systematic approach involves the construction of tree diagrams. Tree diagrams provide a more informative visual presentation than simple listings and are easily constructed. However, if the number of outcomes is large, mathematical formulae are used to determine the number of possible outcomes. Example 4–7 demonstrates how a tree diagram can be developed.

Example 4–7   A young man is considering possible jobs with three companies: A, B, or C. He also must choose if he will work the day or night shift. How many outcomes are possible?

Solution   The total possible outcomes the young man can choose are calculated by multiplying the number of firms by the number of shifts. Figure 4–4 illustrates the construction of this tree diagram. Since there were three companies and two shifts, six (3 × 2) outcomes are possible.

Revised Probabilities

Frequently, probabilities can be revised after additional information becomes available, which makes probability techniques valuable in business decision making. The idea of obtaining revised probabilities is attributed to the Reverend Thomas Bayes who lived in England during the eighteenth century. Equation 4–11, frequently referred to

FIGURE 4–4
Tree diagram

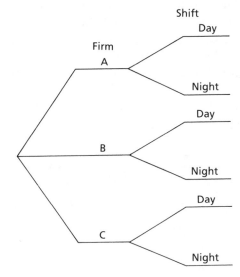

as *Bayes' Theorem,* is used to revise probabilities when additional information is available.

$$P(A|B) = \frac{P(A \text{ and } B)}{P(B)} \qquad \textbf{(4-11)}$$

> Bayes' Theorem is a method used to revise probability estimates on the basis of sample data.

Example 4–8 Consider the case of a manufacturer who has an automatic machine that produces an important part. Past records indicate that at the beginning of the day the machine is set up correctly 70 percent of the time. Past experience also shows that if the machine is set up correctly it will produce good parts 90 percent of the time. If it is set up incorrectly, it will produce good parts 40 percent of the time. Since the machine will produce 60 percent bad parts 30 percent of the time, the manufacturer is considering using a testing procedure. If the machine is set up and produces a good part, what is the revised probability that it is set up correctly?

Solution Table 4–4 summarizes the probabilities based on past experience.

The application of Bayes' Theorem is represented by the tree diagram in Figure 4–5. The following steps are necessary to revise the probabilities and are coded in parentheses in Figure 4–5.

1. The mutually exclusive event for which probabilities are provided for this tree diagram.
2. Past experience indicates that the machine is set up correctly 70 percent of the time.
3. If the probability that the machine will be set up correctly is .7, then Table 4–4 shows the probability that the machine will be set up incorrectly is .3 = (1 − .7).
4. Given that the machine is set up correctly, past experience

TABLE 4–4
Revised probabilities

Event	*P*(Event)	*P*(Good Part|Event)
Correct	.7	.9
Incorrect	.3	.4
Total	1.0	

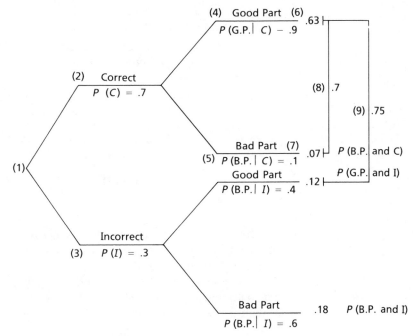

FIGURE 4–5
Tree diagram for
revised probabilities

indicates that the probability that it will produce a good part
is $P(\text{G.P.}|C) = .9$.

5. Since it is given that the machine is set up correctly, the
probability that it will produce a good or bad part is a mutually exclusive event. Therefore, if the probability of a good
part is .9, then the probability of a bad part is $.1 = (1 - .9)$.

6. The multiplication rule shown in Equation 4–9 is applied to
determine the probability that the machine will be set up
correctly and produce a good part.

$$P(\text{G.P. and } C) = P(\text{G.P.}|C) \times P(C)$$

$$P(\text{G.P. and } C) = .9 \times .7$$

$$P(\text{G.P. and } C) = .63$$

7. The multiplication rule shown in Equation 4–9 is also applied
to determine the probability that the machine will be set up
correctly and produce a bad part.

$$P(\text{B.P. and } C) = P(\text{B.P.}|C) \times P(C)$$

$$P(\text{B.P. and } C) = .1 \times .7$$

$$P(\text{B.P. and } C) = .07$$

8. Note that the two endpoints for the branch labeled correct sum to .7 = (.63 + .07).

9. The probability of a good part, the sum of the probabilities of the two outcomes that produce a good part, is .75 = (.63 + .12).

10. The revised probability that the machine is set up correctly, given it produced a good part, is .84.

$$P(C|\text{G.P.}) = \frac{P(C \text{ and G.P.})}{P(\text{G.P.})}$$

$$P(C|\text{G.P.}) = \frac{.63}{.75}$$

$$P(C|\text{G.P.}) = .84$$

This is better, but suppose two parts are tested. Table 4–5 shows a summary of the computations. Given the machine is set up correctly, the probability that it will produce two good parts is .81 = (.9 × .9). Thus, the probability that the machine will be set up correctly and produce two good parts is .567 = (.7 × .81). Since the probability that the machine will be set up incorrectly and produce two good parts is .048 = (.3 × .4 × .4), the probability that the machine will produce two good parts is .615 = (.567 + .048). Therefore, if the machine produces two good parts when tested, the revised probability that it was set up correctly is

$$P(C|2 \text{ G.P.}) = \frac{P(C \text{ and 2 G.P.})}{P(2 \text{ G.P.})}$$

$$P(C|2 \text{ G.P.}) = \frac{.567}{.615}$$

$$P(C|2 \text{ G.P.}) = .92$$

It seems wise to revise probabilities whenever additional information becomes available.

TABLE 4–5
Revised probabilities with joint events

Event	P(Event)	P(Good Part|Event)	P(2 Good Parts|Event)	P(Event and 2 Good Parts)
Correct	.7	.9	(.9 × .9) = .81	(.7 × .81) = .567
Incorrect	.3	.4	(.4 × .4) = .16	(.3 × .16) = .048
Total	1.0			P(2 Good Parts) = .615

SUMMARY

There are numerous times in business where it is necessary to know the likelihood that some future event will occur. Probabilities are used to express these likelihoods. The probability that a particular event will occur ranges from a value of 0 to 1. The complement of an event involves all the other possible outcomes of the event. Two events are mutually exclusive if they cannot occur at the same time.

There are two types of probability: subjective and objective. Subjective probability uses estimates made by people of the likelihood of an event's occurrence. Objective probability is known or determined through experimentation.

Two events are independent if the occurrence of one is unrelated to the occurrence of the other. The probability that events A or B or both will occur is found by the addition rule $P(A \text{ or } B) = P(A) + P(B) - P(A \text{ and } B)$. When events A and B are mutually exclusive, the addition rule is $P(A \text{ or } B) = P(A) + P(B)$. Conditional probability is the likelihood that an event will occur, given that another event has already taken place. The probability that events A and B will occur simultaneously is found by the multiplication rule $P(A \text{ and } B) = P(A|B) \times P(B)$. When events A and B are independent the multiplication rule is $P(A \text{ and } B) = P(A) \times P(B)$.

Counting techniques are used to determine the total number of possible outcomes for an event or combination of events.

Frequently probabilities can be revised after additional information becomes available. Bayes' Theorem is the method used to revise probability estimates on the basis of sample data. The formula is

$$P(A|B) = \frac{P(A \text{ and } B)}{P(B)}.$$

CASE STUDY: THE MURPHY BROTHERS' CLEANING COMPANY

The Murphy Brothers' Cleaning Company currently has 25 percent of the floor wax market in the Inland Empire region of the Northwest. The remaining 75 percent of the market is controlled by the Cascade Corporation.

Jim Murphy met with his staff to discuss the development of a new product. Roger Murphy, manager of the research and development department, reported substantial progress on a much improved product. Based on the chemist's estimate, Roger felt there was an 85 percent chance of developing the improved floor wax. Next, the discussion moved to an analysis of what Cascade's reaction might be. Michael Murphy, manager of the marketing department, indicated that if the new floor wax was developed and marketed by Murphy Brothers, the probability was about 60 percent that Cascade would develop a similar product. When questioned about what effect this would have on the total market picture, Michael responded with the following analysis. If Cascade develops a similar product, the chances are .25 that Murphy Brothers will have an 80 percent market share, .35 that Murphy Brothers will have a 60 percent market share, and .40 that Murphy Brothers will have a 40 percent market share. If Cascade is not able to develop a new floor wax, then the chances are .75 that Murphy Brothers will have an 80 percent market share and .25 that Murphy Brothers will have a 40 percent share. If Murphy Brothers does not develop a new floorwax, the market share will remain 25 percent.

Joseph Murphy, the controller, felt that Murphy Brothers should proceed with this project if they could be assured of gaining at least 60 percent of the market. At this point in the meeting Jim turned the analysis over to the company's statistician, Jack Murphy. He told Jack that he wanted a presentation everyone could understand by the end of the week.

Questions
1. How should Jack present his analysis so everyone can understand it?
2. What is the probability that Murphy Brothers will gain at least 60 percent of the market?
3. What decision do you think Murphy Brothers should make? Why?

EXERCISES

1. Briefly describe the different approaches to assigning probabilities.
2. What are the advantages and disadvantages of the objective approach to assigning probabilities?
3. What is the relationship between odds and probabilities?
4. Define the term *mutually exclusive* and give a business example.
5. Define the term *complement* and give a business example.
6. What does the expression *independent events* mean?
7. Why must the probabilities of complementary events add up to one?
8. Explain the difference in the addition rule for mutually exclusive events and events that are not mutually exclusive.

9. Why is it useful to revise probabilities?

10. How is Bayes' Theorem used?

11. A single card is drawn from a deck of 52 cards. What is the probability of obtaining
    a. a ten?
    b. a face card?
    c. a red card?
    d. a club?
    e. a four of hearts?

12. What is the complement of each of the events in Problem 11?

13. List the pairs of events that are mutually exclusive in Problem 11.

14. Given the following events:

    ■ A = A person died of cancer yesterday
    ■ B = A person ran 5 miles today
    ■ C = A person had an automobile accident today

    a. Are events A and B mutually exclusive?
    b. Are events A and C mutually exclusive?
    c. Are events B and C mutually exclusive?

15. When a stockbroker predicts that the probability of the stock market rising is 40 percent, what are the odds it will rise?

16. When a consultant indicates the odds are 3:2 he will get the bid for a particular job, what is the probability that the job will be awarded to him?

17. A small appliance store has collected data on video game sales for the last 50 days. The results are as follows:

Number of Games Sold	Number of Days
0	15
1	10
2	8
3	11
4 or more	6

    a. How many outcomes are possible?
    b. What approach would be used to assign probabilities to the outcomes?
    c. Assign the probabilities.
    d. What is the probability that one video game will be sold on a particular day?
    e. What is the probability that 2 or more games will be sold?
    f. What is the probability that no video games will be sold on the next two days?

18. An emergency room service at the local hospital keeps records on patient problems. The records for the past three months are as follows:

accident victims	45
poisoning	8
heart attacks	19
respiratory illness	18
other	10

a. What is the probability that a patient has either a heart attack or respiratory illness?

b. What is the probability that the next patient is not an accident victim?

c. What is the probability that the next two patients will be classified in the last category?

19. A firm is currently testing a product and has done an analysis of a price promotion campaign. The test market showed that 15% of the people interviewed were both aware of the promotion and had made a purchase. It was also determined that 75% of the people were aware of the promotion and 25% were purchasers of the product prior to the promotion.

   a. Are the events "made a purchase" and "aware of the promotion" dependent?

   b. Given that a person is aware of the promotion, what is the probability he or she will make a purchase?

   c. Should the company introduce this promotion on a national scale? Why or why not?

20. Management believes a special safety program will reduce accidents during the current year. Records show that 9% of the employees had accidents last year. It is estimated that 15% of those employees who had accidents last year will have another one during the current year. The safety program should reduce the number of accidents to 5% during the current year.

   a. What percentage of the employees will have accidents in both years?

   b. What percentage of the employees will have one accident over the two-year period?

   c. What percentage of the employees will not have accidents over the two-year period?

21. Sharon Shark spends Friday evening at the pool hall. She especially likes to play two brothers, Jim and John Pigeon. Sharon feels that her chance of winning on any Friday night is .85 regardless of which Pigeon she plays. She also feels that what happens on one night does not influence her chances on other nights.

   a. What is the probability that both Pigeon brothers will beat Sharon on Friday night?

   b. What is the probability that Sharon will beat one of the brothers and lose to the other next Friday night?

   c. What is the probability that Sharon will beat both Pigeons two weeks in a row?

22. The owner of Cheney Realty is interested in determining the likelihood that a piece of property will be sold within a certain period of time. Sales of the firm were analyzed for the previous year's listings. The results of 1000 listings were compared to the asking price in the following table:

Asking Price	Days Listed until Sold			
	Under 30	31–60	Over 60	Totals
Under $25,000	60	60	20	140
$25,000–50,000	20	200	120	340
$50,000–75,000	20	300	120	440
Over $75,000	20	40	20	80
Totals	120	600	280	1000

    a. What is the likelihood that the initial asking price is over $75,000?

    b. What is the likelihood that a home will be listed for less than 30 days?

    c. What is the likelihood that both a and b will occur?

    d. Assume a home has just been listed for $60,000. What is the likelihood that it will take Cheney Realty more than 60 days to sell it?

    e. Are these events dependent?

23. A clerk is told to place a clock, a radio, and a watch in a row on a display shelf. How many displays can he create? Draw a tree diagram of the different outcomes.

24. A production line for a tire manufacturer is sampled by the selection and inspection of three tires. Each tire is classified as okay or defective. If a tire is defective, it may be fixed or discarded. Construct a tree diagram for the sampling of the production line.

25. Bank records indicate that 80% of its loans are completely repaid. An analysis of the repaid loans shows that 75% were made to applicants who had been employed at their present position for over five years. Of the defaulted loans, 30% were made to applicants who had been employed at their present position for less than five years.

    a. Given that a particular loan applicant has been employed for seven years, what is the revised probability that this person will repay the loan?

    b. If an applicant has only been employed for one year, what is the probability that this individual will repay the loan?

26. The owner of a stereo store has kept records on customers who visited her store for the past year and found 70% were males. She reports that 50% of her male customers purchased a stereo whereas only 25% of the females made a purchase.

    a. What is the probability that the next customer who enters the store will purchase a stereo?

    b. If the next two customers who enter the store are males, what is the probability that one of them will purchase a stereo? What is the probability that neither one of them will buy a stereo?

    c. If the last customer did not make a purchase, what is the probability that the customer was female?

27. A consulting company has submitted a bid to do a computer feasibility study. The company's management initially estimated a 70–30 chance of getting the job. However, the firm that requested the bid has now asked for additional information. Past experience indicates that on 90% of the successful bids and 25% of the unsuccessful bids additional information was requested. What is the revised probability that the consulting company will get the job?

28. Each week an automated machine must be set up to produce parts used in the production of integrated circuits. Records have been kept and past experience indicates that the machine was set up correctly 85% of the time. If the machine was set up correctly, it produced good parts 95% of the time. If it was set up incorrectly, it produced good parts 60% of the time.
    a. If the machine was set up and the first part tested is defective, what is the revised probability that the machine was set up correctly?
    b. If the machine was set up and the first two parts tested are good, what is the revised probability that the machine was set up correctly?
    c. What is the probability that the first part tested will be bad?
    d. What decision criteria would you use if the cost of producing bad parts was extremely high?

29. This question refers to the class data base. Calculate the probability that a person chosen at random is a sophomore.

5

Discrete Probability Distributions

Where You   In previous chapters you have examined various ways of summarizing
Have Been   data collections so that the important information contained in the
                data may be used in decision making. You have learned how to de-
                scribe the essential characteristics of data arrays with summary val-
                ues such as the mean and standard deviation. The basic ideas of
                probability have also been examined.

Where You   In this chapter you will look at methods for describing the possible
Are Going   occurrences of a variable whose values, from case to case, are randomly
                determined and will use these methods in decision-making situations.
                In addition, two specific types of variables that are often used in
                organizations will be examined.

DISCRETE VERSUS CONTINUOUS RANDOM VARIABLES

A *random variable* is an essential concept in the study of the uncertain
future with regard to numerical values. This is a data value that takes
on different numerical values from one occurrence to another, as discussed in Chapter 3, and whose value in a particular instance is
determined by chance.

> A random variable is a numerical quantity that takes on dif-
> ferent values from trial to trial on a random basis.

An example of a random variable is age because different people have
different ages. It is a random variable because if people are randomly
chosen from a population of interest, the age of each person cannot be
predetermined; that is, such values are determined randomly. Other
examples of random variables include the ounces of fill per container
on a filling assembly line, the weight of aluminum ingots produced in a
foundry, the number of overtime hours worked per employee in an
office, and the number of cars sold per week on a used car lot. In each of
these cases, the numerical value of interest varies from case to case,
and the specific values of these variables cannot be predetermined.
     It is important to understand the difference between two types of
random variables that are frequently used in organizations. If only
certain values, usually integers, are possible for the random variable,
it is known as a *discrete random variable*.

> A discrete random variable is one for which only certain speci-
> fied values are possible; these are usually integers.

Discrete random variables are those values for which some counting process is conducted. For example, the number of overdrawn checking accounts at a bank, the number of employees calling in sick, the number of boxcars arriving per day to be unloaded, and the number of active accounts in a salesperson's territory are all examples of discrete random variables. In these cases the possible values the random variable can assume are 0, 1, 2, 3, and so forth. That is, only the integer values, including zero, are possible because in each case items are being counted and fractions or decimals are not possible.

In contrast, there are other random variables for which any value within some range is possible. These are known as *continuous random variables*.

A continuous random variable is one for which any value within some range may be assumed.

In general, a continuous random variable is associated with a measuring device. The weights, lengths, heights, and volumes of objects are continuous random variables. Other examples include the ounces of fill placed in containers by an automatic filling machine, the time between breakdowns for an automatic welding machine, the length of cables produced in a cable factory, and the miles per gallon of a fleet of rental cars. In these cases the numerical value of a specific case is variable, randomly determined, and measured on a continuous scale; that is, within some reasonable range, any numerical value is possible including fractions or decimals.

In this chapter discrete random variables and the distribution of their possible outcomes will be examined. In the next chapter the subject of continuous random variables will be discussed.

THE PROBABILITY DISTRIBUTION

A very useful way of presenting the possible outcomes of a discrete random variable as well as the likelihood that each of these values might be assumed in a particular case is the *probability distribution*.

A probability distribution displays the possible outcomes for a random variable and specifies the probability that such an outcome will occur in a particular case.

Consider, for example, the probability distribution shown in Table 5–1.

TABLE 5–1
Discrete probability
distribution

Units Sold X	Probability P(X)
0	.10
1	.15
2	.20
3	.25
4	.20
5	.10
Total:	1.00

Suppose the X value in this distribution represents the number of generators sold each month by a heavy equipment manufacturer.

Every probability distribution for a discrete random variable has the format of Table 5–1. That is, X, the possible values that the random variable can assume, is listed in one column, and $P(X)$, the probability that such a value can occur, is listed in a second column. Notice that this second column of probabilities adds up to 1.00 or 100%. This must always be the case because the list of X's must include every possible occurrence; therefore, there is a 100% chance that one outcome will occur.

Table 5–2 presents another probability distribution for a discrete random variable. In this case X is the number of absent employees per day in a small business. Notice that this distribution meets the requirements for a probability distribution. That is, the various values that the random variable X can assume are listed along with the

TABLE 5–2
Discrete probability
distribution

Number of Absent Employees X	P(X)
0	.20
1	.10
2	.10
3	.05
4	.05
5	.10
6	.15
7	.10
8	.15
Total:	1.00

probabilities that each event will occur. Notice that these probabilities add up to 1.00, indicating that all possible values of X have been included.

Expected Value

It is frequently of interest to determine the average value that a random variable will assume over many trials. In statistics, this is known as the *expected value*.

> The expected value of a random variable is the average value the variable assumes over many trials.

The expected value of a discrete random variable, as summarized by its probability distribution, is found by multiplying each possible value of X by its probability of occurrence and summing these products. Equation 5–1 is a shorthand way of stating this calculation.

$$E(X) = \Sigma\, X \cdot P(X) \qquad\qquad (5\text{–}1)$$

To find the expected value of the probability distribution shown in Table 5–1, each X is multiplied by its corresponding probability; these six products are then added as follows:

$$0(.10) + 1(.15) + 2(.20) + 3(.25) + 4(.20) + 5(.10) = 2.6$$

Thus, the expected value of the number of generators sold each month (see Table 5–1) is 2.6 units. This value is also known as the average or mean. Since the expected value is, in fact, the average value of the distribution over time, the terms expected value, average, and mean are all synonymous.

The expected value of the number of absent employees per day (see Table 5–2) can also be found using Equation 5–1. Again, each value of X in the distribution is multiplied by its probability of ocurrence and these products are added.

$$0(.20) + 1(.10) + 2(.10) + 3(.05) + 4(.05) + 5(.10)$$
$$+ 6(.15) + 7(.10) + 8(.15) = 3.95$$

It can now be said that the expected number of absent employees is 3.95 per day, based on the probability distribution shown in Table 5–2. This value, of course, represents the average number of absent employees over many days; hence, a decimal value is not surprising. However, notice that the expected value is not actually the value expected on any individual occurrence. That is, 3.95 persons cannot be absent on a particular day because only the integer values can occur when count-ing people. Instead, the value 3.95 represents the mean or average value of the distribution of absent persons in the company over a large number of days.

BINOMIAL DISTRIBUTION

Several theoretical distributions are of interest to business organiza-tions because these distributions closely resemble real situations. The first distribution that will be examined is the *binomial distribution*.

> The binomial distribution represents the probabilities of vari-ous numerical outcomes over several identical, independent trials, where there are two possible outcomes for each trial.

To approximate a real situation by using a theoretical binomial dis-tribution, the following key points must exist in the situation:

1. On each of n identical trials, only two outcomes are possible; these are usually called success and failure.
2. Probabilities of success and failure remain constant from trial to trial (for a small population this requires sampling with replacement).
3. Trials are independent.

If these three conditions are met, the binomial distribution can be used as a model of the real situation. The advantage of this modeling process is that the binomial distribution can be used to estimate proba-bilities instead of using expensive manipulations of the real situation.

For example, suppose that two suppliers of a particular compo-nent part in a company each provide half the parts necessary for the final assembly process. If the parts are randomly placed in inventory as they arrive from the two suppliers, the necessary conditions exist to model this situation with the binomial distribution. That is, the three conditions for a binomial distribution are met. There are only two possible outcomes each time a part is drawn (supplied by A or by B), the probabilities that selected parts will be from Supplier A remain constant (.50) from one part selection to another because the parts are randomly placed in inventory, and the selections of parts (the trials) are independent, again, because the inventory is randomly distributed. If the binomial distribution is now used to find any desired proba-bilities, these will represent the correct probabilities for the actual inventory selection situation.

The following equation is used to estimate probabilities for binomial distributions:

$$P(X) = C_x^n \, \pi^X (1 - \pi)^{n-x} \qquad \textbf{(5-2)}$$

Where π = probability of success on each trial
n = number of trials
X = desired number of successes
C_x^n = combination of n things taken X at a time.

$$C_x^n = \frac{n!}{X!(n - X)!}$$

The ! sign means factorial; for example, $3! = 3 \cdot 2 \cdot 1$, and $5! = 5 \cdot 4 \cdot 3 \cdot 2 \cdot 1$.

The second half of Formula 5-2 represents the probability that the desired outcome, X successes in n trials, will occur in any particular order. In the case of the inventory example, suppose the inventory manager wanted to know the probability of finding exactly three parts provided by Supplier A if five parts are randomly selected from the inventory. The second half of the binomial formula can be solved as follows:

$$\pi^x(1 - \pi)^{n-x} = .5^3(.5)^2 = .03125$$

Thus, there is a .03125 probability of observing three parts from Supplier A out of five parts selected in a certain order such as three parts from A followed by two parts from B. But there are many other outcomes; for example, two parts from B followed by three parts from A. The first part of Equation 5-2 computes the number of different ways to observe X successes in n trials; this is called the *combination* of n items taken X at a time. In the inventory example, there are ten different ways to end up with three parts from A and two parts from B as the five parts are drawn one at a time from inventory. This value is computed as follows:

$$C_3^5 = \frac{5!}{3!2!} = \frac{5 \cdot 4 \cdot 3 \cdot 2 \cdot 1}{3 \cdot 2 \cdot 1 \cdot 2 \cdot 1} = 10$$

Notice that the factorial sign, !, calls for multiplying the given value times the next smaller digit, times the next smaller, and so on through the digit one.

The binomial formula can now be combined to compute the desired probability:

$$P(X = 5) = C_3^5(.5)^3(.5)^2 = 10(.03125) = .3125$$

Thus, there is a .3125 probability of obtaining exactly three parts from Supplier A and two parts from Supplier B if five parts are randomly selected from the inventory. The theoretical binomial distribution formula resulted in this value, and since the requirements for a binomial experiment are met in the actual situation, this value represents the probability that the desired outcome will occur in this situation. The value of this modeling process is that outcomes in real situations can be computed without the time and expense of real-life experiments. It is not necessary, in the inventory example, to draw five parts hundreds or thousands of times to find the probability of getting three parts from Supplier *A*. It is only necessary to recognize that a binomial experiment is being conducted and to use Equation 5–2 to compute the desired probability.

Suppose a process that produces electronic components has a 95% quality level; that is, 95% of the parts produced by the process function properly and 5% do not. If eight parts are randomly chosen from the inventory and shipped to a customer, what is the probability that all eight function properly? If the requirements of the binomial distribution are met in this situation, it will be possible to solve the binomial formula for the desired answer. If the probability that all eight parts will function properly is acceptable to management, the shipment will be made without the expense of testing all the components prior to shipment.

The requirements for a binomial distribution are indeed met in this case. For eight identical trials, there are only two possible outcomes (part works or part does not work); the probability of an acceptable part remains constant from trial to trial due to the randomness of part selection from the inventory; and the trials are independent, again due to the randomness of the part selection. Thus

$$n = 8 \qquad \pi = .95 \qquad X = 8$$

The binomial formula can now be solved as follows:

$$P(X = 8) = C_8^8 (.95)^8 (.05)^0 = \frac{8!}{8!0!} (.95)^8 = (1)(.95)^8 = .6634$$

Note that $0! = 1$; any number to the 0 power equals 1.

The probability that all eight of the components in the shipment will work properly is .6634. Management now has the information necessary to decide whether to spend money on a complete test of all components. The desired decision-making information, the probability of a perfect shipment, has resulted from modeling the real situation with the binomial distribution.

TABLE 5-3
Partial table of individual terms of the binomial distribution

π

n	X	.05	.10	.15	.20	.25	.30	.35	.40	.45	.50	.55	.60	.65	.70	.75	.80	.85	.90	.95
4	0	.8145	.6561	.5220	.4096	.3164	.2401	.1785	.1296	.0915	.0625	.0410	.0256	.0150	.0081	.0039	.0016	.0005	.0001	.0000
	1	.1715	.2916	.3685	.4096	.4219	.4116	.3845	.3456	.2995	.2500	.2005	.1536	.1115	.0756	.0469	.0256	.0115	.0036	.0005
	2	.0135	.0486	.0975	.1536	.2109	.2646	.3105	.3456	.3675	.3750	.3675	.3456	.3105	.2646	.2109	.1536	.0975	.0486	.0135
	3	.0005	.0036	.0115	.0256	.0469	.0756	.1115	.1536	.2005	.2500	.2995	.3456	.3845	.4116	.4219	.4096	.3685	.2916	.1715
	4	.0000	.0001	.0005	.0016	.0039	.0081	.0150	.0256	.0410	.0625	.0915	.1296	.1785	.2401	.3164	.4096	.5220	.6561	.8145
5	0	.7738	.5905	.4437	.3277	.2373	.1681	.1160	.0778	.0503	.0313	.0185	.0102	.0053	.0024	.0010	.0003	.0001	.0000	.0000
	1	.2036	.3281	.3915	.4096	.3955	.3602	.3124	.2592	.2059	.1563	.1128	.0768	.0488	.0284	.0146	.0064	.0022	.0004	.0000
	2	.0214	.0729	.1382	.2048	.2637	.3087	.3364	.3456	.3369	.3125	.2757	.2304	.1811	.1323	.0879	.0512	.0244	.0081	.0011
	3	.0011	.0081	.0244	.0512	.0879	.1323	.1811	.2304	.2757	.3125	.3369	.3456	.3364	.3087	.2637	.2048	.1382	.0729	.0214
	4	.0000	.0004	.0022	.0064	.0146	.0283	.0488	.0768	.1128	.1562	.2059	.2592	.3124	.3601	.3955	.4096	.3915	.3281	.2321
	5	.0000	.0000	.0001	.0003	.0010	.0024	.0053	.0102	.0185	.0312	.0503	.0778	.1160	.1681	.2373	.3277	.4437	.5905	.7738
6	0	.7351	.5314	.3771	.2621	.1780	.1176	.0754	.0467	.0277	.0156	.0083	.0041	.0018	.0007	.0002	.0001	.0000	.0000	.0000
	1	.2321	.3543	.3993	.3932	.3560	.3025	.2437	.1866	.1359	.0938	.0609	.0369	.0205	.0102	.0044	.0015	.0004	.0001	.0000
	2	.0305	.0984	.1762	.2458	.2966	.3241	.3280	.3110	.2780	.2344	.1861	.1382	.0951	.0595	.0330	.0154	.0055	.0012	.0001
	3	.0021	.0146	.0415	.0819	.1318	.1852	.2355	.2765	.3032	.3125	.3032	.2765	.2355	.1852	.1318	.0819	.0415	.0146	.0021
	4	.0001	.0012	.0055	.0154	.0330	.0595	.0951	.1382	.1861	.2344	.2780	.3110	.3280	.3241	.2966	.2458	.1762	.0984	.0305
	5	.0000	.0001	.0004	.0015	.0044	.0102	.0205	.0369	.0609	.0937	.1359	.1866	.2437	.3025	.3560	.3932	.3993	.3543	.2321
	6	.0000	.0000	.0000	.0001	.0002	.0007	.0018	.0041	.0083	.0156	.0277	.0467	.0754	.1176	.1780	.2621	.3771	.5314	.7351
7	0	.6983	.4783	.3206	.2097	.1335	.0824	.0490	.0280	.0152	.0078	.0037	.0016	.0006	.0002	.0001	.0000	.0000	.0000	.0000
	1	.2573	.3720	.3960	.3670	.3115	.2471	.1848	.1306	.0872	.0547	.0320	.0172	.0084	.0036	.0013	.0004	.0001	.0000	.0000
	2	.0406	.1240	.2097	.2753	.3115	.3177	.2985	.2613	.2140	.1641	.1172	.0774	.0466	.0250	.0115	.0043	.0012	.0002	.0000
	3	.0036	.0230	.0617	.1147	.1730	.2269	.2679	.2903	.2918	.2734	.2388	.1935	.1442	.0972	.0577	.0287	.0109	.0026	.0002
	4	.0002	.0026	.0109	.0287	.0577	.0972	.1442	.1935	.2388	.2734	.2918	.2903	.2679	.2269	.1730	.1147	.0617	.0230	.0036
	5	.0000	.0002	.0012	.0043	.0115	.0250	.0466	.0774	.1172	.1641	.2140	.2613	.2985	.3177	.3115	.2753	.2097	.1240	.0406
	6	.0000	.0000	.0001	.0004	.0013	.0036	.0084	.0172	.0320	.0547	.0872	.1306	.1848	.2471	.3115	.3670	.3960	.3720	.2573
	7	.0000	.0000	.0000	.0000	.0001	.0002	.0006	.0016	.0037	.0078	.0152	.0280	.0490	.0824	.1335	.2097	.3206	.4783	.6983
8	0	.6634	.4305	.2725	.1678	.1001	.0576	.0319	.0168	.0084	.0039	.0017	.0007	.0002	.0001	.0000	.0000	.0000	.0000	.0000
	1	.2793	.3826	.3847	.3355	.2670	.1977	.1373	.0896	.0548	.0313	.0164	.0079	.0033	.0012	.0004	.0001	.0000	.0000	.0000
	2	.0515	.1488	.2376	.2936	.3115	.2965	.2587	.2090	.1569	.1094	.0703	.0413	.0217	.0100	.0038	.0011	.0002	.0000	.0000
	3	.0054	.0331	.0839	.1468	.2076	.2541	.2786	.2787	.2568	.2188	.1719	.1239	.0808	.0467	.0231	.0092	.0026	.0004	.0000
	4	.0004	.0046	.0185	.0459	.0865	.1361	.1875	.2322	.2627	.2734	.2627	.2322	.1875	.1361	.0865	.0459	.0185	.0046	.0004
	5	.0000	.0004	.0026	.0092	.0231	.0467	.0808	.1239	.1719	.2188	.2568	.2787	.2786	.2541	.2076	.1468	.0839	.0331	.0054
	6	.0000	.0000	.0002	.0011	.0038	.0100	.0217	.0413	.0703	.1094	.1569	.2090	.2587	.2965	.3115	.2936	.2376	.1488	.0515
	7	.0000	.0000	.0000	.0001	.0004	.0012	.0033	.0079	.0164	.0312	.0548	.0896	.1373	.1977	.2670	.3355	.3847	.3826	.2793
	8	.0000	.0000	.0000	.0000	.0000	.0001	.0002	.0007	.0017	.0039	.0084	.0168	.0319	.0576	.1001	.1678	.2725	.4305	.6634

The Binomial Table

Although binomial probabilities can always be found by using Equation 5–2, this can be time consuming, and errors are possible. It would, therefore, be handy to have several hundred binomial problems solved and placed in a table that could be used as a reference in each binomial situation. For these reasons, binomial tables appear in almost all statistics and operations/production textbooks and handbooks.

Table 5–3 presents a portion of this binomial table. The full table is found in Appendix A, and even larger tables can be found in statistical table handbooks. Notice that Table 5–3 is arranged in groups of n units, the number of binomial trials. For example, to find the probability of flipping three heads in five flips of a fair coin, find the $n = 5$ block. Next, look to the right until you find the number under the $\pi = .50$ column, since the probability of success in the experiment is .50. The probability of $X = 3$ appears in the fourth row of the $n = 5$ group. This value, .3125, was calculated earlier using Equation 5–2 and also represents the probability of obtaining three parts from Supplier A out of five parts drawn from inventory. The entire binomial probability distribution for this example appears in the binomial table in the $n = 5$ block, under the column $\pi = .50$. This distribution appears as a histogram in Figure 5–1.

Likewise, the probability of eight good parts in a shipment of eight can be found. In this case, $n = 8$, $\pi = .95$, and $X = 8$. The $n = 8$ block of Table 5–3 is used, where $X = 8$ and $\pi = .95$. The probability in the table for these values is .6634, the same value computed using the binomial formula. Also appearing in the table is the entire probability distribution for this example. This distribution appears as a histogram in Figure 5–2.

FIGURE 5–1
Binomial distribution,
$N = 5$, $\pi = .50$

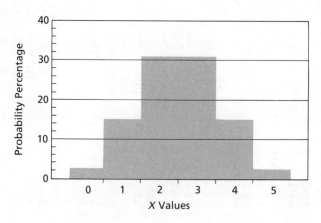

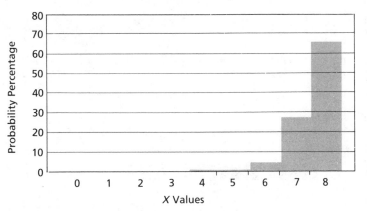

FIGURE 5–2
Binomial distribution,
$N = 8, \pi = .95$

The binomial table, then, contains the results of solving the binomial formula hundreds of times. It is, therefore, not necessary to solve this formula every time a binomial probability is needed, because the correct answer can be found by consulting the table.

Although Table 5–3 is useful for individual binomial probabilities, cumulative binomial probabilities are sometimes desired. For example, suppose in the inventory situation the probability of no more than two parts from A is desired; that is, the probability that $X \leq 2$ is needed. This probability can be obtained from Table 5–3, since the desired probability is equal to $P(X = 0) + P(X = 1) + P(X = 2)$. These three values, obtained from Table 5–3, can be added together as follows:

$$.0313 + .1563 + .3125 = .5001$$

However, it is often easier to look up the desired cumulative probability in a table that presents cumulative binomial values. Table 5–4 is a portion of the Cumulative Binomial Table that appears in Appendix B. This table has the same format as the individual binomial table. First, locate the appropriate group of probabilities, in this case, the block for $n = 5$. Next, find the $\pi = .50$ column since .50 is the probability of success on each trial. Finally, locate the X row for 2. However, in Table 5–4 this represents the probability that $X \leq 2$, not $X = 2$. The probability from Table 5–4 in this position is .5000, the same value that was calculated by adding the values from Table 5–3 (disregarding rounding errors).

Suppose, in the example involving the shipment of eight parts, management wanted to know the probability of no more than one defective in the shipment. In other words

$$n = 8 \qquad \pi = .95 \qquad P(X \geq 7) = ?$$

TABLE 5-4
Partial table of cumulative binomial probabilities

π

n	X	.05	.10	.15	.20	.25	.30	.35	.40	.45	.50	.55	.60	.65	.70	.75	.80	.85	.90	.95
4	0	.8145	.6561	.5220	.4096	.3164	.2401	.1785	.1296	.0915	.0625	.0410	.0256	.0150	.0081	.0039	.0016	.0005	.0001	.0000
	1	.9860	.9477	.8905	.8192	.7383	.6517	.5630	.4752	.3910	.3125	.2415	.1792	.1265	.0837	.0508	.0272	.0120	.0037	.0005
	2	.9995	.9963	.9880	.9728	.9492	.9163	.8735	.8208	.7585	.6875	.6090	.5248	.4370	.3483	.2617	.1808	.1095	.0523	.0140
	3	1.0000	.9999	.9995	.9984	.9961	.9919	.9850	.9744	.9590	.9375	.9085	.8704	.8215	.7599	.6836	.5904	.4780	.3439	.1855
	4	1.0000	1.0000	1.0000	1.0000	1.0000	1.0000	1.0000	1.0000	1.0000	1.0000	1.0000	1.0000	1.0000	1.0000	1.0000	1.0000	1.0000	1.0000	1.0000
5	0	.7738	.5905	.4437	.3277	.2373	.1681	.1160	.0778	.0503	.0313	.0185	.0102	.0053	.0024	.0010	.0003	.0001	.0000	.0000
	1	.9974	.9185	.8352	.7373	.6328	.5282	.4284	.3370	.2562	.1875	.1312	.0870	.0540	.0308	.0156	.0067	.0022	.0005	.0000
	2	.9988	.9914	.9734	.9421	.8965	.8369	.7648	.6826	.5931	.5000	.4069	.3174	.2352	.1631	.1035	.0579	.0266	.0086	.0012
	3	1.0000	.9995	.9978	.9933	.9844	.9692	.9460	.9130	.8688	.8125	.7438	.6630	.5716	.4718	.3672	.2627	.1648	.0815	.0226
	4	1.0000	1.0000	.9999	.9997	.9990	.9976	.9947	.9898	.9815	.9688	.9497	.9222	.8840	.8319	.7627	.6723	.5563	.4095	.2262
	5	1.0000	1.0000	1.0000	1.0000	1.0000	1.0000	1.0000	1.0000	1.0000	1.0000	1.0000	1.0000	1.0000	1.0000	1.0000	1.0000	1.0000	1.0000	1.0000
6	0	.7351	.5314	.3771	.2621	.1780	.1176	.0754	.0467	.0277	.0156	.0083	.0041	.0018	.0007	.0002	.0001	.0000	.0000	.0000
	1	.9672	.8857	.7765	.6554	.5339	.4202	.3191	.2333	.1636	.1094	.0692	.0410	.0223	.0109	.0046	.0016	.0004	.0001	.0000
	2	.9978	.9842	.9527	.9011	.8306	.7443	.6471	.5443	.4415	.3438	.2553	.1792	.1174	.0705	.0376	.0170	.0059	.0013	.0001
	3	.9999	.9987	.9941	.9830	.9624	.9295	.8826	.8208	.7447	.6563	.5585	.4557	.3529	.2557	.1694	.0989	.0473	.0159	.0022
	4	1.0000	.9999	.9996	.9984	.9954	.9891	.9777	.9590	.9308	.8906	.8364	.7667	.6809	.5798	.4661	.3446	.2235	.1143	.0328
	5	1.0000	1.0000	1.0000	.9999	.9998	.9993	.9982	.9959	.9917	.9844	.9723	.9533	.9246	.8824	.8220	.7379	.6229	.4686	.2649
	6	1.0000	1.0000	1.0000	1.0000	1.0000	1.0000	1.0000	1.0000	1.0000	1.0000	1.0000	1.0000	1.0000	1.0000	1.0000	1.0000	1.0000	1.0000	1.0000
7	0	.6983	.4783	.3206	.2097	.1335	.0824	.0490	.0280	.0152	.0078	.0037	.0016	.0006	.0002	.0001	.0000	.0000	.0000	.0000
	1	.9556	.8503	.7166	.5767	.4449	.3294	.2338	.1586	.1024	.0625	.0357	.0188	.0090	.0038	.0013	.0004	.0001	.0000	.0000
	2	.9962	.9743	.9262	.8520	.7564	.6471	.5323	.4199	.3164	.2266	.1529	.0963	.0556	.0288	.0129	.0047	.0012	.0002	.0000
	3	.9998	.9973	.9879	.9667	.9294	.8740	.8002	.7102	.6083	.5000	.3917	.2898	.1998	.1260	.0706	.0333	.0121	.0027	.0002
	4	1.0000	.9998	.9988	.9953	.9871	.9712	.9444	.9037	.8471	.7734	.6836	.5801	.4677	.3529	.2436	.1480	.0738	.0257	.0038
	5	1.0000	1.0000	.9999	.9996	.9987	.9962	.9910	.9812	.9643	.9375	.8976	.8414	.7662	.6706	.5551	.4233	.2834	.1497	.0444
	6	1.0000	1.0000	1.0000	1.0000	.9999	.9998	.9994	.9984	.9963	.9922	.9848	.9720	.9510	.9176	.8665	.7903	.6794	.5217	.3017
	7	1.0000	1.0000	1.0000	1.0000	1.0000	1.0000	1.0000	1.0000	1.0000	1.0000	1.0000	1.0000	1.0000	1.0000	1.0000	1.0000	1.0000	1.0000	1.0000
8	0	.6634	.4305	.2725	.1678	.1001	.0576	.0319	.0168	.0084	.0039	.0017	.0007	.0002	.0001	.0000	.0000	.0000	.0000	.0000
	1	.9428	.8131	.6572	.5033	.3671	.2553	.1691	.1064	.0632	.0352	.0181	.0085	.0036	.0013	.0004	.0001	.0000	.0000	.0000
	2	.9942	.9619	.8948	.7969	.6785	.5518	.4278	.3154	.2201	.1445	.0885	.0498	.0253	.0113	.0042	.0012	.0002	.0000	.0000
	3	.9996	.9950	.9786	.9437	.8862	.8059	.7064	.5941	.4770	.3633	.2604	.1737	.1061	.0580	.0273	.0104	.0029	.0004	.0000
	4	1.0000	.9996	.9971	.9896	.9727	.9420	.8939	.8263	.7396	.6367	.5230	.4059	.2936	.1941	.1138	.0563	.0214	.0050	.0004
	5	1.0000	1.0000	.9998	.9988	.9958	.9887	.9747	.9502	.9115	.8555	.7799	.6846	.5722	.4482	.3215	.2031	.1052	.0381	.0058
	6	1.0000	1.0000	1.0000	.9999	.9996	.9987	.9964	.9915	.9819	.9648	.9368	.8936	.8309	.7447	.6329	.4967	.3428	.1869	.0572
	7	1.0000	1.0000	1.0000	1.0000	1.0000	.9999	.9998	.9993	.9983	.9961	.9916	.9832	.9681	.9424	.8999	.8322	.7275	.5695	.3366
	8	1.0000	1.0000	1.0000	1.0000	1.0000	1.0000	1.0000	1.0000	1.0000	1.0000	1.0000	1.0000	1.0000	1.0000	1.0000	1.0000	1.0000	1.0000	1.0000

In this case, the desired probability cannot be looked up directly from Table 5–4 because it is a greater-than-or-equal value whereas the table contains less-than-or-equal values. However, the probability can be rewritten so that Table 5–4 can be used to find the correct answer. This is done as follows:

$$P(X \geqslant 7) = 1 - P(X \leqslant 6)$$
$$= 1 - .0572$$
$$= .9428$$

Since the probabilities on each side of the equal sign are complements (one or the other must happen), this equation holds. Since the probability on the right side of the equation is a value presented in Table 5–4, its value can be found and subtracted from 1.00. As a result, management sees that there is about a 94% chance that the shipment contains at least seven good parts.

Mean and Standard Deviation of Binomial Variables

It is often of interest to know the average value that a binomial random variable will assume over many trials as well as the standard deviation of such values. The following formulas for the mean (expected value) and standard deviation for binomial random variables have been developed:

$$\mu = n\pi \qquad \qquad \textbf{(5–3)}$$
$$\sigma = \sqrt{n\pi (1 - \pi)} \qquad \qquad \textbf{(5–4)}$$

These equations can be used in any binomial experiment if the mean and standard deviation are desired. In the inventory example, these two values are calculated as follows:

$$\mu = (5)(.5) = 2.5$$
$$\sigma = \sqrt{(5)(.5)(.5)} = 1.12$$

Therefore, if five parts are repeatedly drawn from inventory, the average number of parts from Supplier A will be 2.5 with a standard deviation of 1.12.

Likewise, these values can be found for the part shipment example. Since $n = 8$ and $\pi = .95$:

$$\mu = (8)(.95) = 7.6 \text{ good parts}$$
$$\sigma = \sqrt{(8)(.95)(.05)} = .62 \text{ good parts}$$

POISSON DISTRIBUTION

Another theoretical distribution of interest in many business situations is the *Poisson distribution*. Like the binomial distribution, the Poisson describes the probability of various numbers of occurrences and involves discrete random variables. It is used as a model for random arrivals of events in time or space.

> The Poisson distribution represents the random arrival of events per unit of time or space.

A common example used to illustrate the Poisson distribution is the arrival of cars at a toll bridge. If these arrivals are randomly generated, the theoretical Poisson formula can be used to find the probability that any number of cars will arrive at any given minute or second. The following equation is used for the Poisson distribution:

$$P(X) = \frac{\mu^x e^{-\mu}}{X!} \qquad\qquad \textbf{(5–5)}$$

where μ = average number of occurences per unit of time or space
$\quad\ e$ = natural log base (2.71828)
$\quad\ X$ = number of occurrences of interest

This equation indicates that one parameter is needed to specify a particular Poisson distribution: the mean number of occurrences per unit of time or space (μ). If this value is known, the probability of any value of X occurring in the next unit of time or space can be computed.

For example, suppose that previously collected traffic data indicate that, during the afternoon rush hour, an average of 3.5 cars arrive at a toll bridge each second. If it is assumed that cars arrive randomly, and can thus be modeled with the Poisson distribution, what is the probability that in the next second, no cars will arrive? Rather than spending several days at the toll bridge observing car arrivals, you can answer this question by using Equation 5–5 because the situation meets the requirements of a Poisson process (random generation of arrivals). Given that the average number of car arrivals per second is 3.5, the Poisson formula is solved for the answer as follows:

$$P(X = 0) = \frac{(3.5)^0 \, (2.71828)^{-3.5}}{0!} = \frac{1}{2.71828^{3.5}} = .0302$$

It can now be concluded that if an average of 3.5 cars arrive at a toll bridge per second, then there is about a 3% chance that no cars will arrive at any particular second. Again, this value was calculated after modeling the real situation with a theoretical distribution whose specifications were met.

Suppose a certain valuable tool is kept in a central location, called a tool crib, on the factory floor. Mechanics who wish to use the tool must check it out and return it when they are finished. Assuming that mechanics arrive randomly at the tool crib, the Poisson distribution becomes a good model of this situation. If an average of one mechanic arrives at the tool crib in each ten-minute period, what is the probability that within the next ten minutes, exactly one mechanic will arrive? Again, the Poisson formula can be used to find the answer; in this case, $X = 1$ and $\mu = 1.0$.

To save time in making calculations using the Poisson formula, hundreds of such calculations have been made and placed in a table, a portion of which is shown in Table 5-5.

In this table the column headings represent the mean of the Poisson distribution. Since $\mu = 1.0$ and $X = 1$, the probability from Table 5-5 is .3679. Since the Poisson distribution is a valid model of the tool crib situation, this is the probability of one arrival in a ten-minute period whose average number of arrivals is one. Likewise, the probability computed for the toll bridge example can be found in Table 5-5. In this case, the mean of the distribution is 3.5 and the desired value of X is 0. Using Table 5-5, the probability that no cars will arrive at the toll bridge is .0302, which is the same value that was found by using Equation 5-5.

Just as with the binomial distribution, it is sometimes necessary to find cumulative probabilities for the Poisson distribution. Table 5-6 can be used to find the probability that X is less than or equal to some value in a Poisson problem.

Suppose there are an average of .42 defects per 100 yards of cloth made by a weaving machine. Assuming such defects arrive randomly from time to time, what is the probability of no more than one defect on any particular 100-yard length of cloth? In other words, using the Poisson process,

$$\mu = .42$$
$$P(X \leq 1) = \ ?$$

The answer can be found in Table 5-6 by looking in the column headed $\mu = .42$. The values found in this column represent the probabilities that X is less than or equal to the X value of the row. Therefore, the probability that there will be no more than one defect on a 100-yard length of cloth is .9330 because this value is in the $X \leq 1$ row.

Finally, it should be noted that it is sometimes necessary to convert the mean arrival rate to the desired time or units of space

TABLE 5–5
Partial table of
individual terms
of the Poisson
distribution

					μ					
X	0.10	0.20	0.30	0.40	0.50	0.60	0.70	0.80	0.90	1.00
0	.9048	.8187	.7408	.6703	.6065	.5488	.4966	.4493	.4066	.3679
1	.0905	.1637	.2222	.2681	.3033	.3293	.3476	.3595	.3659	.3679
2	.0045	.0164	.0333	.0536	.0758	.0988	.1217	.1438	.1647	.1839
3	.0002	.0011	.0033	.0072	.0126	.0198	.0284	.0383	.0494	.0613
4	.0000	.0001	.0002	.0007	.0016	.0030	.0050	.0077	.0111	.0153
5	.0000	.0000	.0000	.0001	.0002	.0004	.0007	.0012	.0020	.0031
6	.0000	.0000	.0000	.0000	.0000	.0000	.0001	.0002	.0003	.0005
7	.0000	.0000	.0000	.0000	.0000	.0000	.0000	.0000	.0000	.0001

					μ					
X	1.10	1.20	1.30	1.40	1.50	1.60	1.70	1.80	1.90	2.00
0	.3329	.3012	.2725	.2466	.2231	.2019	.1827	.1653	.1496	.1353
1	.3662	.3614	.3543	.3452	.3347	.3230	.3106	.2975	.2842	.2707
2	.2014	.2169	.2303	.2417	.2510	.2584	.2640	.2678	.2700	.2707
3	.0738	.0867	.0998	.1128	.1255	.1378	.1496	.1607	.1710	.1804
4	.0203	.0260	.0324	.0395	.0471	.0551	.0636	.0723	.0812	.0902
5	.0045	.0062	.0084	.0111	.0141	.0176	.0216	.0260	.0309	.0361
6	.0008	.0012	.0018	.0026	.0035	.0047	.0061	.0078	.0098	.0120
7	.0001	.0002	.0003	.0005	.0008	.0011	.0015	.0020	.0027	.0034
8	.0000	.0000	.0001	.0001	.0001	.0002	.0003	.0005	.0006	.0009
9	.0000	.0000	.0000	.0000	.0000	.0000	.0001	.0001	.0001	.0002

					μ					
X	2.10	2.20	2.30	2.40	2.50	2.60	2.70	2.80	2.90	3.00
0	.1225	.1108	.1003	.0907	.0821	.0743	.0672	.0608	.0550	.0498
1	.2572	.2438	.2306	.2177	.2052	.1931	.1815	.1703	.1596	.1494
2	.2700	.2681	.2652	.2613	.2565	.2510	.2450	.2384	.2314	.2240
3	.1890	.1966	.2033	.2090	.2138	.2176	.2205	.2225	.2237	.2240
4	.0992	.1082	.1169	.1254	.1336	.1414	.1488	.1557	.1622	.1680
5	.0417	.0476	.0538	.0602	.0668	.0735	.0804	.0872	.0940	.1008
6	.0146	.0174	.0206	.0241	.0278	.0319	.0362	.0407	.0455	.0504
7	.0044	.0055	.0068	.0083	.0099	.0118	.0139	.0163	.0188	.0216
8	.0011	.0015	.0019	.0025	.0031	.0038	.0047	.0057	.0068	.0081
9	.0003	.0004	.0005	.0007	.0009	.0011	.0014	.0018	.0022	.0027
10	.0001	.0001	.0001	.0002	.0002	.0003	.0004	.0005	.0006	.0008
11	.0000	.0000	.0000	.0000	.0000	.0001	.0001	.0001	.0002	.0002
12	.0000	.0000	.0000	.0000	.0000	.0000	.0000	.0000	.0000	.0001

					μ					
X	3.10	3.20	3.30	3.40	3.50	3.60	3.70	3.80	3.90	4.00
0	.0450	.0408	.0369	.0334	.0302	.0273	.0247	.0224	.0202	.0183
1	.1397	.1304	.1217	.1135	.1057	.0984	.0915	.0850	.0789	.0733
2	.2165	.2087	.2008	.1929	.1850	.1771	.1692	.1615	.1539	.1465
3	.2237	.2226	.2209	.2186	.2158	.2125	.2087	.2046	.2001	.1954
4	.1734	.1781	.1823	.1858	.1888	.1912	.1931	.1944	.1951	.1954

TABLE 5–6
Partial table of cumulative Poisson probabilities

					μ					
X	.30	.32	.34	.36	.38	.40	.42	.44	.46	.48
0	.7408	.7261	.7118	.6977	.6839	.6703	.6570	.6440	.6313	.6188
1	.9631	.9585	.9538	.9488	.9437	.9384	.9330	.9274	.9217	.9158
2	.9964	.9957	.9949	.9940	.9931	.9921	.9910	.9898	.9885	.9871
3	.9997	.9997	.9996	.9995	.9994	.9992	.9991	.9989	.9987	.9985
4	1.0000	1.0000	1.0000	1.0000	1.0000	.9999	.9999	.9999	.9999	.9999

					μ					
X	.50	.55	.60	.65	.70	.75	.80	.85	.90	.95
0	.6065	.5769	.5488	.5220	.4966	.4724	.4493	.4274	.4066	.3867
1	.9098	.8943	.8781	.8614	.8442	.8266	.8088	.7907	.7725	.7541
2	.9856	.9815	.9769	.9717	.9659	.9595	.9526	.9451	.9371	.9287
3	.9982	.9975	.9966	.9956	.9942	.9927	.9909	.9889	.9865	.9839
4	.9998	.9997	.9996	.9994	.9992	.9989	.9986	.9982	.9977	.9971
5	1.0000	1.0000	1.0000	.9999	.9999	.9999	.9998	.9997	.9997	.9995
6	1.0000	1.0000	1.0000	1.0000	1.0000	1.0000	1.0000	1.0000	1.0000	.9999

					μ					
X	1.0	1.1	1.2	1.3	1.4	1.5	1.6	1.7	1.8	1.9
0	.3679	.3329	.3012	.2725	.2466	.2231	.2019	.1827	.1653	.1496
1	.7358	.6990	.6626	.6268	.5918	.5578	.5249	.4932	.4628	.4337
2	.9197	.9004	.8795	.8571	.8335	.8088	.7834	.7572	.7306	.7037
3	.9810	.9743	.9662	.9569	.9463	.9344	.9212	.9068	.8913	.8747
4	.9963	.9946	.9923	.9893	.9857	.9814	.9763	.9704	.9636	.9559
5	.9994	.9990	.9985	.9978	.9968	.9955	.9940	.9920	.9896	.9868
6	.9999	.9999	.9997	.9996	.9994	.9991	.9987	.9981	.9974	.9966
7	1.0000	1.0000	1.0000	.9999	.9999	.9998	.9997	.9996	.9994	.9992
8	1.0000	1.0000	1.0000	1.0000	1.0000	1.0000	1.0000	.9999	.9999	.9998
9	1.0000	1.0000	1.0000	1.0000	1.0000	1.0000	1.0000	1.0000	1.0000	1.0000

					μ					
X	2.0	2.1	2.2	2.3	2.4	2.5	2.6	2.7	2.8	2.9
0	.1353	.1225	.1108	.1003	.0907	.0821	.0743	.0672	.0608	.0550
1	.4060	.3796	.3546	.3309	.3084	.2873	.2674	.2487	.2311	.2146
2	.6767	.6496	.6227	.5960	.5697	.5438	.5184	.4936	.4695	.4460
3	.8571	.8386	.8194	.7993	.7787	.7576	.7360	.7141	.6919	.6696
4	.9473	.9379	.9275	.9162	.9041	.8912	.8774	.8629	.8477	.8318
5	.9834	.9796	.9751	.9700	.9643	.9580	.9510	.9433	.9349	.9258
6	.9955	.9941	.9925	.9906	.9884	.9858	.9828	.9794	.9756	.9713
7	.9989	.9985	.9980	.9974	.9967	.9958	.9947	.9934	.9919	.9901
8	.9998	.9997	.9995	.9994	.9991	.9989	.9985	.9981	.9976	.9969
9	1.0000	.9999	.9999	.9999	.9998	.9997	.9996	.9995	.9993	.9991
10	1.0000	1.0000	1.0000	1.0000	1.0000	.9999	.9999	.9999	.9998	.9998
11	1.0000	1.0000	1.0000	1.0000	1.0000	1.0000	1.0000	1.0000	1.0000	.9999
12	1.0000	1.0000	1.0000	1.0000	1.0000	1.0000	1.0000	1.0000	1.0000	1.0000

before using the Poisson tables. For example, if 120 cars arrive randomly per hour at an intersection, what is the probability that one car will arrive in the next minute? The mean arrival rate must first be converted to the desired units of time, which, in this case, is minutes. Since the average is 120 per hour, the average per minute is 120/60 = 2 per minute. Since $\mu = 2$ and $X = 1$, the probability can be found by using the Poisson table. This value is .2707, which means there is about a 27% chance of exactly one arrival in any minute.

Poisson Approximation of Binomial

The binomial tables discussed earlier in this chapter can be used to find various probabilities of interest. This is not possible, however, if the sample size in a particular problem is larger than the largest value of n in the table. Under these circumstances another method must be used to find desired probability values.

Figure 5–3 summarizes procedures that can be followed when dealing with binomial distribution problems. As shown in the lower part of this figure, if n is less than or equal to 20, the correct probability can be determined by referring to the binomial table.

In the next chapter, the approximation of binomial probabilities using the so-called normal distribution will be discussed. As shown in Figure 5–3, this approximation method is appropriate when n is larger than 20, so that the binomial table cannot be used, and the probability of success is neither very small nor very large. Under these conditions, the normal distribution provides accurate binomial probability estimates.

FIGURE 5–3
Solving binomial problems

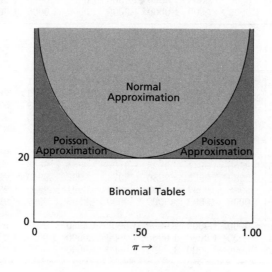

Also shown in Figure 5–3 is the method of approximating binomial probabilities when n is larger than 20 and the probability of success is either quite close to 0 or quite close to 1.00. Under these conditions, using the normal distribution to approximate the desired probabilities is not as accurate as using the Poisson distribution. In general, the Poisson distribution provides very close approximations of the binomial distribution when $n\pi \le 5$ or $n(1 - \pi) \le 5$.

As mentioned in the discussion of the Poisson distribution earlier in this chapter, the mean of the Poisson process must be known to identify which Poisson distribution to use. If the Poisson distribution is used to approximate binomial probabilities, the mean of the binomial process is calculated and used to locate probabilities in the Poisson table.

For example, suppose that .6% of the jackets made in a clothing factory have defects that prevent them from being sold at full retail price. If 200 jackets are randomly drawn from inventory and sent to a retailer, what is the probability that the shipment contains no defective jackets? What is the probability that the shipment contains no more than one defective jacket? Since $n = 200$, it is not possible to find the answers to these questions in a binomial table, and since the probability of success is quite small (.006), it is not appropriate to use the normal approximation to estimate these probabilities.

Figure 5–3 suggests that the Poisson distribution can be used to approximate the desired probability values. First, the average number of defective units to be found in a shipment is determined. In other words, the mean of the binomial distribution is calculated as follows:

$$\mu = n\pi = (200)(.006) = 1.2$$

Since $n\pi$ is less than 5, the Poisson distribution can be used to approximate the desired probability. Assume that, instead of a binomial experiment, we are dealing with a Poisson process in which defects randomly arrive in shipments of 200 jackets. The average number of arrivals per unit is 1.2. The following probabilities are desired:

$$P(X = 0) \qquad P(X \le 1)$$

The first probability can be found from Table 5–5 or from the larger Poisson table in Apppendix C. For $\mu = 1.2$, the probability of $X = 0$, found in the Poisson table, is .3012. There is about a 30% chance that the shipment will contain no defective jackets.

The second probability can be found by using the values in Table 5–5 and by adding the probability that none of the jackets will be defective to the probability that one jacket will be defective. Using Table 5–5, the two probabilities are .3012 and .3614. Therefore, the desired probability is the sum of these two values, or .6626. Or the probability can be looked up in the cumulative Poisson probability table in Table 5–6 or Appendix D.

It can now be said that the probabilities .3012 and .6626 represent the exact probabilities of 0 and 1.00 or less occurrences in a Poisson process with a mean of 1.2. More importantly, since the Poisson distribution closely approximates the binomial distribution in this situation, these two probabilities are quite close to the precise binomial probabilities for 0 and for 1.00 defective jackets in the shipment. For practical purposes, the approximation is so close that binomial tables for n values larger than 25 are rarely found in books of statistical tables.

SUMMARY

This chapter has presented two important theoretical distributions that are often useful in business situations. This is because many practical situations can be modeled by using these theoretical distributions. In these cases, it is not necessary to observe the process over a long period of time to assess the likelihood of various outcomes of interest. Rather, if the modeling process has been done properly and either the binomial or Poisson process is used, probabilities of randomly determined numerical outcomes can be computed from these distributions.

Both binomial and Poisson formulas can be used to find probabilities if one of these distributions closely models the real process. It is easier, however, to use the binomial or Poisson tables that are found in books of statistical tables and in most statistic books. In the case of the binomial, the sample size (n) must be known along with the probability of success on each trial (π). The individual term binomial table, therefore, provides the probabilities of various values of the random variable, whereas the cumulative binomial table provides the probabilities that an outcome is equal to or less than a desired value.

In the case of the Poisson distribution, the mean or average number of arrivals per unit of time or space is need (μ). The individual term Poisson table, therefore, yields the probabilities of specified values of the random variable, whereas the cumulative table gives the probabilities that an outcome is equal to or less than a specified value.

CASE STUDY: THE CARLSON COMPANY

The Carlson Company manufactures keyboards for installation in home computers. The company has recently experienced difficulties in the quality of one of its major components, a small electronics device, that it purchases from a supplier in California. Carlson's purchasing agent, Nancy Woodmann, recently attended a trade show and talked with an agent for another supplier who could supply a similar part at about the same price. The agent for the new company claimed that the defective percentage of its manufacturing process is .4%, a substantial improvement over the defective rate of Carlson's current supplier.

Ms. Woodmann's boss expressed doubt about the claimed defective rate of the new supplier. After discussing the amount Carlson could save if the claimed defective rate were true, it was decided that a shipment would be ordered from the new supplier. Then, each component in the shipment could be tested to determine the number of defective parts. After computing the percentage of defective parts in this shipment, it would be possible to decide whether the supplier's claim seemed reasonable, and a recommendation on the matter could be prepared for the president of the company.

The company decided to order a batch of 1000 parts and test all units. It was decided that the cost involved in testing such a large quantity would be justified in view of the potential savings to Carlson if the supplier's claim could be verified and the account switched.

Ms. Woodmann recognized that this situation could be modeled by the bionomial distribution because each of the 1000 parts would either be defective or not defective, and because she presumed that the supplier would simply take a shipment from inventory; if so, the 1000 parts represented a random sample of the supplier's output. The binomial problem was then briefly stated as follows: $n = 1000$, $\pi = .004$.

It was next necessary to decide what would constitute verification of the supplier's claim. The discussion focused on how many parts could be defective without making the supplier's claim false. Ms. Woodmann decided to temporarily accept their claim ($\pi = .004$) and computed the distribution of possible defective outcomes under this assumption. She thought that this distribution would help her decide whether to believe the supplier after the tests were conducted.

Since the sample size, 1000, was much too large for any binomial table, she recognized that an approximation of the probabilities of various outcomes would have to be made. Since the probability of success (defective) was quite low, she decided to approximate the desired binomial probabilities with the Poisson distribution. She calculated the mean, or expected number of defectives, as follows:

$$\mu = (1000)(.004) = 4$$

Since this value was less than 5, the Poisson approximation seemed appropriate.

Next, the probability distribution for a mean of 4 was obtained from the Poisson probability table. Ms. Woodman decided to begin adding the probabilities in this table until a fairly high value resulted. She concluded that there was a high probability of obtaining a certain number of defectives or less, if the claim of a .4% defective rate was true. The first six probabilities in the table, for 0 through 5 defective parts inclusive, was found to be .7852. In other words,

$$P(X \leq 5) = .7852$$

where $\mu = 4$

Ms. Woodmann then presented the following decision rule to her boss and the president of Carlson: "Five or fewer defective units in the lot of 1000 seems reasonable in view of the supplier's claim; in this event I recommend that we switch Carlson's account to the new supplier. If there are more than five defective units in the lot, the supplier's claim, although it might be true, seems suspect. Under these circumstances I recommend that we work with our present supplier to improve quality."

Ms. Woodmann's boss agreed with her reasoning and suggested that the shipment be ordered from the new supplier. Carlson's president then asked how many people it would take to test the 1000 parts and how long it would take them. When Ms. Woodmann's boss looked to her for an answer, she replied, "It will probably take three lab people about a week to do the job." The president then said, "Wouldn't it be better to take a sample?"

Questions   1. Do you think the binomial distribution is a good model of the process in the case?
2. How would you react to the president's question?
3. Comment on Ms. Woodmann's decision rule (to accept the supplier's claim if five or fewer defective units are found).

EXERCISES

1. Both the frequency distribution and the probability distribution list the possible outcomes associated with a discrete random variable. What is the difference between the two?

2. Identify the following random variables as either discrete or continuous in nature:
   a. Range, in miles, of a company's delivery trucks.
   b. Number of overdue accounts per month.
   c. Monthly cost of goods sold.
   d. Children per family in a shopping area.
   e. Defective units per shift.
   f. Lifetime of light bulbs.
   g. Phone calls arriving per hour.
   h. Pounds of feed per bag.

3. An insurance company estimates that there is a 1% chance of a total loss on a building that it will insure against fire, a 2% chance of a partial loss, and a 3% chance of a small loss. The costs to the company of these losses are estimated to be $500,000, $100,000, and $50,000 respectively. What is the dollar figure to which the company should add overhead and profit in pricing this policy?

4. The following is the probability distribution of the number of defective units produced by a certain electronics component assembly line during a week. What is the expected value of this distribution? What is the average number of defective units produced per week?

X	P(X)
0	.30
1	.20
2	.20
3	.20
4	.10

5. A new car salesman estimates that he has a 25% chance of selling a car to a person who walks into the showroom, based on five years of selling experience. On a certain day, he talks with 10 potential customers.
   a. Using the binomial distribution, what is the probability that he will sell cars to 5 of these people?
   b. How appropriate is the binomial distribution for modeling this situation?

6. In a flour mill it is found that 1% of the 50-pound flour bags have tears or are not sewn shut properly. This defective condition seems to occur randomly during the day. What is the probability that the next 300 bags are defect free? What is the probability that there will be no more than 2 defective bags in this lot?

7. It is known that 40% of the bank card accounts have balances in excess of $1000. Suppose five of the bank card accounts are selected at random.

   a. What is the probability that the first two accounts are over $1000 and the next three are $1000 or under?

   b. What is the probability that the first three are $1000 or under and the last two are over $1000?

   c. How many ways are there for two accounts to be over $1000 and three accounts $1000 or under?

   d. What is the probability that two accounts will be over $1000 and three will be $1000 or under?

8. Twenty percent of the beer cans filled by an automatic filling machine are either over filled or under filled. On the next six-pack produced by this machine:

   a. What is the probability that all cans are filled properly?

   b. What is the probability that at least five cans are filled properly?

   c. What is the probability that at least one can is filled improperly?

9. On the average, there are .5 defects per bolt of cloth in a textile factory. What is the probability of a defect-free bolt?

10. Customers arrive randomly at a small shop at the rate of 120 per hour. If the owner leaves the shop for one minute, what is the probability that no customers will arrive?

11. In the accounting department of a large corporation it is known that 99% of the accounts tallied each month are error free and do not need additional attention. There are a total of 350 such accounts.

   a. What is the mean and standard deviation of the number of correct accounts each month?

   b. What is the probability that all accounts will be tallied correctly the first time in a particular month?

12. In each of the following binomial situations, indicate the method to be used in determining the probabilities of various numbers of successes.

   a. $n = 16, \ \pi = .60$.

   b. $n = 500, \pi = .03$.

   c. $n = 17, \ \pi = .05$.

   d. $n = 350, \pi = .98$.

   e. $n = 100, \pi = .50$.

13. Indicate whether or not the binomial distribution might be used to model the following situations:

   a. The number of defective units produced by a certain person during the workday.

   b. The number of errors made by a computerized billing process each week.

   c. The number of defective units per shipment.

   d. The number of people in a neighborhood who intend to vote for the Democratic candidate in the next election.

14. The average number of calls that arrive at a police station per day during an eight-hour day shift is 96. What is the probability that no calls will arrive during a randomly chosen minute of the day shift? What is the probability that the station will receive at least one call?

15. Calls are received at a fire station on the average of three per day. Can the Poisson process be used to model this situation so that the probabilities of various numbers of calls per day can be found?

16. What is the advantage of attempting to find a mathematical model of a real-life situation?

17. Use the data base in Appendix I to select the first 30 persons from variables X8 and X9, which represent annual salary and age. Construct a probability distribution for each variable based on this sample and use an appropriate number of classes. Use these probability distributions to estimate the average salary and age of the sample.

6

Continuous Probability Distributions

Where You   In Chapter 5 you discovered that business data are observed values of
Have Been   random variables and learned how to determine the probabilities of
                specific numerical outcomes. You learned that probability
                distributions show the proportion of times a random variable tends to
                assume various values. You also learned how to compute the
                probabilities of possible numbers of successes in different two-outcome
                situations by using the binomial or Poisson distributions.

Where You   Business data are often derived from observations of continuous or
Are Going   discrete random variables. This chapter will consider some continuous
                random variables that are prevalent in business. One of the most
                useful distributions in business statistics, the normal probability
                distribution, will be introduced.

CONTINUOUS PROBABILITY DISTRIBUTIONS

So far, probability distributions of discrete variables have been considered where the random variable could assume only certain specified
values. Probability distributions of continuous random variables are
also important in statistical applications. A probability distribution is
continuous when the random variable may assume any value within
some specified range.

> A probability distribution is continuous when the random
> variable may assume any value within some specified range.

Figure 6–1 shows a smoothed curve that might appear from
graphing the probability distribution for a continuous random variable
X. The areas under the curve correspond to probabilities for X. For
example, the shaded area between the two points a and b is the
probability that X assumes a value within the shaded area ($a < X < b$).

FIGURE 6–1
Graph of a probability
distribution for a con-
tinuous random
variable X

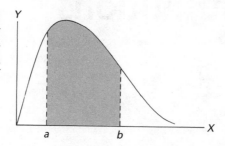

For continuous random variables, probabilities can be interpreted graphically only in terms of areas between two values. As discussed in Chapter 5, the total area of a probability distribution is equal to 1 $[\Sigma P(X) = 1.0]$. Finally, the shapes of probability distributions for continous random variables differ depending on the relative frequency distributions of the real data to be modeled.

The area under a continuous probability distribution is obtained by the use of calculus. Since this can be a difficult task, the areas of the most common distributions will be given in tabular form in the Appendices. To detemine the area between two values of X (the shaded area between a and b in Figure 6-1), we simply consult the appropriate table.

THE NORMAL DISTRIBUTION

The normal distribution shown in Figure 6-2 is important for the following three reasons:

1. The distributions for many continuous random variables in business and economics resemble this theoretical distribution.
2. The normal distribution can be used to approximate binomial probabilities when n is sufficiently large.
3. The distribution of both sample means and sample proportions of large samples tend to be normally distributed.

In the eighteenth century, astronomers observed that repeated measurements of the same value (such as the distance to the moon) tended to vary. When a large number of these observations were recorded and organized into a frequency distribution, the shape shown in Figure 6-2 kept reappearing. It was discovered that the distribution could be closely approximated with a continuous distribution called the *normal distribution*. This continuous probability distribution is shown in Figure 6-3. The curve for a normal distribution is bell-shaped and is determined by the mean, μ, and standard deviation, σ.

FIGURE 6-2
Normal frequency distribution for a large sample

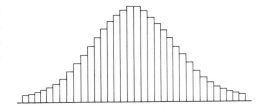

FIGURE 6–3
Normal frequency
curve for a population

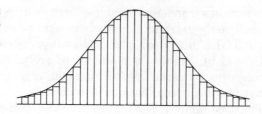

The normal curve is continuous and has a bell-shaped probability curve that is determined by the mean, μ, and standard deviation, σ.

Properties of the Normal Curve

Normal curves have the following characteristics that involve its shape, definition, and use:

1. Only the mean (μ) and standard deviation (σ) need to be known to compute probabilities for the normal distribution. Each combination of mean and standard deviation has a unique normal curve, and different combinations produce different normal curves. Figure 6–4 shows three normal curves with the same mean and different standard deviations. Since the standard deviation for curve C is relatively large, the values for this curve are more widely dispersed around the mean than the values for curves A and B.

2. The graph of the normal distribution in Figure 6–4 is bell shaped and symmetrical around its mean. The curve extends indefinitely in either direction from the mean.

3. Since the normal curve is measured on a continuous scale, the probability of obtaining a precise value is approximately 0.

FIGURE 6–4
Normal distribution
curves for variables
that have the same
mean and different
standard deviations

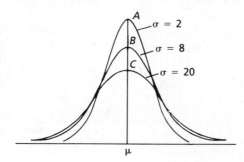

4. The probability that a random variable will have a value between any two points is equal to the area under the curve between those points. The total area under a normal curve is 1.0 or 100% of the probability associated with a particular variable. Since the normal curve is symmetrical around the mean, 50% of the area is below the mean and 50% of the area is above the mean.

5. The area under the normal curve between the mean and any other point can be determined by knowing how many standard deviations this point is from the mean.

Areas Under the Normal Curve

Computing the area under the normal probability distribution is a difficult task requiring knowledge of calculus. Fortunately, these areas have already been calculated and placed in a table. Since there are an infinite number of normal curves, one for each combination of μ and σ, the table of areas is constructed as a function of a Z score. The number of standard deviations from the mean for an observation X is defined as a Z *score*.

$$Z = \frac{(\text{Value} - \text{Mean})}{\text{Standard Deviation}}$$

$$Z = \frac{(X - \mu)}{\sigma} \tag{6-1}$$

where Z = the number of standard deviations from the mean
$\quad\quad X$ = the value of interest
$\quad\quad \mu$ = the mean of the distribution
$\quad\quad \sigma$ = the standard deviation of the distribution

To determine areas under the curve for any normal distribution, the scale must be converted from actual units to standard units or Z scores. The mean of a distribution is always equal to a Z score of 0, and the standard deviation measures the relative distance from the mean. A vertical axis is drawn at the mean or $Z = 0$ where the curve reaches its maximum point. Figure 6–5 shows the normal curve after the values have been converted to Z scores. Only three standard deviation units are shown on either side of the mean because this Z value includes 99.72% of the total area under the normal curve.

The Z score is the number of standard deviations from the mean of the normal curve to some point of interest.

FIGURE 6–5
Normal distribution of
Z scores

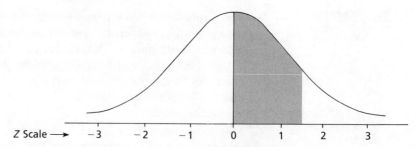

Z Scale ⟶   −3   −2   −1   0   1   2   3

Finding Probabilities from the Normal Table

The normal table is designed so that it can be read in terms of Z scores. Table 6–1, which also appears in Appendix E, shows the area under the curve between the mean and a selected value of Z (the shaded area in Figure 6–5). Since the normal curve is symmetrical around its mean, the vertical line drawn at $Z = 0$ divides the curve into two equal halves. Each half contains 50% of the total area under the curve, and the normal table is used to find areas on either side of the mean. For each segment on the right side of the mean, there is a corresponding segment on the left side.

Example 6–1   Suppose that a manager knows that the mileages of a large fleet of her company's rental cars can be closely approximated by a normal distribution. She knows that the mean of this distribution is 24 miles per gallon and the standard deviation is 4 mpg. Figure 6–6 illustrates this population of automobile mileages.

What is the probability that a rental car selected at random will average between 24 and 28 miles per gallon? An alternative way of posing this question is, what percentage of the normal curve area lies in the interval 24 to 28 mpg? These two questions are the same because the total area under the curve is equal to 1.0 or 100%. The area represented by the interval 24 to 28, shown as the shaded area in Figure 6–7, is the likelihood that an individual car drawn randomly from the distribution will average between 24 and 28 mpg.

Solution   If equation 6–1 is applied,

$$Z = \frac{(X - \mu)}{\sigma}$$

$$Z = \frac{(28 - 24)}{4}$$

$$Z = 1.00$$

TABLE 6-1
Table of areas for
standard normal prob-
ability distribution

Z	.00	.01	.02	.03	.04	.05	.06	.07	.08	.09
0.0	.0000	.0040	.0080	.0120	.0160	.0199	.0239	.0279	.0319	.0359
0.1	.0398	.0438	.0478	.0517	.0557	.0596	.0636	.0675	.0714	.0753
0.2	.0793	.0832	.0871	.0910	.0948	.0987	.1026	.1064	.1103	.1141
0.3	.1179	.1217	.1255	.1293	.1331	.1368	.1406	.1443	.1480	.1517
0.4	.1554	.1591	.1628	.1664	.1700	.1736	.1772	.1808	.1844	.1879
0.5	.1915	.1950	.1985	.2019	.2054	.2088	.2123	.2157	.2190	.2224
0.6	.2257	.2291	.2324	.2357	.2389	.2422	.2454	.2486	.2518	.2549
0.7	.2580	.2612	.2642	.2673	.2704	.2734	.2764	.2794	.2823	.2852
0.8	.2881	.2910	.2939	.2967	.2995	.3023	.3051	.3078	.3106	.3133
0.9	.3159	.3186	.3212	.3238	.3264	.3289	.3315	.3340	.3365	.3389
1.0	.3413	.3438	.3461	.3485	.3508	.3531	.3554	.3577	.3599	.3621
1.1	.3643	.3665	.3686	.3708	.3729	.3749	.3770	.3790	.3810	.3830
1.2	.3849	.3869	.3888	.3907	.3925	.3944	.3962	.3980	.3997	.4015
1.3	.4032	.4049	.4066	.4082	.4099	.4115	.4131	.4147	.4162	.4177
1.4	.4192	.4207	.4222	.4236	.4251	.4265	.4279	.4292	.4306	.4319
1.5	.4332	.4345	.4357	.4370	.4382	.4394	.4406	.4418	.4429	.4441
1.6	.4452	.4463	.4474	.4484	.4495	.4505	.4515	.4525	.4535	.4545
1.7	.4554	.4564	.4573	.4582	.4591	.4599	.4608	.4616	.4625	.4633
1.8	.4641	.4649	.4656	.4664	.4671	.4678	.4686	.4693	.4699	.4706
1.9	.4713	.4719	.4726	.4732	.4738	.4744	.4750	.4756	.4761	.4767
2.0	.4772	.4778	.4783	.4788	.4793	.4798	.4803	.4808	.4812	.4817
2.1	.4821	.4826	.4830	.4834	.4838	.4842	.4846	.4850	.4854	.4857
2.2	.4861	.4864	.4868	.4871	.4875	.4878	.4881	.4884	.4887	.4890
2.3	.4893	.4896	.4898	.4901	.4904	.4906	.4909	.4911	.4913	.4916
2.4	.4918	.4920	.4922	.4925	.4927	.4929	.4931	.4932	.4934	.4936
2.5	.4938	.4940	.4941	.4943	.4945	.4946	.4948	.4949	.4951	.4952
2.6	.4953	.4955	.4956	.4957	.4959	.4960	.4961	.4962	.4963	.4964
2.7	.4965	.4966	.4967	.4968	.4969	.4970	.4971	.4972	.4973	.4974
2.8	.4974	.4975	.4976	.4977	.4977	.4978	.4979	.4979	.4980	.4981
2.9	.4981	.4982	.4982	.4983	.4984	.4984	.4985	.4985	.4986	.4986
3.0	.49865	.4987	.4987	.4988	.4988	.4989	.4989	.4989	.4990	.4990
4.0	.4999683									

FIGURE 6-6
Distribution of auto-
mobile mileages

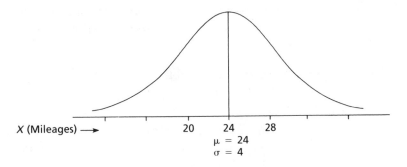

X (Mileages) ⟶   20   24   28

$\mu = 24$
$\sigma = 4$

101

FIGURE 6–7
Probability that a car
will average between
24 and 28 mpg

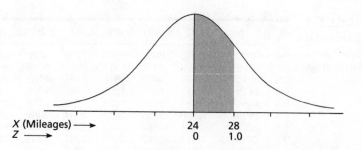

X (Mileages) ⟶   24   28
Z ⟶   0   1.0

The value for X (28) is one standard deviation from the mean (24). On any normal curve, one standard deviation from the mean involves the same amount of area. The normal curve table gives this area. One peculiarity of a normal curve table is that the values of Z are shown in two parts. The column labeled Z in the left margin gives the Z score in tenths. The column headings give the Z score in hundredths. Since $Z = 1.00$ in the example, look down the left margin column until you find the value 1.0. Since $Z = 1.00$, the .00 column is used (if $Z = 1.01$, the .01 column would be used). The area shown in the table opposite $Z = 1.0$, in the .00 column, is .3413. This is the area under the normal curve from the mean to one standard deviation away. There is approximately a 34% chance that a rental car selected at random will average between 24 and 28 mpg.

Any area under the normal curve can be determined by computing intervals from the mean. For example, the following questions from Example 6–1 can be answered. What is the probability that a randomly chosen car will average

    a. 22 to 28 mpg?
    b. 29 or more mpg?
    c. less than 21 or more than 26 mpg?
    d. 27 to 30 mpg?

Figure 6–8 shows the appropriate shaded areas for the four intervals. The probabilities for these shaded areas are found in Examples 6–2 through 6–5.

Example 6–2   What is the probability that a car selected at random will average between 22 and 28 mpg?

Solution   The Z scores are calculated for the interval from the mean (24) to 28 and for the interval from the mean to 22. The Z scores are looked up in the normal curve table to find the appropriate areas, and the two areas are then added together.

FIGURE 6–8
Intervals representing
the number of miles
per gallon a car can
travel

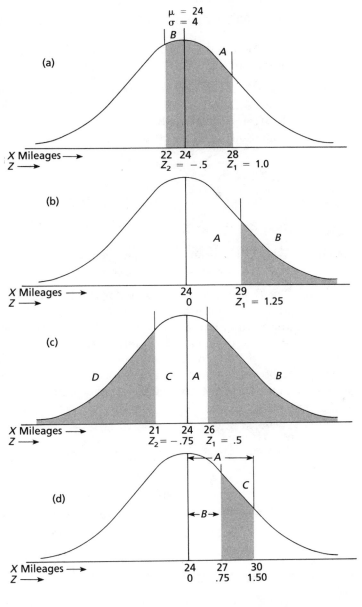

$$Z_1 = \frac{(28 - 24)}{4} = 1.00 \rightarrow \text{Area } A = .3413$$

$$Z_2 = \frac{(22 - 24)}{4} = -.50 \rightarrow \text{Area } B = \underline{.1915}$$

Total shaded area = .5328
Answer: 53.28%

Note that the minus sign for Z_2 simply means that X is below μ.

Example 6–3   What is the probability that a car selected at random will average 29 mpg or more?

Solution   The Z score is calculated for the interval from the mean (24) to 29. The Z score is looked up in the normal curve table to find the area. To determine the area above 29, the area between 24 and 29 is subtracted from .5000 because 50% of the curve is above the mean.

$$Z_1 = \frac{(29 - 24)}{4} = 1.25 \rightarrow \text{Area } A = .3944$$

$$\text{Area } B = (.5000 - .3944) = .1056$$

$$\text{Answer: } 10.56\%$$

Example 6–4   What is the probability that a car selected at random will average less than 21 mpg or more than 26 mpg?

Solution   The Z scores are calculated for the interval from the mean (24) to 26 and for the interval from the mean to 21. The Z scores are looked up in the normal curve table to find the areas of the intervals from the Z scores to the mean. To determine the area above 26, the area between 24 and 26 is subtracted from .5000. The area below 21 is found by subtracting the area between 21 and 24 from .5000. The area above 26 is added to the area below 21 to determine the answer.

$$Z_1 = \frac{(26 - 24)}{4} = .50 \longrightarrow \text{Area } A = .1915$$

$$\text{Area } B = (.5000 - .1915) = .3085$$

$$Z_2 = \frac{(21 - 24)}{4} = -.75 \longrightarrow \text{Area } C = .2734$$

$$\text{Area } D = (.5000 - .2734) = .2266$$

$$\text{Area } B + \text{Area } D = .3085 + .2266 = .5351$$

Example 6–5   What is the probability that a car selected at random will average between 27 and 30 mpg?

Solution   The Z scores are calculated for the interval from the mean (24) to 30 and the interval from the mean to 27. The Z scores are looked up in the normal curve table and the areas of the intervals are determined. The area for the interval 24 to 27 is then subtracted from the area for the interval 24 to 30.

$$Z_1 = \frac{(30 - 24)}{4} = 1.50 \longrightarrow \text{Area } A = .4332$$

$$Z_2 = \frac{(27 - 24)}{4} = .75 \longrightarrow \text{Area } B = \underline{.2734}$$

$$\text{Shaded area } C = .1598$$

Sometimes the area under the normal curve is known and some value of X can be obtained.

Example 6–6 Suppose a local tire manufacturer has determined from actual road tests that the mean tire mileage is $\mu = 30,000$ miles and the standard deviation is $\sigma = 3,000$ miles. In addition, the data collected are normally distributed. Assume that the manufacturer wishes to offer a guarantee that will provide a discount on a new set of tires if the original tires do not exceed the mileage stated in the guarantee. If the manufacturer wishes no more than 15% of the tires to be eligible for the discount, what should the guaranteed mileage be? Figure 6–9 shows the shaded area of interest to the manufacturer.

Solution To use the normal curve table, reverse the procedure used before and look up an area from the mean to where the shaded area begins. This area equals (.5000 − .1500 = .3500). Instead of looking for the area for a Z score, look for the Z score that coincides with the area of interest. The area that is closest to .3500 is .3508, which is found at the intersection of the 1.0 row and the .04 column ($Z = -1.04$). (Note that the minus sign is used because the area of interest is below the mean.) To find the mileage X corresponding to $Z = -1.04$ use Equation 6–1.

$$Z = \frac{(X - \mu)}{\sigma}$$

$$-1.04 = \frac{(X - 30,000)}{3,000}$$

$$-3,120 = X - 30,000$$

$$X = 26,880$$

FIGURE 6–9
Distribution of tire
mileage

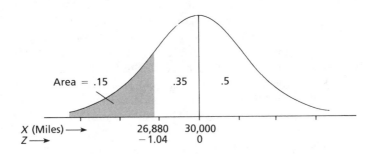

Area = .15   .35   .5

X (Miles) ⟶   26,880   30,000
Z ⟶   − 1.04   0

A guarantee of 26,880 miles will meet the requirement that 15% of the tires will be eligible for the guarantee. With this information, the manufacturer might set the tire mileage guarantee policy at 27,000 miles.

Again, note that probability distributions play an important role in providing information for decision making. Once a probability distribution is determined for a problem, it can be used to provide timely probability data. This type of information helps managers to reach quick and accurate decisions.

Properties of the Normal Curve Distribution

1. To compute probabilities for any normal distribution, only the mean and standard deviation need to be known.

2. The normal distribution is bell-shaped.

3. It is symmetrical around the mean.

4. The total area under the curve is 1.0 or 100%.

5. The normal distribution extends indefinitely in either direction from the mean.

6. The probability that a random variable will have a value between any two points is equal to the area under the normal curve between those points.

7. The probability that a normally distributed variable will equal an exact given value is approximately zero.

NORMAL DISTRIBUTION AS AN APPROXIMATION OF BINOMIAL PROBABILITIES

As discussed in the last chapter, binomial probability tables for values of n greater than 20 are usually not available. When n is large ($n > 20$) and π is small ($\pi < .05$), the Poisson distribution was used to approximate binomial probabilities. The normal curve can be used to approximate binomial probabilities when $n\pi > 5$ or $n(1 - \pi) > 5$.

The use of the normal curve to approximate binomial probabilities causes one difficulty that is not a problem when Poisson approximations are used. Both the Poisson and binomial distributions are discrete, whereas the normal curve is continuous. Since discrete variables involve integer values only, intervals will have to be assigned to the continuous normal distribution to represent binomial values. For example, continuous values in the range 9.5 to 10.5 relate to the discrete value 10. The addition and subtraction of .5 to the X value is commonly referred to as the *continuity correction factor*. It is the method of converting a discrete variable into a continuous variable. To find the binomial probability of exactly 10 successes, the normal curve approximation would be used based on the probability (area under the normal curve) between 9.5 and 10.5.

Example 6–7 Suppose that a State Revenue Department has found from experience that 50% of the individual state income tax returns filed contain arithmetic errors. What is the probability that a randomly drawn sample of 20 returns will contain exactly ten with errors? We will use the binomial table to solve this problem and then solve the same problem using the normal approximation and compare results.

Solution Binomial solution:

$$n = 20, \pi = .5, X = 10; \quad \text{probability} = .1762$$

Normal curve approximation:

Since the normal distribution is expressed by its mean and standard deviation, the μ and σ must be calculated as follows:

$$\mu = n\pi \qquad \sigma = \sqrt{n\pi (1 - \pi)}$$
$$\mu = 20(.5) \qquad \sigma = \sqrt{20(.5)(1 - .5)}$$
$$\mu = 10 \qquad \sigma = 2.236$$

Figure 6–10 shows the normal distribution with the interval 9.5 to 10.5 as the shaded area. The Z scores are calculated for the interval from the mean (10) to 10.5 and for the interval from the mean to 9.5. The Z scores are looked up in the normal curve table to find the appropriate area. The two areas are then added as follows:

FIGURE 6–10
Distribution of errors
on state income tax
returns

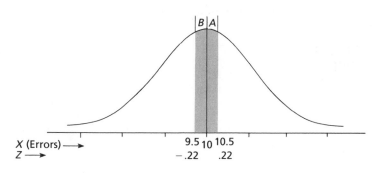

$$Z_1 = \frac{(10.5 - 10)}{2.236} = .22 \quad \rightarrow \text{Area } A = .0871$$

$$Z_2 = \frac{(9.5 - 10)}{2.236} = -.22 \rightarrow \text{Area } B = \underline{.0871}$$

$$\text{Total shaded area} = .1742$$

Note that the approximation of .1742 is close to the true binomial value .1762; the error is only .002, which is quite small.

Example 6-8   Over a long period of time, a firm has hired hundreds of employees and has found that 80% of those applying for jobs are satisfactory. Suppose 50 workers apply for jobs. What is the probability that 45 or more will be satisfactory?

Solution   First the mean and standard deviation are calculated as follows:

$$\mu = n\pi \qquad \sigma = \sqrt{n\pi\,(1 - \pi)}$$
$$\mu = 50(.8) \qquad \sigma = \sqrt{50(.8)(1 - .8)}$$
$$\mu = 40 \qquad \sigma = 2.8$$

Figure 6-11 shows the normal distribution with the interval above 44.5 as the shaded area. Note that to include 45 workers, one must start at 44.5. The Z score is calculated for the interval from the mean (40) to 44.5. The Z score is looked up in the normal curve table to find the area, which is then subtracted from .5000.

$$Z = \frac{(44.5 - 40)}{2.8} = 1.61 \rightarrow \text{Area } A = .4463$$

$$\text{Area } B = (.5000 - .4463) = .0537$$

$$\text{Answer: } 5.37\%$$

Finally, it should be noted that the nearer π is to .5, and the larger the value of n, the more closely the normal curve areas will approximate binomial probabilities.

FIGURE 6-11
Distribution of
qualified applicants

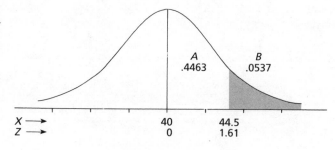

NORMAL CURVE APPLICATIONS

Normally distributed sets of data arise from several sources in business and management. Some examples are the following:

- Repetition of certain kinds of industrial processes over and over again (such as using a filling machine to fill cans of beer with 12 ounces of fluid).
- Weights of loads of produce shipped to a supermarket.
- Percentage of monthly gains (or losses) of a stock's price.
- Annual sales of a firm or corporation.
- The demand for a product.
- Scores on standardized personnel tests.
- Various kinds of errors that characterize measurements, including chance fluctuations in random sampling, errors due to the unreliability of measuring instruments, errors of observation or judgement, and errors in predictions or forecasts.

These types of errors and the uses of the normal curve to analyze statistics will be discussed in later chapters.

An understanding of how to determine normal curve areas is important to several statistical applications. We will learn in Chapter 8 that these techniques are frequently used with populations that are not normally distributed as well as with those that can be approximated by the normal curve.

When solving problems that involve normal curves, it is advisable to sketch a graph of the appropriate normal curve and shade the area of interest. Whenever the normal curve table is used, the population is assumed to approximate the normal distribution. The normal curve is *not* the only continuous probability distribution. It is used frequently because many real-life situations closely resemble it and because the technique for finding areas under such a curve is easy to use. However, normal distributions do not accurately describe all variables. For example, consider the distribution of the lifetimes of a

FIGURE 6-12
Distribution of the
lifetimes of batteries

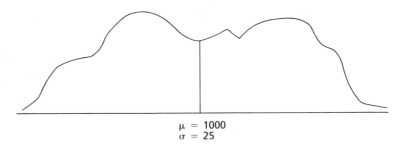

$\mu = 1000$
$\sigma = 25$

population of batteries presented in Figure 6–12. The mean lifetime of a battery is 1,000 hours with a standard deviation of 25 hours, and the variable is measured on a continuous scale, time. However, the normal distribution is not appropriate for analyzing this situation. Other continuous distributions, such as the uniform and exponential distributions, can be used to describe populations.

SUMMARY

A continuous probability distribution is used both to describe continuous random variables and to approximate discrete random variables (binomial). Probabilities of continuous distributions are computed in terms of the area under a curve between two points. The probability of obtaining an exact given value is approximately zero.

The normal distribution is actually a series of unique distributions, each with a different combination of mean and standard deviation. The normal distribution is bell-shaped and symmetrical around the mean and it extends indefinitely in either direction from the mean. The total area under the curve of a normal distribution is equal to 1.0. The process of obtaining probabilities is simplified by expressing the values of a normally distributed random variable in terms of the number of standard deviations a given value is from the mean (Z score).

The normal distribution is frequently used to approximate binomial probabilities. The approximation works best when n is large ($n > 20$) and the probability for each trial (π) is close to .5.

CASE STUDY: EUREKA DAIRY

Jim Black is in charge of quality control at the Eureka Dairy located in Deer Park, Washington. Jim is very concerned about the bacteria count per cubic centimeter of Grade A milk. On July 15 the bacteria count was 31,000. Jim's problem is to determine whether something is wrong with the production process. The Eureka Dairy over a long period of time has regulated its processing so that it has a mean bacteria count of 21,000 with a standard deviation of 3,000. A distribution made from the bacteria counts over a long period of time indicated that the distribution is normal in form. Each day the count is plotted on a chart similar to that shown in Figure 6–13. Jim needs to determine whether this chart is useful.

FIGURE 6–13
Bacteria counts in
Grade A milk

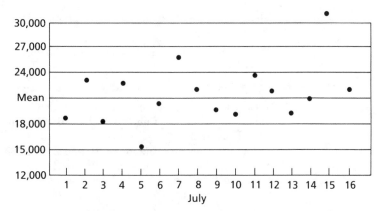

Questions

1. What are the chances in 1,000 that the bacteria count will exceed 30,000 if the day-to-day variation shown in Figure 6–13 is purely random?
2. What is the probability of a bacteria count of 31,000 or more?
3. Which is the more reasonable assumption: That a bacteria count of 31,000 might reasonably be expected or that something is wrong? Why?
4. Is the charting device shown in Figure 6–13 helpful in maintaining a high standard of quality? Explain.
5. Why would it be important for this dairy to find the mean value of these bacteria counts every month?

EXERCISES

1. Which of the following statements are true concerning the normal probability distribution?
    a. It is symmetrical.
    b. It is completely specified when the mean and standard deviation are known.
    c. The mean of a normal curve could be negative.
    d. The standard deviation of a normal curve could be negative.
    e. The normal curve is used as an approximation for the Poisson distribution.
    f. The normal distribution represents the probability distribution for a continuous random variable.
    g. The mean and median of a normal curve will usually not be equal.

2. Explain the difference between a discrete random variable and a continuous random variable.

3. Why do we use Z scores?

4. What is the relationship between probability and area for continuous distributions?

5. What is the reference point when using the normal curve table to look up Z scores?

6. Why does the normal curve table only show areas on one-half of the curve?

7. Draw a normal curve for each of the following parts. Shade in the area under the curve and find the probability that an item would fall in the shaded interval.
   a. The area between the mean (0) and $Z = 1.25$.
   b. The area between the mean (0) and $Z = -2.00$.
   c. The area to the right or above $Z = 1.75$.
   d. The area to the left or below $Z = 1.00$.
   e. The area between $Z = -.50$ and $Z = .50$.
   f. The area between $Z = .62$ and $Z = 1.62$.

8. Find the Z score that corresponds to the following areas of probabilities:
   a. One-half or 50% of the area lies above this Z score.
   b. One-third or 33.3% of the area lies above this Z score.
   c. One-fourth or 25% of the area lies below this Z score.

9. A machine automatically fills pop cans with an average (mean) of 12 ounces and a standard deviation of .1 ounces of pop. It has been observed that the ounces of fill closely approximate a normal distribution.
   a. What percentage of the cans contain more than 12.1 ounces?
   b. What percentage of the cans contain less than 11.95 ounces?
   c. What percentage of the cans contain between 11.97 and 12.03 ounces?
   d. What percentage of the cans contain between 12.1 and 12.2 ounces?
   e. A can is tested and contains only 11.7 ounces. What is the probability that a can will have 11.7 or less ounces?

10. Spokane Auto Sales is considering offering a service contract covering the cost of service work required on leased vehicles. From past records the manager determines that yearly service costs are approximately normally distributed with a mean of $200 and a standard deviation of $30. Spokane Auto Sales is considering offering the service contract for a yearly charge of either $250 or $275. What is the probability that any one customer's service costs will exceed a contract price of $250? Of $275?

11. The number of days that guests stay at the Grambo Resort is an approximately normally distributed random variable with a mean of 10 and a standard deviation of 2. Next month 1,000 guests are expected.
    a. How many can be expected to stay more than 6 days?
    b. How many can be expected to stay more than 13 days?
    c. How many can be expected to stay between 9 and 15 days?
    d. How many can be expected to stay fewer than 7 days?
    e. Eighty percent of the guests will stay longer than how many days?
    f. Ten percent of the guests leave after how many days?

12. The bid prices on a section of real estate are assumed to be normally distributed with a mean of $100,000 and a standard deviation of $10,000.

A single bid is randomly selected from all of those received.
a. What is the probability that the bid will be less than $75,000?
b. What is the probability that it will exceed $110,000?
c. What is the probability that the bid will exceed $95,000?
d. What is the probability that it will be less than $120,000?
e. What is the probability that the bid will be between $85,000 and $90,000?
f. Twenty-five percent of the bids will exceed what amount?
g. Fifteen percent of the bids will be less than what amount?

13. The amount of mail handled daily by the postal department in a local bank is normally distributed with a mean of 2,000 and a standard deviation of 50. The manager of the postal department would like to know the following:
a. The probability that the volume of mail will exceed 2,150.
b. The probability that the volume of mail will exceed 1,950.
c. The probability that the volume of mail will be between 1,875 and 1,975.
d. The probability that the volume will be less than 2,100.
e. Can the volume ever exceed 2,300?
f. Seventy-five percent of the time volume will be less than what amount?

14. The department in charge of selling advertising for CBA Television claims the number of homes (based on the Nielsen ratings) viewing its evening news program has a mean of 5 million and a standard deviation of .5 million. The number of homes reached per evening by this program is normally distributed.
a. What percentage of the evenings does this program reach fewer than 4.1 million homes?
b. What percentage of the evenings does this program reach between 4.8 and 5.3 million homes?
c. What is the probability that on two randomly selected evenings this program will reach fewer than 4 million homes on both days?
d. On 70% of the evenings this program is seen by at least how many homes?

15. The mean and standard deviation of a distribution of 1,500 accounts receivable for a large department store are $60 and $20, respectively. Assume that they are normally distributed.
a. How many accounts in this distribution will lie above the point $85 on the scale?
b. Above what point on the scale will one-third of the accounts lie?
c. What percentage of all the cases will lie between $60 and $85?
d. What dollar amounts on either side of the mean would include the middle 60% of the accounts in the distribution?
e. What are the chances in 100 that a single account selected at random will lie above $35?
f. The chances are 95 in 100 that a single account selected at random will lie above what point along the scale?

g. What is the probability that a single account selected at random will lie between $80 and $90?

h. The chances are 1 in 10 that a single account selected at random will deviate from the mean by more than what amount?

i. Five percent of the measures will lie more than what distance from the mean?

16. The lives of Extra-Life light bulbs are normally distributed with a mean of 1,500 hours and a standard deviation of 20 hours.

a. What percentage of the bulbs will have a life between 1,500 and 1,525 hours?

b. What percentage of the bulbs will have a life between 1,475 and 1,490 hours?

c. The 5% of the bulbs with the longest life will last longer than how many hours?

d. The 10% of the bulbs with the shortest life will last no longer than how many hours?

e. What percentage of the bulbs will burn out during the 1,500th hour?

17. Suds Beverages is interested in placing advertisements in *Sports Digest*. After considerable research, a study is located that indicates the probability that a reader will read an advertisement in *Sports Digest* is .03. If Suds Beverages places 50 ads in *Sports Digest*, what is the probability that a person reads

a. no Suds advertisements?

b. exactly two Suds advertisements?

c. more than four Suds advertisements?

d. fewer than three Suds advertisements?

18. To check the effectiveness of a new production process, 500 photo flash devices were randomly selected from a production line. If the process actually is supposed to produce only 8% defectives, what is the probabiliy that

a. fifty or more defectives appear in the sample of 500?

b. fewer than 40 defectives appear in the sample of 500?

c. exactly 45 defectives appear in the sample of 500?

19. The Layrite Products Company has a history of making errors in 9% of its invoices. A sample of 200 invoices has been taken. What is the probability that

a. exactly 20 invoices contain errors?

b. more than 25 invoices contain errors?

c. fewer than 20 invoices contain errors?

d. fewer than 15 invoices contain errors?

20. Decision Science Associates (DSA) is a market firm that forecasts sales for its client companies. DSA measures errors made in past forecasts by obtaining actual sales data from companies and computing the percent difference between actual and forecasted sales. If sales of a particular item were forecasted to be 420 units and actual sales turned out to be 400 units, the error would be 20 in 400, or 20/400 = 5%. Decision Science claims that its errors average 6% with a standard deviation of 2 percentage points. Assuming errors are normally distributed, what is the probability that the error percentage in a forecast is

a. between 9 and 11 percent?

b. over 12 percent?

c. less than 3 percent?

d. 20% of the time DSA's forecasts will be within what percentage of actual sales?

21. Given the same information in Exercise 20,

a. within what interval centered at the mean did 68% of the forecast errors lie?

b. within what interval centered at the mean did 95% of the forecast errors lie?

22. In a large plant, the maintenance department has been instructed to replace light bulbs before they burn out. A study shows that the life of light bulbs is normally distributed with a mean life of 500 hours and a standard deviation of 50 hours. When should the light bulbs be replaced so that no more than 4% of them will ever burn out?

23. A college bookstore's records show that attendance in the Statistics course is normally distributed with a mean of 200 students a quarter and a standard deviation of 25 students. How many textbooks should be ordered if the bookstore would like to allow for no more than a 5% chance of running out of stock?

24. This question refers to the class data base. Assume that High School Grade Point Average is a normally distributed variable. What percentage of the class had an average higher than 3.0?

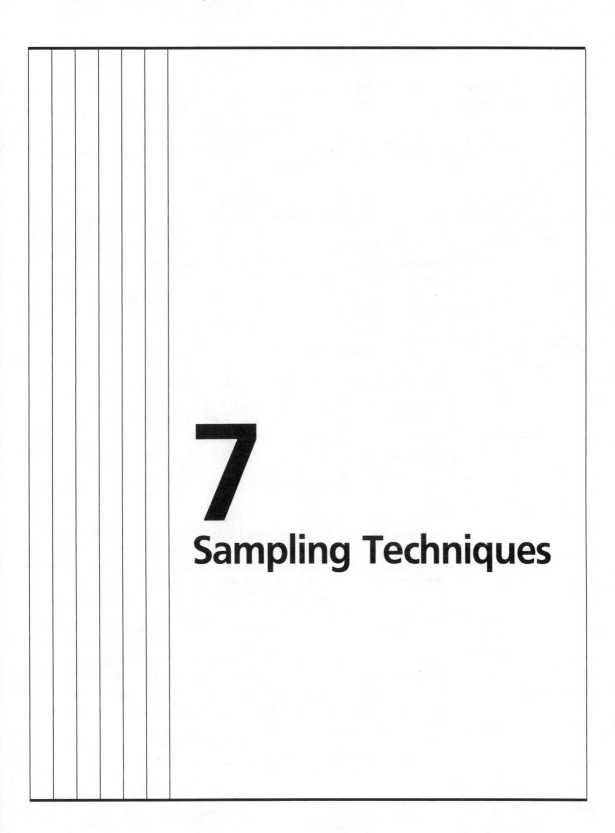

7
Sampling Techniques

In previous chapters a number of topics have been discussed to prepare you for the most essential task of statistics, which is to make inferences about populations on the basis of sample data. This preparatory work has involved a study of the basic concepts of statistical analysis that must be understood before moving on to the data analysis techniques used widely in management.

Before turning to a study of data analysis techniques, it is important to understand the various methods of selecting those items to be included in the sample. There are several ways of making such selections but some are more appropriate than others in certain situations. The purpose of this chapter is to examine several methods used to select sample items from populations.

SAMPLING TECHNIQUES

Sampling versus Taking a Census

It is sometimes possible to conduct a census of the population under study; this involves a measurement of every single item constituting the population of interest. Such a census is feasible when the population is quite small and easy to access or when the population is listed on a computer file. In this latter case, a good deal of time and money are typically spent in writing and debugging a survey computer program; however, the run-time involved is quite small even for a complete census.

Analysts are almost always forced to examine only a few of the population items because of time and money restraints; these few items are known as the sample. In this chapter we will look at various ways of sampling objects from populations before moving on to a study of the techniques used to extract useful information from sample data.

The basic objective to keep in mind when searching for a method of selecting items for the sample is that the sample must be *representative* of the entire population. Various measurements will be made on the sampled items, and it will be inferred that the population possesses these same characteristics. Obviously then, the analyst will want the sampled items to be a miniature population; that is, each sampled item must be a good representative of the many nonsampled population items it represents.

One way of assuring that the sample has a good chance of representing the population well is to give every population item the same chance of being selected for the sample. If this is done, the result is called a *random sample*.

A random sample is one in which each item in the population has the same chance of being selected to be in the sample.

Random versus Nonrandom Sampling

Statistical procedures always assume that the sample items being analyzed are randomly chosen from the population. This is because these procedures make statements of inference about the population from which the sample items were selected. Thus, it must be assumed that the sample is a good representation of the population, and a random sample provides this assurance. More specifically, if the sample is selected randomly it is possible to calculate the probability that sample estimates are within certain distances of the population parameters they estimate; if the sample is not random such calculations are not possible.

In practice, it is often difficult to select a sample on a genuinely random basis, and the analyst must be extremely careful to choose a sample in such a way as to assure that the sample is truly representative of the population. What appears to be a representative sampling procedure at first glance may, in fact, involve hidden biases. If the sample chosen under these conditions does not represent the population well, the inferential statements made about the population will be erroneous.

For example, hidden researcher biases are often involved when selecting people for interviews. Interviewers may claim there is no bias in this selection process but may subconsciously select only persons of the same age, sex, and race as themselves. Again, great care must be taken to assure that the sample is representative of the population.

Particular care must be taken in sampling situations where the results may be controversial or subject to attack by the study recipients. If the researcher cannot defend the randomness of the sample selection process, the study results may be rejected even though the sample may actually represent the population quite well. Analysts often pay too little attention to the requirement that the sampled items must be good representatives of the population of interest. Questions at the end of this chapter invite you to assess the randomness of the sample in several situations.

NONRANDOM SAMPLING

Judgement Sampling

A nonrandom sample is one in which not every population item has the same chance of being selected for the sample. One common example of such a sampling procedure is called the *judgement sample* because the analyst's judgement is used in selecting the sampled items.

> A judgement sample is one in which population items are sampled on the basis of the analyst's judgement as to which items will constitute a representative sample.

Many national polls are conducted on a judgement basis because it would be impossible to obtain a list of everyone's name so that persons could be selected for the sample on a truly random basis. Instead, experienced pollsters have determined those types of people, areas of the country, and sample sizes for each substrata that will produce a representative picture of the entire nation. If pollsters exercise good judgement in the selection process, their results are subsequently verified, and their services are engaged by political candidates, businesses, and TV networks. However, if pollsters select samples that are not representative of the entire population, their results are shown to be inaccurate, and they are soon out of business.

Judgement sampling can be either good or bad depending upon the experience and judgement of the persons selecting the sampled items. Even when their judgement is quite good, however, the sample results are often open to question because such pollsters cannot totally defend their sampling process: it is, in fact, not random. Attacks on pollsters are especially prevalent when money or political power rises and falls with ratings. TV ratings and political candidate ratings, for example, almost always generate controversy.

Quota or Convenience Sampling

If little or no thought is given to the importance of selecting a representative sample, a *convenience sample* often results. The required sample size is selected in the most convenient and timely manner. If several persons are each assigned a target number of items to sample without any instructions as to how these items should be selected, the resulting process is sometimes called a *quota sample*.

> A convenience sample or quota sample is one in which the objective is to obtain the required sample size as quickly and conveniently as possible regardless of whether the sample represents the population.

If a convenience sample results in a representative sample it is because of coincidence rather than design. Convenience samples usually result in oversampling some population elements and undersampling others. For this reason, experienced analysts reject such sampling procedures. Unfortunately, these procedures are often followed by less experienced samplers. The resulting analyses, no matter how sophisticated they might be, do not accurately describe the characteristics of the population under study because the data that were analyzed do not reflect the true nature of the population. Experienced analysts who are interested in obtaining an accurate picture of some population take great pains to assure that the sampled items present as accurate a picture of that population as possible before turning their attention to the analysis that will be conducted on the collected data.

RANDOM SAMPLING

Simple Random Sampling

One of the most common random sampling procedures frequently employed by analysts is the *simple random sample*. Such a sampling procedure results when the sample items are selected, one at a time, by some simple procedure such as drawing names from a hat.

> A simple random sample results from randomly choosing the sample items one at a time from the population so that each item has the same chance of being selected.

For example, suppose an analyst wants to choose a representative group of 10 students from a large class. One way of doing this would be to write each person's name on an identical-sized piece of paper, put these pieces of paper into a large container, and reach in without looking to select the 10 names. Such a sampling procedure would result in a random sample because each person in the class would have the same chance of being selected and there would be no sampling bias involved. The procedure would constitute a *simple* random sample because the sample items are simply picked randomly from the population one at a time.

When simple random samples are selected by drawing sample items from a hat, the sampling technique is easy to defend because there can be no charge of bias; if the sample size is large enough, the statistics measured in the sample can clearly be inferred to the population. In other cases it would be time consuming to literally write out the list of the entire population and place pieces of paper into a container. In such cases a random number table can often be used.

The random number table is a large listing of many digits randomly generated, usually by a computer program. These digits are displayed in tables usually found at the back of statistics and production/operations textbooks; Appendix F in this textbook contains a random number table. Table 7–1 is a partial listing of such a table.

To illustrate the use of the random number table shown in Table 7–1, suppose there are 85 people in a class and 5 of them will be randomly selected to constitute a committee. If there is a class list, one could number the persons on the list from 1 to 85. Then, five random numbers can be drawn from Table 7–1, and the persons that correspond to these numbers can be identified and appointed to the committee.

To select five random numbers from Table 7–1, it is necessary to begin at some arbitrarily chosen starting point and move systemat-

TABLE 7–1 Partial random number table						
64270	01638	92477	66969	98420	04880	45585
82765	34476	17032	87589	40836	32417	70002
46473	23219	53416	94970	25832	69975	94884
67245	68350	82948	11398	42878	80287	88267
07391	58745	25774	22987	80059	39911	96189
29992	65831	38857	50490	83765	55657	14361
31926	14883	24413	59744	92351	97473	89286
25388	61642	34072	81249	35648	50891	69352
70765	10592	04542	76463	54328	02349	17247
38391	91132	21999	59516	81652	27195	48223
53381	79401	21438	83035	92350	36693	31238
91962	04739	13092	97662	24822	94730	06496
87637	99016	71060	88824	71013	18735	20286
49323	45021	33132	12544	41035	80780	45393
14422	15059	45799	22716	19792	09983	74353

ically though the table until five numbers are chosen. If it was decided to start at the upper-left corner of the table and move across rows, the first random number would be 64. Two-digit random numbers are chosen because the largest numbered population item is a two-digit number (85). The following five random numbers were chosen from Table 7–1 using this procedure:

$$64 \quad 27 \quad 00 \quad 16 \quad 38$$

Since one of these numbers has no corresponding population item (00), another number must be chosen. The next number is 92, but no one in the class is assigned to the number 92 because the population contains only 85 people. The next random number is 47, and finally the following five usable numbers have been drawn: 64, 27, 16, 38, and 47. The five persons who are on the above positions on the class list have now been selected. These persons were selected randomly and this randomness is easily defensible.

Some of the problems at the end of this chapter ask you to use the random number table in Appendix F in conjunction with the data base at the end of the text in taking simple random samples. To use this larger random number table, turn to one of the pages, begin at a predetermined point (for example, the upper-left or lower-right), and move systematically through the table (for example, across rows or down columns). It is important to move systematically through the table so that no sampling bias can be introduced. Continue drawing random numbers until the desired sample size is reached. Duplicate numbers and those for which no population item exists will have to be replaced. The result is n random numbers: the population items with those numbers constitute the sample.

In many situations it is not possible to take a simple random sample. Such cases arise when it is not possible or convenient to obtain a listing of the entire population. Such a listing is sometimes called a *sampling frame*; it is necessary to have such a list before randomly selected numbers can be matched with population items. For example, suppose an analyst wished to randomly sample people in a shopping mall. As mentioned earlier in this chapter, when selecting persons to interview, the possibility of interviewer bias must be carefully guarded against. Therefore, it is important to assure that the persons who will be interviewed are selected on a genuinely random basis. However, it is impossible to obtain, for example, a complete list of those persons who frequent the shopping mall so that those who match random numbers can be interviewed. The next section describes a sampling procedure that will produce a random sample in such situations.

Systematic Sampling

When the population is lined up in some random fashion or flows randomly past some point, it is possible to choose every kth item to be in the sample. For example, one could choose every 15th root beer bottle from a filling machine or every 25th person to pass a point in a shopping mall. Such a sampling procedure generates a *systematic sample*.

A systematic random sample is one in which every kth item in the population is chosen for the sample; the population items must form some sort of line or sequence.

If the population items are randomly distributed in the sequence, such a sampling procedure generates a truly random sample. In the shopping mall case, for example, any researcher biases are eliminated because every 25th person will be interviewed regardless of that person's age, sex, race, or apparent economic condition. Notice also that a population frame is not needed. There exists no list of everyone who frequents the shopping mall. Nevertheless, it is possible to randomly sample such persons through the systematic process.

The customers at a shopping mall and the bottles of root beer on a production line represent what are sometimes called *infinite populations*. Although the population sequence will not literally go on forever, the population is extremely large and can be thought of as infinite in length. Smaller, or *finite populations*, are sometimes sampled using systematic sampling even though the items might be numbered and chosen using a simple random sample. An example of such a population is a series of personnel files in a file drawer. It would take longer to look through an entire file drawer to find certain numbered files that correspond to the chosen random numbers than it would to take every 10th or 25th file.

When systematically sampling from a finite population, it is first necessary to divide the population size by the sample size to determine the sample interval. For instance, if a file drawer contained 1000 files and a sample of 100 was desired, then every 10th file would be chosen (1000/100 = 10). A random starting point would be selected from the first ten files by drawing a random number between one and ten. Suppose the number four was chosen. The sampled files would then be files 4, 14, 24, 34, . . . 994. If the files were placed in the drawer alphabetically or arranged in some other arbitrary way, a truly random sample of 100 files would result, and the characteristics of this sample could be inferred to the population.

Care must be taken when using systematic sampling to make sure that the order of the population being sampled does not follow a pattern. If it does, systematic sampling may lead to a sampling bias. For example, suppose an automatic liquid filling machine has 10 filling heads. It would be a mistake to systematically sample every 10th container coming off the line because the entire sample would have been filled by the same filling head and all the other population items would not have been sampled at all. Before using systematic sampling it is necessary to check the population to be sure there is no periodic variation in the stream of population items. For most populations, such cycling does not exist and systematic sampling will produce a random sample.

The exercises at the end of this chapter ask you to use the systematic sampling procedure to select certain items from the data base at the back of the book. Remember to determine the sample interval (N/n) first, then select a random starting point from the first N/n items, and then choose every N/n item after that.

Stratified Sample

Suppose a lumber company wants to choose a number of logs from its log yard for a sample. The sampled logs will be measured for a number of important characteristics such as moisture content and board feet, and the results will then be used to estimate these characteristics for the entire log inventory. Because the results will be used to report inventory to the Internal Revenue Service, company management wants to be sure that the randomness of the sampling procedure is totally defensible.

It would be possible to conduct a simple random sample if each log were numbered. Then n random numbers could be drawn and the logs that correspond to these numbers could be removed and measured. The problem with using a simple random sample procedure is that the logs are arranged in the yard in piles of 10 to 15 logs and it would be too expensive to remove only one log from each of many stacks. On the other hand, the logs are not moving past a point so that every 20th or 30th could be selected. Even if the logs were sequentially numbered, many stacks would have to be broken up if a systematic sample were used, and this would be very expensive.

Before dealing with the problem of these log clusters, management decides to break the entire population of logs into three subgroups because the log stacks were formed during different periods of time and each stack can be regarded as old, middle aged, or new. Since the measurements of interest (moisture content and board feet) depend heavily on the age of the logs, such a population division is useful.

When meaningful subgroups are formed in a population before the sample is selected, the result is called a *stratified sample*.

A stratified sample results from forming subgroups in the population on a basis that is relevant to the sampling study; elements within each stratum should be similar, whereas the differences between strata should be great.

Notice from the definition of a stratified sample that the method of forming the subgroups must be relevant to the study being conducted. In the example, it might be possible to stratify the logs on the basis of who cut down the tree. But since this has nothing to do with moisture content and board feet, it would be a waste of time. On the other hand, the characteristics being measured are different for logs of different ages, and therefore, a stratification on age is worthwhile.

The principle advantage of stratifying a population prior to sampling is that, if the stratification is done on a relevant characteristic, the desired sampling accuracy can be obtained for a smaller sample size than would be possible with a simple random sample. If a simple random sample were used, given the desired degree of accuracy in estimating population parameters, a sample size of 200 might be needed, for example. A rather large sample is necessary so that a representative sample is obtained. This means continuing to sample until representative numbers of old, middle-aged, and new logs have been chosen. If, however, the population is stratified according to age, there will be enough old logs because the analyst goes to the place in the log yard where they are stacked and samples them. Likewise, the desired number of middle-aged logs and new logs are chosen. The resulting sample size might be only 100, and the study cost would be half of what would be required for a simple random sample.

Stratified samples are commonly used in human population studies. Skilled pollsters often make stratifications such as male/female, white/black/other, young/middle-aged/elderly, rural/suburban/city, northeast/south/midwest/west, and so forth. By carefully stratifying the population into such meaningful subgroups, these pollsters are able to obtain representative samples at a much lower cost and in much less time than would be possible with a simple random sample.

The question of how samples are obtained from the subgroups is another matter. As mentioned previously, many national pollsters conduct judgement samples. The point is that these judgements might be made within each subgroup after the stratifications are made.

Returning to the log yard example, management must now decide how to randomly select sample logs from within each age subgroup, and the problem of how to deal with the large log stacks remains.

Cluster Sample

When population items are gathered in groups, it is possible to randomly select entire clusters on a random basis and include all their items in the sample. Such a procedure is called a *cluster sample*.

> A cluster sample results from randomly choosing several population groups and including all members of these groups in the sample.

Management of the log yard agrees on a numbering system for the stacks of logs in each age subgroup. Suppose that there are 23 stacks of old logs and that about 36 old logs are needed for the total sample. Since each stack contains about 12 logs, three of the stacks will be totally sampled. Three random numbers are drawn from a random number table, and the stacks that correspond to these three numbers are broken up and each log is measured. The same procedure is followed for the middle-aged and new log stacks in the yard.

The final result is a random sample. Every log has the same chance of having its stack picked for the sample and there is no bias in selecting any particular log even if it is in the back of the yard and difficult to remove for measurement.

The sampling procedure employed in this example also uses both the stratified and cluster sampling procedures. First, the population was stratified on a meaningful characteristic (age), and the number of sampled items to be drawn from each subgroup was determined. This latter determination was made on the basis of the total sample size needed and the percent of the studied population made up by each subgroup. Next, instead of using a simple random sample for each subgroup, clusters of items were randomly chosen and sampled. This was done to avoid having to tear down a large number of log stacks.

Clustering and stratification techniques are often used in studies involving people. Stratification samples are used to determine economic well-being; that is, families living in areas of a city or county might be classified as high, medium, or low income. Next, entire clusters of persons (city blocks) are surveyed. This is not only convenient because it saves driving time, but because it is not possible to

TABLE 7–2
Sampling procedures

Sampling Procedure	Characteristics
Non-random	
Judgement	Quality depends on sampler's judgement
Convenience or Quota	Sample obtained as easily as possible
Random	
Simple	Items randomly chosen one at a time
Systematic	Every kth item chosen
Stratified	Relevant substrata sampled
Cluster	Items selected in groups

conduct simple random samples in the economic subgroups. There exists no list of persons residing in a particular middle-income subgroup, for example. However, the city map contains a list of where these persons live. The blocks on the map can be numbered and constitute the numbered clusters within each stratum. Random numbers are drawn, the corresponding clusters (city blocks) are identified, and trips are made to each selected block to interview every person living there. If the sample size is large enough, the study accurately reflects the entire population because each person in the area has the same chance of being selected. Also, the time and money required to complete the study are reduced because effective stratification on an important characteristic precedes the actual sampling.

Table 7–2 summarizes the sampling procedures discussed in this chapter.

DATA-GATHERING TECHNIQUES

When the population items to be sampled and measured are non-human, the method of measuring them is usually straightforward and obvious. For example, if one wishes to learn about the length of steel beams, the amount of fill on a bottling machine, or the average account balance in a bank, it is not difficult to measure the sample items without bias.

However, when the sampled objects are people, difficulties almost always arise. The reason is that most of these studies are conducted to learn what people are *thinking* about the subject of interest. Depending on whether questions are asked in written form, over the telephone, or in person, the answers may or may not reflect the true feelings of the sampled people and, thus, of the population of interest. In other words, the possibility of bias must always be guarded against when sampling people. In this section three common methods of learning about the attitudes of sampled persons are examined.

Questionnaire Construction

Written questionnaires are commonly used by researchers to learn about people's attitudes and demographics (age, income, type of job, number of children, and so forth). The questionnaire is usually the cheapest method of gathering information as compared with telephone and personal interviewing. However, the questions must be very carefully prepared because the lines of inquiry cannot be adjusted after the instrument is mailed. In contrast, skilled telephone and personal interviewers can change the direction of the interview based on responses to the first few key questions.

A major problem with using mailed questionnaires is called *nonresponse bias*. Suppose that 500 questionnaires are mailed out but only 250 are filled out and returned; the response rate is 50%. Are those who did not return the questionnaire different from those who did? If so, the results of the research are biased because an important segment of the population (those who do not respond to questionnaires) has not been sampled and measured. Skilled researchers take great pains to minimize the possible distortion effects of nonresponse bias. The following strategies are sometimes used:

1. Include a cover letter that has the person's name and address typed by the same machine that types the letter.
2. Personally sign the cover letter (one researcher uses a ball-point pen with a soft pad of paper under the letter so the pen will indent the letter as it is signed).
3. Make sure the questionnaire is attractive and professional looking (i.e., has adequate margins, is typed or printed in high quality fashion, and so forth).
4. Include a premium (coins or a dollar bill, for example).
5. Use a secret key so that names can be crossed off as returns come in. Two weeks after the mailing send a post card follow-up to people who have not returned their questionnaires.
6. Use a telephone follow-up after the post card follow-up and mail a new questionnaire if necessary.

It may not seem necessary to go to all this trouble to get a few nonresponders to return the questionnaire; why not just mail out a few more? The answer is that those who initially decide not to respond may differ in some very important respects from those who promptly return the instrument. If a very high response rate is achieved, the danger of nonresponse bias has been eliminated.

In constructing the questionnaire the following points should be considered:

1. Write a questionnaire that is reasonably short. People will not spend an hour filling it out.

2. Begin with questions that people will not mind answering (for example, how many children under the age of 18 reside at your residence?) and put more controversial questions near the end (for example, in which of the following categories is the annual income of your household?). People are more inclined to answer the tough questions if they have answered easy ones first.

3. Be very careful to make the questions unbiased so that the true feelings of the respondents come through. The following three questions are designed to measure the popularity of the President; however, only one of them will provide an unbiased response:

    a. Since there are more unemployed people in this country than at any time in its history, do you think this President is doing a good job?

    b. Do you think this President is doing a good job of getting this country moving again after the mess that was left by the previous President?

    c. Considering both international and domestic affairs, would you rate the President's performance in office as excellent, good, fair, or poor?

The proper steps for constructing questionnaires can be summarized as follows:[1]

1. Define your objectives. Although this seems an obvious first step to any research effort, we find that those who are about to embark on an expensive and time-consuming data-gathering effort are often unable to verbalize the objectives they wish to achieve.

2. Formulate the questions and put together a series of questions that will assure reliable responses. Remember that the results of the sample will be inferred to a much larger population.

3. Determine the tabulation method. We find in our consulting work that this point is very often overlooked. If the results of the data-gathering effort are to be tabulated so that manage-

---

[1] We are indebted to Dr. William R. Wynd of Eastern Washington University for providing an essay on questionnaire construction from which this list was taken.

ment can assimilate the results for decision-making purposes, it is important to formulate the questions so that meaningful tabulations are possible. For example, the following questions can be used to explore a consumer's attitudes toward a company's product quality.

a. What quality image do you have of our product?

b. Put an X in one of the five spaces below to indicate your attitude toward the quality of our product:

Low   High

Quality |___|___|___|___|___| Quality

One of these questions can be easily computer tabulated, the other cannot.

4. Prepare the instrument. Keeping in mind the physical appearance, length, letter of introduction, and order of questions, prepare a questionnaire that will assure the highest possible return rate.

5. Pretest the instrument. No questionnaire should be distributed until it has been thoroughly tested. A pretest should be given to a group of knowledgeable people and also to a group of persons selected from the target population, who then comment on the strengths and weaknesses of the questionnaire. After improvements are made, the pretest should be repeated until the instrument is as perfect as possible.

Telephone and Personal Interviewing

Telephone interviewing is more expensive than using written questionnaires because people must be recruited and trained to conduct the interviews. If the questions are rigidly formulated in advance, the possibility of interviewer bias is reduced; on the other hand, highly skilled interviewers can extract more information from respondents if the question format is less structured. This latter approach is more expensive because much interviewer training and monitoring is required.

Telephone interviewing produces results very rapidly. For this reason, it is often used for exploratory purposes or for updating population attitudes on a regular and timely basis. Television ratings or public figure ratings can be quickly tabulated by telephone, for example.

The disadvantage of using the telephone is that a representative sample is often difficult to achieve. Persons listed in the telephone book are not representative because some people do not have telephones and many others have unlisted numbers. Also, many people do not wish to be bothered in their homes with unsolicited phone calls. For these reasons, the possibility of bias is always present in telephone interviewing.

Personal one-on-one interviewing is the most expensive method of gathering attitude information but offers the most flexible method if conducted by skilled interviewers. The skill level of the interviewer must be extremely high for indepth interviews so that the greatest range of information can be extracted from interviewees. However, since a rapport must be established between the two parties, the greatest potential for interviewer bias exists and must be guarded against.

A more casual form of personal interviewing using structured and simple questions is the *mall intercept* often used by researchers. This method is so named because many of the interviews are conducted in shopping malls. A brief set of stuctured questions is asked of those persons intercepted in a shopping area; care must be taken to include a representative group of people in the sample (a systematic sample is often used for this purpose). The questions must be brief and easy to answer since people are not willing to pause for a long period of time. Quick and fairly accurate results can be achieved using this method.

Focus Groups

The *focus group* technique is widely used in marketing research to explore the beliefs and feelings of usually from five to ten people per session. To eliminate possible bias from the peculiarities of a single group, several focus groups are usually conducted in the course of a research project. Since the reactions of these persons represent the entire target population, it is important that good representatives of this population be chosen to participate. The correct mix of men and women, age groups, racial groups, and so forth, must be used in each group.

A skilled moderator acts as the session chair and attempts to explore the feelings and beliefs of the focus group on a number of questions of importance to the research. The moderator's task is to frame the discussion along the desired lines and to make sure that as many opinions as possible are presented by the participants.

More than one session is usually conducted because each group can take a different tack depending on its dominant members. There is a tendency for such groups to achieve a consensus rather than for each person to express an opinion. For this reason, several groups are conducted and the common themes across all groups are taken to be the prevailing attitudes of the target population. Again, it is vital to make sure that the participants in the focus groups are good representatives of the population of interest.

CASE STUDY: PORT DISTRICT STUDY

In June of 1982 a survey was conducted for Spokane County, Washington, to determine citizen awareness and attitudes toward the proposed formation of a port district. The following is a portion of the report that resulted from this study.

Port District Study

The purpose of this study was to determine how much Spokane County registered voters know about the proposed Port District. Four hundred and one telephone interviews were conducted on June 4 and 5.

The population was stratified by location and gender. Approximately fifty percent (50%) of the sample was randomly chosen from the county while the remainder was selected from within the Spokane city limits. The sample was also proportioned to provide a balance of male and female respondents.

The sample size was selected so that the results could be generalized to the population with a ninety-five percent (95%) degree of confidence that the reported percentages would be within five percent (5%) of the actual population values.

Summary of Survey Results

When the respondents were asked if they had heard the term "Port District," 72.1% replied "yes" and 27.9% replied "no."

When the 289 respondents who had heard the term were asked if they knew what a Port District is, 47.8% said "yes" and 52.2% replied "not sure." Therefore, 34.4% of the total group of respondents thought they knew what a Port District is.

All of the interviewees were also asked "Is there already enough developed land available for industrial use in Spokane County?" Forty-eight percent (48%) replied "yes," twenty-six percent (26%) said "no" and twenty-six percent (26%) were "not sure."

Next, the 289 respondents who had heard the term "Port District" responded as follows to several specific questions:

3. Does a Port District require a navigable waterway?

YES: 12.9%   NO: 68.6%   NOT SURE: 18.5%

PORT DISTRICT QUESTIONNAIRE

Are you a registered voter of Spokane County? (IF "NO", TERMINATE INTERVIEW)
(IF "YES" . . .)

Would you be willing to spend less than five minutes of your time answering a few questions concerning some ideas about Spokane County's future? (IF "NO", TERMINATE INTERVIEW)

(IF "YES" . . .)

1. Have you heard the term Port District?   YES ___   NO ___
    (IF "NO" SKIP TO #14)   (IF "YES". . .)

2. Do you know what a Port District is?   YES ___   NOT SURE ___

3. Does a Port District require a navigable waterway?   YES ___   NO ___   NOT SURE ___

4. Does a Port District have the right to tax?   YES ___   NO ___   NOT SURE ___

5. Does a Port District generate activities that create new jobs?   YES ___   NO ___   NOT SURE ___

6. Would a Port District create another layer of government?   YES ___   NO ___   NOT SURE ___

7. Would a Port District help develop land in order to attempt to bring new business and industry to Spokane County?   YES ___   NO ___   NOT SURE ___

8. Would a Port District become financially self-sufficient within six years?   YES ___   NO ___   NOT SURE ___

9. Would a Port District promote Spokane County internationally?   YES ___   NO ___   NOT SURE ___

10. Would a Port District take over ownership of both Felts Field and Spokane International Airport?   YES ___   NO ___   NOT SURE ___

11. Would a Port District benefit economic development in Spokane County?   YES ___   NO ___   NOT SURE ___

12. Would four elected Port Commissioners run the Port District?   YES ___   NO ___   NOT SURE ___

13. Does a Port District have the right of eminent domain?   YES ___   NO ___   NOT SURE ___

14. Is there already enough developed land available for industrial use in Spokane County?   YES ___   NO ___   NOT SURE ___

15. What is your occupation? _____

16. If the Port District question is placed on the ballot, would you: VOTE YES ___   VOTE NO ___   VOTE UNDECIDED __

May I ask why:

Would you like more informaton concerning the
Port District issue: IF YES: ADDRESS: _____
                     (NO NAME)
                                                        _____

                                                        _____

County _____·___   City Limits _____

Male _____   Female _____

4. Does a Port District have the right to tax?

   YES: 56.3%   NO: 10.4%   NOT SURE: 33.3%

5. Does a Port District generate activities that create new jobs?

   YES: 71.9%   NO: 7.3%   NOT SURE: 20.8%

6. Would a Port District create another layer of government?

   YES: 55.2%   NO: 16.3%   NOT SURE: 28.5%

7. Would a Port District help develop land in order to attempt to
   bring new business and industry to Spokane County?

   YES: 69.8%   NO: 8.0%   NOT SURE: 22.2%

8. Would a Port District become financially self-sufficient
   within six years?

   YES: 25.7%   NO: 23.6%   NOT SURE: 50.7%

9. Would a Port District promote Spokane County internationally?

   YES: 46.1%   NO: 19.4%   NOT SURE: 34.4%

10. Would a Port District take over ownership of both Felts Field
    and Spokane International Airport?

    YES: 18.1%   NO: 30.3%   NOT SURE: 51.6%

11. Would a Port District benefit economic development in
    Spokane County?

    YES: 65.3%   NO: 12.5%   NOT SURE: 22.2%

12. Would four elected Port Commissioners run the Port District?

YES: 27.1%   NO: 7.6%   NOT SURE: 65.3%

13. Does a Port District have the right of eminent domain?

YES: 34.0%   NO: 20.5%   NOT SURE: 45.5%

Finally, the respondents were asked "If the Port District question is placed on the ballot, how would you vote?" Nineteen point two percent (19.2%) said they would vote "yes," 19.5% "no," and 61.2% were undecided.

The responses were cross-classified on the "heard term Port District," "know what it is," and "how a person would vote" variables. Significant relationships at the .05 significance level were found in the following situations:

1. A higher proportion of male respondents had heard the term "Port District" versus a lower proportion of females.
2. A higher proportion of respondents who knew what a Port District is would vote either "yes" or "no" if the issue were on the ballot. A higher proportion of people who said they were "not sure" were in the "undecided" vote category.
3. A higher proportion of male respondents would vote either "yes" or "no" while a higher proportion of females were "undecided."
4. A higher proportion of male respondents thought they knew what a Port District is than females.

Questions   1. What are the strengths and weaknesses of the questionnaire used in this case?
2. Are there any biased questions in the questionnaire? If so, how should these questions be asked in an unbiased manner?
3. The method used to select the sample of persons to be questioned was not discussed in the case. How would you select the sampled persons in this situation?

EXERCISES

1. Under what conditions would a census be taken rather than a sample?
2. Describe the conditions under which the following statement could be true: "I am considering taking a systematic sample because it is impossible to take a simple random sample."
3. Why do national pollsters sometimes use a judgement sample that, by definition, is not random?

4. Refer to the data bank in Appendix I. Using the random number table, take a simple random sample of X1 (number of years with company) and compute the mean. Use a sample size of 50.

5. Use the data bank to take a systematic random sample ($n = 25$) of employees and compute the percent that is female.

6. What is the advantage of stratifying a population prior to sampling from it?

7. Suppose a political candidate wished to learn about the voting preferences of a certain state. Using the following variables, discuss the extent to which stratification would be useful prior to sampling:

Gender	Shoe size
Income	Years lived in state
Age	Number of children
Number of cars	Farm versus urban

8. A cluster sample is usually not as expensive as a simple random sample. Why?

9. Under what conditions would a cluster sample be possible whereas a simple random sample would be impossible?

10. Suppose you are interested in exploring the attitudes that the buying public has of your brand of toothpaste. Write three questions designed (1) to be biased for your product; (2) to be biased against your product, and (3) to be an unbiased investigation of this matter.

11. Write one unbiased question to explore the feelings of people with regard to the following:
    a. The attitude of your company employees toward unionizing.
    b. The attitude of county residents toward a sales tax on food versus a state income tax.
    c. Consumers' preferences regarding the most desired size of a certain boxed soap product.
    d. Your employees' preferences regarding the most desirable number of paydays per month.

12. Refer to the data bank in Appendix I. Use the random number table to select 20 company employees from this population and compute the average age.

13. Take a systematic random sample of 35 employees from the data bank and estimate the number of sick days taken in the last six months.

14. What is meant by an infinite population, and what sorts of sampling techniques can be used to deal with such populations?

The following questions refer to the class data base generated from the student questionnaire.

15. Refer to Question 6 on the student questionnaire involving average number of hours worked per week during the current school term. Use the

random number table in Appendix F to take a simple random sample of students and compute the sample mean hours worked per week.

16. Suppose it is desired to take a random sample of approximately 25% of the class questionnaires. Use a systematic random sample to select the questionnaires for the sample and compute the mean college GPA for these students (see Question 4 on the questionnaire).

8

Sampling
Distributions

In the last chapter you learned that the purpose of sampling is to make inferences about a population after inspecting only a small segment. Samples are selected so they will represent the population from which they are drawn. The probability of accomplishing this goal is good when random sampling is used. The primary advantage of using random sampling techniques is that the degree of sampling variability can be determined and inferences can be made about a population. You also discovered that under certain conditions variations of simple random sampling such as systematic, stratified, or cluster sampling can be more efficient.

Now that you know how to select a random sample from a population of interest, the goal is to use information from the sample to make an inference about the population. Frequently, the objective will be to estimate a numerical characteristic, such as the mean of the population, using information from the sample. Since the value of a statistic may lead to either a poor or a good inference, one needs to understand its probability distribution. A sampling distribution is used because it characterizes the distribution of values of the statistic over a large number of samples. You will learn how to evaluate the accuracy of population parameter estimates.

INTRODUCTION

To make inferences about population parameters, one needs to understand more about sample statistics. When the sample proportion (p) is calculated, is this value the same as the population proportion? For example, if a random sample of people are asked whether they will purchase a particular product, will the proportion of people who say "yes" exactly equal the proportion of people who would say "yes" in the population? Of course, the proportions would not be exactly equal. Analysts are satisfied with a sample proportion that is close to the population proportion. If another sample is selected, would the proportion of people indicating they would purchase the product be the same as the first sample? Again, the two sample proportions would not be exactly equal. One does, however, hope these values are close. In fact, it is hoped that every sample proportion is close to the population proportion.

Suppose 1000 shoppers who test the product are sampled, and 200, or 20%, say they will purchase it. What can be said about the population proportion? Is the population proportion 20%? Is it close to 20%? If another 1000 shoppers were sampled, where does the calculated sample proportion fit into the distribution of all possible sample proportions that could have been calculated from samples of 1,000?

The key question is how close is the sample statistic to the actual population parameter? This is determined by the answers to the following questions:

1. Which sample statistic is being considered? Different distributions are used to describe the sampling variability of sample statistics such as the mean, proportion, or standard deviation.

2. How much variability exists in the population being sampled? Populations with a great deal of variability will produce sample statistics that are not as reliable as populations with little variation.

3. How large is the sample? There is less variation among statistics of large samples.

All three questions are concerned with the variability of the distribution from which the sampling statistic will be selected. The probability distribution of sample statistics is referred to as the sampling distribution. A *sampling distribution* consists of every possible sample statistic of a certain sample size that can be drawn from a population.

A sampling distribution includes every possible sample statistic of a certain sample size that can be drawn from a population.

SAMPLING DISTRIBUTIONS

Understanding a sampling distribution is difficult because the concept is theoretical. Sampling distributions exist in theory but are usually just assumed to exist when real-world problems are solved. For this reason, a real-life example of a sampling distribution will be presented to help you understand the concept.

Suppose a local realty firm employs five persons and has kept a record of how many years each person has worked for the firm. The mean and standard deviation of this population are calculated and the results are presented in Table 8–1. Suppose a random sample of $n = 2$ is selected from the population of $N = 5$. If the sample is chosen with replacement (a sampled item is returned to the population and could be drawn as the second item), 25 different samples of two items could be selected. Table 8–2 presents the 25 samples along with each sample's mean. This listing of all possible sample means ($\overline{X}$'s) is called the

TABLE 8–1
Population of em-
ployee years of service

Worker	Years of Service X	Computation of Mean and Standard Deviation
A	1	$\mu_x = \dfrac{\sum X}{N} = \dfrac{15}{5} = 3.0$
B	2	
C	3	
D	4	
E	5	$\sigma_x = \sqrt{\dfrac{\sum X^2 - \dfrac{(\sum X)^2}{N}}{N}}$
	$\sum X = 15$	
		$\sigma_x = \sqrt{\dfrac{55 - \dfrac{(15)^2}{5}}{5}} = \sqrt{2} = 1.4$

TABLE 8–2
Sampling distribution
of $n = 2$

Sample	Sample Values	Sample Means $\overline{X}$	Computation of Mean and Standard Deviation
1	1,1	1.0	$\mu_{\bar{x}} = \dfrac{\sum \overline{X}}{N} = \dfrac{75}{25} = 3.0$
2	1,2	1.5	
3	1,3	2.0	
4	1,4	2.5	$\sigma_{\bar{x}} = \sqrt{\dfrac{\sum \overline{X}^2 - \dfrac{(\sum \overline{X})^2}{N}}{N}}$
5	1,5	3.0	
6	2,1	1.5	
7	2,2	2.0	
8	2,3	2.5	$\sigma_{\bar{x}} = \sqrt{\dfrac{250 - \dfrac{(75)^2}{25}}{25}}$
9	2,4	3.0	
10	2,5	3.5	
11	3,1	2.0	
12	3,2	2.5	$\sigma_{\bar{x}} = \sqrt{\dfrac{250 - 225}{25}}$
13	3,3	3.0	
14	3,4	3.5	
15	3,5	4.0	$\sigma_{\bar{x}} = \sqrt{\dfrac{25}{25}} = \sqrt{1}$
16	4,1	2.5	
17	4,2	3.0	$\sigma_{\bar{x}} = 1.0$
18	4,3	3.5	
19	4,4	4.0	
20	4,5	4.5	
21	5,1	3.0	
22	5,2	3.5	
23	5,3	4.0	
24	5,4	4.5	
25	5,5	5.0	
		$\sum \overline{X} = 75.0$	

sampling distribution of sample means and appears in the third column of Table 8–2. In this example every possible sample mean of sample size $n = 2$ has been shown for a population of $N = 5$. One of these values will result when the sample is selected. How close will the sample mean $(\overline{X})$ be to the population mean of $\mu = 3$?

Relationships Between Populations and Sampling Distributions

Whenever a sample is selected from a population, it is important to understand the difference between sample statistics, sampling distribution statistics, and population parameters. Table 8–3 presents the symbols used to describe sampling distribution statistics.

DISTRIBUTIONS OF SAMPLE MEANS

The sampling distribution of means presented in Table 8–2 is a function of sample size, along with the mean and standard deviation of the population shown in Table 8–1. For each combination of population mean, population standard deviation, and sample size, there will be a unique sampling distribution of sample means. The mean of the sampling distribution, $\mu_{\overline{x}} = 3$, is computed in Table 8–2 and is exactly equal to the population mean, $\mu = 3$, computed in Table 8–1. This is not a coincidence. The mean of a sampling distribution will always equal the mean of the sampled population.

$$\mu_{\overline{x}} = \mu_x \qquad (8\text{–}1)$$

where $\mu_{\overline{x}}$ = the mean of a sampling distribution
μ_x = the population mean

Table 8–2 shows the computation of the standard deviation of the sampling distribution of means. When the population is very large or infinite (sampling with replacement), the standard deviation of the sampling distribution of sample means can be computed using Equation 8–2.

	Population Parameter	Sample Statistic	Sampling Distribution Statistic
Mean	μ_x	$\overline{X}$	$\mu_{\overline{x}}$
Standard Deviation	σ_x	S_x	$\sigma_{\overline{x}}$
Proportion	π	p	μ_p

TABLE 8–3
Symbols for populations, samples, and sampling distribution statistics

$$\sigma_{\bar{x}} = \frac{\sigma_x}{\sqrt{n}} \qquad\qquad (8\text{-}2)$$

where $\sigma_{\bar{x}}$ = the standard deviation of the sampling distribution
σ_x = the population standard deviation
n = the sample size

Note that Equation 8-2 gives the same standard deviation, $\sigma_{\bar{x}} = 1$, which is calculated in Table 8-2.

$$\sigma_{\bar{x}} = \frac{\sigma_x}{\sqrt{n}} = \frac{1.4}{\sqrt{2}} = 1$$

Equation 8-2 indicates that the amount of variability in the sampling distribution depends on the following two factors:

1. Sample size
2. Variability in the population

The standard deviation of the sampling distribution of a statistic is usually called the standard error of the statistic. In this case, we call $\sigma_{\bar{x}}$ the standard error of the mean.

> The standard error of the mean is the standard deviation of the sampling distribution of sample means.

The Central Limit Theorem

Estimating the mean useful life of tires, batteries, picture tubes, automobiles, or comptuers; the mean breaking strength of cable, line, or wire; and the mean sales of many products are common practical problems. In many practical business situations analysts are interested in making an inference about the mean μ of some population. The analyst needs a sample statistic that is a good estimator of μ and has a probability distribution that can be defined. The sample mean $\overline{X}$ is a good estimator of the population mean μ. The probability distribution for this sample statistic can be defined. If the population distribution is normal, the sampling distribution of sample means is normal for any sample size. For the situation where the population distribution is unknown, statisticians rely on the *central limit theorem*. This theorem assumes that the sampling distribution of sample means can be approximated by a normal probability distribution whenever the sample size is large. General practice is to assume that a sample size of 30 or more is large.

If all possible samples, each of size n, are selected from any population, the central limit theorem states that the sampling distribution of sample means will

1. have a mean μ equal to the population mean μ.

$$\mu_{\bar{x}} = \mu_x$$

2. have a standard deviation $\sigma_{\bar{x}}$ equal to the population standard deviation divided by the square root of the sample size $\sigma_x/\sqrt{n}$.

$$\sigma_{\bar{x}} = \frac{\sigma_x}{\sqrt{n}}$$

3. be approximately normally distributed regardless of the shape of the population distribution.

The n referred to in the central limit theorem is the size of each sample in the sampling distribution. Finally, the approximation to the normal distribution improves as n gets larger.

Figure 8–1 shows the sampling distribution of the sample means of sample size $n = 2$ from Table 8-2. This distribution has a mean of $\mu_{\bar{x}} = 3$ and a standard deviation equal to $\sigma_{\bar{x}} = 1$. Taking a random sample of the number of years two workers were employed and calculating its mean is equivalent to randomly drawing a sample mean from the sampling distribution shown in Figure 8–1. Thus, one of the 25 sample means is selected when one takes a random sample of $n = 2$.

FIGURE 8–1
Distribution of sample means

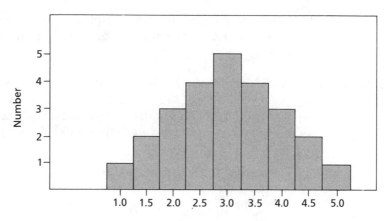

Notice that the sampling distribution shown in Figure 8–1 is symmetrical. Most of the sample means fall in the center of the distribution and only a few are at the ends. Count the number of sample means in Table 8–2 that fall within one standard deviation from the mean (2.0 to 4.0). Nineteen of the 25 sample means or 76% are within one standard deviation of the distribution mean. The sampling distribution is assumed to be approximately normally distributed whenever the sample size is large. Since plus or minus one standard deviation from the mean contains 68% of the items on a normal curve, the sampling distribution begins to approximate the normal distribution even with the small sample size of $n = 2$.

In summary, the central limit theorem allows one to assume that the sampling distribution of means is approximately normally distributed whenever a large random sample is used (when $n \geq 30$). When the sample is small (when $n < 30$), the sampling distribution can be considered normal only if the population is normally distributed.

Using the Sampling Distribution of Means

If the mean and standard deviation of a normal distribution are known, the areas under the curve can be determined. In Chapter 6 Equation 6–1 was used to describe the standard normal variable.

$$Z = \frac{\text{value of random variable} - \text{mean of random variable}}{\text{standard deviation of random variable}}$$

Since the normally distributed random variable of interest is the sample mean, the formula becomes

$$Z = \frac{(\overline{X} - \mu_{\bar{x}})}{\sigma_{\bar{x}}} \qquad \textbf{(8–3)}$$

Values of Z calculated using Equation 8–3 can be used to determine areas under the normal curve by using the standard normal distribution.

Example 8–1 The hourly wages of employees at the TEL Telephone Company have a mean wage rate of $10.00 per hour with a standard deviation of $1.20. What is the probability that the mean hourly wage of a random sample of 36 employees will be larger than $10.30? Assume the company has a total of 1000 employees.

Solution The analyst is given $\mu = \$10.00$ and $\sigma = \$1.20$ and is interested in the sampling distribution of all possible sample means of sample size 36. The mean of the sampling distribution is $\mu_{\bar{x}} = \mu_x$, therefore, $\mu_{\bar{x}} =$

FIGURE 8–2
Sampling distribution
of average wages

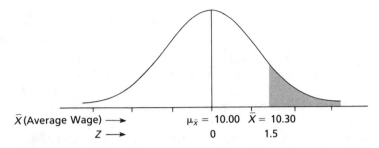

$\bar{X}$(Average Wage) ⟶ $\mu_{\bar{x}}$ = 10.00 $\bar{X}$ = 10.30
                Z ⟶   0   1.5

$10.00. The standard deviation of the sampling distribution or the standard error of the mean $\sigma_{\bar{x}}$ is

$$\sigma_{\bar{x}} = \frac{\sigma_x}{\sqrt{n}} = \frac{\$1.20}{\sqrt{36}} = \$.20$$

Figure 8-2 shows the sampling distribution that has a mean equal to $10.00 and a standard deviation equal to $.20. Because $n = 36$ satisfies the $n \geq 30$ rule, the distribution of sample means is assumed to be normal. Note that the variable shown on the horizontal axis is the mean of samples of size $n = 36$. A Z value is obtained using Equation 8-3.

$$Z = \frac{(\bar{X} - \mu_{\bar{x}})}{\sigma_{\bar{x}}}$$

$$Z = \frac{(10.30 - 10.00)}{.20}$$

$$Z = 1.5$$

The solution is the shaded area above a Z value of 1.5 shown in Figure 8-2. The area associated with a Z value of 1.5 is .4332. The probability that the mean hourly wage for a random sample of 36 employees is larger than $10.30 is .0668 (.5000 − .4332).

SAMPLING FROM A FINITE POPULATION

Equation 8-2 is correct if the population is infinitely large or if the sampling is done with replacement. This formula is also used when the sample is a small part (5% or less) of a finite population. When the sample comprises a large part of the population (whenever $n/N > .05$) and is selected without replacement, $\sigma_x/\sqrt{n}$ should be multiplied by $\sqrt{(N - n)/(N - 1)}$.

$$\sigma_{\bar{x}} = \frac{\sigma_x}{\sqrt{n}} \sqrt{\frac{(N - n)}{(N - 1)}} \qquad \text{(8–4)}$$

The adjustment $(N - n)/(N - 1)$ is called the *finite correction factor* and measures the proportion of the population not included in the sample. Its use always reduces the standard error since it is a value less than one.

Example 8–2   In Example 8–1 the analyst assumed the company employed 1000 people. What is the probability of choosing a random sample of 36 employees without replacement and finding a sample mean wage larger than $1.30 if the firm only has 100 persons?

Solution   Since $n/N > .05$ (36/100 = .36), the standard error of the mean should be calculated using Equation 8–4.

$$\sigma_{\bar{x}} = \frac{\sigma_x}{\sqrt{n}} \sqrt{\frac{(N - n)}{(N - 1)}}$$

$$\sigma_{\bar{x}} = \frac{1.20}{\sqrt{36}} \sqrt{\frac{(100 - 36)}{(100 - 1)}}$$

$$\sigma_{\bar{x}} = .2\sqrt{.646}$$

$$\sigma_{\bar{x}} = .2(.8)$$

$$\sigma_{\bar{x}} = .16$$

The standard error of the mean equals $.16 whereas in Example 8–1 when the correction factor was not used it equalled $.20. Since the mean of the sampling distribution is $10.00, the Z value is

$$Z = \frac{(10.30 - 10.00)}{.16}$$

$$Z = 1.88$$

The solution is represented by the shaded area above a Z value of 1.88 shown in Figure 8–3. The area associated with a Z value of 1.88 is .4699. The probability of obtaining a sample mean larger than $10.30 is .0301 (.5000 − .4699).

The finite correction factor is used whenever the sample size is more than 5% of the population.

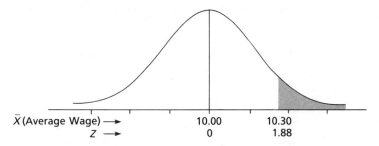

FIGURE 8–3
Sampling distribution
of wages

$\bar{X}$ (Average Wage) ⟶   10.00   10.30
              Z ⟶   0   1.88

DISTRIBUTIONS OF SAMPLE PROPORTIONS

Analysts are frequently interested in estimating population proportions or percentages. They want to know what percentage of the
population will buy their product, what percentage of items are defective on an assembly line, or what percentage of the population will vote
for their candidate. Therefore, an understanding of the sampling distribution of proportions is necessary, and a real-world example will be
used to explain this theoretical concept.

Suppose an analyst is interested in studying the population of five
realty firm employees and uses a simple random sample of two employees to estimate the percentage of females. Table 8–4 shows the population and each employee's gender. When the binomial distribution was
discussed, π was called the probability of success. Now π will be called
the proportion of successes or the population proportion. In this example, the presence of a female employee is the variable of interest;
therefore, there are two successes (females) in the population of five

TABLE 8–4
Population of workers

Worker	Sex
A	M
B	F
C	F
D	M
E	M

$X = 2$ (number of female workers)

$$\pi = \frac{X}{N} = \frac{2}{5} = 40\%$$

where π = population percentage
       N = population size
       X = number of female workers

FUNDAMENTALS OF BUSINESS STATISTICS

TABLE 8–5
Sampling distribution
of $n = 2$

Sample	Sample Combinations	Sample Characteristics	Sample Percentage of Females P
1	A, B	M, F	.5
2	A, C	M, F	.5
3	A, D	M, M	.0
4	A, E	M, M	.0
5	B, C	F, F	1.0
6	B, D	F, M	.5
7	B, E	F, M	.5
8	C, D	F, M	.5
9	C, E	F, M	.5
10	D, E	M, M	.0
			$\Sigma P = 4.0$

$$\mu_p = \frac{\Sigma P}{N} = \frac{4}{10} = .4$$

$$\sigma_p = \sqrt{\frac{\Sigma P^2 - \frac{(\Sigma P)^2}{N}}{N}} = \sqrt{\frac{2.5 - \frac{(4)^2}{10}}{10}} = \sqrt{.09} = .3$$

employees. The population proportion of females is $X/N = 2/5$ or 40%. Table 8–5 lists the sampling distribution of all possible proportions if a sample of two employees is chosen (without replacement) and the percentage of females is observed. The mean of the sampling distribution is computed in Table 8–5. Note that the mean of the sampling distribution is .40, which is the same as the population percentage. The mean of a sampling distribution of proportions with random samples of size n is equal to the population proportion.

$$\mu_p = \pi \tag{8–5}$$

Table 8–5 shows the computation for the standard deviation of the sampling distribution of proportions. The standard deviation of this sampling distribution equals .30. As noted earlier, the standard deviation of a statistic is usually called the standard error of the statistic; therefore, this standard deviation is called the standard error of the proportion. Equation 8–6 is used to compute the standard error of the proportion when the population is very large or infinite.

$$\sigma_p = \sqrt{\frac{\pi(1 - \pi)}{n}} \tag{8–6}$$

When the sample size is more than 5% of the population, the *finite correction factor* is used and the formula becomes

$$\sigma_p = \sqrt{\frac{\pi(1 - \pi)}{n}} \sqrt{\frac{(N - n)}{(N - 1)}} \qquad \text{(8-7)}$$

Since the sample size of two is more than 5% of the population size of five for the sampling distribution shown in Table 8-5, Equation 8-7 is used to compute the standard deviation of the distribution.

$$\sigma_p = \sqrt{\frac{\pi(1 - \pi)}{n}} \sqrt{\frac{(N - n)}{N - 1}}$$

$$\sigma_p = \sqrt{\frac{.4(1 - .4)}{2}} \sqrt{\frac{(5 - 2)}{(5 - 1)}}$$

$$\sigma_p = \sqrt{.12} \sqrt{.75}$$

$$\sigma_p = \sqrt{.09}$$

$$\sigma_p = .30$$

The standard error of the proportion σ_p is .30, which is the same as the standard deviation of the sampling distribution computed in Table 8-5. Sample proportions follow the binomial distribution; however, we discovered in Chapter 6 that the normal approximation can be used when $n\pi$ and $n(1 - \pi)$ are above five. Most business survey samples are large enough so analysts can use the normal approximation of the binomial. Finally, the *continuity correction factor* is omitted to make the computations simpler.

> The sampling distribution of proportions can be approximated by a normal probability distribution whenever the sample size n satisfies the conditions $n\pi > 5$ and $n(1 - \pi) > 5$.

Using the Sampling Distribution of Proportions

To use the normal curve probabilities to approximate the binomial distribution, the mean and standard deviation of the sampling distribution of proportions need to be computed. Substituting in the standard normal formula shown in the earlier discussion of sample means yields

$$Z = \frac{(p - \mu_p)}{\sigma_p} \qquad \text{(8-8)}$$

The normally distributed random variable of interest is the sample proportion, and values of Z can be used to determine areas under the normal curve.

Example 8–3   Suppose 50% of the television audience population watched a particular special on Friday evening. If a random sample of 100 viewers is selected, what is the probability that fewer than 40 of them watched the special?

Solution   The random variable is p and the mean of the sampling distribution is $\mu_p = \pi = .50$. Since the population is very large, the standard error of the proportion is calculated using Equation 8–6.

$$\sigma_p = \sqrt{\frac{\pi(1 - \pi)}{n}}$$

$$\sigma_p = \sqrt{\frac{.5(1 - .5)}{100}}$$

$$\sigma_p = \sqrt{.0025}$$

$$\sigma_p = .05$$

Figure 8–4 shows the sampling distribution of sample proportions. The distribution has a mean equal to .50 and a standard deviation equal to .05. Because $n\pi > 5$ and $n(1 - \pi) > 5$, the normal distribution can be used to approximate the binomial distribution. Note that the variables shown on the horizontal axis are the proportions of samples of size 100. A Z value is obtained using Equation 8–8.

$$Z = \frac{(p - \mu_p)}{\sigma_p}$$

$$Z = \frac{(.40 - .50)}{.05}$$

$$Z = \frac{-.10}{.05}$$

$$Z = -2.0$$

The solution is the shaded area below a Z value of -2.0 shown in Figure 8–4. The area associated with a Z value of -2.0 is .4772. The

FIGURE 8–4
Sampling distribution
of proportions

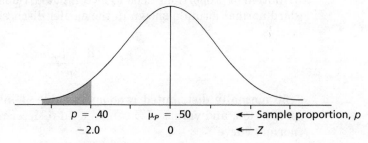

probability that less than 40% of the sample watched the special is .0228 (.5000 − .4772).

SUMMARY

The purpose of sampling is to learn about a population without examining all of it. Sampling distributions are used to accomplish this task because they possess characteristics that result in representative samples. The central limit theorem is one of the most important concepts of statistical inference. It helps analysts define the sampling distribution of sample means even when the nature of the population distribution is not known. The most important probability distribution for describing sampling distributions is the normal curve. The central limit theorem states that large samples tend to yield a sampling distribution that is approximately normal even though the population being sampled is not normal. Finally, sampling without replacement from a finite population when the sample size is larger than 5% of the population requires a modification of the formulas for computing the standard deviation of a sampling distribution. The standard error is multiplied by the finite correction factor.

CASE STUDY: WELK METALS

Mary Welk, President of Welk Metals, is concerned with the problem of quality control. She has recently received complaints concerning a plastic pipe that her firm produces. Ms. Welk is puzzled because the complaints say that the pipe is sometimes too small and sometimes too large. The machine that produces the plastic pipe is supposed to be adjusted so the pipe is 3 inches in diameter. Ms. Welk calls Jim Thompson, a recent business school graduate, into her office and asks him to develop a system to monitor the machine's performance. Mr. Thompson feels that the machine's output can be viewed statistically as a set of data generated by successive repetition of the same physical process. He checks the specifications for the machine and finds that the mean is 3.0 inches, the standard deviation is .09 inches, and the diameters of the pieces of pipe are normally distributed. Jim now has enough information to construct a control chart. He decides to take a simple random sample of nine pieces of pipe each hour and calculates the mean diameter of each sample. The machine is operated for 12 hours on the first day of Jim's test, so he records the 12 sample means that are presented in the table. Because the machine is extremely expensive to repair, Jim wants to make sure something is really wrong before production is stopped and a technician is brought in to inspect and adjust the machine.

Mean Pipe Diameters (in inches)

3.04	3.01	3.02
2.99	2.98	3.04
3.07	2.95	3.00
2.97	2.97	2.96

Questions

1. If the machine is operating according to specifications, one can be 99% sure that a sample mean will fall within what limits?
2. If the machine is operating according to specifications, what is the probability of obtaining a sample with a mean equal to 3.2?
3. Construct a chart that plots the 12 sample means.
4. Construct a control chart showing that the machine will be checked whenever a sample mean falls more than three standard deviations from the population mean.
5. If the population is not normally distributed, is Jim's approach valid? What can be done to check the machine under this assumption?

EXERCISES

1. Is the mean of the sampling distribution of means related to the population mean?
2. What is a sampling distribution?
3. When does a sampling distribution approximate the normal probability distribution?
4. Why is the central limit theorem important?
5. Why is it possible to make probability statements about the value of a sample mean if the population mean is known?
6. What effect does sampling from a finite population have on the variability of a sampling distribution?
7. What effect does each of the following have on the variability of a sampling distribution of means?
   a. Population mean
   b. Population standard deviation
   c. Sample size
   d. Population size

8. When do we use the finite correction factor?

9. When does the sampling distribution of proportions approximate the normal probability distribution?

10. Consider the following data indicating how many sales that a population of four salespersons made today and how many salespeople were college graduates.

Salesperson	Sales	College Graduate
A	3	yes
B	1	no
C	2	yes
D	2	no

a. Compute the mean and standard deviation for the random variable number of sales today.

b. List the sampling distribution of all possible sample means of $n = 3$ selected without replacement for the variable sales.

c. Using the sampling distribution of mean sales, compute the mean and standard deviation of the sample mean.

d. Compute the mean and standard deviation of the sample mean using the appropriate formulas and compare your results to Part c.

e. Compute the mean and standard deviation for the population of the proportion of salespersons who said they were college graduates.

f. List the sampling distribution of all possible sample proportions for samples of $n = 2$ selected with replacement for the college graduate variable.

g. Using the sampling distribution of the proportion of college graduates, compute the mean and standard deviation of the sample proportion.

h. Compute the mean and standard deviation of the sample proportion using the appropriate formulas and compare your results to Part g.

i. If two salespersons are selected at random from the group of four, what is the probability that the sample contains two college graduates?

11. An automatic machine that is used to fill cans of soda pop has a mean fill $\mu = 16.0$ fluid ounces and a standard deviation $\sigma = .4$ ounces.

a. Graph the sampling distribution of sample means for samples of 30 cans selected randomly by a quality control inspector.

b. What is the probability that the inspector will find a sample with a mean less than 15.9 ounces?

12. The Dow Jones industrial average is an average of the prices of 30 stocks that vary from day to day. Suppose 10 stocks were used in computing the average. Would you expect the 10-price average to have smaller or greater variations than the 30-price average? Why?

13. The research department of a major automobile manufacturer claims that the engine they are developing will average 50 miles per gallon with a

standard deviation of 2 miles per gallon. In nine trial runs to test the claim, the engine averaged

49   48   49   50   47   45   46   49   48

Does the claim seem reasonable? Why or why not?

14. A random sample of 100 factory workers at a large plant are surveyed by management to determine what proportion of a population of 500 employees favor unionizing. Find the probability of obtaining a sample proportion that differs by more than 4% from the actual proportion if the actual proportion of employees who favor unionizing is 50%.

15. Suppose that from 9 to 10 P.M. on a Friday night, 1 million people watched television and 300,000 of them viewed a special on the problems caused by drug use. If we select a sample of 700 people who were watching television between 9 and 10 on Friday night, what is the probability that more than 200 were viewing the special about drugs?

16. In a population of 1,000 employees, a simple random sample of 100 employees is selected to estimate what proportion would participate in a physical fitness program.
    a. Would you use the finite correction factor in calculating the standard error of the proportion?
    b. If the population proportion is $\pi = .10$, compute the standard error of the proportion both using and not using the finite correction factor.
    c. Why is the finite correction factor used whenever $n/N \geq .05$?

17. The Chamber of Commerce of Pullman, Florida, publishes a booklet that states that the average cost of new homes built within the city's limits is $50,000. Jill Black, a local real estate appraiser believes this cost is too low. She obtains the sales records for 64 randomly selected new homes built in the city and computes the mean.
    a. How should Jill select her sample?
    b. If the population standard deviation of the cost of new homes in Pullman is actually $24,000, what is the probability that the average cost of a random sample of 64 new homes is larger than $55,000?
    c. Suppose Jill selects her sample and computes a sample mean equal to $60,000. Does the figure quoted in the Chamber of Commerce's booklet seem reasonable?

18. The mean hourly wage of workers in an industry is $7.50 per hour with a standard deviation of $.50. If we select a sample of 49 workers, the probability is 30% that the sample will have a mean wage rate above what amount?

19. Five percent of a population of valve stems are defective. If samples of 400 are drawn, what percentage of the sample proportions might be expected to range betweeen 3% and 7%?

20. The Good Taste Bottling Company has discovered that an average of 8% of the bottles that run through their machine are overfilled. If a sample of

121 bottles is selected randomly from a production run of 500 bottles, what is the probability that the sample proportion of overfilled bottles will be from 6% to 10%?

21. This question refers to the class data base. If the class is a random sample of all students attending your school, what is the probability that the mean age of another class of exactly the same size will be greater than 20?

9
Estimation

Where You Have Been

In preceding chapters you learned how to calculate numerical descriptive measures to describe population parameters. You were introduced to probability theory and learned how probability concepts can be used to deal with problems of uncertainty. You learned about both discrete and continuous probability distributions. You found out how to generate a random sample from a population of interest. In the last chapter you learned that sample statistics vary in a random manner from sample to sample and that inferences are subject to uncertainty. You studied sampling distributions so you can use knowledge of probability and probability distributions to make inferences about population parameter values based on sample statistics.

Where You Are Going

You are now ready to apply the material you learned in preceding chapters. You will estimate population means and proportions based on a sample selected from the population of interest. You will learn how to use a sample statistic as a point estimate of a population parameter and will evaluate the accuracy of these estimates. Finally, you will consider the problem of determining sample size.

INTRODUCTION

Suppose that an increase of four percentage points in the Kirby Average Ratings from 25% to 29% can move a show from a ranking of 30 into the top ten and that a few points in the ratings determines whether a show is canceled or whether an advertiser is willing to pay $100,000 per minute for commercial time. Unfortunately, the problem with television ratings is that no one really knows what percentage of the population actually watches a particular TV show. The Kirby Ratings are based on a sample of approximately 1,500 families. The values we see published in the newspaper each week are sample estimates of population parameters. A rating of 30 for *60 Minutes* was obtained by using a sample proportion to estimate that 30% of the viewing population watched the show. An error of two percentage points in estimating this rating could change the rankings dramatically. How good is the estimate of the percentage of people who view *60 Minutes*? The case at the end of this chapter attempts to answer this question.

TYPES OF ESTIMATES

Point Estimates

Sample statistics are used to estimate population parameters. A sample mean ($\overline{X}$) is used to estimate the population mean (μ); a sample standard deviation (*s*) is used to estimate the population standard deviation (σ); and the proportion of items in a sample with a given characteristic (*p*) is used to estimate the proportion of items in the population with the same characteristic (π). These estimates are called *point estimates*. A point estimate is a single value that is calculated from a sample and is used to estimate some population parameter.

For example, how far does the average customer live from the local Save-Mart store? The analyst takes a sample from the population and calculates the sample mean ($\overline{X}$). Suppose a random sample of 36 customers is selected and a sample mean of 5.0 miles is calculated. What is the population mean? If the sample mean is used as the estimate, the analyst is making a point estimate. It is known that the population mean distance is not exactly 5.0 miles. However, the best estimate of the population mean is 5.0 miles. The analyst hopes the point estimate of 5.0 miles is close to the population mean.

> A point estimate is a single value that is calculated from a sample and is used to estimate some population parameter.

Interval Estimates

The problem with point estimates is that they do not provide information about how close the estimate is to the population parameter. The analyst does not know how close the point estimate of 5.0 miles is to the actual distance the average Save-Mart customer lives from the store. This single value does not consider information about the sample size or the variability of the population from which the sample was selected. However, both of these facts will affect the accuracy of the estimate. This problem is solved through the use of *interval estimates*.

> An interval estimate of a population parameter is a range of possible values computed from sample data in which a population parameter is thought to be.

An analyst's ability to estimate a population parameter by using sample data is dependent upon knowledge of the sampling distribution of the statistic being estimated. The sample mean for the distance Save-Mart customers lived from the store was $\overline{X} = 5.0$ miles. This sample mean is a member of the sampling distribution of all possible sample means computed from samples of size 36. Since the central limit theorem describes this sampling distribution, the following five steps can be used to prepare an interval estimate:

FIGURE 9-1
Area for a confidence
level of 95%

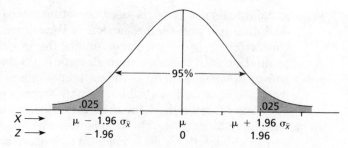

1. Calculate the sample statistic.
2. Determine the appropriate sampling distribution and compute its standard deviation.
3. Decide on the degree of confidence needed to ensure that the interval estimate actually includes the population parameter. This is called the confidence level.
4. Divide the confidence level by 2. If the sampling distribution is normally distributed, look up this area in the normal curve table to obtain the appropriate Z value. Figure 9-1 shows an example for a confidence level of 95%. Table 9-1 provides the Z values for the most common confidence levels.
5. Calculate the *confidence interval* using Equation 9-1.

$$\text{sample statistic} \pm Z \text{ (standard error)} \qquad \textbf{(9-1)}$$

> A confidence interval of a population parameter is a range of possible values computed from sample data in which a population parameter is thought to be with a known risk of error.

ESTIMATING POPULATION PARAMETERS

Estimating the Population Mean for Large Samples

The central limit theorem is the source for the information needed to construct interval estimates for population means. The question of how

TABLE 9-1
Z values for common
confidence levels

Confidence Level	Z Value
90%	1.65
95%	1.96
98%	2.33
99%	2.58

close a particular sample mean might be to the population mean depends on the variability in the sampling distribution. The central limit theorem describes sampling distributions of sample means as approximately normally distributed with a mean $\mu_{\bar{x}} = \mu_x$ and a standard deviation of $\sigma_{\bar{x}} = \sigma_x/\sqrt{n}$. Enough information has now been provided to prepare an interval estimate that will have a high probability of containing the actual population mean, μ.

The method used to estimate the population mean depends on whether the population standard deviation is known. When the population standard deviation σ is known, the interval estimate of the population mean is calculated using Equation 9–2:

$$\overline{X} \pm Z \frac{\sigma_x}{\sqrt{n}} \qquad\qquad (9\text{–}2)$$

The interval estimate of the population mean is based on the assumption that the sampling distribution of sample means is normally distributed. For large samples $n \geq 30$, the central limit theorem applies. However, for small samples $n < 30$, the population being sampled must be approximately normally distributed in order for the sampling distribution to be normal. Small sample procedures will be discussed later in the chapter. An example of the five-step interval estimation procedure follows:

Example 9–1 The Quality Bolt Company has an automatic machine that produces bolts which have lengths that are normally distributed with a standard deviation of .1 millimeter. A random sample of 16 bolts is selected that have a mean diameter of 26 millimeters. Use the 90% confidence level to construct an interval estimate for the mean diameter of all bolts made by the machine.

Solution Use the five step procedure shown in the previous section.

1. The sample mean has been calculated and is equal to $\overline{X} = 26$ millimeters.

2. The population standard deviation is known to be .1 millimeter. Since the population is normally distributed, it can be assumed that the sampling distribution is normally distributed.

3. The Quality Bolt Company has decided on a 90% confidence level.

4. The 90% confidence level is divided by 2, .90/2, resulting in an area equal to .4500. The Z value is looked up in the normal curve table and is equal to 1.65. This result could have been obtained from Table 9–1.

5. Equation 9-2 is used to calculate the confidence interval.

$$\overline{X} \pm Z\left(\frac{\sigma_x}{\sqrt{n}}\right) = 26 \pm 1.65\left(\frac{.1}{\sqrt{16}}\right)$$

$$= 26 \pm 1.65(.025)$$

$$= 26 \pm .04125$$

$$= 25.96 \text{ millimeters to } 26.04 \text{ millimeters}$$

Can we be sure that the true population mean (μ) is within the interval 25.96 to 26.04 millimeters? Although we cannot be certain, we can be reasonably confident. This confidence comes from the knowledge that if we were to repeatedly draw random samples of 16 bolts and a 1.65 standard deviation interval was formed around the sample mean $\overline{X}$ each time, 90% of the intervals would contain the population mean. Figure 9-2 shows what might happen when ten samples are drawn from this population and confidence intervals are calculated for each. The location of μ is indicated by the vertical line in the figure. Note that nine out of ten intervals shown as horizontal line segments actually contain the population mean (μ). One of the intervals, interval 6, does not contain μ. An analyst is never sure whether the interval estimate contains μ. However, the probability is that 9 out of 10 or 90% of the intervals constructed in this manner will actually contain μ.

Usually, the value of the population standard deviation (σ) is not known. In these instances the standard deviation of the sample (s) is

FIGURE 9-2
Confidence intervals
for ten samples of
bolts

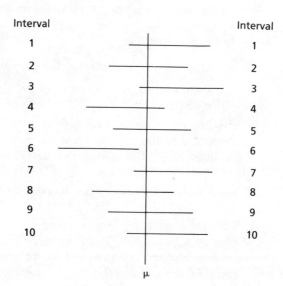

used as a point estimate of the population standard deviation (σ). Equation 9–3 shows how the standard error of the mean is estimated:

$$s_{\bar{x}} = \frac{s_x}{\sqrt{n}} \qquad (9\text{–}3)$$

The $s_{\bar{x}}$ notation is used for the estimate of $\sigma_{\bar{x}}$ just as s is used for the estimate of σ. When sample size is at least 30, it can be concluded from the central limit theorem that the sampling distribution of means will be approximately normal. When the sample size is less than 30, the t distribution discussed in the next section will be used.

Example 9–2 The Zing Corporation manufactures home computers. Zing does not manufacture one of the components of the computer so it must be supplied by another company. A new supplier, Perfect Electronics, has submitted a bid to supply the component. Zing is particularly concerned about the life expectancy of this component. A sample of 81 of the new supplier's components are tested to determine the life expectancy. The sample mean life expectancy of the 81 sampled components is $\bar{X}$ = 990 hours and the standard deviation is s = 45 hours. Set up a 95% confidence interval for the true life expectancy of the component.

Solution
1. The sample mean has been calculated and is equal to $\bar{X}$ = 990 hours.
2. The population standard deviation σ is unknown, so the sample standard deviation s = 45 hours will be used to estimate it. Since n = 81, it is assumed that the sampling distribution is normally distributed.
3. The Zing Corporation has decided on a 95% confidence level.
4. The 95% confidence level is divided by 2, .95/2, resulting in an area equal to .4750. The Z value is looked up in the normal curve table and is equal to 1.96. This result could have been obtained from Table 9–1.
5. Equation 9–1 is used to calculate the confidence interval.

$$\bar{X} \pm Z\left(\frac{s_x}{\sqrt{n}}\right) = 990 \pm 1.96\left(\frac{45}{\sqrt{81}}\right)$$

$$= 990 \pm 1.96(5)$$

$$= 990 \pm 9.80$$

$$= 980.2 \text{ hours to } 999.8 \text{ hours}$$

If the analyst were to repeatedly draw random samples of 81 components and a 1.96 standard deviation interval was formed around the sample mean each time, 95% of the intervals would contain the population mean. Therefore, the analyst is 95% confident that the population mean μ falls within the range 980.2 hours to 999.8 hours.

Estimating the Population Mean for Small Samples

Many estimates in business applications must be made on the basis of very limited information. Cost or time limitations often restrict the sample size that may be obtained. For example, whenever items are tested to determine their average life, TV picture tubes for instance, the sample must be small due to cost constraints. When small samples are used, the following two problems arise:

1. The central limit theorem applies only to large samples, $n \geq 30$. For small samples, $n < 30$, the assumption that the sampling distribution of $\overline{X}$ is approximately normally distributed cannot be made. In this case, the sampling distribution of $\overline{X}$ depends on the shape of the population being sampled.

2. If the sample size is small, the sample standard deviation (s) may not be a good approximation of the population standard deviation (σ).

Fortunately, an analyst may proceed with estimation techniques for small samples assuming that the population being sampled is approximately normally distributed. An interval estimate of the population mean can be based on a probability distribution known as the t *distribution*. The t distribution is a family of probability distributions that are similar to the Z distribution (standard normal probability distribution). A specific t distribution depends upon the parameter *degrees of freedom* (df), which is equal to $n - 1$. There is a unique t distribution with 1 degree of freedom, with 5 degrees of freedom, with 13 degrees of freedom, and so forth. As the number of degrees of freedom increases, the difference between the t distribution and the Z distribution becomes smaller. The t distribution has the following properties:

1. The t distribution is symmetrical and has a mean of zero.
2. The t distribution is less peaked at the mean and has more area in the tails than the normal distribution.
3. There is a family of t distributions based on the parameter degrees of freedom ($n - 1$). The t distribution approaches the normal distribution as the sample size increases.

Figure 9–3 shows the Z distribution and its relationship to t distributions with 10 and 20 degrees of freedom. Table 9–2 shows an example of t values for one-tailed areas of various t distributions.

FIGURE 9–3
Relationship of the Z
distribution to two t
distributions with dif-
ferent degrees of
freedom

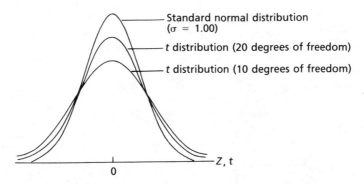

FIGURE 9–3
Relationship of the Z
distribution to two t
distributions with dif-
ferent degrees of
freedom

Observe that the t values in each column decrease as degrees of freedom increase and the last entry is the normal curve value. A more
complete table is found in Appendix G. Note that the table contains
degrees of freedom from 1 to 30. Since statisticians generally use the
normal curve table for sample sizes of 30 or more, the table contains
few values above 30.

When the population is normally distributed but the population
standard deviation is unknown, the interval estimate of the population
mean is calculated for small samples by replacing Z in Equation 9–2
with t. The flowchart in Figure 9–4 summarizes the steps in determining when the t distribution is appropriate. The small sample confidence interval is computed using Equation 9–4 where the t distribution is based on $n - 1$ degrees of freedom.

$$\overline{X} \pm t \left(\frac{s_x}{\sqrt{n}} \right) \tag{9–4}$$

The reason for using $n - 1$ degrees of freedom is that the sample
standard deviation (s) is used as an estimator of the population standard deviation (σ) in computing the standard error of the mean $(s_{\bar{x}})$.
The $n - 1$ value may be interpreted as the number of independent
deviations of $(X - \overline{X})$ present in the computation of s. The total of the

TABLE 9–2
t distribution
(selected one-tailed
areas)

df	.10	.05	.025	.01
		One-Tailed Area		
5	1.48	2.02	2.57	3.36
15	1.34	1.75	2.13	2.60
25	1.32	1.71	2.06	2.49
30	1.31	1.70	2.04	2.46
60	1.30	1.67	2.00	2.39
∞	1.28	1.65	1.96	2.33

FIGURE 9-4
Flowchart of
steps used in
determining
whether to
use the t
distribution

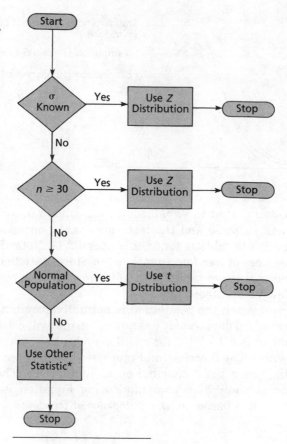

* A nonparametric statistic would be used in this case.

deviations $\sum(X - \overline{X})$ for n observations always equals zero, and only $n - 1$ of the deviations of $(X - \overline{X})$ are independent. The nth $(X - \overline{X})$ would be determined by the condition that the sum of n deviations have to equal zero. Whenever the population standard deviation is estimated, it is said that there are $n - 1$ degrees of freedom present if an $n - 1$ divisor is used in the estimator.

Example 9-3   Interest rates on mortgages play a significant role in the housing market. Pacific Construction Company desires to estimate the average interest rate charged for a 30-year loan to new home buyers in California last year. The 30-year mortgage statements for a random sample of $n = 25$ new home buyers in California were selected, and the interest rate charges were recorded. Estimate μ, the average interest rate charged for a 30-year mortgage last year to new home buyers in

California, with a 95% confidence level if the sample mean was $\overline{X} = 14\%$, the sample standard deviation was $s = 1\%$, and the population was assumed to be normally distributed.

Solution

1. The sample mean has been calculated and is equal to $\overline{X} = 14\%$.

2. Since the population standard deviation σ is unknown, the sample standard deviation $s = 1\%$ will be used to estimate it. Since $n = 25$ and the population is normally distributed, it is assumed that the sampling distribution is based on the t distribution. Figure 9–4 summarizes how this decision was made.

3. The Pacific Construction Company has decided on a 95% confidence level.

4. The 95% confidence level is divided by 2, .95/2, resulting in an area equal to .4750. When the t distribution is used, this area is subtracted from .5000 (.5000 − .4750 = .0250). The degrees of freedom are calculated $df = (n - 1) = (25 - 1) = 24$. The t value is looked up in the t table and is equal to 2.064. Note that this value is slightly larger than 1.96, which would have been determined if the Z distribution had been used.

5. Equation 9–4 is used to calculate the confidence interval.

$$\overline{X} \pm t\left(\frac{s_x}{\sqrt{n}}\right) = .14 \pm 2.064\left(\frac{.01}{\sqrt{25}}\right)$$

$$= .14 \pm 2.064(.002)$$

$$= .14 \pm .004128$$

$$= 13.6\% \text{ to } 14.4\%$$

If an analyst were to repeatedly draw random samples of 25 mortgage statements and a 2.064 standard deviation interval was formed around the sample mean each time, 95% of the intervals would contain the population mean. Therefore, the analyst is reasonably confident that the population mean interest rate falls within the range 13.6% to 14.4%.

Estimating the Population Proportion

In Chapter 8 you learned that the mean of the sampling distribution of proportions is equal to the population proportion. This allows the use of the sample proportion (p) as an unbiased estimator of the population proportion (π). You also learned that if the sample size is sufficiently large, the sampling distribution approximates the normal distribution. Thus, probability statements about the interval estimates of π are based on sample proportions. The confidence interval for p may be constructed using a procedure similar to the one used for estimating a population mean. For large samples, the sampling distribution of p is approximately normal with mean equal to $\mu_p = \pi$ and standard deviation equal to $\sigma_p = \sqrt{p(1 - p)/n}$. Substituting in Equation 9–1, the interval estimate of the population proportion is

$$p \pm Z\sqrt{\frac{p(1 - p)}{n}} \qquad\qquad (9\text{–}5)$$

Note that the sample value p was substituted for the corresponding population value π. This approximation is valid for large samples.

Example 9–4   The Seafirst Mortgage Corporation is interested in estimating the proportion of customers who default on loans within the first 5 years after receiving them. A random sample of 200 accounts is selected for people who received loans in 1985. If 20 of these people defaulted on their loans in the past 5 years, estimate the proportion of all Seafirst customers who defaulted within 5 years using a 90% confidence interval.

Solution

1. The sample porportion is equal to $p = X/n$ or 20/200 or 10%.
2. Since the sample size is large, the sampling distribution is assumed to be normally distributed. The standard deviation is equal to the standard error of the proportion.
3. The Seafirst Mortgage Corporation has decided on a 90% confidence level.
4. The 90% confidence level is divided by 2, .90/2, resulting in an area equal to .4500. The Z value is looked up in the normal curve table and is equal to 1.65.
5. Equation 9–5 is used to calculate the confidence interval.

$$p \pm Z\sqrt{\frac{p(1 - p)}{n}} = .10 \pm 1.65\sqrt{\frac{.10(.90)}{200}}$$

$$= .10 \pm 1.65(.021)$$

$$= .10 \pm .03465$$

$$= 6.5\% \text{ to } 13.5\%$$

If an analyst were to repeatedly draw random samples of 200 customers and a 1.65 standard deviation interval around the sample mean was formed each time, 90% of the intervals would contain the population proportion. Therefore, the analyst can be reasonably confident that the population proportion π falls within the range 6.5% to 13.5%.

ESTIMATION ERROR

The error (e) in an interval estimate refers to the difference between the sample statistic and the actual population parameter. Since the interval estimate is centered around the sample statistic, the error is one-half of the interval width. For example, the interval

$$\overline{X} \pm Z \frac{\sigma_x}{\sqrt{n}}$$

can be written as

$$\overline{X} \pm \text{error } (e)$$

with the error (e) equal to

$$e = Z \frac{\sigma_x}{\sqrt{n}} \tag{9--6}$$

If the interval estimate involves estimating a population proportion, the maximum error of estimate is equal to

$$e = Z \sqrt{\frac{p(1 - p)}{n}} \tag{9--7}$$

The *maximum error of estimate* is one-half of the width of the confidence interval.

Sometimes it is necessary to calculate the amount of accuracy that can be acquired with a particular sample size.

Example 9–5   A manufacturer of flash cubes wants to estimate the probability that a flash cube will flash with 95.5% confidence. Since destructive testing is involved, the firm has decided that the largest sample size it could use would be $n = 100$. The manufacturer estimates from past research that the population proportion of flash cubes that flash is .90. Calculate the maximum error of estimate that a sample size of 100 might provide in estimating the population proportion.

Solution   For a 95.5% confidence level, a Z value of 2.0 is appropriate. Since $n = 100$ and the manufacturer's estimate of π equals .90, the maximum error of estimate involved is calculated using Equation 9–7.

$$e = Z \sqrt{\frac{p(1 - p)}{n}}$$

$$e = 2.0 \sqrt{\frac{.90(.10)}{100}}$$

$$e = 2.0(.03)$$

$$e = .06$$

A sample size of 100 will provide an interval estimate accurate within 6% on either side of the sample proportion.

Sample Size Determination for Estimating Means

Analysts take samples because it is usually too costly to gather data for the whole population. The collection of sample data also costs money, and the smaller the sample, the less the cost. Analysts are faced with the dilemma of wanting a small sample to hold down cost and wanting a large sample to provide a good estimate of the population parameter of interest. How large should a sample be? The answers to the following two questions specify the required sample size.

1. What degree of precision is desired, or how much error can be tolerated?
2. How confident must one be that the interval estimate contains the population parameter?

For example, suppose that the average outstanding balance of signature loans issued by a bank varies from month to month and that the amounts are normally distributed with a standard deviation of $400. The bank wishes to compute an interval estimate of the population mean so that the probability is .90 that the point estimate will not differ from μ by more than $75. How large a sample should the bank select?

The bank has indicated that the sample mean $(\overline{X})$ must be within $75 of the population mean (μ), so

$$e = \overline{X} - \mu = \$75$$

Since e was defined in Equation 9-6 to be

$$e = Z \frac{\sigma_x}{\sqrt{n}}$$

then the bank is saying they want $Z \sigma_{\bar{x}}$ to equal $75.

The necessary sample size can now be determined by solving $Z \sigma_x/\sqrt{n} = \$75$. Since a confidence level of 90% is desired in the estimation of μ, the Z value is 1.65. Substituting in Equation 8-2 yields

$$e = Z \frac{\sigma_x}{\sqrt{n}}$$

$$\$75 = 1.65 \frac{\$400}{\sqrt{n}}$$

Since there is one equation with one unknown,

$$\sqrt{n} = \frac{1.65(400)}{75}$$

$$\sqrt{n} = 8.8$$

$$n = 78$$

The bank should choose a sample size of 78 accounts.

Equation 9-6 can be manipulated to find the value of n. Thus,

$$e = Z \frac{\sigma_x}{\sqrt{n}}$$

$$\sqrt{n} = \frac{Z\sigma_x}{e}$$

$$n = \left(\frac{Z\sigma_x}{e}\right)^2 \qquad \textbf{(9-8)}$$

Equation 9-8 indicates that the necessary sample size will depend on (1) the amount of tolerable error, (2) the degree of confidence desired, and (3) the variability in the population.

The required sample size can be estimated by using the following four steps:

1. Determine the accuracy required. What is the maximum error that can be tolerated? The size of e will depend on how important it is to estimate μ accurately. Since e is inversely related to n, a small e will require a large sample size. The error that can be tolerated is usually a judgemental decision made by the analyst or manager.

2. Decide on a confidence level. The higher the confidence level, the larger the sample size required. The appropriate Z value is determined just as in the confidence interval procedure by the analyst or manager.

3. Determine the population standard deviation. If σ is unknown, it must be estimated from past experience or past research.

4. Use the results of steps 1 through 3 in Equation 9-8.

Example 9-6   Live Rite Placement Services wants to estimate the mean monthly rent charged for two-bedroom apartments in the Chicago metropolitan area. A random sample will be used to estimate the mean to within ± $10 per month, with a confidence of 98%. The best information Live Rite can obtain is that past studies have indicated a population standard deviation of $60. What size should the sample be?

Solution   Use the four-step procedure shown in the previous section:

1. Live Rite wants to obtain an estimate of the population mean monthly rent within $10. They can tolerate a maximum error of e = $10.

2. Live Rite wants to be 98% confident in the maximum error of $10. The 98% confidence level is divided by 2, .98/2, resulting in an area equal to .4900. The Z value is looked up in the normal curve table and is equal to 2.33.

3. The population standard deviation is estimated from past studies to be $60.

4. The results of Steps 1 through 3 are substituted into Equation 9–8.

$$n = \left(\frac{Z\sigma_x}{e} \right)^2$$

$$n = \left(\frac{2.33(60)}{10} \right)^2$$

$$n = (13.98)^2$$

$$n = 195.44$$

In cases where the computed n is a fraction, analysts round up to the next higher integer value, thus making the recommended sample size 196. To be 98% confident that the sample mean will be within $10 of the actual population mean monthly rent, Live Rite needs to select a sample of at least 196 observations.

Sample Size Determination for Estimating Proportions

If the analyst is concerned about estimating a proportion, the procedure for determining the appropriate sample size is similar to the one described in the last section. The analyst uses the same steps as those for determining sample sizes for means with the exception of Step 3, which involved estimating the population standard deviation. Instead of estimating σ, the analyst needs to estimate the population proportion. If there is no basis for estimating π, an estimate of .50 is used because it provides the largest most conservative sample size recommendation. Equation 9–7 can be manipulated so that the analyst can solve for the value of n. Thus

$$e = Z\sqrt{\frac{\pi(1-\pi)}{n}}$$

$$\sqrt{n} = Z\sqrt{\frac{\pi(1-\pi)}{e}}$$

$$n = \frac{Z^2\pi(1-\pi)}{e^2} \qquad\qquad \text{(9–9)}$$

Example 9–7   A bank credit card firm is interested in estimating the proportion of credit card holders who incur an interest charge at the end of each month. Assume that the desired precision for the proportion estimate is ± 4% at a 95% confidence level. How large a sample should be selected if approximately 75% of the firm's cardholders incur interest each month?

Solution   Use the four-step procedure:

1. The bank credit card firm wants to obtain an estimate of the population proportion of customers who incur interest charges within 4%. They can tolerate a maximum error of $e = .04$.
2. The firm wants to be 95% confident. The 95% confidence level is divided by 2, .95/2, resulting in an area equal to .4750. The Z value is looked up in the normal curve table and is equal to 1.96.
3. The population proportion of customers who incur interest charges is estimated to be approximately 75%.
4. The results of steps 1 to 3 are substituted into Equation 9–9.

$$n = \frac{Z^2\pi(1-\pi)}{e^2}$$

$$n = \frac{(1.96)^2.75(1-.75)}{(.04)^2}$$

$$n = 450.19$$

To be 95% confident that the sample proportion will be within 4% of the actual population proportion of customers who incur interest charges, the bank credit card firm needs to select a sample of at least 451 customers.

Example 9–8   How large a sample would be recommended for the bank credit card firm in Example 9–7 if no estimate of the population proportion could be specified?

Solution   Whenever it is difficult to estimate the population proportion, $\pi = .50$ is used because it provides the largest, most conservative sample size recommendation. Now the substitution into Equation 9–9 is

$$n = \frac{Z^2 \pi (1 - \pi)}{e^2}$$

$$n = \frac{(1.96)^2 .5(1 - .5)}{(.04)^2}$$

$$n = 600.25$$

The larger recommended sample size of 601 reflects the caution taken in using a conservative estimate of population proportion.

SUMMARY

Population means and proportions are estimated based on one sample selected from the population of interest. These estimates can be point

TABLE 9–3
Summary of formulas

A. Estimating means

Point estimate	$\overline{X}$
Interval estimate	
σ_x known	$\overline{X} \pm Z \dfrac{\sigma_x}{\sqrt{n}}$
σ_x unknown	$\overline{X} \pm t \dfrac{s_x}{\sqrt{n}}$
Sample size	$n = \left(\dfrac{Z\sigma_x}{e}\right)^2$
Maximum probable error	
σ_x known	$e = Z \dfrac{\sigma_x}{\sqrt{n}}$
σ_x unknown	$e = t \dfrac{s_x}{\sqrt{n}}$

B. Estimating proportions

Point estimate	p
Interval estimate	$p \pm Z \sqrt{\dfrac{\pi(1 - \pi)}{n}}$
Sample size	$n = \dfrac{Z^2 \pi (1 - \pi)}{e^2}$
Error	$e = Z \sqrt{\dfrac{\pi(1 - \pi)}{n}}$

estimates for single values or interval estimates for a range of values in which the population parameter is thought to be. Confidence intervals are interval estimates that include a probability statement indicating the risk of error.

Interval estimates of μ or π are constructed on the basis of the properties of the sampling distribution. If the sample size is sufficiently large, these sampling distributions approximate the normal distribution. If μ is estimated for a small sample, the sampling distribution approximates a t distribution if the population is normally distributed.

The sample size is important because it affects the degree of precision of interval estimates and confidence in their accuracy. The necessary sample size depends on the amount of error that can be tolerated, the degree of confidence desired, and the variability in the population. Frequently, sample size determination becomes a practical decision based on cost, time, and availability constraints. Table 9–3 presents a review of the formulas discussed in this chapter.

CASE STUDY: THE KIRBY RATINGS

The Kirby ratings service is sold to TV networks, program suppliers, ad agencies, and advertisers who pay fees based on a portion of their total business. A top ad agency may pay $350,000 a year for the Kirby service and networks pay more. Subscribers receive a series of reports filled with estimates of TV-show popularity from Kirby. Networks base their charges for commercial time on these ratings. A commercial minute on a top-rated show like *60 Minutes* might cost an advertiser $188,000, compared with a charge of $75,000 or less for shows low in the rankings. Tough, big-money decisions are based on the ratings. Clients and agencies both take the numbers very seriously. The clients want to know how many people they are reaching with their TV money.

Kirby sets up a panel of approximately 1200 homes and uses about 1,500 people to measure TV viewing for the whole population each week. Sampling error is a major concern and Kirby tells users the standard error of the proportion is $\pm$ 1.3 points at a rating of 20. That means a show with a rating of 20 might have as few as 18.7% or as many as 21.3% of all American homes watching. Kirby statisticians minimize the extent of their sampling error by using a concept called level of confidence. When Kirby reports ratings, the

TABLE 9–4

Kirby average ratings
(top 40 regular shows,
Sept. 11, 1977
through
Dec. 10, 1977)

Rank	Program	Average Rating
1	Laverne & Shirley	37.6
2	Happy Days	37.0
3	Three's Company	32.6
4	Charlie's Angels	31.9
5	All in the Family	31.5
6	Alice	29.9
7	60 Minutes	29.8
8	NBC Monday Movie	29.1
9	On Our Own	28.3
10	Little House on Prairie	28.2
11	ABC Sunday Movie	27.7
12	Eight is Enough	27.6
12	Rhoda	27.6
12	Soap	27.6
15	Monday Night Football	27.3
16	M*A*S*H	27.2
17	One Day at a Time	27.1
18	Barney Miller	27.0
19	Six Million Dollar Man	26.5
20	The Love Boat	26.4
20	What's Happening!!	26.4
20	Barnaby Jones	26.4
20	Welcome Back, Kotter	26.4
24	The Big Event	26.2
25	Donny & Marie	25.9
26	Family	25.6
27	ABC Friday Movie	25.5
28	Hawaii Five-O	25.4
29	Baretta	25.2
30	Starsky & Hutch	25.0
31	CBS Sunday Movie	24.8
31	Carter Country	24.8
31	The Betty White Show	24.8
34	NBC Saturday Movie	24.7
35	The Waltons	24.4
36	CBS Wednesday Movie	24.2
37	Good Times	24.0
38	World of Disney	23.8
38	Tabitha	23.8
40	Maude	23.7

report will say their numbers are true two out of three times or 68% of the time.

Kirby also claims that when repeated measurements of the same people are taken many times, the sampling error is lowered. Kirby statisticians have a special formula that reduces the standard error of the proportion from 1.3 to .9 over a 13-week period. Table 9–4 presents the ratings from September 11, 1977 through December 10, 1977.

Questions 1. What can be said about the ratings for *Barney Miller*?

2. Do you feel the Kirby ratings are accurate? Why?

EXERCISES

1. What is the difference between a point estimate and an interval estimate?

2. What is the disadvantage of a point estimate?

3. What effect does increasing the sample size have on an interval estimate?

4. What effect does increasing the level of confidence have on an interval estimate?

5. What effect does the population variability have on an interval estimate?

6. When is it appropriate to use the t distribution?

7. When is the normal distribution used as an approximation of the t distribution?

8. How are the Z distribution and the t distribution similar? How do they differ?

9. What is the correct interpretation of the following statement? "I am 99% confident that the interval estimate contains the population proportion."

10. When should the finite correction factor be used in an interval estimate?

11. How is the error in an interval estimate measured?

12. How large should a sample be?

13. Determine the Z value for the following confidence levels:
    a. 90%
    b. 80%
    c. 96%

14. Suppose you have a sample of 21 items and the population standard deviation is unknown. Would you use a Z distribution or a t distribution in your interval estimate?

15. Determine the appropriate t value for the following interval estimates:
    a. $n = 16$, 90% confidence level

b. $n = 27$, 99% confidence level
c. $n = 10$, 95% confidence level

16. A sample of 25 customers at Bob's Service Station purchases an average of 12.8 gallons of gasoline. If the population standard deviation is 2.5 gallons, what is the 98% confidence interval estimate of the mean number of gallons purchased per customer?

17. The annual health insurance claims for a random sample of 225 women between the ages of 30 and 35 were obtained to determine the necessity of a rate increase. The sample mean was $536 and the sample standard deviation was $30. Find the 95% confidence interval for the population mean claim.

18. The Keytronics Company would like to compare the annual salaries of its employees against industry-wide salaries. From past experience the company knows the standard deviation of these salaries is $7,000. A random sample of 22 companies is selected and the average salary is found to be $23,400. Find the 90% confidence interval for the population mean salary.

19. The regional manager of Value Mart, a local supermarket chain, is attempting to estimate the average fat content per pound of hamburger sold in Dallas, Texas. To do so, he purchases one pound of hamburger from each of the stores in his area on nine randomly selected days. The hamburger is then cooked and the fat is poured off and weighed. The average results for each of the nine days were recorded in ounces of fat as follows:

    3.3   4.8   5.1   4.5   4.0   3.9   4.7   5.0   3.6

    Find the 95% confidence interval for the population mean.

20. The auditors of Litho-Art Printers would like to know the proportion of accurate accounts receivable based on an audit verification letter sent to customers. On the basis of the letter, 180 out of 200 responses were verified as accurate. Find the 99% confidence interval for the true proportion of accurate accounts receivable.

21. A random sample of 75 savings accounts at the Third National Bank is examined to see what the balance was at the end of the last month. The mean for the 75 accounts was $3,076 and the standard deviation was $500. Find a 90% confidence interval for the population mean for all savings accounts at the end of last month.

22. Goodmonth Tire Corporation wants to be sure that their estimate of the average mileage of a new brand of tires deviates no more than 400 miles from the true average. The standard deviation for this type of tire is typically 3000 miles. If Goodmonth wants to be 95% certain that the sample mean is within the desired interval, how many tires should be tested?

23. Vesta Bodily, Inc. is a research firm that does telephone interviews to test advertising recall. Kershaw's has just developed a new advertising campaign and has asked Vesta to bid on a contract to test people's recall. Kershaw's wants to be 95% confident that the sample proportion is within

5% of the actual population proportion of individuals who recall the new advertising slogan. How many telephone interviews should Vesta obtain?

24. Using the sample size decided on in Exercise 23, Vesta completed the telephone interviews and found that 120 respondents recalled the new advertising slogan. Find the appropriate confidence interval.

25. Heart Medical Center desires to estimate the mean time that a staff member spends with each patient. If the population standard deviation is estimated to be 6 minutes, how large should the sample be if the precision of the estimate is to be 1 minute?

26. The Boulevard Restaurant wants to be sure that it will not run out of a special dessert. A survey of 200 customers indicates that 40 of the customers order this dessert. Next weekend the restaurant anticipates 1000 customers. Would they be safe in stocking 200 special desserts? What percent of the time would they run out? If the restaurant desires that there would be only a 3% chance of running out of the dessert, what stock policy should be followed?

27. The personnel officer of the Johnson & Jackson Corporation would like to estimate the proportion of employees within two years of mandatory retirement. She selects a simple random sample of 100 employee records and determines that 13 are within two years of retirement. Find a 90% confidence interval for the true proportion of employees nearing retirement in the entire corporation.

28. Mutual Savings Bank is considering offering its customers the possibility of investing in a money market fund. A random sample of 90 savings account holders is chosen and called on the telephone. Thirty-two of them indicate an interest in investing in the money market fund. Find a 90% confidence interval for the population proportion of all savings account holders interested in the money market fund.

29. Greenwood's Advertising Agency would like to measure the proportion of the population that would respond favorably to a particular TV commercial. If the agency estimates that the population proportion is .70, how many people should be included in a random sample used for estimating the true proportion of favorable respondents within .03 with a confidence of .90? What sample size should be used if Greenwood's does not know what the population proportion might be?

30. This question refers to the class data base. Take a random sample of ten students from the class data base. Develop a 90% confidence interval for the variable age. Develop a 95% confidence interval for the proportion of males in the class.

10

General Concepts of Hypothesis Testing

Where You Have Been   So far you have learned how to gather, present, analyze, and interpret sample data. You found that statistical inference is the process of drawing conclusions about population parameters based on information contained in a sample. You learned how to use probability theory to make estimates about populations on the basis of sample information. You know how to make point and interval estimates of means and proportions in these populations. You are prepared to continue this type of statistical analysis and will try to frame your inferences so that they lead to useful decisions.

Where You Are Going   Another type of statistical inference is hypothesis testing. This approach is used to make a decision about the validity of a statement, claim, or assumption that may have been made about the population. You will learn how to answer such questions as the following: Should a shipment of goods be accepted? Is a manufacturer's claim valid? Does an advertising campaign lead to increased sales? Will customers prefer a new product? To answer these questions, you will learn how to set up hypotheses about the characteristic of the population you wish to study.

INTRODUCTION

In many situations an analyst is interested in testing some claim about the population rather than estimating one of its parameters. This procedure is called *hypothesis testing* and involves the following steps:

1. State the hypothesis being tested (called the null hypothesis) and the alternative hypothesis (the one accepted if the null hypothesis is rejected).

2. Identify the appropriate sampling distribution; this is the distribution from which the sample statistic will be drawn.

3. Determine the level of significance (the probability of rejecting the null hypothesis when it is true).

4. State a decision rule indicating what value or values of the sample statistic will lead to a rejection of the null hypothesis.

5. Select a random sample of items from the population and compute the appropriate sample statistic.

6. Make the statistical decision and formulate a conclusion to be acted on by the appropriate decision maker.

Hypothesis testing involves using sample data to test statements, claims, or assumptions about population parameters.

HYPOTHESIS-TESTING PROCEDURE

Hypothesis Development

In hypothesis testing the statement, claim, or assumption to be tested is called the *null hypothesis* and is denoted by H_0. It is frequently a version of the statement that any difference between a sample statistic and its hypothesized population parameter is most likely due to chance variation in sampling. Since we are concerned with a hypothesis of no change or difference, we call it the null hypothesis.

> The null hypothesis usually states that the difference between the sample statistic and its claimed population parameter is due to chance variation in sampling.

A hypothesis gives an analyst the opportunity to test whether a change has occurred or a real difference exists. Why not state that the difference between the sample statistic and population parameter is due to a specific variable? The problem is that this type of hypothesis is incapable of definitive testing. Evidence that is consistent with a hypothesis can almost never be taken as conclusive grounds for accepting it. A finding that is consistent with a hypothesis would be consistent with other hypotheses too and, thus, does not demonstrate the truth of the given hypothesis. For instance, the finding that 52 tails were obtained out of 100 flips of a coin is consistent with the hypothesis that the coin is biased in favor of tails, but this finding is also consistent with the hypothesis that the coin is fair. On the other hand, the finding that 65 tails were obtained out of 100 flips can be assumed to contradict the hypothesis that the coin is fair. A look at the appropriate sampling distribution demonstrates that a fair coin has 1 chance in 1,000 of showing as many as 70 tails. Therefore, it can be concluded with small risk of error that the coin was biased in favor of tails.

Suppose that the mean family income in Chico, California, was determined to be $17,500 with a standard deviation of $2,000 for a particular year and that five years later we want to determine whether the mean income has changed. With no evidence to the contrary, we tentatively assume that the mean income is still $17,500. The null hypothesis is that the mean income in Chico is not different or has not changed from $17,500. This hypothesis will either be accepted or rejected based on sample evidence. An alternative hypothesis must be stated and is what will be believed if the null hypothesis is rejected. The alternative hypothesis is that the mean income in Chico is different or has changed from $17,500. The null hypothesis H_0 and an alternate hypothesis H_1 are set up with appropriate symbols as follows:

$$H_0: \mu = \$17,500$$
$$H_1: \mu = \$17,500$$

Errors in Hypothesis Testing

The hypothesis-testing procedure begins by assuming that the null hypothesis, H_0, is true. The goal is to reach a decision whether to accept or reject H_0. A sample is selected and a decision is made after the sample results are compared with the results expected if the null hypothesis were true. Ideally, an analyst wants to accept the null hypothesis, H_0, when it is true, or reject H_0 when it is false. However, this will not always be the case.

From the study of sampling distributions, it is realized that the value of a sample statistic cannot be expected to equal the population parameter exactly. Therefore, the hypothesis-testing procedure will possibly lead to a wrong decision. If H_0 is rejected when it is true or accepted when it is false, an error has been made. For example, if the null hypothesis, H_0, reflects the true population situation, the hypothesis-testing procedure should lead the analyst to accept H_0. If, instead, the procedure leads the analyst to reject H_0, a *Type I error* has been made. A Type I error occurs if H_0 is rejected when it is actually true. It is important to note that the only time a Type I error can occur is when the null hypothesis is rejected.

Consider the case where the mean income in Chico is actually $17,500. The null hypothesis, $\mu = \$17,500$, is true. The analyst hopes that the hypothesis-testing procedure will lead to the conclusion that H_0 should be accepted or that the mean income in Chico is not different from $17,500. If the procedure leads to the conclusion that H_0 should be rejected, a Type I error has been made.

What happens if the null hypothesis is actually false? The analyst hopes that the hypothesis-testing procedure will lead to the rejection of H_0. If, instead, the procedure leads to the conclusion to accept H_0, the analyst will be making what is called a *Type II error*. A Type II error occurs if H_0 is accepted when it is actually false. It is important to note that the only time a Type II error can occur is when the null hypothesis is accepted.

Consider the case where the mean income in Chico has actually changed in the last five years and is not $17,500. If the null hypothesis, $\mu = \$17,500$, is false, it is hoped that the hypothesis-testing procedure will allow the analyst to reject H_0 and accept the alternative hypothesis H_1, which states that the mean income in Chico has changed from

$17,500. If the procedure leads to the conclusion that H_0 should be accepted, a Type II error will be made.

> A Type I error occurs if a null hypothesis is rejected when it is true.
> A Type II error occurs if a null hypothesis is accepted when it is false.

Determining the Appropriate Sampling Distribution

The hypothesis test is based on whether some observed sample statistic could reasonably have come from a population with the claimed parameter. It is important to take into account the sampling variability that might arise given the claimed population parameter value. The analyst needs to identify the appropriate sampling distribution that will fully describe chance variation. The probability distribution of a sample statistic is determined by the assumption that the null hypothesis is true.

Suppose the analyst selects a sample of 400 Chico residents and tests the null hypothesis that the mean income in Chico has not changed from $17,500. Since the population standard deviation is known, $\sigma = \$2,000$, the appropriate sampling distribution is the normal distribution with a mean of $\mu = \$17,500$ and a standard deviation of $\sigma/\sqrt{n} = \$2,000/\sqrt{400} = \$100$. Thus if the mean income has not changed, the sample mean should come from a sampling distribution with a mean of $17,500 and a standard deviation of $100 as shown in Figure 10-1.

The probability that the sample mean will be exactly $17,500 is approximately zero. If the sample mean is close to $17,500, it would

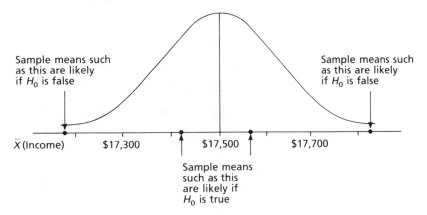

FIGURE 10-1
Sampling distribution of the mean income for Chico residents

Sample means such as this are likely if H_0 is false

Sample means such as this are likely if H_0 is false

$\bar{X}$ (Income) $17,300 $17,500 $17,700

Sample means such as this are likely if H_0 is true

seem to suggest that chance alone could account for the discrepancy. The distinction between what might reasonably be regarded as chance variation and what might be regarded as meaningful variation is discussed in the next section.

Determining the Significance Level

The analyst always hopes that the correct decision concerning the null hypothesis will be reached after examining sample evidence, but there is always a possibility of rejecting a true H_0 and failing to reject a false H_0. The probabilities of these events are known as alpha ($\propto$) and beta (β), respectively.

The probability of rejecting a null hypothesis that is true is called the *level of significance* of a hypothesis test. In most textbook examples it is common to designate a signficance level, usually .01, .02, or .05, without a discussion of why such values are chosen. In a real-world decision-making situation the analyst must choose the significance level. The appropriate question to be answered is what probability of rejecting a true null hypothesis am I willing to accept? It is important to understand that a low probability of committing a Type I or alpha error generates a high probability of committing a Type II or beta error, and vice versa, for any given sample size.

> The level of significance of a hypothesis test is the probability of rejecting a null hypothesis that is true. It is designated by the symbol $\propto$ (Greek alpha).

How does an analyst choose an appropriate value for alpha? The answer depends on the penalties associated with Type I and II errors. If rejecting a true H_0 is more costly than accepting a false H_0, a small alpha should be chosen. If accepting a false H_0 is more costly than rejecting a true H_0, a large alpha should be chosen. The case study at the end of this chapter illustrates some of the factors considered in selecting a significance level.

Once a hypothesis test has been completed, only one type of error is possible. If the null hypothesis was rejected, the danger is that a true H_0 was rejected (Type I error). If the null hypothesis is accepted, the danger is that a false H_0 was accepted (Type II error).

Stating the Decision Rule

Decision rules are specified in terms of when the null hypothesis will be rejected. The significance level is selected and the appropriate sampling distribution constructed. Figure 10–2 shows the sampling

FIGURE 10–2
Sampling distribution
for the null hypothesis
of the mean income
for Chico residents

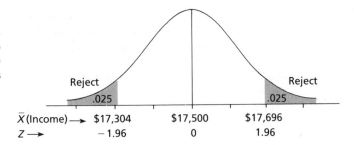

distribution for the null hypothesis of the Chico income example ana-lyzed at the .05 significance level. The $\propto$ = .05 has been divided by two, resulting in an area of .025 in each tail of the curve. By using the normal curve table in Appendix E, one can determine that the Z value associated with an area of .025 is 1.96. To state the decision rule, one needs to determine the *critical values* (sample means that are equiv-alent to Z values of -1.96 and $+1.96$ in Figure 10–2). The critical values are calculated using Equation 10–1:

$$c = \text{population parameter} \pm Z(\text{standard error}) \qquad \textbf{(10–1)}$$

In this case the standard deviation of the sampling distribution or the standard error of the mean is $\sigma_{\bar{x}} = \sigma_x/\sqrt{n} = \$2,000/\sqrt{400} = \$100$. The critical values are

$$c = \$17,500 \pm 1.96(\$100)$$
$$c = \$17,500 \pm \$196$$
$$c = \$17,304 \text{ and } \$17,696$$

With these critical values, the decision rule that provides a .05 proba-bility of making a Type I error when $\mu = \$17,500$ is

$$\text{Reject } H_0 \text{ if } \bar{X} < \$17,304 \text{ or if } \bar{X} > \$17,696$$

Making the Decision

The analyst is now ready to select a sample, compute the sample statistic, and accept or reject the null hypothesis. The decision rule for the Chico Income study requires that the analyst reject H_0 if the sample mean is less than $17,304 or greater than $17,696 and accept H_0 otherwise. Suppose that the sample mean for the 400 residents is $17,800. Following the decision rule, the analyst would reject H_0 and accept the alternative hypothesis that the mean income in Chico has changed from $17,500. The sampling distribution in Figure 10–2 shows that a sample mean of $\bar{X} = \$17,800$ is unlikely if the population mean is $17,500. In fact, this sample mean is so unlikely that it may not have come from this sampling distribution. Of course, the analyst might be wrong in rejecting the null hypothesis and might be making a Type I error. The probability of a Type I error in this case is $\propto = .05$. Figure 10–2 shows that there is a 5% chance of obtaining a sample mean outside the 17,304 to 17,696 range even though the actual population mean is $17,500.

ONE- AND TWO-TAILED TESTS

An alternative hypothesis may indicate a change from the H_0 in a particular direction, or it may merely indicate a change without specifying a direction. In the Chico Income study the analyst rejected the null hypothesis if the sample mean was either too large or too small. This is a *two-tailed test*. Frequently, analysts are only concerned with one alternative. They might be testing a manufacturer's claim or determining how many people prefer a particular product. In the Chico Income study the analyst might only be interested in whether the mean income has increased. When the variable of interest concerns only one direction, a *one-tailed test* should be used. If an increase in the mean income of Chico residents is of interest, the null and alternative hypotheses are

$$H_0: \mu = \$17,500$$
$$H_1: \mu > \$17,500$$

A one-tailed test is one in which the alternative hypothesis is directional and includes either the symbol $<$ or $>$.
A two-tailed test is one in which the alternative hypothesis does not specify a direction and includes the symbol $\neq$.

Example 10–1 Suppose the sponsor of the television program, *F Team*, states that the program should be canceled if there is convincing evidence that the program's share of the viewing audience is less than 20%. State the null and alternative hypotheses to test this situation.

Solution Since the sponsor is only interested in an outcome of less than 20%, the analyst should form a directional or one-tailed alternative hypothesis.

$$H_0: \pi = .20$$
$$H_1: \pi < .20$$

The hypothesis-testing procedure is illustrated in the following example.

Example 10–2 The Mountaintop Corporation is attempting to take over the Hilltop Company. Mountaintop's securities consultant reports that 55% of Hilltop's shareholders support the takeover bid. The president of Mountaintop wants to make sure of this and requests a telephone survey of Hilltop's shareholders. The staff polls 500 shareholders and finds that 260 support the takeover bid. At the $\alpha = .02$ significance level, does the sample proportion refute the consultant's report?

Solution Use the six step hypothesis-testing procedure:

1. State the null and alternative hypotheses. Since the president is only interested in the situation where the sample proportion is less than 55%, direction is implied and a one-tailed test should be used.

$$H_0: \pi = .55$$

$$H_1: \pi < .55$$

2. The sample size is large enough to use the normal approximation of the binomial distribution. The sampling distribution of sample proportions is assumed to be normally distributed.

3. An $\alpha = .02$ has been selected as the significance level and is the probability of making a Type I error.

4. Figure 10–3 shows the sampling distribution of sample proportions. By using the normal curve table in Appendix E, one can determine that the Z value associated with an area of .02 is 2.05. Equation 10–1 is used to calculate the appropriate critical value (sample proportion that is equivalent to a Z value of -2.05). In this case the standard deviation of the sampling distribution or the standard error of the proportion is:

FIGURE 10–3
Sampling distribution of sampling proportions for a one-tailed test

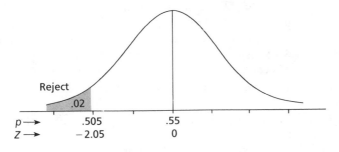

$$\sigma_p = \sqrt{\frac{\pi(1 - \pi)}{n}}$$

$$\sigma_p = \sqrt{\frac{.55(1 - .55)}{500}}$$

$$\sigma_p = .022$$

The critical value is

$$c = \pi + Z(\text{standard error})$$
$$c = .55 + (-2.05)(.022)$$
$$c = .55 - .045$$
$$c = .505$$

The decision rule is

Reject H_0 if $p < .505$

5. The sample proportion is equal to $p = X/n = 260/500 = .52$.
6. Since the sample proportion, $p = .52$, is not less than the critical value, $c = .505$, the null hypothesis is accepted. Based on the sample evidence, the staff has failed to reject that the population proportion is .55. At the .02 significance level the president's poll tends to support the consultant's report that 55% of the shareholders support the takeover bid, even though only 52% of the sampled shareholders do so. The fact that 52% < 55% is attributed to chance variation in sampling rather than a lack of support for the takeover.

TYPE II ERROR

Since the hypothesis-testing procedure in Example 10-2 led to the conclusion that H_0 should be accepted, a Type II error is possible. A Type II error would occur if the actual population proportion is less than .55. What is the probability of making a Type II error? To compute this probability, the analyst would need to know the actual population proportion. If the actual population proportion were known, a hypothesis test would not need to be performed in the first place. Therefore, the probability of Type II errors can only be calculated for assumed population proportions.

Example 10-3   Calculate the probability of making a Type II error if it is assumed that the actual population proportion of shareholders who support the takeover bid in Example 10-2 is .50.

FIGURE 10–4
(a) The probability
that a Type I error
will be made; (b) the
probability that a
Type II error will be
made

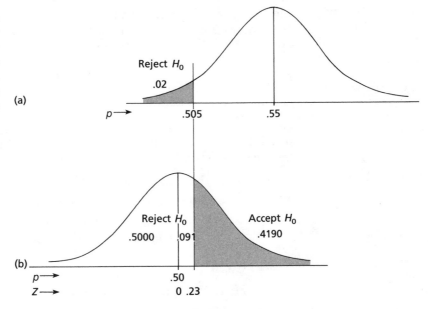

(a)

(b)

Reject H_0
.02

$p \longrightarrow$ .505   .55

Reject H_0 Accept H_0
.5000   091   .4190

$p \longrightarrow$ .50
$Z \longrightarrow$ 0 .23

Solution   Figure 10–4(a) shows the situation under the condition that the null hypothesis is true. The shaded area is the probability of making a Type I error, .02. Figure 10–4(b) shows the situation under the condition that the true population proportion is .50. Notice that the shaded area in Figure 10–4(b) represents H_0 being accepted, even though it is false. This is the probability of making a Type II error. Note also that .505 is the critical value for both curves. To calculate the probability of a Type II error the analyst uses the normal distribution as follows:

$$Z = \left(\frac{p - \pi}{\sigma_p} \right)$$

$$Z = \frac{(.505 - .500)}{\sqrt{\dfrac{.5(.5)}{500}}}$$

$Z = .23$ Area $= .091$ (from the normal curve table)

From the normal curve table the probability of making a Type II error is $.4090 = (.5000 - .0910)$. In other words, if $\propto = .02$ is chosen, the analyst is running a .419 chance of accepting H_0 when the true proportion is $\pi = .50$.

In Example 10–4 the level of significance was set at .02. The analyst could have set alpha or the probability of making a Type I error at .05. If this is done, the probability of making a Type II error is approximately 28% (see if you can compute this percentage). As alpha increases, beta decreases; and as alpha decreases, beta increases when the sample size is kept constant. To reduce the probability of making either a Type I or a Type II error, the sample size must be increased.

SUMMARY

Analysts are frequently interested in testing a specific claim about the population. The procedure to do this is called hypothesis testing and includes the following steps:

1. State the null and alternative hypotheses.
2. Determine the appropriate sampling distribution.
3. Determine the level of significance.
4. State a decision rule indicating when the null hypothesis will be rejected.
5. Select a random sample and compute the sample statistic.
6. Make the statistical decision.

The hypothesis-testing procedure begins with a statement about the value of a population parameter. This statement is called the null hypothesis and is assumed to be true. The null hypothesis usually states that there is no difference between the sample statistic and its claimed population parameter. A sampling distribution is constructed based on this premise and indicates the extent to which sample outcomes might vary simply because of chance variation in sampling. A maximum allowable probability of rejecting H_0 when it is true is used as the level of significance. A critical value is computed for a decision rule that can be used to make the decision to reject or accept H_0. A Type I error occurs if a null hypothesis is rejected when it is true. A Type II error occurs if a null hypothesis is accepted when it is false.

The choice of the sampling distribution depends on sample size, type of data being analyzed, and assumptions made about the underlying population. The next chapter will deal with the application of the hypothesis-testing procedure to different types of situations.

CASE STUDY: FARRIS BREWING COMPANY

The Farris Brewing Company announced that it would broadcast on live television a taste test featuring 100 beer drinkers. The test would be conducted at halftime of a basketball game. The Farris

Company claimed that the people selected for the taste test were loyal Brewmaster beer drinkers. Each participant was to be served two beers, one Brewmaster beer and one Farris beer, in unlabelled mugs. Prior to the test, the tasters would be informed that one mug contained Brewmaster beer and the other Farris beer. The percentage of loyal Brewmaster drinkers who preferred Farris beer would then be tabulated.

The results of the live television taste test indicated that 46% of the loyal Brewmaster beer drinkers preferred Farris beer. In an advertisement, the Farris Brewing Company concluded that the outcome of the test was an impressive showing. The President of Brewmaster wished to counter this argument and called in the firm's statistician to discuss whether the test could show that a significantly higher proportion of the taste testers preferred Brewmaster.

Questions

1. What are the null and alternative hypotheses for this test?

2. If you were the statistician, what significance level would you use?

3. What is the proper conclusion for this test?

4. Do you think that it is possible to select a sample of 100 loyal Brewmaster beer drinkers?

5. How could the Farris Brewing Company have selected a sample to bias the results of the test in their favor?

EXERCISES

1. What is the purpose of hypothesis testing?

2. How does hypothesis testing differ from estimation?

3. Explain the difference between each of the following:
   a. Null hypothesis and alternative hypothesis
   b. Type I error and Type II error
   c. One-tailed test and two-tailed test
   d. .01 level and .10 level
   e. Alpha and level of significance
   f. Level of significance and Type I error

4. What are the two possible conclusions of a hypothesis test?

5. Evaluate the statement that an analyst will not make very many errors if a very low significance level (i.e., alpha equal to .01) is used.

6. Is it more important to control Type I errors or Type II errors?

7. How would you decrease the probability of making either a Type I error or a Type II error in a particular hypothesis test?

8. When can an analyst risk making a Type II error?

9. When can an analyst risk making a Type I error?

10. In a hypothesis test, is the size of the region of rejection increased or decreased when the level of significance is reduced?

11. If the null hypothesis is true, what type of error might the analyst make?

12. If the null hypothesis is false, what type of error might the analyst make?

13. State the null and alternative hypotheses that would be used to test each of the following statements:
    a. The average time for the delivery of Kaypro Computers is 40 days.
    b. The average age of Sears customers is 30 years.
    c. A manufacturer claims that the average life of a certain transistor is at least 1000 hours.
    d. A pharmaceutical firm maintains that the average time for a certain drug to take effect is 15 minutes.
    e. A supplier of metal casing has agreed to send a manufacturing firm shipments that contain no more than 3% defectives.
    f. A random sample of invoices was checked to determine whether the proportion incorrectly recorded had changed from 3%.

14. Assume that the government requires that hamburger have no more than 20% fat content by weight on the average. Design a hypothesis-testing procedure that will allow a government inspector to determine whether restaurants are meeting this requirement.

15. The City Manager is considering putting an increase in the city sales tax on the November ballot. She would like to have some idea as to the possibility of its succesful passage. She calls on you as a consultant to tell her how to get an estimate of the necessary information. What would you recommend to the City Manager?

16. An auditor is working for a person who is considering purchasing a defunct business. The business has stated that no more than 20% of its accounts receivable are more than 60 days past due. A sample of 100 accounts is selected and the sample proportion tested at the .02 significance level. State the null and alternative hypotheses and the appropriate decision rule.

17. State the appropriate conclusion for Exercise 16, if the sample proportion is equal to $p = .22$. Explain what type of error might be made.

18. The manufacturer of K-Brand Cereal is producing 24-ounce packages. The automated packaging device needs frequent checking to see whether it is actually putting 24 ounces in each package. The weights of the packages are known to be normally distributed with a standard deviation of .4 ounce. State the null and alternative hypotheses. State the decision rule if the hypothesis is to be tested at the 5% significance level for a sample of 36 packages.

19. State the appropriate conclusion for Exercise 18 if the sample mean is equal to $\overline{X} = 25$ ounces. Explain what type of error might be made.

20. The manager of the Phoenix Resort Hotel believes that the mean guest bill is at least $300. The population is normally distributed with a standard deviation of $50. What is the decision rule for a significance level of .10 if a sample of 49 guest bills is surveyed?

21. State the appropriate conclusion for Exercise 20 if the sample mean is equal to $\overline{X}$ = $280. Explain what type of error might be made.

22. An automobile assembly line operation has a scheduled mean completion time of 3 minutes. The population is normally distributed with a standard deviation of .3 minutes. State the decision rule for a sample size of 64 observations tested at the .01 significance level.

23. State the appropriate conclusion for Exercise 22 if the sample mean is equal to $\overline{X}$ = 3.75 minutes. Explain what type of error might be made.

24. An automobile manufacturer claims that a new economy model will average at least 40 miles per gallon of gasoline. The population is normally distributed with a standard deviation of 4 miles per gallon. State the decision rule for a sample of 35 cars tested at the .05 significance level.

25. What is the probability in Exercise 24 of committing a Type II error if the actual mileage is 38 miles per gallon?

26. What is the probability in Exercise 24 of committing a Type II error if the actual mileage is 41 miles per gallon?

27. State the appropriate conclusion for Exercise 24 if the sample mean is equal to $\overline{X}$ = 38 miles per gallon.

28. This question refers to the class data base. Set up the correct hypothesis to test whether an equal number of males and females attend your school.

11

Hypothesis-testing Applications

Where You Have Been   You have learned how to use hypothesis testing to make a decision about the validity of a statement, claim, or assumption that has been made about the population. You learned how to state null and alternative hypotheses, determine the appropriate sampling distribution, determine the level of significance, state decision rules, and make the statistical decision.

Where You Are Going   In this chapter you will learn how to apply the hypothesis-testing procedure to several different types of situations. A claim might involve the mean or proportion of a single population, which requires a one-sample test. Or a claim might be that the means or the proportions of two populations are equal, which requires a two-sample test.

HYPOTHESIS TEST ABOUT A POPULATION MEAN

A *one-sample test* is used to test a claim about a single population mean. A sample mean, $\overline{X}$, is computed and compared to the claimed population mean, μ. The analyst must take into account the degree that the sample mean might vary from the claimed population parameter because of chance variation in sampling. This is analyzed using a sampling distribution with a mean equal to the value of the claimed population parameter. The sampling distribution will be normally distributed for samples selected from a normal population with a known standard deviation and will have a t distribution when the population standard deviation is estimated using the sample standard deviation. The need to assume that we are sampling from a normal population can be relaxed when the sample size is 30 or more.

> A one-sample test is used to test a claim about a single population mean.

Large Samples

When the population standard deviation (σ) is known for a normal population, the appropriate sampling distribution is the normal distribution for all sample sizes. When the standard deviation is known for a population that is not normally distributed, the appropriate sampling distribution is the normal distribution for sample sizes of 30 or more.

When the population standard deviation (σ) is unknown, it must be estimated using the sample standard deviation (s), and the appropriate sampling distribution is the t distribution. Actually, the t distribution is only required when the sample size is less than 30. For larger samples, the values of t and Z are approximately the same, and the normal distribution can be used in place of the t distribution.

If the sample size is sufficiently large ($n \geq 30$), the central limit theorem permits the assumption that the sampling distribution is approximately normally distributed for all cases.

Example 11–1 Prior to the installation of a new type of equipment, the average number of on-the-job accidents per day at a factory was 3.2. The population distribution was nonnormal in shape with a standard deviation of .9. To determine whether the new equipment affected the number of on-the-job accidents per day, a random sample of 36 days was selected and the number of accidents per day was recorded. If the sample mean is 3, is there sufficient evidence to conclude that the average number of on-the-job accidents per day at the factory changed since the installation of the new equipment?

Solution Use the six-step hypothesis-testing procedure:

1. State the null and alternative hypotheses.

$$H_0: \mu = 3.2$$

   To determine whether the number of on-the-job accidents per day has changed, a two-tailed test is used because the direction of the change has not been specified.

$$H_1: \mu \neq 3.2$$

2. Determine the appropriate sampling distribution. Since the population is nonnormal, the population standard deviation is known, and the sample size is 30 or more, the appropriate sampling distribution of sample means, $\overline{X}$'s, is normal with a mean of μ and the standard error of the mean (standard deviation of the sampling distribution) is equal to $\sigma_{\overline{x}} = \sigma_x/\sqrt{n}$.

3. Determine the level of significance. What are the implications of making a Type I error? If the population mean has changed from 3.2 accidents per day, what decision will be made? No major decision will be made. Actually the decision has already been made, and the factory is interested in determining whether the new equipment has had any effect on the number of accidents. Since the research is exploratory, the .10 significance level is chosen.

FIGURE 11–1
Two-tailed test
with a .10 level
of significance

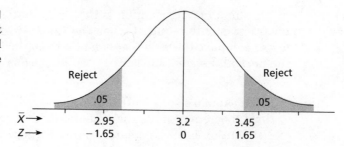

4. State a decision rule. Figure 11–1 shows the sampling distribution of sample means. The mean of the sampling distribution is assumed to be 3.2 and the standard error of the mean (standard deviation of the sampling distribution) is

$$\sigma_{\bar{x}} = \frac{\sigma_x}{\sqrt{n}}$$

$$\sigma_{\bar{x}} = \frac{.9}{\sqrt{36}}$$

$$\sigma_{\bar{x}} = .15$$

By using the normal curve table in Appendix E, the Z value as determined for a total area of .10 in two tails, or an area of .05 in one tail, is equal to 1.65. The critical values are

$c_1 = 3.2 + (-1.65)(.15)$ $c_2 = 3.2 + (1.65)(.15)$

$c_1 = 3.2 - .2475$ $c_2 = 3.2 + .2475$

$c_1 = 2.95$ $c_2 = 3.45$

The decision rule is

Reject H_0 if $\bar{X} < 2.95$ or if $\bar{X} > 3.45$

5. The random sample of 36 days had a sample mean equal to 3 accidents per day.

6. Since the sample mean, $\bar{X} = 3$, is not less than the critical value, $c_1 = 2.95$, nor greater than the critical value, $c_2 = 3.45$, the null hypothesis is accepted. Based on the sample evidence, the hypothesis that the population mean number of on-the-job accidents is 3.2 per day cannot be rejected. The sample evidence does not indicate that the new equipment has affected the number of accidents per day. However, a Type II error might have been committed. Whenever H_0 is accepted, the sample evidence suggests it is true. There is no way to be absolutely sure unless a person could check on the number of

accidents for each day in the future. To determine the probability of making a Type II error, the actual population mean needs to be known. Since it can not be determined, only the probability of making a Type II error for assumed population means can be calculated.

Example 11–2   The Kix Company manufactures cereal and wants to test to see whether their filling machine is set to load boxes with an average of 12 ounces per box. Suppose that 81 boxes of cereal are selected randomly and the contents are weighed. Test to see whether the sample mean filling weight differs from 12 ounces if the sample mean is $\overline{X} = 12.23$ ounces and the sample standard deviation is $s = .45$.

Solution   1. State the null and alternative hypotheses.

$$H_0: \mu = 12$$

Since Kix is interested in testing whether the mean filling weight is different from 12 ounces, a two-tailed test is used because the direction of the change has not been specified.

$$H_1: \mu \neq 12$$

2. Determine the appropriate sampling distribution. Since the standard deviation is unknown and the sample size is 30 or greater, the appropriate sampling distribution of sample means, $\overline{X}$'s, is the normal distribution with a mean of μ and the standard error of the mean (standard deviation of the sampling distribution of sample means) is equal to $s_{\overline{x}} = s_x/\sqrt{n}$.

3. Determine the level of significance. What are the implications of making a Type I error? Kix might conclude that the machine underfills or overfills the boxes when the actual population mean is 12 ounces. The machine would be set up a second time and another test would be necessary. What are the implications of making a Type II error? The machine would be allowed to continue operating when it is underfilling or overfilling. The cost of each contingency would decide what significance level. An alpha level of .05 is used in this example.

4. State a decision rule. Figure 11–2 shows the sampling distribution of sample means. The mean of the sampling distribution is assumed to be 12 ounces and the standard error of the mean (standard deviation of the sampling distribution) is

$$s_{\overline{x}} = \frac{s_x}{\sqrt{n}}$$

FIGURE 11–2
Two-tailed test
with a .05 level
of significance

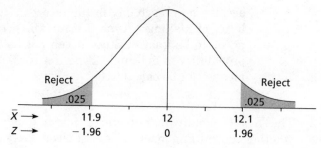

$$s_{\bar{x}} = \frac{.45}{\sqrt{81}}$$

$$s_{\bar{x}} = .05$$

By using the normal curve table in Appendix E, the analyst can determine that the Z value for a total area of .05 in two tails, .025 in one tail, is equal to 1.96. The critical values are

$$c_1 = 12 + (-1.96)(.05) \qquad c_2 = 12 + (1.96)(.05)$$
$$c_1 = 12 - .098 \qquad\qquad c_2 = 12 + .098$$
$$c_1 = 11.9 \qquad\qquad\qquad c_2 = 12.1$$

The decision rule is

$$\text{Reject } H_0 \text{ if } \bar{X} < 11.9 \text{ or if } \bar{X} > 12.1$$

5. The random sample of 81 boxes had a sample mean equal to 12.2 ounces.

6. Since the sample mean, $\bar{X} = 12.2$, is greater than the critical value, $c_2 = 12.1$, the null hypothesis is rejected. Kix concludes that the average machine fill is different from 12 ounces and the machine should be set up again. However, the analyst might be committing a Type I error. There is a 5% probability that the analyst obtained a sample mean that allowed H_0 to be rejected when the population mean actually equaled 12 ounces.

Small Samples

When the sample size is small (less than 30) the analyst must be able to assume that the relative frequency distribution of the population from which the sample was selected is approximately normal. If the analyst can make this assumption and knows the population standard deviation, the sampling distribution or sample means can be assumed to be normally distributed. If the population standard deviation is unknown, the sampling distribution of sample means is described by the t distribution. When the sample size is small and the population is not normally distributed, a statistical approach not discussed in this text is used. Figure 9–4 showed a flowchart that summarizes the procedure for determining the appropriate sampling distribution of sample means.

Example 11–3   The Firm Tread Tire Company requires that the tires it makes withstand a mean pressure of at least 160 psi (pounds per square inch) before bursting. The population of pressures that cause the tires to burst has been found to be normally distributed with a standard deviation of 4 psi. From each large batch of tires made, a random sample of 16 tires is selected and subjected to increasing pressures until they burst. If the last sample had a mean of 155 psi, what should the analyst conclude?

Solution   Use the six-step hypothesis-testing procedure:

1. State the null and alternative hypotheses.

$$H_0: \mu = 160 \text{ psi}$$

Since the Firm Tread Tire Company requires that its tires withstand a mean pressure of at least 160 psi, they are only interested in the situation where the tires cannot withstand 160 psi. Direction is indicated and the test is one-tailed.

$$H_1: \mu < 160 \text{ psi}$$

2. Determine the appropriate sampling distribution. Since the population standard deviation is known and the population is assumed to be normally distributed, the appropriate sampling distribution of sample means, $\overline{X}$'s, is normal with a mean of μ and the standard error of the mean (standard deviation of the sampling distribution) is equal to $\sigma_{\overline{x}} = \sigma_x/\sqrt{n}$.

3. Determine the level of significance. What are the implications of making a Type I error? If the company concludes that the population mean is less than 160 psi, what decision will be made? If the decision will be to scrap the whole batch, the company cannot afford to make a Type I error. For this reason, the .01 significance level is chosen. Thus the probability of scrapping a batch when the mean really is 160 psi is only 1 out of 100.

4. State a decision rule. Figure 11–3 shows the sampling distribution of sample means assuming the null hypothesis is true. The mean of the sampling distribution is assumed to be

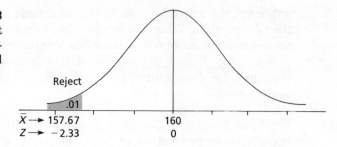

FIGURE 11–3
One-tailed test
with a .01 sig-
nificance level

160 psi and the standard error of the mean (standard deviation) of the sampling distribution) is

$$\sigma_{\bar{x}} = \frac{\sigma_x}{\sqrt{n}}$$

$$\sigma_{\bar{x}} = \frac{4}{\sqrt{16}}$$

$$\sigma_{\bar{x}} = 1$$

By using the normal curve table in Appendix E, the analyst can determine that the Z value for an area of .01 in one tail is equal to 2.33. The critical value is

$$c = 160 + (-2.33)(1)$$
$$= 160 - 2.33$$
$$= 157.67$$

The decision rule is

$$\text{Reject } H_0 \text{ if } \bar{X} < 157.67$$

5. The random sample of 16 tires had a sample mean equal to 155 psi.
6. Since the sample mean, $\bar{X} = 155$, is less than the critical value, $c = 157.67$, the null hypothesis is rejected. The company concludes that the average pressure at which this batch of tires will burst is less than 160 psi. However, this conclusion may result in a Type I error. Whenever H_0 is rejected, the sample evidence suggests it is not true. There is no way to be absolutely sure unless every tire in the whole batch is checked. There is a 1% probability that they obtained a sample mean that allowed them to reject the H_0 when the population mean is actually equal to 160 psi.

Example 11–4   Because of the expense involved in manufacturing a new chemical fertilizer, the fertilizer must produce an average yield of more than 10,000 pounds of tomatoes per half-acre within a specified growing period to be economically feasible. The average yield of tomatoes is thought to be normally distributed. An independent agricultural testing organization chose 25 half-acres of farmland at random in various geographical regions, fertilized each with the new chemical fertilizer, and planted tomatoes. The results show that the 25 half-acres had an average yield of 10,200 pounds with a standard deviation of 500 pounds. Can the testing organization conclude that the true population mean really exceeds 10,000 pounds?

Solution   1. State the null and alternative hypotheses.

$$H_0: \mu = 10,000$$

Since the testing organization is interested in concluding that the fertilizer results in a population mean that exceeds 10,000 pounds, direction is indicated and a one-tailed test is used.

$$H_1: \mu > 10,000$$

2. Determine the appropriate sampling distribution. Since the population is thought to be normally distributed, the population standard deviation is unknown, and the sample size is less than 30, the appropriate sampling distribution of sample means, $\overline{X}$'s, is described by the t distribution with a mean of $\mu_{\overline{x}}$ and the standard error of the mean (standard deviation of the sampling distribution) is equal to $s_{\overline{x}} = s_x/\sqrt{n}$.

3. Determine the level of significance. What are the implications of making a Type I error? The testing organization might conclude that the fertilizer produced the desired level of yield when it did not. A firm might buy the new fertilizer at a higher cost without better results. This could lead to financial failure. Therefore, the .01 significance level is chosen.

4. State a decision rule. Figure 11–4 shows the sampling distribution of sample means. The mean of the sampling distribution is assumed to be 10,000 pounds and the standard error of the mean (standard deviation of the sampling distribution) is

$$s_{\overline{x}} = \frac{s_x}{\sqrt{n}}$$

$$s_{\overline{x}} = \frac{500}{\sqrt{25}}$$

$$s_{\overline{x}} = 100$$

FIGURE 11–4
One-tailed test
with a .01 level
of significance

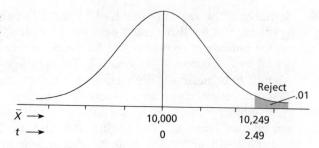

To use the t table in Appendix G, the testing organization must determine the appropriate degrees of freedom. Since the sample standard deviation is used to estimate the population standard deviation in a computation, one degree of freedom is lost. Therefore, the degrees of freedom in this case are $(n - 1) = (25 - 1) = 24$. The t value for an area of .01 in one tail for 24 degrees of freedom is equal to 2.49. The critical value is

$$c = 10,000 + (2.49)(100)$$
$$c = 10,000 + 249$$
$$c = 10,249$$

The decision rule is

$$\text{Reject } H_0 \text{ if } \overline{X} > 10,249$$

5. The random sample of 25 half-acres had a sample mean equal to 10,200 pounds.
6. Since the sample mean, $\overline{X} = 10,200$, is not greater than the critical value, $c = 10,249$, the null hypothesis is accepted. Based on the sample evidence, the testing organization cannot reject the hypothesis that the population mean yield is 10,000 pounds at the .01 significance level. The experimental yields have not been large enough to provide convincing proof of the economic feasibility of the new chemical fertilizer.

Suppose that the economic goal of running a profitable operation had been outweighed by the need to produce a larger food supply as soon as possible. In that case, the precise level of mean yield would be less important than the ability of the fertilizer to produce a larger yield. Therefore, the testing organization would not want to make a Type II error that would result in their rejecting the use of the fertilizer in some situations when it would be effective. To avoid a Type II error, the testing organization could increase probability of a Type I error by raising the significance level from .01 to .05.

HYPOTHESIS TEST OF POPULATION PROPORTIONS

A one-sample test is also used to test claims about a single population proportion. A sample proportion (p) is computed and compared to the claimed population proportion (π). The analyst must consider the degree that the sample proportion might vary from the claimed population parameter because of chance variation in sampling and must choose the hypothesis test based on whether the sample size is small or large. In Chapter 5 you learned that the binomial distribution is applied in situations where one is interested in the number of successes that occur in a set of n trials. With samples of 20 or less, the binomial distribution should be used. With samples of more than 20 observations, the normal distribution is usually a good approximation of the sampling distribution if the population proportion is not too close to 0 or 1. This section will concentrate on large samples where the appropriate sampling distribution of sample proportions, p, is normal with a mean of μ and the standard error of the proportion (standard deviation of the sampling distribution) is equal to $\sigma_p = \sqrt{\pi(1 - \pi)/n}$.

Example 11–5   The Sweet Grape Wine Company buys thousands of boxes of grapes each year. The Sweet Grape buyer visits vineyards and samples grapes on the vine. If the sample convinces the buyer that at least 85% of the total crop of a vineyard is of high wine-making quality, the buyer purchases the entire crop. Would the buyer recommend the purchase of a crop if a random sample of 600 grapes contains 500 high quality grapes?

Solution   1. State the null and alternative hypotheses.

$$H_0: \pi = .85$$

Since Sweet Grape is interested in testing to determine whether the crop contains at least 85% high quality grapes, direction is indicated and the one-tailed test is used.

$$H_1: \pi < .85$$

2. Determine the appropriate sampling distribution. Since the sample size is large, the appropriate sampling distribution of sample proportions, p's, is the normal distribution with a mean of π and the standard error of the proportion (standard deviation of the sampling distribution) is equal to $\sigma_p = \sqrt{\pi(1 - \pi)/n}$.

3. Determine the level of significance. What are the implications of making a Type I error? The company might reject a crop that actually contains 85% high quality grapes. The Type II

error would involve accepting a crop that does not contain 85% high quality grapes. The Type II error seems to be more serious. Sweet Grapes can probably afford to pass up a high quality crop but might lose money on a crop that did not contain enough high quality grapes. The company will use a .10 level of significance.

4. State a decision rule. Figure 11–5 shows the sampling distribution of sample proportions. The mean of the sampling distribution is assumed to be 85% and the standard error of the proportion (standard deviation of the sampling distribution) is

$$\sigma_p = \sqrt{\frac{\pi(1 - \pi)}{n}}$$

$$\sigma_p = \sqrt{\frac{.85(1 - .85)}{600}}$$

$$\sigma_p = .0146$$

By using the normal curve table in Appendix E, the analyst determines that the Z value for an area of .10 in one tail is equal to 1.28. The critical value is

$$c = .85 + (-1.28)(.0146)$$

$$c = .85 - .019$$

$$c = .831$$

The decision rule is

Reject H_0 if $p < .831$

5. The random sample of 600 contained 500 high quality grapes or $p = 500/600 = .833$.

6. Since the sample proportion, $p = .833$, is not less than the critical value, $c = .831$, the null hypothesis is accepted. Based on the sample evidence, the company cannot reject the hypoth-

FIGURE 11–5
One-tailed
test with a
.10 signifi-
cance level

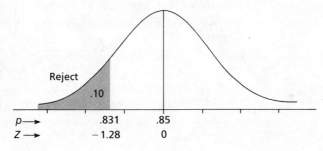

esis that the population proportion is .85 at the .10 significance level. Therefore, the crop should be purchased. By using a high alpha level, .10, the company has decreased the probability of making a Type II error.

HYPOTHESIS TEST OF THE DIFFERENCE BETWEEN TWO POPULATION MEANS

A *two-sample test* is used to test a claim about two population means or proportions. The claim to be tested is that the means of the two populations are equal. The null hypothesis is $\mu_1 = \mu_2$. The test looks at the relative difference between the means of two independent samples, one selected from each population. The analyst must take into account the degree that the sample means might differ from each other because of chance variation in sampling. This is analyzed using a sampling distribution with a mean difference equal to zero. In other words, the null hypothesis is assumed to be true, $\mu_1 = \mu_2$ or $\mu_1 - \mu_2 = 0$. Therefore, the two samples can be regarded as coming from the same population. The variances for the two populations can be combined and the standard deviation of the sampling distribution can be computed. The standard deviation of the sampling distribution of differences between sample means is called the standard error of the difference $(\sigma_{\bar{x}_1 - \bar{x}_2})$. Equation 11–1 shows how the standard error of the difference is calculated when σ_1 and σ_2 are known.

$$\sigma_{\bar{x}_1 - \bar{x}_2} = \sqrt{\frac{\sigma_1^2}{n_1} + \frac{\sigma_2^2}{n_2}} \qquad \textbf{(11–1)}$$

When σ_1 and σ_2 are unknown, s_1 and s_2 are used as estimates and can be substituted into Equation 11–1 forming the following equation:

$$s_{\bar{x}_1 - \bar{x}_2} = \sqrt{\frac{s_1^2}{n_1} + \frac{s_2^2}{n_2}} \qquad \textbf{(11–2)}$$

> A two-sample test is used to test a claim about two population means or proportions.

The sampling distribution will be normally distributed for samples selected from normal populations with a known standard deviation and will have a t distribution when the population standard deviations are estimated using the sample standard deviations. The need to assume that the sample came from a normal population can be relaxed when both n_1 and n_2 are 30 or more.

Large Samples

When the sample size is sufficiently large, the same principles that applied to one-sample tests about a population mean apply to two-sample tests. If both n_1 and n_2 are 30 or more, the sampling distribution of sample differences between sample means is approximately normally distributed for all cases.

Example 11-6 A test is to be conducted with respect to the driving distance of two brands of golf balls. The balls are tested with a mechanical driver that is known to provide normally distributed distances with a standard deviation of 20 yards. Each ball is tested 25 times. Brand A averages 275 yards and Brand B averages 255 yards. Is there a significant difference in the driving distance of the two brands of balls?

Solution
1. State the null and alternative hypotheses.

$$H_0: \mu_1 = \mu_2$$

Since the analyst is interested in determining whether there is a difference in the driving distance of the two balls, no direction is indicated and a two-tailed test is used.

$$H_1: \mu_1 \neq \mu_2$$

2. Determine the appropriate sampling distribution. Since the population standard deviations are known and the populations are assumed to be normally distributed, the appropriate sampling distribution of differences between sample means, $\overline{X}_1 - \overline{X}_2$, is normal with a mean of 0 and a standard error of the difference (standard deviation of the sampling distribution of differences between sample means) is computed using Equation 11-1.

3. Determine the level of significance. What are the implications of making a Type I error? If the analyst concludes that the driving distance of one ball is greater than the other, the firm will purchase that ball. What happens if the ball purchased is not really better (Type I error)? Unless this ball costs more, the error will not be too serious and the .05 significance level is chosen.

4. State a decision rule. Figure 11-6 shows the sampling distribution of differences in sample means assuming the null hypothesis is true. The mean of the sampling distribution is 0 and the standard error of the difference (standard deviation of the sampling distribution) is

FIGURE 11–6
Two-tailed test with a
.05 level of signifi-
cance

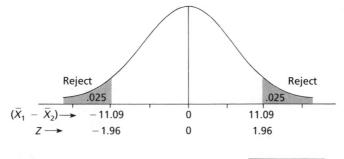

$$\sigma_{\bar{x}_1 - \bar{x}_2} = \sqrt{\left(\frac{\sigma_1^2}{n_1}\right) + \left(\frac{\sigma_2^2}{n_2}\right)}$$

$$\sigma_{\bar{x}_1 - \bar{x}_2} = \sqrt{\left(\frac{20^2}{25}\right) + \left(\frac{20^2}{25}\right)}$$

$$\sigma_{\bar{x}_1 - \bar{x}_2} = 5.66$$

By using the normal curve table in Appendix E, the analyst can determine that the Z value for an area of .05 in two tails or .025 in one tail is 1.96. The critical values are

$c_1 = 0 + (-1.96)(5.66)$	$c_2 = 0 + (1.96)(5.66)$
$c_1 = 0 - 11.09$	$c_2 = 0 + 11.09$
$c_1 = -11.09$	$c_2 = 11.09$

The decision rule is

Reject H_0 if $(\bar{X}_1 - \bar{X}_2) < -11.09$ or if $(\bar{X}_1 - \bar{X}_2) > 11.09$

5. The random samples showed a difference in sample means, $(275 - 255) = 20$ yards.

6. Since the difference in sample means, $(\bar{X}_1 - \bar{X}_2) = 20$, is more than the critical value, $c_2 = 11.09$, the null hypothesis is rejected. The analyst concludes there is a difference in the driving distance between Brand A and Brand B. However, the analyst might be committing a Type I error. There is a 5% probability that the selected samples showed a significant difference when the two population means are actually equal.

Example 11–7   The TDC Corporation is considering the location of a new plant in either Greeley, Colorado, or Medford, Oregon. A decision has been made to choose Medford unless the cost of new homes is lower in Greeley. A study is conducted to determine whether the cost of new homes is lower in Greeley. The results are presented in Table 11–1. Where should TDC locate their new plant?

TABLE 11–1
TDC Corporation test

Greeley	Medford
$n_1 = 100$	$n_2 = 80$
$\overline{X}_1 = \$60,000$	$\overline{X}_2 = \$64,000$
$s_1 = \$\ 7,000$	$s_2 = \$\ 8,000$

Solution

1. State the null and alternative hypotheses.

$$H_0: \mu_1 = \mu_2$$

Since TDC is interested in determining whether the cost of new homes is lower in Greeley, direction is indicated and a one-tailed test is used.

$$H_1: \mu_1 < \mu_2$$

2. Determine the appropriate sampling distribution. Since the population standard deviation is unknown and both n_1 and n_2 are 30 or more, the appropriate sampling distribution of differences between sample means, $(\overline{X}_1 - \overline{X}_2)$, is the normal distribution with a mean of 0 and a standard error of the difference (standard deviation of the sampling distribution of differences between sample means) computed using Equation 11–2.

3. Determine the level of significance. What are the implications of making a Type I error? If TDC concludes that the cost of new homes is lower in Greeley, they will build their new plant there. What happens if there is no difference in the cost of new homes in the two cities and a Type I error is committed? The plant would end up in Greeley when it should be located in Medford. This might be a serious error so the .02 significance level is chosen.

4. State a decision rule. Figure 11–7 shows the sampling distribution of differences in sample means assuming the null hypothesis is true. The mean of the sampling distribution is 0

FIGURE 11–7
One-tailed test with a .02 level of significance

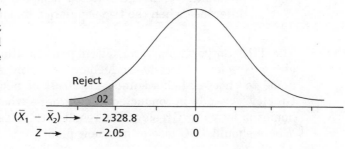

and the standard error of the difference (standard deviation of the sampling distribution) is

$$s_{\bar{x}_1 - \bar{x}_2} = \sqrt{\left(\frac{s_1^2}{n_1}\right) + \left(\frac{s_2^2}{n_2}\right)}$$

$$s_{\bar{x}_1 - \bar{x}_2} = \sqrt{\left(\frac{7,000^2}{100}\right) + \left(\frac{8,000^2}{80}\right)}$$

$$s_{\bar{x}_1 - \bar{x}_2} = \sqrt{490,000 + 800,000}$$

$$s_{\bar{x}_1 - \bar{x}_2} = 1136$$

By using the normal curve table in Appendix E, TDC determined that the Z value for an area of .02 in one tail is 2.05. The critical value is

$$c = 0 + (-2.05)(1136)$$

$$c = 0 - 2328.80$$

$$c = -2328.80$$

The decision rule is

$$\text{Reject } H_0 \text{ if } (\bar{X}_1 - \bar{X}_2) < -2328.80$$

5. The random samples showed a difference in sample means, $(60,000 - 64,000) = -4,000$.

6. Since the difference in sample means, $(\bar{X}_1 - \bar{X}_2) = -4,000$, is less than the critical value, $c = -2,328$, the null hypothesis is rejected. TDC concludes that the cost of new homes in Greeley is lower. They might be committing a Type I error, however. There is a 2% probability that the selected samples showed Greeley's new home cost to be lower when the two population means are actually equal.

Small Samples

When either n_1 or n_2 are less than 30, the same principles that applied to one-sample tests about a population mean apply to two-sample tests. The population must be approximately normally distributed. If the population standard deviation is known, the sampling distribution of differences between sample means is normally distributed. If the population standard deviations are unknown, the sampling distribution of differences between sample means is described by the t distribution. In this case, the standard error of the difference (standard deviation of the differences between sample means) is computed using Equation 11–3:

$$s_{\bar{x}_1 - \bar{x}_2} = \sqrt{\frac{s_1^2(n_1 - 1) + s_2^2(n_2 - 1)}{n_1 + n_2 - 2}\left(\frac{1}{n_1} + \frac{1}{n_2}\right)} \qquad \textbf{(11-3)}$$

Example 11-8   The Environmental Protection Agency (EPA) frequently conducts studies designed to estimate gas mileages for automobiles. The EPA has been asked to compare city mileages for cars using unleaded and leaded gasoline. The EPA selects 22 cars and tests the number of miles per gallon obtained for each. Table 11-2 summarizes the results. What should the EPA conclude if the two populations being sampled are normally distributed?

Solution   1. State the null and alternative hypotheses.

$$H_0\colon \mu_1 = \mu_2$$

Since the EPA is interested in testing to determine whether there is a difference in city mileages for the two types of gasoline, no direction is indicated and a two-tailed test is used.

$$H_1\colon \mu_1 \neq \mu_2$$

2. Determine the appropriate sampling distribution. Since the populations are normal, the population standard deviations are unknown, and the sample size is 30 or less, the appropriate sampling distribution of the differences in sample means, $(\bar{X}_1 - \bar{X}_2)$, is described by the t distribution with a mean of 0 and the standard error of the difference (standard deviation of the sampling distribution) is computed using Equation 11-3.

3. Determine the level of significance. What are the implications of making a Type I error? If the EPA concludes that one of the gasolines gets better mileage, people will probably believe the study and purchase that kind of gas. If the population mean gas mileages are actually equal, a Type I error might occur, and the EPA could possibly lose their credibility. For this reason they might choose the .01 level of significance.

4. State a decision rule. Figure 11-8 shows the sampling distribution of differences in sample means assuming the null hypothesis is true. The mean of the sampling distribution is 0

TABLE 11-2
EPA test

Unleaded	Leaded
$n_1 = 12$	$n_2 = 10$
$\bar{X}_1 = 21.2$ mpg	$\bar{X}_2 = 20.4$ mpg
$s_1 = 1.3$ mpg	$s_2 = 1.2$ mpg

FIGURE 11–8
Two-tailed test
with a .01 level
of significance

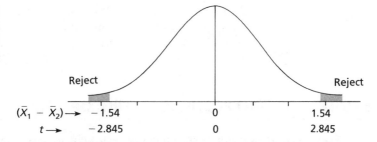

and the standard error of the difference (standard deviation of the sampling distribution) is

$$s_{\bar{x}_1 - \bar{x}_2} = \sqrt{\frac{s_1^2 (n_1 - 1) + s_2^2 (n_2 - 1)}{n_1 + n_2 - 2}\left(\frac{1}{n_1} + \frac{1}{n_2}\right)}$$

$$s_{\bar{x}_1 - \bar{x}_2} = \sqrt{\frac{(1.3)^2(12 - 1) + (1.2)^2(10 - 1)}{12 + 10 - 2}\left(\frac{1}{12} + \frac{1}{10}\right)}$$

$$s_{\bar{x}_1 - \bar{x}_2} = \sqrt{(1.5775)(.1833)}$$

$$s_{\bar{x}_1 - \bar{x}_2} = .54$$

To use the t table in Appendix G, the appropriate degrees of freedom must be determined. Since two sample standard deviations are used to estimate two population standard deviations in a computation, two degrees of freedom are lost. The degrees of freedom, in this case, are $(n_1 - 1) + (n_2 - 1) = (n_1 + n_2 - 2) = (12 + 10 - 2) = 20$. The t value for an area of .01 in two tails or .005 in one tail for 20 degrees of freedom is equal to 2.845. The critical values are

$$c_1 = 0 + (-2.845)(.54) \qquad c_2 = 0 + (2.845)(.54)$$
$$c_1 = 0 - 1.54 \qquad c_2 = 0 + 1.54$$
$$c_1 = -1.54 \qquad c_2 = 1.54$$

The decision rule is

Reject H_0 if $(\bar{X}_1 - \bar{X}_2) < -1.54$ or if $(\bar{X}_1 - \bar{X}_2) > 1.54$

5. The random samples showed a difference in sample means, $(21.2 - 20.4) = .8$.
6. Since the difference in sample means, $(\bar{X}_1 - \bar{X}_2) = .8$, is not less than the critical value, $c_1 = -1.54$, or greater than the critical value, $c_2 = 1.54$, the null hypothesis is accepted. Based on the sample evidence, the EPA cannot reject the hypothesis

that the two types of gasoline obtain the same city gas mileage. They might commit a Type II error, however. This type of error would occur if the city gasoline mileages actually did differ for leaded and unleaded gasoline.

HYPOTHESIS TEST OF TWO POPULATION PROPORTIONS

A two-sample test is used to test a claim about two population proportions. The claim to be tested is that the proportions of the two populations are equal, and the null hypothesis is stated $\pi_1 = \pi_2$. The test looks at the relative difference between the proportions of two independent samples, one selected from each population. The analyst must take into account the degree to which the sample proportions might differ from each other because of chance variation in sampling. This is analyzed using a sampling distribution with a mean difference equal to zero. In other words, the null hypothesis is assumed to be true, $\pi_1 = \pi_2$ or $\pi_1 - \pi_2 = 0$. Now the two samples can be regarded as coming from the same population. Due to the larger sample size, the two samples provide a better estimate of the true population proportion. If the sample sizes are equal, their sample proportions are averaged. If the sample sizes are unequal, Equation 11–4 is used to compute the combined estimate of π:

$$\pi = \frac{(p_1 n_1 + p_2 n_2)}{(n_1 + n_2)} \qquad \textbf{(11–4)}$$

The combined estimate of π is used to compute the standard error of the difference (the standard deviation of the sampling distribution of differences in sample proportions). This computation is similar to computing the standard error of the proportion except that now it must be weighted by the two sample sizes as shown in Equation 11–5:

$$\sigma_{p_1 - p_2} = \sqrt{\pi(1 - \pi)\left(\frac{1}{n_1} + \frac{1}{n_2}\right)} \qquad \textbf{(11–5)}$$

Example 11–9   The People-Say Research Company does telephone interview surveys. For most surveys, they call between 5:00 and 9:00 P.M. so as not to obtain too many female respondents. People-Say has decided that the ratio of males to females has changed in the past years and they wonder if the number of females who answer in the afternoon equals the number who answer in the evening. They call 500 households in the afternoon and 400 in the evening and record whether a male or female answers. The results are summarized in Table 11–3. Does a higher proportion of females still answer in the afternoon?

TABLE 11–3
People-Say research

Afternoon	Evening
$n_1 = 500$	$n_2 = 400$
$p_1 = 63\%$	$p_2 = 55\%$

Solution

1. State the null and alternative hypotheses.

$$H_0: \pi_1 = \pi_2$$

Since People-Say is interested in testing to determine whether a higher proportion of females will answer, direction is indicated and a one-tailed test is used.

$$H_1: \pi_1 > \pi_2$$

2. Determine the appropriate sampling distribution. Since the sample sizes are large, the appropriate sampling distribution of differences between sample proportions, $(p_1 - p_2)$, is the normal distribution with a mean of 0, and the standard error of the difference (standard deviation of the sampling distribution of differences between sample proportions) is computed using Equation 11–4.

3. Determine the level of significance. What are the implications of making a Type I error? If People-Say concludes that the proportion of females answering in the afternoon is higher, they will continue to call between 5:00 and 9:00. What happens if there is no difference in the proportion of females who answer in the afternoon and evening? People-Say could be calling at both times. They could increase their number of calls by two. This would probably be a serious error so the .01 significance level is chosen.

4. State a decision rule. Figure 11–9 shows the sampling distribution of differences in sample proportions assuming the

FIGURE 11–9
One-tailed test with a .01 level of significance

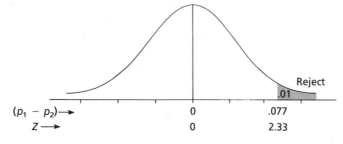

null hypothesis is true. The mean of the sampling distribution is 0 and the standard error of the difference (standard deviation of the sampling distribution) is computed using Equations 11–4 and 11–5. The combined estimate of π is

$$\pi = \frac{(p_1 n_1 + p_2 n_2)}{(n_1 + n_2)}$$

$$\pi = \frac{(.63)(500) + (.55)(400)}{(500 + 400)}$$

$$\pi = .594$$

The standard error of the difference is

$$\sigma_{p_1 - p_2} = \sqrt{\pi(1 - \pi)\left(\frac{1}{n_1} + \frac{1}{n_2}\right)}$$

$$\sigma_{p_1 - p_2} = \sqrt{.594(1 - .594)\left(\frac{1}{500} + \frac{1}{400}\right)}$$

$$\sigma_{p_1 - p_2} = \sqrt{.241(.0045)}$$

$$\sigma_{p_1 - p_2} = .033$$

By using the normal curve table in Appendix E, People-Say determines that the Z value for an area of .01 for a one-tailed test is 2.33. The critical value is

$$c = 0 + (2.33)(.033)$$

$$c = 0 + .077$$

$$c = .077$$

The decision rule is

$$\text{Reject } H_0 \text{ if } (p_1 - p_2) > .077$$

5. The random samples showed a difference in sample proportions, $(.63 - .55) = .08$.

6. Since the difference in sample proportions, $(p_1 - p_2) = .08$, is greater than the critical value, $c = .077$, the null hypothesis is rejected. People-Say Research concludes that a higher proportion of females answer in the afternoon than in the evening. They might be making a Type I error. There is a 1% probability that People-Say obtained a difference in sample proportions that allowed them to reject the H_0 when the population proportions were actually equal.

HYPOTHESIS TEST OF CROSS-CLASSIFIED DATA

The examples used so far in this chapter involve numerical data; that is, each hypothesis test uses data values measured on a numerical scale. However, many business studies involve data that are measured in categories rather than as numerical values. For example, the gender of employees or a supervisor's rating of excellent, good, fair, or poor would consitute non-numerical data.

It is often of interest to determine whether one method of classifying objects is statistically dependent on another method. In these cases, the Chi-square test or *contingency table test* is used.

> The contingency table test measures the dependence between two methods of classifying sample objects.

Example 11–10   Suppose a company has classified each employee in a certain plant as being excellent, good, fair, or poor. In addition, each employee is classified as being with the company for less than one year, from one to three years, or over three years. The data collected from a sample of plant employees appear in Table 11–4 where the cell values indicate the number of employees occurring in each cross classification.

Solution   In addition to showing the cell counts for each cross classification, Table 11–4 indicates the row and column totals for the table. These totals will be used to develop the expected frequencies of each cell under the null hypothesis to be tested.

In a contingency table test, the null hypothesis states that there is independence between the two methods of classifying objects. In this example, independence means that an employee's tenure with the company is independent of the quality of work performed. In other words, knowing an employee's row classification is of no help in determining the column classification.

TABLE 11–4
Contingency table

	Excellent	Good	Fair	Poor	Total
Less than year	8	14	15	12	49
1-3 years	18	26	30	22	96
Over 3 years	18	17	10	8	53
Total	44	57	55	42	198

If the null hypothesis is true, the expected number of employees in each cell of the contingency table can be computed. Assuming that the two classification methods are independent (H_0 is true), the expected frequency in the first contingency table cell can be found by first computing the percentage of employees in the sample who have worked less than one year. Since 49 people out of a total of 198 sampled employees have worked for the company for less than one year, this fraction is

$$\left(\frac{49}{198}\right)$$

Since there is assumed independence between rows and columns, this fraction of the 44 excellent employees would be expected to be in cell one. This expected value is

$$\left(\frac{49}{198}\right)(44) = 10.89$$

The expected number of employees in the second cell of the contingency table (employees who have worked for the company for less than one year and who are given a good rating) is likewise calculated as

$$\left(\frac{49}{198}\right)(57) = 14.11$$

All expected values in the contingency table can be found in this fashion. First, the row total for the cell is divided by the total sample size. This fraction is then multiplied by the column total to produce the expected value for the cell. Table 11–5 shows the revised contingency table with the expected values shown in the upper left-hand corner of each cell.

TABLE 11–5
Contingency table

	Excellent	Good	Fair	Poor
Less than year	10.89 8	14.11 14	13.61 15	10.39 12
1–3 years	21.33 18	27.64 26	26.67 30	20.36 22
Over 3 years	11.78 18	15.25 17	14.72 10	11.25 8

A certain statistic can be computed from the data shown in Table 11–5 if the null hypothesis of independence of classification is true. This statistic is known as the *Chi-square statistic* and is computed by comparing the observed and expected frequencies in each cell of the table. If these differences are large, a large Chi-square statistic will result and the null hypothesis of independence will be rejected. If the observed and expected frequencies are close to the same value in each cell, a small Chi-square statistic will result and the null hypothesis will not be rejected. The following formula is used to compute the Chi-square statistic.

$$\sum_{\substack{\text{all} \\ \text{cells}}} \frac{(f_o - f_e)^2}{f_e} \qquad \textbf{(11–6)}$$

where f_o = observed frequency
f_e = expected frequency

The Chi-square statistic is computed by comparing the observed and expected frequencies in each cell of the contingency table.

The Chi-square statistic for the contingency table shown in Tables 11–4 and 11–5 can now be computed as shown in Table 11–6. Once the contingency table has been formed and the sample statistic has

TABLE 11–6
Chi-square calculation

f_o	f_e	$(f_o - f_e)^2$
8	10.89	.7669
14	14.11	.0009
15	13.61	.1420
12	10.39	.2495
18	21.33	.5199
26	27.64	.0973
30	26.67	.4158
22	20.36	.1321
18	11.78	3.2842
17	15.25	.2008
10	14.72	1.5135
8	11.25	.9389
		8.2618 = Chi-square

been computed, it is possible to perform the hypothesis test of interest using the six-step hypothesis-testing procedure used throughout this chapter.

1. State the null and alternative hypotheses.

   H_0: Independence of classification exists between rows and columns.

   H_1: Independence of classification does not exist.

2. Determine the appropriate sampling distribution. The Chisquare distribution is the appropriate sampling distribution if the sample statistic is computed from the contingency table using Equation 11–6.

3. Determine the level of significance. A significance level of 5% is often chosen in hypothesis tests regardless of the consequences associated with rejecting a null hypothesis when it is true. Such a low level of Type I risk is sometimes criticized by business people as being too conservative. For the test now being conducted, assume that a significance level of 10% is acceptable to management.

4. State a decision rule. The Chi-square value can be found in Appendix H as soon as the appropriate degrees of freedom for this test is found. In contingency table tests, the appropriate degrees of freedom is found by multiplying the number of table rows minus one by the number of table columns minus one. Equation 11–7 shows this calculation.

$$df = (r - 1)(c - 1) \qquad \textbf{(11–7)}$$

where r = number of rows
       c = number of columns

In the present hypothesis test, the degrees of freedom is determined to be

$$df = (3 - 1)(4 - 1) = (2)(3) = 6$$

Using Appendix H, the Chi-square value for a .10 level of significance and 6 degrees of freedom is 10.64. The decision rule can now be stated as follows:

$$\text{If } \sum \frac{(f_o - f_e)^2}{f_e} > 10.64, \text{ reject } H_0$$

5. The sample statistic computed earlier for this contingency table is 8.26.

6. Since the Chi-square statistic, 8.26, is less than the table Chi-square value, 10.64, the null hypothesis cannot be rejected. At the 10% significance level, company management must assume that the length of time that employees work at the company is independent of the performance rating of employees. Based on the sample evidence collected, more experienced workers are getting neither better nor worse performance ratings than less experienced workers.

SUMMARY

A one-sample test is used to test a claim about a single population parameter; a two-sample test is used to test the claim that two populations have the same parameter. Claims are tested by constructing a sampling distribution that assumes the null hypothesis is true. A significance level is chosen and a decision rule stated. A sample statistic is calculated and compared to the decision rule. Sample statistics that result in small differences from the claimed value are considered to be due to chance variation, whereas large differences are interpreted as evidence that the claim is untrue. The contingency table test is used to measure the dependence between two methods of classifying sample objects.

CASE STUDY: THE BROWN BOTTLING COMPANY

The Brown Bottling Company distributes four soft drink beverages in Clinton, Iowa. The Company owns a large bottle-filling machine and usually bottles a different type of soft drink each week.

The bottles used by Brown will hold almost 13 ounces, although they are considered 12-ounce bottles. Dick Brown, the company president, is concerned that the machine is overfilling the bottles, resulting in lower profits. He decides that a sample of bottles should be taken and their contents measured to determine if, in fact, the machine is providing an average fill in excess of 12 ounces. If it is, an expensive adjustment can be made in the machinery to reduce the average fill to 12 ounces.

Mr. Brown's daughter, Jill, has recently joined the company after graduating with a degree in business. She explains to her father that the sample of bottles must be chosen randomly and that

their average fill must be significantly greater than 12 ounces
before it can be concluded that the machine is out of adjustment. He
agrees to test the following hypotheses:

$$H_0: \mu = 12 \text{ ounces}$$
$$H_1: \mu > 12 \text{ ounces}$$

He understands that the first hypothesis cannot be rejected unless
the sample mean is significantly above 12 ounces, although he
admits he is not quite sure what that means.

His daughter also convinces him that the variability of fill
amounts will be a factor in the outcome, and the standard deviation
of fill amounts is obtained from past studies of the machine.
Regardless of the average fill amount, the standard deviation has
always been very close to .1 ounce. Therefore, it is agreed that this
is the current standard deviation.

Mr. Brown then asks Jill how large the sample should be. His
daughter is not sure, so Mr. Brown decides to use a sample of 100
because, as he explains, "that should be plenty."

Finally, a significance level must be chosen. Jill explains to her
father that this represents the probability of the sample showing
that the machine is overfilling when it really is not. Mr. Brown then
says this probability should be zero. Jill points out that it is not
possible to obtain a sample in an error-free environment and that a
low alpha increases the likelihood of accepting the null hypothesis
when it is false. To explain these matters to her father, Jill
assembles the material shown in Table 11–7, the last column of
which represents her father's judgement after reviewing the table.

Mr. Brown's comments in Table 11–7 lead his daughter to
suggest that alpha should be set fairly high; this will lower the

TABLE 11–7
Type I and Type II
errors

Error	Description	Penalty	Mr. Brown's Reaction
Reject H_0 when true (α)	The machine is operating properly but the sample evidence advises machine repair	$2,000 to fix a properly operating machine	Would like to avoid this unnecessary cost, but worse things could happen.
Accept H_0 when false (β)	The machine is overfilling but the sample evidence fails to detect this fact.	Continuing to sell a bottle that contains more than 12 ounces.	Does not want to be overfilling bottles for the next several months. This would be very expensive.

FIGURE 11–10
Probability of a
Type II error

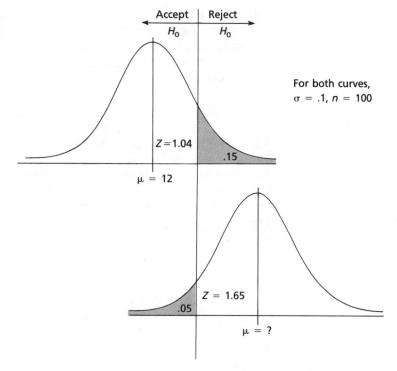

probability that a flaw in the machine will not be detected. It is agreed that alpha will be set at .15.

Mr. Brown then asks, "How far above 12 ounces does the average fill have to be before we can detect it?" Before attempting to compute the answer, Jill points out that the ability to detect a flaw in the machine is entirely dependent on sample size.

Jill decides to compute the point at which there is a 95% chance of detecting a false null hypothesis and writes the following statement: It is very likely that if the mean fill of the machine has risen to _____ , it will be detected.

Jill proceeds to fill in the blank by constructing the curves shown in Figure 11–10. The decision rule point becomes

$$12 + 1.04 \left(\frac{.1}{\sqrt{100}} \right) = 12.0104$$

The unknown mean can then be found as follows:

$$\mu - 1.65 \left(\frac{.1}{\sqrt{100}} \right) = 12.0104$$

$$\mu = 12.0269$$

Jill then tells her father there is a 95% chance of detecting a flaw in the machine if the true mean of the machine is 12.03 ounces. Jill reminds her father that this accuracy is based on the population standard deviation, the significance level, and the sample size. Mr. Brown decides to accept the risks and tells Jill to proceed with the sampling plan.

Questions
1. How can a hypothesis be proved?
2. What factors should Jill consider in deciding exactly how to select the sample of 100 bottles?
3. How can the assumptions be checked after the sample data have been collected?
4. What rationale did Mr. Brown use in accepting a significance level of .15?

EXERCISES

1. How does a hypothesis-testing procedure with a known population standard deviation differ from a hypothesis-testing procedure with an unknown population standard deviation?

2. What are the differences between the test procedure for means and the test procedure for proportions?

3. What is meant by a significant difference in hypothesis testing?

4. What does a significance level of .01 mean?

5. Assuming that the population is normally distributed, indicate whether the Z distribution or the t distribution applies for the following situations:
   a. $n = 21$, $\sigma = 3$
   b. $n = 26$, $s = 15$
   c. $n = 38$, $s = 10$
   d. $n = 45$, $\sigma = 5$

6. Describe the appropriate sampling distribution for each of the following situations:
   a. One-sample test of population means
   b. One-sample test of population proportions
   c. Two-sample test of population means
   d. Two-sample test of population proportions

7. Why must an estimated standard error of the difference between proportions be used in hypothesis testing?

8. Does testing and rejecting a null hypothesis disprove the hypothesis? Why or why not?

9. Does a sample result that is inconsistent with a hypothesis lead to the rejection of that hypothesis? Why or why not?

10. Under what conditions is it necessary to assume that the population being sampled is approximately normal?

11. When should the t distribution be used for two-sample tests?

12. Which sampling distribution is appropriate for tests of proportions when the sample size is small?

13. Which sampling distribution is appropriate for tests of proportions when the sample size is large?

14. Is it necessary to assume that the population in a test of proportions is approximately normal? Why or why not?

15. A bank analyst is attempting to determine a way of measuring profitable customers. Three years ago a study was conducted that showed the average service charge for checking accounts was $2.40 with a standard deviation of $.30. The population of service charges is thought to be normally distributed. The analyst is interested in detecting a situation in which the average service charge is either greater than or less than $2.40. What should the analyst conclude at the .10 significance level if a sample of 200 accounts had a mean service charge of $2.50?

16. The employees' union claims that the average seniority is at least 9 years for the Canton Manufacturing Corporation. A random sample of 64 employees is selected, and the average seniority is 8.5 years with a standard deviation of 2 years. Test the union's claim at the .02 significance level.

17. The Sampson Toy Company buys batteries for their electric toys. Their supplier guarantees that their brand of batteries will last an average of 9.5 hours. After receiving customer complaints, Sampson randomly selects 9 batteries from their stock and tests them for life expectancy. The results are presented below.

Battery	Lifetime (Hours)
1	9.0
2	9.2
3	9.5
4	10.1
5	9.8
6	9.3
7	9.7
8	9.6
9	10.0

Assuming that the lifetime of these batteries is normally distributed, test the supplier's guarantee at the .01 significance level.

18. Past experience has shown that 8% of the recipients of home mortgages from Sea-First Mortgage Company default within the first two years. Sea-First feels that the default rate is increasing. If they obtain evidence that the proportion of customers who default is now greater than 8%, the company will revise its guidelines for granting mortgages. A random

sample of 200 customers who received loans two years ago indicated that 20 have since defaulted. Test the appropriate hypothesis at the .05 significance level.

19. The Alton Corporation has been buying Unisupreme tires to mount on new automobiles. A representative of the Goodweek Tire Corporation claims that the mean mileage for their brand is greater than the mean mileage for Unisupreme tires. Alton submits random samples of 25 tires of each brand to simulated road wear until the tires wear out. The results are summarized below. Test Goodweek's claim at the .01 significance level.

Unisupreme	Goodweek
$n_1 = 25$	$n_2 = 25$
$X_1 = 31,000$ miles	$X_2 = 34,000$ miles
$s_1 = 4,000$ miles	$s_2 = 3,000$ miles

20. The St. Michelle Wine Company wants to determine whether a different marketing strategy is needed for their California market as compared with their marketing strategy for the state of Washington. One of their best red wines is taste tested in both regions. The proportion of wine drinkers who liked the wine are presented below. Using the .01 significance level, test whether there is a difference in the proportion of wine drinkers who liked the wine in the two regions.

California	Washington
$n_1 = 300$	$n_2 = 400$
$p_1 = .62$	$p_2 = .68$

21. A television network wants to determine whether major sports events or soap operas attract more viewers in the afternoon. The network selected 42 afternoons; of these, 22 had progams devoted to sports events and the remaining 20 had soap operas. The number of viewers was estimated by a television viewer rating firm and recorded for each afternoon. The following table summarizes the results. Test at the .02 significance level to determine whether there is a difference between the number of viewers who watch sports events and the number of viewers who watch soap operas.

Soap Operas	Sports Events
$n_1 = 20$	$n_2 = 22$
$X_1 = 7.5$ million	$X_2 = 6.9$ million
$s_1 = 1.4$ million	$s_2 = 1.8$ million

22. The Svroco Manufacturing Company produces faucets. Past experience shows that the diameters of the faucets are normally distributed with an average diameter of 1.6 inches and a standard deviation of .07 inches. Fifteen faucets are randomly selected from the production process and have a mean diameter of 1.5 inches. What would you conclude if you tested at the .05 significance level?

23. A national magazine says that 80% of the owners of new cars are satisified with their purchases. A car manufacturer wants to determine if this is true

for their customers. Forty-seven recent customers are contacted and 35 indicate they are satisified with their cars. Is the proportion of satisfied customers as high as the national magazine indicates? Test at the .05 significance level.

24. The Sharp Corporation manufactures razor blades and wishes to test whether men and women are equally satisfied with its new extra sharp blade. The company hires a research firm to recruit people to test the new blade. The research firm randomly selects 50 women and 75 men to use the blade for one week. At the end of the experiment the participants are asked if they would purchase the new blade. Thirty-five percent of the women and 40% of the men indicate they would buy the new blade. At the .01 significance level, is there a difference between the proportion of men and women who would purchase the blade?

25. A photographic-processing stage is supposed to last an average of 40 seconds. If the amount of time taken to process the film is either shorter or longer than 40 seconds, the quality of the picture will be low. The Quality Film Company decides to check on the process stage and selects and runs 20 pieces of film through the process. If the sample mean is equal to 35 seconds and the sample standard deviation is 4 seconds, what should Quality Film conclude if they test at the .10 significance level? Assume that the amount of time needed to process the film is normally distributed.

26. The WWP Company wants to determine whether the mean residential electricity usage per household has increased for the month of December. A simple random sample of 50 households was selected for December of last year and was compared to a sample of 50 households for December of this year. The sample results are recorded below. Test at the .05 significance level to determine whether the mean residential electricity usage per household has increased during December of this year.

Last Year	This Year
$n_1 = 50$	$n_2 = 50$
$\overline{X}_1 = 1{,}432$ KWH	$\overline{X}_2 = 1{,}498$ KWH
$s_1 = 312$ KWH	$s_2 = 322$ KWH

27. The Vice-President of Marketing for the Lanier Corporation claims that the average salary for accountants is higher than for marketing personnel. A random sample of 75 employees is selected independently from each of the two departments. A study of company records reveals the following results. Test at the .10 significance level to determine whether the average salary for accountants is higher.

Marketing Department	Accounting Department
$n_1 = 75$	$n_2 = 75$
$\overline{X}_1 = \$23{,}462$	$\overline{X}_2 = \$24{,}112$
$s_1 = \$5{,}832$	$s_2 = \$6{,}002$

28. The Northwestern Publishing Company hires college students to market textbooks during the summer. Each student participates in one of two training programs. To measure the efficiency of each training program a

company representative randomly selects a group of salespeople and records the number of textbook adoptions in the past month. The following table summarizes the results. Is there sufficient evidence to indicate a difference in the mean number of monthly sales for the populations associated with the two training programs if the data are tested at the .02 significance level? Assume sales are normally distributed.

Training Program A	Training Program B
$n_1 = 9$	$n_2 = 17$
$\overline{X}_1 = 72$	$\overline{X}_2 = 69$
$s_1 = 5$	$s_2 = 4$

29. Consider the population of 200 family sizes presented in the following table.

(1) 3	(35) 1	(69) 2	(102) 1	(135) 5	(168) 6
(2) 2	(36) 2	(70) 4	(103) 2	(136) 2	(169) 3
(3) 7	(37) 4	(71) 3	(104) 5	(137) 1	(170) 2
(4) 3	(38) 1	(72) 7	(105) 3	(138) 4	(171) 3
(5) 4	(39) 4	(73) 2	(106) 2	(139) 2	(172) 4
(6) 2	(40) 2	(74) 6	(107) 1	(140) 4	(173) 2
(7) 3	(41) 1	(75) 2	(108) 2	(141) 1	(174) 2
(8) 1	(42) 3	(76) 7	(109) 2	(142) 2	(175) 1
(9) 5	(43) 5	(77) 3	(110) 1	(143) 4	(176) 5
(10) 3	(44) 2	(78) 6	(111) 4	(144) 1	(177) 3
(11) 2	(45) 1	(79) 4	(112) 1	(145) 2	(178) 2
(12) 3	(46) 4	(80) 2	(113) 1	(146) 2	(179) 4
(13) 4	(47) 3	(81) 3	(114) 2	(147) 5	(180) 3
(14) 1	(48) 5	(82) 5	(115) 2	(148) 3	(181) 5
(15) 2	(49) 2	(83) 2	(116) 1	(149) 1	(182) 3
(16) 2	(50) 4	(84) 1	(117) 4	(150) 2	(183) 1
(17) 4	(51) 1	(85) 3	(118) 2	(151) 6	(184) 2
(18) 4	(52) 6	(86) 3	(119) 1	(152) 2	(185) 4
(19) 3	(53) 2	(87) 2	(120) 3	(153) 5	(186) 3
(20) 2	(54) 5	(88) 4	(121) 5	(154) 1	(187) 2
(21) 1	(55) 4	(89) 1	(122) 1	(155) 2	(188) 5
(22) 5	(56) 1	(90) 2	(123) 2	(156) 1	(189) 3
(23) 2	(57) 2	(91) 3	(124) 3	(157) 4	(190) 4
(24) 1	(58) 1	(92) 3	(125) 4	(158) 2	(191) 3
(25) 4	(59) 5	(93) 2	(126) 3	(159) 2	(192) 2
(26) 3	(60) 2	(94) 4	(127) 2	(160) 7	(193) 3
(27) 2	(61) 7	(95) 1	(128) 1	(161) 4	(194) 2
(28) 3	(62) 1	(96) 2	(129) 6	(162) 2	(195) 5
(29) 6	(63) 2	(97) 4	(130) 1	(163) 1	(196) 3
(30) 1	(64) 6	(98) 3	(131) 2	(164) 7	(197) 3
(31) 2	(65) 4	(99) 2	(132) 5	(165) 2	(198) 2
(32) 4	(66) 1	(100) 6	(133) 2	(166) 7	(199) 5
(33) 3	(67) 2	(101) 4	(134) 1	(167) 4	(200) 1
(34) 2	(68) 1				

Ten years ago the average family size was 2.9. Randomly select a sample of 30 sizes and test the hypothesis that the average family size has not changed in the last ten years. (Hint: Make sure your sample is randomly drawn from the population. Consult your instructor if you do not know how to do this.)

30. A company classifies its accounts receivable as either paid on time or overdue. It also decides to classify the accounts as local, regional, or national. Use a significance level of 10% to test whether the proximity of the debtor has any bearing on payment status, given the following data:

	Paid	Overdue
Local	25	73
Regional	19	84
National	85	22

31. Do males and females have the same voting preference in a coming election? The following data resulted from a recent poll:

	Democrat	Republican
Males	25	38
Females	52	22

32. Several people in a large club were classified as to whether or not they smoke cigarettes. Their ages were also recorded and each person was placed into an age category. On the basis of the following data, is smoking dependent on age?

Smoker	Young	Middle	Older
Yes	10	15	38
No	53	22	24

33. Is there a relationship between a person's college status and grade point average? A class polled several campus students to answer this question and found the following data:

Rank	3.5+	3.0–3.4	2.5–2.9	Below 2.5
Freshman	17	25	38	18
Sophmore	25	33	42	14
Junior	19	42	25	9
Senior	25	32	34	12

The following questions refer to the class data base. Treat the class as a representative sample of your school. You may use any significance level you or your instructor chooses.

34. Test to determine whether an equal number of males and females attend your school.

35. Test to determine whether the mean age is less than 20.

36. Determine whether there is a relationship between sex and preference for a quiz each week.

12

Correlation and Regression Analysis

You have used sample characteristics to make inferences about a population and have learned that the answers to many business questions require knowledge about the mean or proportion of a population. Means and proportions play a major role in estimating the consequences of business decisions. The mean or proportion of a sample is often used as the predicted or estimated value of a population. Finally, you learned how to test hypotheses about means, proportions, the differences between means, and the differences between proportions.

You previously learned techniques to estimate a single population parameter. In business many problems require the analysis of more than one variable. You often attempt to determine whether two or more variables are related, and if so, you will need to describe how they are related. The techniques presented in this chapter are used to estimate a relationship that may exist in the population. You will explore the graphical presentation of data when more than one variable is analyzed. Scatter diagrams will be used to describe data instead of frequency polygons and histograms. You will learn how to determine the degree of relationship between two variables (correlation) and describe that relationship mathematically (regression).

INTRODUCTION

Correlation and regression analysis are used to determine if two variables are related to each other in the population. Correlation analysis focuses on the strength of the relationship between two variables and is used in exploratory work when a researcher or analyst attempts to determine which variables are important. Regression analysis involves a mathematical equation that describes the relationship. The regression equation can be used to estimate or predict future values for one variable based on knowledge of the values for the other variable.

Businesspeople and economists frequently draw conclusions and make recommendations based upon an observed relationship between two variables. For example, a marketing manager may project sales volume based upon an observed relationship between advertising expenditures and sales volume. A personnel director may hire job applicants who score high on an aptitude test that predicts good job performance. A book publisher may increase or decrease the size of its sales force based on its relationship with yearly revenue. A concessions manager may base the decision on how many hot dogs to order according to the estimated attendance at a baseball game.

THE SCATTER DIAGRAM

The first step in determining whether a relationship exists between two variables is to plot or graph the available data. Suppose that a mail-order business has recorded the data shown in Table 12–1. The sales manager's objective is to determine whether there is a relationship between the number of catalogs distributed and the number of mail orders received. The data are plotted on a graph with the number of catalogs distributed on the horizontal axis and the number of mail orders received on the vertical axis. Figure 12–1 is a graph of the data presented in Table 12–1 and is called a *scatter diagram* because it shows how points are scattered on the graph. An examination of a scatter diagram usually allows an analyst to determine whether a relationship exists between two variables and to describe the kind and the degree of this relationship.

> A scatter diagram is a two-dimensional plot of X-Y data points.

In correlation and regression analysis, variables are commonly classified as either independent or dependent. An independent variable does the explaining and a dependent variable is being explained. In the mail-order example, the number of catalogs distributed is called the independent variable. If a relationship exists, the independent variable will be used to explain the number of mail orders received (dependent variable). The usual practice when constructing a scatter

	Mail Orders Received (Thousands)	Catalogs Distributed (Thousands)
TABLE 12–1 Mail-order business		
City	**Y**	**X**
A	24	6
B	16	2
C	23	5
D	15	1
E	32	10
F	25	7
G	18	3
H	35	11
I	15	2
J	32	12

FIGURE 12–1
Scatter diagram for a
mail-order business

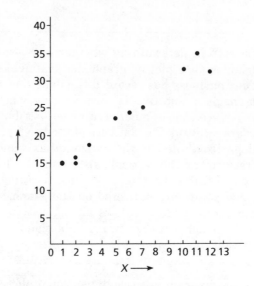

diagram is to plot the data with the dependent variable on the vertical or Y axis and the independent variable on the horizontal or X axis.

Plotting data is informative because it shows whether the variables are negatively or positively related, and whether the relationship is linear (straight line) or nonlinear (curvilinear). If Y increases as X increases (for example, as the number of catalogs mailed increases, the number of mail orders received increases, as shown in Figure 12–1), the relationship between the variables is positive. Figure 12–2(a) provides an example of a positive linear (straight line) relationship whereas Figure 12–2(c) shows a positive nonlinear (curvilinear) relationship. If Y decreases as X increases, the variables are inversely, or negatively, related. If price is related to sales for most products, then as price increases, sales decrease. This is a negative relationship and is shown graphically in Figure 12–2(b) and (d). In Figure 12–2(e), it can be seen that knowledge of X does not tell one anything about Y. There is no apparent relationship between X and Y, or Y does not seem to be affected by the movement of X.

CORRELATION ANALYSIS

Correlation analysis is used to describe the degree or strength of a relationship between two variables. It indicates the extent that values of one variable are related to values of another variable. The amount of relationship between two continuous variables is analyzed by a correlation coefficient, which is called Pearson's r. This technique is

FIGURE 12–2
Positive linear rela-
tionship (a); negative
linear relationship (b);
positive curvilinear
relationship (c); nega-
tive curvilinear
relationship (d); no re-
lationship (e)

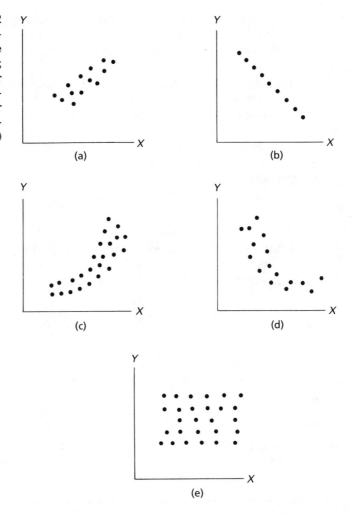

appropriate if the analyst assumes that X and Y are continuous random variables and that they have a joint frequency distribution that is
normal (the distribution of values of X-Y pairs is normal).

> Correlation analysis describes the strength of a relationship
> between two variables.

Pearson's Correlation Coefficient

The *correlation coefficient* tells an analyst two things about the relationship between two variables. The sign ($-$ or $+$) identifies the kind

of relationship, and the magnitude describes the strength of the relationship. Imagine that a straight line is drawn to fit the plotted points in Figure 12–1. The sign of r indicates whether the line has a positive or negative slope, and the magnitude indicates how close the individual points are to the imaginary line. Because of the way it is defined, values of the correlation coefficient are always between -1 and $+1$. If all the plotted points lie on the imaginary line, a perfect relationship exists (r is either -1 or $+1$). Figure 12–2(b) shows a perfect negative relationship ($r = -1$).

The sample correlation coefficient can be computed using Equation 12–1:

$$r = \frac{n\Sigma XY - \Sigma X\Sigma Y}{\sqrt{n\Sigma X^2 - (\Sigma X)^2}\sqrt{n\Sigma Y^2 - (\Sigma Y)^2}} \qquad \textbf{(12–1)}$$

Table 12–2 shows the calculations required to use Equation 12–1 for the data presented in Table 12–1. These calculations are used to compute the sample correlation coefficient r:

$$r = \frac{10(1654) - (59)(235)}{\sqrt{10(493) - (59)^2}\sqrt{10(6033) - (235)^2}}$$

$$r = \frac{2675}{\sqrt{1449}\sqrt{5105}}$$

$$r = \frac{2675}{2720}$$

$$r = .9835$$

The correlation coefficient for the mail-order data is .9835. The sign is positive indicating that as X (number of catalogs distributed) in-

TABLE 12–2 Mail-order business correlation computations	City	Y	X	Y²	X²	XY
	A	24	6	576	36	144
	B	16	2	256	4	32
	C	23	5	529	25	115
	D	15	1	225	1	15
	E	32	10	1,024	100	320
	F	25	7	625	49	175
	G	18	3	324	9	54
	H	35	11	1,225	121	385
	I	15	2	225	4	30
	J	32	12	1,024	144	384
		$\Sigma Y = 235$	$\Sigma X = 59$	$\Sigma Y^2 = 6033$	$\Sigma X^2 = 493$	$\Sigma XY = 1654$

creases, Y (number of mail-orders received) also increases. The magnitude (.9835) is quite high on a scale from 0 to 1. The manager seems to have discovered a high positive linear relationship between the two variables. It appears that the more catalogs distributed, the more mail-orders received.

> The correlation coefficient measures the linear relationship between two variables. This coefficient (r) ranges between -1 and $+1$.

Testing the Population Correlation Coefficient

Since only a sample of data points is usually obtained, the analyst needs to test a hypothesis about the unknown population correlation coefficient ρ (*rho*). If the two variables of interest are not related, the population correlation coefficient is equal to zero ($\rho = 0$). Since a large number of samples can be drawn from a population, the number of possible sample correlation coefficients (r's) is extremely large. These sample r's will be distributed around the population correlation coefficient ($\rho = 0$). Some r's will be negative (less than zero) and others will be positive (greater than zero). In other words, the analyst can create a sampling distribution of r's. Mathematicians have determined that if the two variables of interest are normally distributed and $\rho = 0$, then the sample test statistic is

$$t = r \sqrt{\frac{n-2}{1-r^2}} \qquad \text{(12–2)}$$

and follows the t distribution with $(n-2)$ degrees of freedom.[1] This sampling distribution is used to test the null hypothesis that X and Y are not related, $H_0: \rho = 0$. If H_0 is rejected, the analyst concludes that the two variables of interest, X and Y, are linearly related.

Example 12–1   In the last section a correlation coefficient for the number of catalogs distributed and the number of mail orders received was calculated. If the correlation coefficient is tested at the 5% significance level, are these two variables linearly related in the population?

Solution   Use the six-step hypothesis-testing procedure outlined in chapter 10:

   1. State the null and alternative hypotheses. Since the sales manager is interested in whether increasing the number of

---

[1] Two degrees of freedom are lost because two population parameters (μ_X and μ_Y) are estimated using sample values ($\overline{X}$ and $\overline{Y}$).

catalogs distributed will increase the number of mail orders received, direction is implied and a one-tail test should be used.

$$H_0: \rho = 0$$
$$H_1: \rho > 0$$

2. If the analyst assumes that X and Y are normally distributed and $\rho = 0$, the t distribution with $(n - 2)$ degrees of freedom is the appropriate sampling distribution for the sample statistic $r\sqrt{(n - 2)/(1 - r^2)}$.

3. An $\alpha = .05$ has been selected as the significance level. This is the probability of making a Type I error.

4. Figure 12–3 shows the sampling distribution of $r\sqrt{(n - 2)/(1 - r^2)}$'s assuming H_0 is true. By using the t table in Appendix G, it is determined that the t value associated with an area of .05 for $(n - 2) = (10 - 2) = 8$ degrees of freedom is 1.86. The decision rule is

Reject H_0 if $t > 1.86$

5. The sample correlation coefficient is equal to $r = .9835$. The analyst computes the sample test statistic using Equation 12–2:

$$t = r\sqrt{\frac{n - 2}{1 - r^2}}$$

$$t = .9835 \sqrt{\frac{10 - 2}{1 - .9835^2}}$$

$$t = .9835\sqrt{244.6}$$

$$t = .9835(15.6)$$

$$t = 15.4$$

FIGURE 12–3
Hypothesis test for catalogs and mail orders

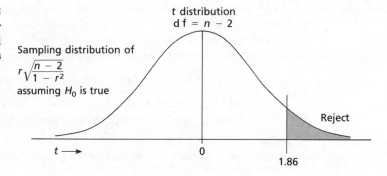

Sampling distribution of
$r\sqrt{\dfrac{n - 2}{1 - r^2}}$
assuming H_0 is true

t distribution
d f = n − 2

Reject

$t \longrightarrow$ 0
     1.86

6. Since the sample test statistic, $t = 15.4$, is greater than the critical value, $t = 1.86$, the analyst rejects the null hypothesis. Based on the sample evidence, the sales manager concludes that the number of catalogs distributed and the number of mail orders received are positively related in the population.

Example 12–2   A mortgage corporation conducted a study to determine the relationship between the current mortgage rate and the number of weekly home loan applications. Twelve weeks were selected at random from among the 208 weeks of the past four years. The data are presented in Table 12–3. Since the president of the corporation feels that there is an inverse linear relationship between these two variables, the statistician tests the hypothesis at the .01 significance level.

Solution   1. State the null and alternative hypotheses. Since the mortgage corporation is interested in whether the current mortgage rate is negatively related to the number of loan applications, direction is indicated and a one-tailed test should be used.

$$H_0\colon \rho = 0$$
$$H_1\colon \rho < 0$$

2. If the statistician assumes that X and Y are normally distributed and $\rho = 0$, the t distribution with $(n - 2)$ degrees of freedom is the appropriate sampling distribution for the sample statistic $r\sqrt{(n - 2)/(1 - r^2)}$.

TABLE 12–3
Mortgage corporation

Week	Number of Loan Applications Y	Mortgage Rate % X	Y^2	X^2	XY
1	75	11.0	5625	121.0	825.0
2	50	14.7	2500	216.1	735.0
3	65	13.5	4225	182.3	877.5
4	58	14.0	3364	196.0	812.0
5	83	11.6	6889	134.6	962.8
6	62	12.9	3844	166.4	799.8
7	54	14.5	2916	210.3	783.0
8	89	10.0	7921	100.0	890.0
9	78	11.1	6084	123.2	865.8
10	76	11.9	5776	141.6	904.4
11	63	13.8	3969	190.4	869.4
12	67	13.1	4489	171.6	877.7
Totals	820	152.1	57602	1953.5	10202.4

3. An $\alpha = .01$ has been selected as the significance level.

4. Figure 12–4 shows the sampling distribution of $r\sqrt{(n-2)/(1-r^2)}$'s assuming H_0 is true. By using the t table in Appendix G, the statistician can determine that the t value associated with an area of .01 for $(n-2) = (12-2) = 10$ degrees of freedom is 2.76. The decision rule is

$$\text{Reject } H_0 \text{ if } t < -2.76$$

5. Based on the calculations shown in Table 12–3, the sample correlation coefficient is equal to

$$r = \frac{n\Sigma XY - \Sigma X \Sigma Y}{\sqrt{n\Sigma X^2 - (\Sigma X)^2}\,\sqrt{n\Sigma Y^2 - (\Sigma Y)^2}}$$

$$r = \frac{12(10202.4) - (152.1)(820)}{\sqrt{12(1953.5) - (152.1)^2}\,\sqrt{12(57602) - (820)^2}}$$

$$r = \frac{-2293.2}{\sqrt{307.6}\,\sqrt{18824}}$$

$$r = \frac{-2293.2}{2406.5}$$

$$r = -.953$$

The sample test statistic is computed using Equation 12–2.

$$t = r\sqrt{\frac{n-2}{1-r^2}}$$

$$t = -.953\sqrt{\frac{12-2}{1-(-.953)^2}}$$

$$t = -.953\sqrt{\frac{10}{.092}}$$

FIGURE 12–4
Hypothesis test for interest and applications

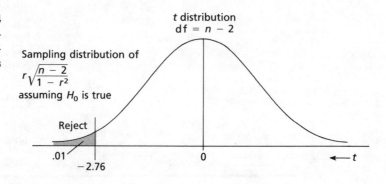

Sampling distribution of
$r\sqrt{\dfrac{n-2}{1-r^2}}$
assuming H_0 is true

t distribution
df $= n - 2$

Reject

.01

-2.76 0 $\leftarrow t$

$$t = -.953\sqrt{108.7}$$
$$t = -.953(10.4)$$
$$t = -9.94$$

6. Since the sample test statistic, $t = -9.94$ is less than the critical value, $t = -2.76$, the statistician rejected the null hypothesis. Based on the sample evidence, the mortgage corporation concluded that the current mortgage rate is inversely or negatively related to the number of loan applications in the population.

Correlation Interpretations

Caution should be used when examining the relationship between two variables on the basis of sample data. A correlation coefficient equal to or close to zero does not imply that two variables are unrelated. The two variables might be related in a *nonlinear* fashion. Equation 12–1, which measures only linear correlation, might produce a zero sample correlation coefficient. Figure 12–5(a) shows an example where r

FIGURE 12–5
Graph showing a non-linear relationship between X and Y(a); graph showing that there is no relationship between X and Y(b).

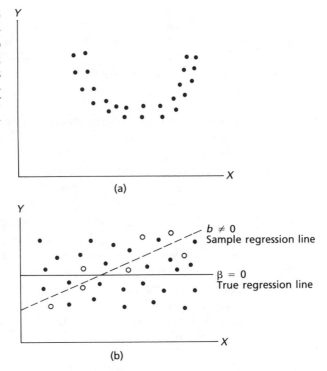

(a)

(b)

would equal zero for two variables that have a strong nonlinear relationship.

Figure 12–5(b) shows a population of data points where no relationship exists. The null hypothesis, $\rho = 0$, is true. The seven circles represent a possible random sample of seven data points selected from this population. Note that the sample suggests a positive linear correlation between X and Y. In fact, the sample correlation coefficient would be positive and fairly large (close to $+1$). This has occurred by chance even though in this population, $\rho = 0$.

Finally, the existence of a high correlation between two variables does not explain why the relationship exists. Specifically, a large correlation coefficient does not mean that one variable is the cause and the other variable is the effect. Also, high correlations often exist because the variables being analyzed are related to other variables. For example, the analyst would expect to find a high positive correlation between church attendance and liquor consumption in most cities. However, these two variables are probably not directly related to each other. Instead, church attendance and liquor consumption are both related to population size. They are both dependent variables and population size is the independent variable.

Summary

The steps that have been taken thus far in determining the relationship between two variables are:

1. A random sample of items is selected from the population, and two numerical measurements (X and Y) are taken on each of these items.

2. The X-Y data points are plotted on a scatter diagram which enables the analyst to determine the kind of relationship that exists between the two variables.

3. The correlation coefficient (r) is computed. This statistic indicates the kind of relationship (positive or negative) that exists between X and Y and also measures the strength or magnitude of the relationship.

4. The null hypothesis that the population correlation coefficient is equal to zero ($\rho = 0$) is tested. If H_0 is rejected, the analyst concludes that there is a linear relationship between X and Y in the population.

REGRESSION ANALYSIS

Once the analyst has established that two variables are linearly related, the next step is to find the straight line that best fits the data on a scatter diagram. This straight line is written in the following form:

$$Y_R = a + bX \qquad \text{(12-3)}$$

where Y_R = estimated value of the dependent variable
X = value of the independent variable
b = the slope of the line
a = the Y-intercept

The first term in Equation 12–3, a, is the Y-intercept since it is the value of Y when X is equal to zero. The slope, b, represents the average amount of change in Y when X increases one unit.

The task is to determine values for a and b for a line that best fits the sample data points. A regression line is commonly defined as a line that minimizes the sum of the squared differences between the line and the data points as measured in the vertical direction. The most widely used method for fitting a straight line using this definition is known as the *least squares* technique. If Y is used to represent the values on the line, $(Y - Y_R)$ represents the vertical distance between a plotted point and the regression line (see Figure 12–6). Since the vertical distances from all the points to the line must be considered, the value that is minimized is

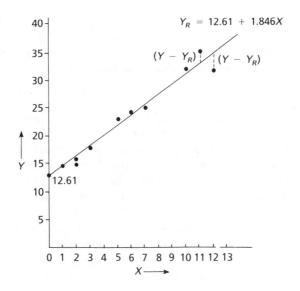

FIGURE 12–6
Regression line for a
mail-order business

$$\Sigma(Y - Y_R)^2 \qquad\qquad \textbf{(12–4)}$$

> The least squares method of fitting a straight line to a set of data points minimizes the sum of the squared vertical distances between the sample X-Y data points and the regression line.

The least squares method of finding the equations to compute a and b requires the use of calculus. The derivations are presented in Appendix J and result in Equations 12–5 and 12–6.

$$b = \frac{n\Sigma XY - \Sigma X \Sigma Y}{n\Sigma X^2 - (\Sigma X)^2} \qquad\qquad \textbf{(12–5)}$$

$$a = \frac{\Sigma Y - b\Sigma X}{n} \qquad\qquad \textbf{(12–6)}$$

Example 12–3   For the mail-order business data presented in Table 12–1, several summations were needed to compute the correlation coefficient. These summations were presented in Table 12–2 and are used in Equations 12–5 and 12–6 to find the least squares regression equation.

$$b = \frac{10(1654) - 59(235)}{10(493) - 59^2}$$

$$b = 1.846$$

$$a = \frac{235 - 1.846(59)}{10}$$

$$a = 12.610$$

When the appropriate values are substituted in Equation 12–3, the least squares regression line becomes

$$Y_R = 12.610 + 1.846X$$

This straight line best fits the data points that were plotted in Figure 12–1 by minimizing the sum of the squared vertical distances between the points and the line. The Y-intercept is equal to 12.610 and is the point at which the regression line crosses the Y axis. Therefore, when $X = 0$, $Y = 12.610$. In this example, $X = 0$ means that the company distributed no catalogs. Even though no catalogs were distributed, the company expects that 12,610 mail orders will be received. This is probably unlikely, and in fact, sometimes a useful interpretation of the Y-intercept can not be made.

The regression line slope usually provides more meaningful information. In Example 12–3, b is equal to 1.85. This means that for each extra catalog the firm sends out, the firm expects an average increase of 1.846 mail orders received.

The regression equation is presented in Figure 12–6. Notice that the vertical distances from the points to the line have been shown as dotted lines. If these distances were squared and added, $\Sigma(Y - Y_R)^2$, this sum would be the lowest possible for any line that could be drawn through the points. Any other line that might be drawn through the points would have a higher sum of squared distances. In accordance with the least-squares procedure, this line represents the best possible fit for the ten sample data points.

The regression equation can now be used to predict Y for assumed values of X. How many mail orders does the sales manager expect to receive if the firm sends out 8,000 catalogs? The regression equation for Y is solved as follows:

$$Y = 12.610 + 1.846(8)$$

$$= 27.378 \text{ thousand}$$

On the basis of the sample evidence, the sales manager predicts that 27,378 mail orders will be received if the firm mails 8,000 catalogs. It is important to note that a linear model based on sample X values within the range 1 to 12 was developed. If the sales manager wants to predict the number of mail orders received if the firm mails 15,000 catalogs, it is assumed that the linear model is still appropriate. Unfortunately, people sometimes predict beyond the scope of their data without making this necessary assumption.

Inferences

The regression line is an estimate of the real, but unknown, linear relationship between two variables in the population. The population relationship or regression line can be shown as

$$Y = \alpha + \beta X + E \qquad \qquad \textbf{(12–7)}$$

where E represents scatter in the population, or the difference between the data points and the population regression line. If the population of paired values were plotted, some degree of scatter or dispersion would usually exist. Scatter exists because there is not a perfect relationship between most pairs of variables in the population and because other variables sometimes influence values of the dependent variable. Sometimes the influence of these other variables is slight and regression analysis provides a good model. Other times the influence is great and the other variables need to be included in the model (multiple regression will be discussed later in the chapter). Most of the time some scatter will be present and sample statistics will tend to differ from actual population parameters. This means that for any given X, there will be several possible values of Y.

The following assumptions are made when regression analysis is used:

1. The population of Y values are normally distributed about the population regression line.
2. The dispersion of population data points around the population regression line remains constant everywhere along the line.
3. The Y values are independent of each other.
4. A linear relationship exists between X and Y in the population.

Standard Error of Estimate

The X-Y data points are fairly close to the regression line in Figure 12–6. This is not surprising since the sales manager established that X and Y are highly correlated, $r = .9835$. Suppose there is a need to determine the scatter or dispersion of data points around the regression line. Specifically, what is the distance between each data point and the regression line as measured in the vertical direction? This statistic is called the standard error of estimate and it can be thought of as the standard deviation of the points around the regression line. Equation 12–8 shows the formula used to compute the standard error of estimate

$$s_{Y.X} = \sqrt{\frac{\Sigma (Y - Y_R)^2}{(n - 2)}} \qquad \text{(12–8)}$$

Note the similarity between this equation and the formula for sample standard deviation in Equation 3–4. The numerator of Equation 12–8 contains the distances between the actual data value (Y) and the average or expected value of the variable, Y_R, as determined by the sample regression line. These distances are squared, summed, and divided by degrees of freedom before the square root is taken. [Note that two degrees of freedom are lost because two sample statistics (a and b) are used to estimate population parameters in the computation.][2] The standard error can be thought of as measuring the typical or average distance from a data point to the sample regression line. A small standard error involves data points very close to the regression line whereas a large standard error involves data points widely scat-

---

[2] Actually, instead of a, the estimate involves the requirement that the point $(\overline{Y}, \overline{X})$ lies on the regression line.

tered around the line. For computation purposes Equation 12–8 can be mathematically converted to

$$s_{Y.X} = \sqrt{\frac{\Sigma Y^2 - a\Sigma Y - b\Sigma XY}{n - 2}} \qquad \text{(12–9)}$$

Example 12–4   In the mail-order business example, all the necessary values have already been computed and $s_{Y.X}$ becomes

$$s_{Y.X} = \sqrt{\frac{[6033 - 12.61(235) - 1.846(1654)]}{(10 - 2)}}$$

$$s_{Y.X} = \sqrt{\frac{16.366}{8}}$$

$$s_{Y.X} = \sqrt{2.046}$$

$$s_{Y.X} = 1.43$$

This is the standard deviation of the distribution of points around the regression line. This value represents the typical distance from the sample data points to the sample regression line. The *standard error of estimate* can be used to compare the dispersion of data points around the regression line in this situation with other situations and can be used by analysts to judge whether the regression line will make accurate predictions. Also, if it is assumed that the population of data points is normally distributed around the population regression line, $s_{Y.X}$ can be used as an estimate of the standard deviation of that normal distribution.

The standard error of estimate measures the scatter of X-Y data points around the regression line.

Predicting the Dependent Variable

Suppose the analyst wants to estimate the value of Y for a given value of X. To obtain a *point estimate,* the regression equation is used. The given value of X is substituted into the equation and the estimated value of Y is determined. For example, suppose the sales manager wishes to estimate the number of mail orders received if the firm sends out 10,000 catalogs. From Equation 12–3, the estimate is 31,070.

$$Y_R = 12.610 + 1.846(10)$$
$$= 31.07 \text{ thousand}$$

Note that Y_R is used to estimate this value because Y_R represents the point on the regression line where $X = 10{,}000$. Of course, the data points that generated the regression line are dispersed around that line as measured by $s_{Y.X}$. To make an *interval estimate* of Y when $X = 10{,}000$, this scatter or dispersion must be taken into account.

If the analyst is working with a population, the interval estimate is computed using Equation 12–10:

$$Y_R \pm Z s_{Y.X} \qquad \text{(12–10)}$$

However, the calculated regression line is a sample regression line since it is computed from a random sample of 10 data points, not from all data points in the population. Other random samples of 10 produce different sample regression lines similar to the case where many samples drawn from a population have different means (see Chapter 8). To make an interval estimate for Y, it is necessary to consider both the dispersion of sample data points around the sample regression line and the dispersion of many sample regression lines around the true population regression line. The *standard error of the forecast* measures the variability of estimated values of Y around the true value of Y for a given value of X and, thus, takes into account both types of dispersion.

Equation 12–11 is used to compute the standard error of the forecast:

$$s_F = s_{Y.X} \sqrt{1 + \frac{1}{n} + \frac{(X - \overline{X})^2}{\sum (X - \overline{X})^2}} \qquad \text{(12–11)}$$

Note that $s_{Y.X}$ is one of the terms in the standard error of the forecast computation since the first value under the radical sign is 1. The other two terms represent the variability of sample regression lines around the true regression line. Also, note that there is a unique standard error of the forecast for each X value. In other words, the forecast error depends on the value of X for which a forecast is desired. The lowest possible forecast error is for $X = \overline{X}$ since the last term under the radical will equal zero. The farther X is from $\overline{X}$, the larger the forecast error. Figure 12–7 shows the 95% interval estimate for various values of X.

The standard error of the forecast measures the variability of estimated values of Y around the true value of Y for a given value of X.

FIGURE 12–7
Interval estimate

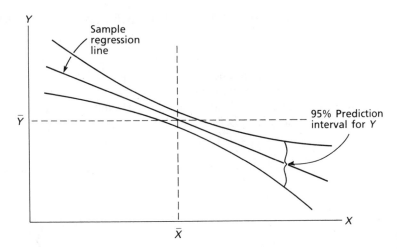

The standard error of the forecast is calculated for $X = 10,000$.

$$s_{Y.X} = 1.43$$
$$s_F = 1.43\sqrt{1.216}$$
$$s_F = 1.43(1.1)$$
$$s_F = 1.57$$

If the sample size is sufficiently large ($n > 30$), the interval estimate becomes

$$Y_R \pm Zs_F \qquad \text{(12–12)}$$

For small sample sizes, the computation is

$$Y_R \pm ts_F \qquad \text{(for } t \text{ value: } df = n - 2) \qquad \text{(12–13)}$$

Example 12–5   In the mail-order business example a 95% interval estimate for Y when $X = 10,000$ catalogs is

$$Y_R \pm ts_F$$
$$10 \pm 2.306(1.57)$$
$$10 \pm 3.62$$

6,380 orders to 13,620 orders

If the sales manager keeps selecting samples of size 10 and computes an interval estimate for each sample, 95% of the intervals will contain the true population Y value for a X of 10,000.

Testing the Population Regression Coefficient

Earlier in this chapter a hypothesis was tested about the unknown population correlation coefficient for a sample of data points. Attention is now turned to determining whether the slope of the unknown population regression line is different from zero. The same hypothesis-testing procedure is used as before. The slope of the population regression line is represented by the symbol, β. The null hypothesis is

$$H_0: \beta = 0$$

A sampling distribution of b's is created. The sample test statistic is

$$t = \frac{b\sqrt{\Sigma(X - \overline{X})^2}}{s_{Y.X}} \qquad \textbf{(12-14)}$$

and follows the t distribution with $(n - 2)$ degrees of freedom. This sampling distribution is used to test the null hypothesis that the population regression line has a slope equal to zero, $H_0: \beta = 0$. If the H_0 is rejected, the conclusion is that the two variables of interest, X and Y, are linearly related.

Example 12-6   In Example 12-1 the sales manager tested the correlation coefficient for the number of catalogs distributed and the number of mail orders received at the 5% significance level. Is the slope of the unknown population regression line greater than zero for these sample data points?

Solution   Use the six step hypothesis-testing procedure outlined in Chapter 10:

1. State the null and alternative hypotheses. Since the sales manager is interested in whether increasing the number of catalogs distributed will increase the number of mail orders received, direction is implied and a one-tailed test is used.

$$H_0: \beta = 0$$
$$H_1: \beta > 0$$

2. If the sales manager assumes that X and Y are normally distributed and $\beta = 0$, the t distribution with $(n - 2)$ degrees of freedom is the appropriate sampling distribution for the sample statistic, $b\sqrt{\Sigma(X - \overline{X})^2}/s_{Y.X}$.

3. An $\alpha = .05$ has been selected as the significance level. This is the probability of making a Type I error.

4. Figure 12-8 shows the sampling distribution of $b\sqrt{\Sigma(X - \overline{X})^2}/s_{Y.X}$'s assuming H_0 is true. By using the t table in Appendix G, it can be determined that the t value associated

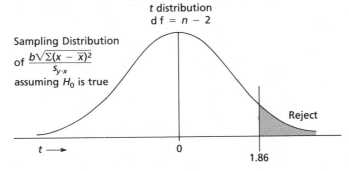

FIGURE 12–8
Hypothesis test for
the slope

with an area of .05 for $(n - 2) = (10 - 2) = 8$ degrees of freedom is 1.86. The decision rule is

$$\text{Reject } H_0 \text{ if } t > 1.86$$

5. The slope of the sample regression line is equal to $b = 1.846$. The sales manager computes the sample test statistic using Equation 12–14:

$$t = \frac{b\sqrt{\Sigma(X - \overline{X})^2}}{s_{Y.X}}$$

$$t = \frac{1.846\sqrt{144.9}}{1.43}$$

$$t = \frac{22.23}{1.43}$$

$$t = 15.55$$

6. Since the sample test statistic, $t = 15.55$, is greater than the critical value, $t = 1.86$, the null hypothesis is rejected. Based on the sample evidence, the sales manager concludes that the population regression line slope is greater than zero and that the number of catalogs distributed and the number of mail orders received are positively related. Note that the same result was obtained when the sales manager tested the population correlation coefficient (a t value of 15.4 was obtained, with the difference due to rounding error).

Coefficient of Determination

Suppose the sales manager wanted to estimate the ten Y values in the sample of X-Y data points presented in Table 12–2 for the mail-order business. If the sales manager knew the mean of Y, but had no knowledge of the X variable, the best estimate for each Y would be $\overline{Y} = 23.5$.

TABLE 12–4
Mail-order business
mean estimation com-
putations

City	Y	X	(Estimated Y) $\overline{Y}$	$(Y - \overline{Y})$	$(Y - \overline{Y})^2$
A	24	6	23.5	.5	.25
B	16	2	23.5	−7.5	56.25
C	23	5	23.5	−.5	.25
D	15	1	23.5	−8.5	72.25
E	32	10	23.5	8.5	72.25
F	25	7	23.5	1.5	2.25
G	18	3	23.5	−5.5	30.25
H	35	11	23.5	11.5	132.25
I	15	2	23.5	−8.5	72.25
J	32	12	23.5	8.5	72.25
Total	235	59		0	510.50

Table 12–4 shows the error that is made each time a Y value is estimated by using the mean of Y. Note that the $\Sigma(Y - \overline{Y})$ is equal to zero. This is true because some data points are above $\overline{Y}$ and some are below $\overline{Y}$. This is the reason that $\Sigma(Y - \overline{Y})^2$ was used to compute the standard deviation. The error found in Table 12–4 is summarized as

$$\Sigma(Y - \overline{Y})^2 = 510.5$$

Knowledge of the linear relationship between X and Y can be used to reduce the error involved in estimating Y. Each Y can be estimated by substituting the appropriate value of X into the regression equation. Each of the estimated Y values will lie on the regression line. Table 12–5 summarizes the computations and the errors found using this approach.

TABLE 12–5
Mail-order business
regression computa-
tions

City	Y	X	$Y_R = a + bX$	$(Y - Y_R)$	$(Y - Y_R)^2$
A	24	6	23.685	.315	.099
B	16	2	16.300	−.300	.090
C	23	5	21.839	1.161	1.348
D	15	1	14.454	.546	.298
E	32	10	31.069	.931	.867
F	25	7	25.531	−.531	.282
G	18	3	18.146	−.146	.021
H	35	11	32.915	2.085	4.347
I	15	2	16.300	−1.300	1.690
J	32	12	34.761	−2.761	7.623
Total	235	59		0	16.665

$$\Sigma(Y - Y_R)^2 = 16.66$$

Note that the sum of squares resulting from using $\overline{Y}$ as an estimator of Y (510.5) is reduced when the knowledge of X or the regression line (Y_R) is used as the predictor (16.66). In fact, only a small percentage of the original error remains when knowledge of X is used to estimate Y:

$$\frac{16.66}{510.5} = .033$$

Therefore, when the linear relationship between X and Y is used to estimate Y, the error is reduced to 3.3% of its former value. Or, to state it another way, 96.7% of the variability in Y is explained through knowledge of X. This value is referred to as r^2 or the *coefficient of determination*. Note that r^2 is simply the coefficient of correlation squared or, $r^2 = (.9835)^2 = .967$. The coefficient of determination can also be computed using Equation 12–15:

$$r^2 = 1 - \frac{\Sigma(Y - Y_R)^2}{\Sigma(Y - \overline{Y})^2} \qquad \textbf{(12-15)}$$

The coefficient of determination is important because it measures the X-Y relationship in terms of an easily understood percentage. Almost 97% of the variability in the number of mail orders received can be explained through a knowledge of the variability in the number of catalogs mailed.

> The coefficient of determination measures the percentage of variability in Y that can be explained through knowledge of a related variable, X.

MULTIPLE REGRESSION

So far, knowledge of an independent variable (X) has been used to predict a dependent variable (Y). Unfortunately, most real business situations are not this simple. More than one independent variable needs to be used to estimate a dependent variable accurately. When more than one independent variable is used, multiple regression analysis is the appropriate technique. Although the basic concepts remain the same, more than one independent variable is used to estimate or predict the dependent variable.

In simple regression the dependent variable is represented by Y and the independent variable by X. In multiple regression analysis, independent variables are represented by X's with subscripts. The dependent variable is still Y and the independent variables are X_2, X_3, ... X_n. Based on this system of notation, a three-variable problem with two independent variables would be represented by Equation 12–16.

$$Y_R = a + b_2X_2 + b_3X_3 \qquad (12\text{–}16)$$

As in simple regression, the method of least squares is used to obtain the best-fitting regression equation. In a two-variable analysis, the least-squares method produced the best-fitting straight line. In a problem involving more than two variables, the least-squares method produces the best-fitting plane. The plane is represented by Y_R and is derived in such a way so that $\Sigma(Y - Y_R)^2$ is at a minimum. The Y-intercept (a) and the slopes (b's) are derived as the best set of weights that minimize the sum of the squared distances between the data points and the multiple regression plane. The computational techniques are complicated, and computer programs are normally used.

The interpretation of the b's or regression coefficients in a multiple regression equation is similar to the definition of the slope in a two-variable regression problem. For example, suppose a computer program produces the following equation:

$$Y_R = 16 + 3X_2 - 5X_3$$

The regression coefficients are interpreted as follows:

1. For each one-unit increase in X_2, Y_R increases by an average of 3, if X_3 is held constant.
2. For each one-unit increase in X_3, Y_R decreases by an average of 5, if X_2 is held constant.

The regression coefficient measures the average change in Y per unit change in the relevant independent variable, if the other independent variables are held constant.

Correlation Matrix

Analysts are frequently faced with the task of deciding which combination of several independent variables to use to estimate a particular dependent variable. A *correlation matrix* is consulted to help with this task. This type of matrix contains the correlation coefficient for each possible pair of two-variable relationships.

Suppose the task is to understand the variability in the prices of lots. The analyst tries to think of as many potential explanatory variables as possible and looks for variables that are related (high correlations) to the price of lots. Eventually, the analyst comes up with the following data on five potential independent variables:

X_2: elevation X_5: slope

X_3: view X_6: number of trees

X_4: area

The data are run on a computer program and the resulting correlation matrix is presented in Table 12-6. Variable 1 (price) is the dependent variable, Y. Variables 2 through 6 are the explanatory variables. In the body of the table are the correlation coefficients (r's) indicating the relationship between each pair of variables. The primary diagonal values are all equal to one because each variable has a perfect positive correlation with itself ($r = 1$). Also notice that the correlation coefficients above the primary diagonal are exactly the same as those below the diagonal. This means that the correlation between variables 2 and 3 ($r = .75$) is the same as the correlation between variables 3 and 2 ($r = .75$).

A correlation matrix indicates the relationship or correlation coefficient between each possible pair of variables.

Since the analyst is particularly interested in the relationship between each potential independent variable and the dependent variable, row one is studied first. As can be seen, X_3 is the variable with the highest potential for explaining the variability in Y ($r = .87$). Also X_2, X_4, and X_5 are fairly highly correlated with Y ($r = .65, .60,$ and $.67$ respectively). Furthermore, X_6 shows a weak relationship to Y ($r = .19$). By studying the correlation matrix, the analyst is able to determine which independent variables have potential for explaining the variability of

TABLE 12-6
Correlation matrix

Variables	Price 1	Elevation 2	View 3	Area 4	Slope 5	Trees 6
1	1.00	.65	.87	.60	.67	.19
2	.65	1.00	.75	.05	.12	.22
3	.87	.75	1.00	.40	.62	.10
4	.60	.05	.40	1.00	.63	.05
5	.67	.12	.62	.63	1.00	.12
6	.19	.22	.10	.05	.12	1.00

the dependent variable. The result is usually a shortened list of explanatory variables.

Actually, the attributes of a good explanatory variable are the following:

1. A good explanatory variable is related to the dependent variable.
2. A good explanatory variable is *not* highly related to any other independent variable.

The first criterion is important because, as you have already learned, in order for an independent variable to explain the dependent variable variance, the two variables must be related. The second criterion is important because if independent variables are highly related to each other, they explain the same dependent variable variance. When this happens, analysts say that collinearity exists. When collinearity is present, the regression coefficients in a multiple regression equation are very unreliable. Specifically,

1. The regression coefficients (b's) may have the wrong sign. A variable that has a positive relationship with Y may have a negative (b).
2. The regression coefficients may vary markedly from one sample to another.

The correlation matrix in Table 12–6 is used to select good explanatory variables based on the criteria listed above. Elevation (X_2), view (X_3), area (X_4), and slope (X_5) are all fairly well related to price (Y). Next, a look at Table 12–7 shows the relationships between these five variables. A final equation containing area and view would probably best explain the price variable variance:

$$Y_R = a + b_3X_3 + b_4X_4$$

To choose the best equation, the analyst runs potentially good models on the computer and consults two types of statistics, r^2 and the t values:

1. The coefficient of determination has the same interpretation as the r^2 in a simple regression analysis. In general, an analyst

TABLE 12–7		
Independent variable relationships	Elevation and View	(X_2 and X_3); $r = .75$, should not be used together
	View and Slope	(X_3 and X_5); $r = .62$, should not be used together
	Area and Slope	(X_4 and X_5); $r = .63$, should not be used together
	View and Area	(X_3 and X_4); $r = .40$, should be used together

wants r^2 to be as high as possible with every independent variable making some contribution to explaining the dependent variable variance.

2. Each regression coefficient (b) in an equation has a t value that is used to test the hypothesis that the corresponding population regression coefficient (β) is equal to zero. The analyst wants every variable in the model to have a regression coefficient that is significantly different from zero.

In multiple regression analysis good judgment should be used in selecting the original independent variables, in forming good explanatory variable combinations, and in selecting the best regression equation after examination of the computer analysis. The ultimate objective is to explain the variability of the dependent variable and to estimate its value given the values of selected independent variables.

SUMMARY

Regression analysis is probably the most widely used statistical tool employed by management when there is a need to evaluate the impact of a single independent variable on a dependent variable. Regression and correlation analysis help the analyst describe the relationships between variables. The analyst can determine both the importance and the kind of relationship.

Most problems using regression analysis involve the more sophisticated version called multiple regression analysis, because most relationships involve the study of more than one independent variable. Multiple regression measures the simultaneous effect of more than one independent variable on one dependent variable. If independent variables are related to the dependent variable but not to each other, they can be used to make predictions about the dependent variable. Regression coefficients measure the average change in the dependent variable per unit change in the relevent independent variable. Because of the cost and tedious labor involved in multiple regression analysis, analysts use computer programs.

CASE STUDY: EVANS & SONS INVESTMENT COMPANY

J. B. Evans, a partner in the Evans & Sons Investment Company, has decided to submit a bid on a new bond issue of the Inland Empire Power Company. Evans & Sons is in the business of making bids on investments offered by various firms that desire additional financing. Mr. Evans has tabulated a bid on the last 25 issues, which was based on each bid's percentage of par value. The bid of Evans's major competitor, the Hayes Corporation, has also been tabulated on these issues. Mr. Evans now wonders if Hayes is using the same rationale in preparing bids. In other words, could the Evans Company's bid be used to estimate the Hayes bid? If not, then Hayes must be evaluating issues differently.

    Mr. Evans takes the data to his daughter Judy who has recently graduated with a business degree from the local university. Judy tells her father that correlation and regression analysis are the appropriate statistical techniques to analyze the data. Judy inputs the data on the company's microcomputer and obtains the following results:

correlation coefficient	$r = .95$
slope	$b = 1.0345$
Y-intercept	$a = -3.25725$
standard error of estimate	$s_{Y.X} = .743$

    Judy schedules a meeting with her father to discuss her findings. Mr. Evans begins the meeting by asking Judy whether the two firms are using the same rationale in preparing their bids. Judy indicates that they are and that knowledge of what the Evans Company intends to bid can be used to estimate what Hayes will bid. Mr. Evans says that they plan to bid 101% of par value on the Inland Empire Power Company bond issue. He asks Judy to estimate what the Hayes Corporation will bid. Judy substitutes in the regression equation and concludes that Hayes will bid 101.2. Since the low bid wins, Mr. Evans asks Judy if she is sure. Judy says no but that she can provide an interval estimate that will give some assurance. Judy does some computations and indicates that she is 95% confident that Hayes will bid somewhere between 99.74 and 102.66. Mr. Evans tells Judy that this interval estimate is worthless. "I need to know the probability that we will win the bid," he says. Judy decides that the estimated Hayes bid can be described by the normal distribution of bids around the regression line. Since the standard error of estimate is the standard deviation of this distribution, the probability that the Evans bid of 101% is lower than the Hayes bid is .6064. She told her father that the probability of winning the bid is 60.6%.

Questions   1. What was Judy's basis for concluding that the firms were using the same rationale in preparing their bids?

2. Was Judy's interval estimate correct? Judy assumed that the data constituted the entire population of bid data. Was this assumption valid?

3. Assuming the data are from a random sample, what changes would be necessary in Judy's computations?

EXERCISES

1. What is the difference between correlation analysis and regression analysis?

2. Why are scatter diagrams important?

3. Why are the sign and magnitude of r important?

4. What is implied when the value of r is close to zero?

5. What does $r = -1$ imply?

6. If the correlation between sales and price is $-.85$ and between sales and advertising expense is $.6$, which independent variable will best estimate sales? Explain.

7. What is the value of $s_{Y.X}$ if $r = 1$? Explain.

8. What is the slope of the regression line if $r = 0$?

9. List the assumptions that are normally made about the observations in regression analysis.

10. Can $s_{X.Y}$ ever be larger than s_Y? Can $s_{Y.X}$ ever be equal to s_Y? Explain.

11. What is the purpose of testing whether or not $\rho = 0$? $\beta = 0$? Will the results differ?

12. Suppose $n = 1000$ and $r = .30$ in a correlation analysis. Can you conclude that the population correlation coefficient is significantly different from 0 at the .05 significance level? Explain what this correlation coefficient indicates.

13. Annual food expenditures in hundreds of dollars are estimated using annual net income (in thousands of dollars). The least squares regression line is $Y_R = 9.850 + 1.959X$.
   a. Interpret the Y-intercept.
   b. Interpret the slope.
   c. Estimate annual food expenditures for a family whose annual net income is $10,000.

14. What are the characteristics of a good explanatory variable for a multiple regression equation?

15. The amount of time required to check out customers in a discount store and the corresponding value of purchases are as follows:

Time Required for Checkout (minutes)	Value of Purchase (dollars)
1.5	6.4
2.8	15.9
0.3	1.9
4.1	40.0
1.8	6.0
3.3	22.0
5.5	43.1
0.7	2.8
4.3	30.0
3.5	30.8

a. Construct a scatter diagram.
b. Compute the sample correlation coefficient.
c. Test the hypothesis that $\rho = 0$ at the .01 significance level.
d. What percentage of the checkout time variance can be explained by the X-Y relationship?

16. In an attempt to relate yearly investment with the average interest rate, the following results were observed during an 8-year period:

Yearly Investment (thousands of dollars)	Average Interest Rate (percentage)
2050	9.6
1800	9.9
1780	10.5
2222	9.8
2750	12.1
4050	7.7
3600	9.5
3100	9.2

a. Construct a scatter diagram.
b. Compute the sample correlation coefficient.
c. Test the hypothesis that $\rho = 0$ at the .01 significance level.
d. What percentage of the yearly investment variance can be explained by the X-Y relationship?

17. The number of hours a salesperson spends with a client and the size of the client's account should be positively related. The following data have been recorded for eight randomly selected clients:

Client	Account Size	Hours Spent
1	$500	9
2	375	5
3	680	14
4	620	10
5	260	4
6	900	18
7	810	17
8	450	8

a. Construct a scatter diagram.
b. Estimate the correlation coefficient.
c. Calculate r and compare it to your estimate in Part b.
d. Is there significant positive correlation tested at the .01 significance level?
e. What percentage of the account size variance can be explained by a knowledge of how many hours a salesperson spends with a client?

18. Since AT&T (American Telephone and Telegraph) is such a large utility, its earnings per share should be related to GNP (gross national product). Based on the data for the nine year period shown below, can AT&T earnings per share be estimated by GNP?

Year	GNP	AT&T Earnings per Share
1977	980.7	1.56
1978	995.5	1.67
1979	1005.1	1.77
1980	1014.6	1.83
1981	1050.9	1.97
1982	1156.0	2.06
1983	1099.1	2.09
1984	1203.9	2.22
1985	1326.5	2.45

a. What is the regression equation?
b. Test H_0: $\beta = 0$.
c. Develop both a point and an interval estimate (90% confidence level) for Y when $X = 1000$.
d. Summarize your results in a report to investors.

19. The Spokane Transit Authority would like to determine whether there is any relationship between the age of a bus and the annual maintenance cost. A sample of eleven buses resulted in the following data:

Age of Bus (Years)	Maintenance Cost (Dollars)
1	425
2	535
2	490
. 3	525
3	580
4	625
4	800
4	720
5	790
7	855
8	975

a. Test H_0: $\beta = 0$.
b. Determine the sample regression equation.
c. Compute the standard error of estimate.
d. Compute the standard error of forecast for a 6-year-old bus.
e. Compute the 95% confidence interval for Part d.

20. An analyst for an insurance company wished to determine the relationship between the amount of life insurance held by families and income. The analyst selected a random sample of twelve families and obtained the following results:

Family	Amount of Life Insurance (Thousands of $)	Income (Thousands of $)
A	65	29
B	79	35
C	70	33
D	49	25
E	45	20
F	50	31
G	90	55
H	100	50
I	75	32
J	40	18
K	90	45
L	25	15

a. Test H_0: $\beta = 0$.
b. Determine the sample regression equation.
c. Compute the standard error of estimate.
d. Compute the standard error of forecast for a family with an income of $40,000.
e. Compute the 98% confidence interval for Part d.

21. The personnel director of the Kaiser Aluminum Company obtained data on the age of his employees and the number of days they were absent.

Using the data presented below, test the hypothesis that $\rho = 0$ at the .01 significance level. Also test the hypothesis that $\beta = 0$.

Age	Days Absent
20	5
31	3
42	10
55	4
25	8
36	6
29	9
61	8
48	7
58	5

22. A concessionaire who sells food at a football stadium must know what size crowd to expect during the coming weekend. Since advance ticket sales give an indication of expected attendance, food needs might be estimated on the basis of the advance sales. The following data have been collected for the last eight weekends.

Hot Dogs Purchased (Thousands)	Advance Ticket Sales (Thousands)
29.2	49.9
36.3	52.8
20.3	38.6
17.8	32.3
25.6	51.5
32.7	47.8
23.4	43.3
15.6	29.5

a. Develop a linear model using advance ticket sales to estimate how many hot dogs to purchase.

b. Calculate r and interpret what it means.

c. Do the data provide sufficient information to indicate that advance ticket sales provide a reliable estimate of hot dog demand?

d. What effect on hot dog purchases does an additional thousand advance ticket sales have?

e. If 40,000 football fans purchased their tickets this week, determine a 90% interval estimate for the number of hot dogs that will be purchased this weekend.

23. The following data represent prevailing interest rates on first mortgages and the number of building permits issued in Lake County over a ten-year span.

Year	Interest Rates	Building Permits
1976	5.9%	1129
1977	6.6%	1976
1978	7.4%	980
1979	8.6%	740
1980	9.3%	495
1981	10.1%	116
1982	9.2%	325
1983	9.8%	296
1984	10.8%	96
1985	11.6%	58

a. What kind of relationship would you expect for these two variables?

b. Construct a linear model of the data.

c. Test H_0: $\beta = 0$. How should H_0 be stated?

d. Interpret the slope and Y-intercept of this model.

e. Develop a point estimate for building permits if economic indicators suggest that the prevailing interest rate on first mortgages will be 12% in 1986.

f. Develop a 98% interval estimate for Part e.

g. What assumption has been made in using the estimates for Parts e and f? Is this a valid assumption to make?

24. Most computer solutions for multiple regression begin with a correlation matrix. This should be the first step when analyzing a problem that involves more than one independent variable. Analyze the following correlations:

Number	1	2	3	4	5	6
1	1.00	0.52	0.19	−0.49	0.81	0.69
2		1.00	0.25	−0.09	0.42	0.45
3			1.00	−0.06	0.19	0.19
4				1.00	−0.41	−0.11
5					1.00	0.70
6						1.00

a. Why are the entries on the primary diagonal equal to one?

b. Why is the bottom half of the matrix below the primary diagonal blank?

c. Which independent variables have the highest degree of relationship with variable 1 (the dependent variable)?

d. What kind of relationship exists between variables 1 and 4?

e. What is the magnitude of the relationship between variables 1 and 3?

f. Which variable or variables will be included in the best model? Explain why.

25. Consider the population of 200 weekly observations that are presented in the accompanying table. The independent variable X is the average weekly temperature of Spokane, Washington. The dependent variable Y is the number of shares of Sunshine Mining Stock traded on the Spokane exchange in a week. Randomly select data for 16 weeks, and compute the coefficient of correlation. Test the hypothesis that the relationship between temperature and the number of shares traded is not significant. (*Hint:* Make sure your sample is *randomly* drawn from the population. Consult your instructor if you do not know how to draw a random sample.)

	Y	X		Y	X
(1)	50.00	37.00	(41)	56.00	61.00
(2)	90.00	77.00	(42)	48.00	18.00
(3)	46.00	55.00	(43)	0.00	45.00
(4)	47.00	27.00	(44)	58.00	4.00
(5)	12.00	49.00	(45)	27.00	23.00
(6)	23.00	23.00	(46)	78.00	68.00
(7)	65.00	18.00	(47)	78.00	79.00
(8)	37.00	1.00	(48)	72.00	66.00
(9)	87.00	41.00	(49)	21.00	80.00
(10)	83.00	73.00	(50)	73.00	99.00
(11)	87.00	61.00	(51)	54.00	86.00
(12)	39.00	85.00	(52)	76.00	48.00
(13)	28.00	16.00	(53)	55.00	48.00
(14)	97.00	46.00	(54)	12.00	15.00
(15)	69.00	88.00	(55)	5.00	70.00
(16)	87.00	87.00	(56)	2.00	9.00
(17)	52.00	82.00	(57)	77.00	52.00
(18)	52.00	56.00	(58)	6.00	71.00
(19)	15.00	22.00	(59)	67.00	38.00
(20)	85.00	49.00	(60)	30.00	69.00
(21)	41.00	44.00	(61)	3.00	13.00
(22)	82.00	33.00	(62)	6.00	63.00
(23)	98.00	77.00	(63)	70.00	65.00
(24)	99.00	87.00	(64)	33.00	87.00
(25)	23.00	54.00	(65)	13.00	18.00
(26)	77.00	8.00	(66)	10.00	4.00
(27)	42.00	64.00	(67)	21.00	29.00
(28)	60.00	24.00	(68)	56.00	21.00
(29)	22.00	29.00	(69)	74.00	9.00
(30)	91.00	40.00	(70)	47.00	8.00
(31)	68.00	35.00	(71)	34.00	18.00
(32)	36.00	37.00	(72)	38.00	84.00
(33)	22.00	28.00	(73)	75.00	64.00
(34)	92.00	56.00	(74)	0.00	81.00
(35)	34.00	33.00	(75)	51.00	98.00
(36)	34.00	82.00	(76)	47.00	55.00
(37)	63.00	89.00	(77)	63.00	40.00
(38)	30.00	78.00	(78)	7.00	14.00
(39)	31.00	24.00	(79)	6.00	11.00
(40)	84.00	53.00	(80)	68.00	42.00

	Y	X		Y	X
(81)	72.00	43.00	(127)	73.00	44.00
(82)	95.00	73.00	(128)	13.00	63.00
(83)	82.00	45.00	(129)	18.00	74.00
(84)	91.00	16.00	(130)	70.00	40.00
(85)	83.00	21.00	(131)	9.00	53.00
(86)	27.00	85.00	(132)	93.00	79.00
(87)	13.00	37.00	(133)	41.00	9.00
(88)	6.00	89.00	(134)	17.00	52.00
(89)	76.00	76.00	(135)	10.00	82.00
(90)	55.00	71.00	(136)	69.00	37.00
(91)	13.00	53.00	(137)	5.00	57.00
(92)	50.00	13.00	(138)	18.00	62.00
(93)	60.00	12.00	(139)	88.00	21.00
(94)	61.00	30.00	(140)	99.00	94.00
(95)	73.00	57.00	(141)	86.00	99.00
(96)	20.00	66.00	(142)	95.00	45.00
(97)	36.00	27.00	(143)	78.00	19.00
(98)	85.00	41.00	(144)	3.00	76.00
(99)	49.00	20.00	(145)	38.00	81.00
(100)	83.00	66.00	(146)	57.00	95.00
(101)	22.00	43.00	(147)	77.00	30.00
(102)	32.00	5.00	(148)	25.00	59.00
(103)	24.00	13.00	(149)	99.00	93.00
(104)	63.00	3.00	(150)	9.00	28.00
(105)	16.00	58.00	(151)	79.00	85.00
(106)	4.00	13.00	(152)	79.00	27.00
(107)	79.00	18.00	(153)	48.00	61.00
(108)	5.00	5.00	(154)	5.00	7.00
(109)	59.00	26.00	(155)	24.00	79.00
(110)	99.00	9.00	(156)	47.00	49.00
(111)	76.00	96.00	(157)	65.00	71.00
(112)	15.00	94.00	(158)	56.00	27.00
(113)	10.00	30.00	(159)	52.00	15.00
(114)	20.00	41.00	(160)	17.00	88.00
(115)	37.00	1.00	(161)	45.00	38.00
(116)	56.00	27.00	(162)	45.00	31.00
(117)	6.00	73.00	(163)	90.00	35.00
(118)	86.00	19.00	(164)	69.00	78.00
(119)	27.00	94.00	(165)	62.00	93.00
(120)	67.00	5.00	(166)	0.00	51.00
(121)	22.00	31.00	(167)	8.00	68.00
(122)	32.00	13.00	(168)	47.00	30.00
(123)	90.00	11.00	(169)	7.00	81.00
(124)	88.00	50.00	(170)	48.00	30.00
(125)	35.00	40.00	(171)	59.00	46.00
(126)	57.00	80.00	(172)	76.00	99.00

	Y	X		Y	X
(173)	54.00	98.00	(187)	90.00	68.00
(174)	95.00	11.00	(188)	78.00	10.00
(175)	7.00	6.00	(189)	60.00	27.00
(176)	24.00	83.00	(190)	96.00	90.00
(177)	55.00	49.00	(191)	51.00	6.00
(178)	41.00	39.00	(192)	9.00	62.00
(179)	14.00	16.00	(193)	93.00	78.00
(180)	24.00	13.00	(194)	61.00	22.00
(181)	36.00	31.00	(195)	5.00	99.00
(182)	62.00	44.00	(196)	88.00	51.00
(183)	77.00	11.00	(197)	45.00	44.00
(184)	32.00	60.00	(198)	34.00	86.00
(185)	12.00	82.00	(199)	28.00	47.00
(186)	85.00	7.00	(200)	44.00	49.00

26. Consider the population of 140 observations that are presented in the accompanying table. The Marshall Printing Company wishes to estimate the relationship between the number of copies produced by an offset-printing technique (X) and the associated direct labor cost (Y). Select a random sample of 20 observations, and determine whether a significant relationship exists between number of copies and total direct labor cost.

	Y	X		Y	X		Y	X
(1)	1.0	10	(23)	1.8	80	(45)	1.6	170
(2)	0.9	10	(24)	1.0	90	(46)	1.9	170
(3)	0.8	10	(25)	2.0	100	(47)	1.7	170
(4)	1.3	20	(26)	0.5	100	(48)	2.2	180
(5)	0.9	20	(27)	1.5	100	(49)	2.4	180
(6)	0.6	30	(28)	1.3	110	(50)	1.6	180
(7)	1.1	30	(29)	1.7	110	(51)	1.8	190
(8)	1.0	30	(30)	1.2	110	(52)	4.1	190
(9)	1.4	40	(31)	0.8	110	(53)	2.0	190
(10)	1.4	40	(32)	1.0	120	(54)	1.5	200
(11)	1.2	40	(33)	1.8	120	(55)	2.1	200
(12)	1.7	50	(34)	2.1	120	(56)	2.5	200
(13)	0.9	50	(35)	1.5	130	(57)	1.7	220
(14)	1.2	50	(36)	1.9	130	(58)	2.0	220
(15)	1.3	50	(37)	1.7	140	(59)	2.3	220
(16)	0.7	60	(38)	1.2	150	(60)	1.8	220
(17)	1.0	60	(39)	1.4	150	(61)	1.3	230
(18)	1.3	70	(40)	2.1	150	(62)	1.6	230
(19)	1.5	70	(41)	0.9	160	(63)	2.8	230
(20)	2.0	70	(42)	1.1	160	(64)	2.2	230
(21)	0.8	80	(43)	1.7	160	(65)	2.6	230
(22)	0.6	80	(44)	2.0	160	(66)	1.4	240

	Y	X		Y	X		Y	X
(67)	1.6	240	(92)	2.8	320	(117)	3.4	420
(68)	1.7	240	(93)	2.4	320	(118)	3.5	420
(69)	1.5	250	(94)	2.5	320	(119)	3.1	420
(70)	2.2	250	(95)	2.0	330	(120)	2.9	420
(71)	2.5	250	(96)	2.4	340	(121)	2.8	430
(72)	2.4	260	(97)	2.2	340	(122)	3.3	430
(73)	2.0	260	(98)	2.0	340	(123)	2.5	440
(74)	2.7	260	(99)	2.5	350	(124)	2.8	440
(75)	2.0	270	(100)	2.8	350	(125)	2.4	450
(76)	2.2	270	(101)	2.3	350	(126)	2.6	450
(77)	2.4	270	(102)	2.7	350	(127)	3.0	450
(78)	1.8	280	(103)	2.8	360	(128)	3.4	460
(79)	2.8	290	(104)	3.1	360	(129)	3.0	460
(80)	2.2	290	(105)	2.5	370	(130)	3.3	470
(81)	2.4	290	(106)	2.9	370	(131)	3.4	470
(82)	2.1	290	(107)	2.6	370	(132)	3.1	470
(83)	1.9	290	(108)	3.0	380	(133)	3.6	480
(84)	2.4	300	(109)	3.2	380	(134)	3.0	480
(85)	2.5	300	(110)	2.9	390	(135)	2.9	480
(86)	2.9	300	(111)	2.6	390	(136)	3.2	480
(87)	2.0	300	(112)	2.5	390	(137)	2.6	490
(88)	1.9	310	(113)	2.7	400	(138)	3.8	490
(89)	2.5	310	(114)	3.1	400	(139)	3.3	490
(90)	2.6	310	(115)	2.4	400	(140)	2.9	500
(91)	3.2	320	(116)	3.0	400			

27. This question refers to the class data bank. Test at the .05 significance level whether there is a relationship between age and cumulative college grade point average.

28. This question refers to the class data bank. Determine whether there is a relationship between high school grade point average and college grade point average. If there is a relationship, determine the appropriate regression equation and discuss its accuracy.

13
Index Numbers

Where You Have Been You have examined numerous statistical techniques, which are all designed to assist the decision-making process by extracting useful information from data. These techniques have included simple descriptive procedures, sampling methods, more advanced estimation and hypothesis-testing techniques, and regression analysis, which is a technique widely used in business and economics.

Where You Are Going Before turning to the final topic of this book, we will examine a topic that is often used in the analysis of time series and is also widely used by itself. Index numbers are not only used regularly by business and government but are also used in popular discussions in newspapers and TV newsprograms. This chapter describes the more popular uses and formulations of these summary numerical values.

PURPOSE OF INDEX NUMBERS

A time-series analysis is conducted when an organization needs to monitor movement of economic variables over time and will be discussed in the next chapter. Often, the problem of following the economic condition of certain aspects of the economy is complicated because a large number of components comprise the area of interest. For example, an automobile manufacturer might be interested in monitoring the cost of materials used in its final assembly plants. Since thousands of parts from hundreds of suppliers make up these assemblies, it would be difficult to summarize component cost without some method of combining these costs into a single indicator.

Following economic indicators is also complicated by the fact that if the indicator is measured in dollars, the inflationary tendencies of the economy distort the analysis. A company would have difficulty, for example, in assessing the impact of union wage demands because devaluation of the dollar occurs on almost a monthly basis. Therefore, *index numbers* were developed to follow complex economic indicators over time and to eliminate the effect of a continually inflating dollar. The case study at the end of this chapter addresses the problem of assessing costs in view of dollar inflation.

> An index number is a ratio of a current economic measurement to the same economic measurement made in an earlier base period.

Suppose a company wishes to follow the cost of living in a community where one of its plants is located. The company begins by defining the market basket, which is a representative collection of items that constitute the cost of living in that community. The cost of living is determined not by a single economic variable but by a composite of many variables. For example, rent, mortgage rates, gasoline prices, grocery prices, clothing costs, entertainment costs, and automobile prices are only a few of the hundreds of components that affect the cost of living. When the company has carefully defined the factors involved in the typical cost of day-to-day living in the area, it is ready to price out these items.

The company lists the quantity of each of the items that are purchased each month by a typical family in the community. When this list is first formulated and priced, the company believes that economic times in the community are normal. That is, the community is not undergoing a recession nor a time of extreme economic prosperity. Therefore, the company chooses the current period as the base period upon which the cost-of-living index for the community will be based. Selection of an appropriate base period will be discussed in the next section.

After defining those items that a typical family in the community will purchase during a month, the company determines that the total price of these items in the community is $432. The base period for the cost-of-living index is the current month, May, 1978. Table 13–1 shows the price of $432 for that month, along with the price of purchasing the same market basket of goods each month thereafter. Finally, Table

TABLE 13–1
Hypothetical cost-of-living index calculation

Month	Cost of Market Basket	Cost-of-Living Index
May, 1978	$432	100.0
June	435	100.7
July	440	101.9
August	438	101.4
September	441	102.1
October	441	102.1
November	445	103.0
December	450	104.2
January, 1979	448	103.7
February	448	103.7
March	452	104.6
April	452	104.6
May	455	105.3
June	460	106.5
July	458	106.0
August	462	106.9

13–1 shows the cost-of-living index for each of these months. The index is defined to be 100 in the base month, May, 1978. Each month thereafter, the price of the market basket is divided by $432 and the decimal place is moved two places to the right to form the index for that month.

For example, the November, 1978 index is calculated by dividing the price of the market basket for that month, $445, by the cost of the same market basket in the base period, $432. After the decimal place has been moved, this ratio is 103.0. This index indicates that in the period May, 1978 to November, 1978, the cost of living in the community has risen by 3%. Likewise, the cost of living has gone up by almost 7% by August, 1979, since the index for that month is 106.9. The company is, thus, able to monitor the cost of living in its community with a single numerical value that is easy to understand, compare, and use.

Suppose the same company wishes to prepare an index that measures its annual dollar sales over several years. The purpose in doing so is to have a simple index that will allow the company to track annual dollar volume as a percentage of a base year rather than tracking the actual dollars. Table 13–2 shows the annual sales in millions of dollars for the company along with the sales index for the years 1975 to 1982.

The company decides that 1977 was a normal year and chooses it as the base period. It then divides each annual sales level by the sales for the base year. After the decimal has been moved two places to the right, the sales indices shown in the last column of Table 13–2 are calculated. Notice that the index for the base year, 1977, is 100. The index for 1975 is 69.2 (42.5/61.4) and for 1982 is 180.3 (110.7/61.4). The company now has a simple index to use in tracking sales volume relative to its chosen base year.

TABLE 13–2
Hypothetical company annual sales index

Year	Annual Sales, Millions	Sales Index
1975	42.5	69.2
1976	55.8	90.9
1977	61.4	100.0
1978	83.8	136.5
1979	85.1	138.6
1980	103.4	168.4
1981	105.6	172.0
1982	110.7	180.3

SELECTION OF BASE PERIOD

The hypothetical company cost-of-living index shown in Table 13–1 used May, 1978 as the base month. If this choice was a good one, it was because that month represented a normal or an average month upon which to base the cost index for the community. Likewise, the company chose 1977 for the base year in computing an annual sales index. Again, this choice might be made because 1977 was a normal year, in the company's opinion.

The base period for the index often represents a time when conditions reflected in the index are normal. That is, the base period would normally not be a depressed period economically nor would it represent a period when economic times are extremely good. Rather, a middle-of-the-road economic period is usually chosen to provide a better standard on which to base the variability in the economic index to be constructed.

The United States Government has chosen 1967 for the base year in constructing the national cost-of-living index. The government will probably move the base period forward at some time so that the index can be formed relative to a more recent year. The choice of a new base year will involve considerable thought on the part of government analysts because an average time period is not always easy to find. The task of changing the base period of an index is discussed later in this chapter.

TYPES OF INDICES

Price Indices

A common index used in business, government, and economics is the *price index*. Tables 13–1 and 13–2 are two hypothetical examples of such an index. The most commonly used price index is the U.S. Bureau of Labor Statistics' *Consumer Price Index*. This index is used as an indicator of inflation and adjusts wages and prices so that measurements in constant dollars can be studied.

The Consumer Price Index (CPI) market basket consists of 400 key items that constitute the typical monthly purchases of American families. The prices of these items are weighted to reflect the proportion of family income devoted to each item. The CPI market basket includes costs for food, clothing, shelter, fuel, drugs, transportation fares, doctors' and dentists' fees, and many other goods and services purchased by families.

The Bureau of Labor Statistics periodically updates the CPI market basket to reflect current purchasing patterns of the American consumer. This updating process requires considerable thought and care. Although the CPI is more relevant if it reflects the most up-to-date collection of goods and services, consistency is desirable if meaningful comparisons are to be made from time period to time period. From this standpoint, the CPI market basket should be changed as little as possible. An example of a shift in the CPI market basket is the percentage of family income spent on food, which has dropped from about 35% to about 20% from 1945 to 1985. Obviously, the Consumer Price Index should take this shift into account in determining the make-up and cost of a family's expenditures.

Formulas used in computing price indices follow. Formula 13–1 is used to compute a *simple price index*. Notice that the denominator is the sum of item costs during the base period. The numerator is the sum of costs of these same items in the current period. This ratio is then multiplied by 100 to produce an index.

$$\text{Simple Price Index: } \frac{\Sigma\ P_K}{\Sigma\ P_B}\ (100) \tag{13–1}$$

where K = current period
$\quad\ B$ = base period

Formula 13–2 shows the calculation for a *weighted index* such as the Consumer Price Index. It is first necessary to determine both the price and quantity of each item in the market basket before summing these costs. The denominator of Equation 13–2, thus, represents the total cost of all purchased items during the base period, and the numerator represents the cost of this same package during the current period. Since an index calculated using Equation 13–2 uses both prices and quantities, it is sometimes called a *value index*.

$$\text{Weighted Index: } \frac{\Sigma\ P_K Q_K}{\Sigma\ P_B Q_B}\ (100) \tag{13–2}$$

where K = current period
$\quad\ B$ = base period

A few values of the Consumer Price Index are shown in Table 13–3. The annual index values for 1981 and 1982 are presented along with monthly indices for the first six months of 1983. Notice that two separate indices have been formed. The first measures the market basket for wage earners and clerical workers whereas the second measures the cost of living for urban consumers. This distinction is a

Annual		**Monthly, 1983**					
1981	1982	JAN	FEB	MAR	APR	MAY	JUN
272.3	288.6	292.1	292.3	293.0	294.9	296.3	297.2

All items, wage earners and clerical workers, revised (CPI-W), 1967 = 100

Annual		**Monthly, 1983**					
1981	1982	JAN	FEB	MAR	APR	MAY	JUN
272.4	289.1	293.1	293.2	293.4	295.5	297.1	298.1

All items, all urban consumers (CPI-U), 1967 = 100

SOURCE: *Survey of Current Business,* July, 1983.

recent addition to the Consumer Price Index (beginning January, 1978), and reflects the increasing urbanization of America.

The index values shown in Table 13-3 were calculated just as the values for the hypothetical company discussed earlier were computed. The market basket of consumer goods was first defined, then a base period was chosen, and finally, the cost of the market basket was determined for each year or month. By dividing the current cost of the defined package of goods by the cost of the same package in the base period, the index for each period was determined.

As Table 13-3 shows, relative to the base period of 1967, there has been an inflationary movement of 288.6% through 1982 for wage earners and clerical workers. That is, the market basket of consumer goods of 1967 would cost 2.88 times as much in 1982. Likewise, the month-by-month movements of the cost of living can be monitored by watching the monthly indices, which are also shown in Table 13-3.

As noted in Table 13-3, the source for the information in that table is a publication called the *Survey of Current Business.* This publication can be found in libraries, government agencies, and businesses and contains many economic index numbers. Another good source of economic index numbers is the annual *Statistical Abstract of the United States,* which is also found in most libraries and businesses.

As mentioned, the Consumer Price Index is used to measure the inflationary movements of the United States' economy. Other commonly used price indices are the following:

Wholesale Price Index   This index is prepared by the Bureau of Labor Statistics and measures the costs of items in primary markets, where the first large volume purchases are made. It is closely watched to detect price changes in the American economy. Changes in this index are often followed by similar changes in the Consumer Price Index.

Industrial Production Index   The Federal Reserve Board calculates this index that measures the volume of U.S. industrial production including manufacturing, mining, and utilities.

Dow-Jones Industrial Average   The New York Stock Exchange calculates this index for each trading day. It measures the movement of 30 selected blue-chip stocks and is used as an indicator of stock market price levels.

Standard and Poor's Stock Index   This index reflects the prices of 425 individual stocks and is regarded by some as more indicative of the general level of stock market prices than the Dow-Jones Average because it involves many more stocks than does the Dow-Jones.

Quantity Indices

The price index is the most popular type of index currently being used. However, sometimes it is desired to follow the movement of quantities relative to a base period rather than monitor prices. The procedure for constructing a quantity index is similar to that used for a price index. First, a base period is selected, and the quantity or quantities of the items of interest are determined. Then, quantities of these same items are measured in subsequent periods and compared with the base value using a ratio. Equation 13–3 shows how these calculations are made.

$$\text{Quantity Index: } \frac{\Sigma \ Q_K}{\Sigma \ Q_B} (100) \tag{13–3}$$

where K = current period
B = base period

Notice from Equation 13–3 that the denominator of the ratio is the sum of those quantities considered to be relevant; these quantities are measured in the base period. The numerator of Equation 13–3 is the sum of these same item quantities in the current period. After this ratio has been multiplied by 100, the quantity index results.

    As an example, suppose a winery wishes to monitor the number of cases of wine shipped from its warehouse each month. Rather than use only the actual volume of cases shipped, the company decides to construct a quantity index. It chooses January, 1975 as the base month, then adds together the number of cases of each type of wine shipped for that month; this total is 749 cases. For the most recent month, November, 1984, the sum of all cases shipped is 2,246 cases. The quantity index for this month is then computed as follows:

$$\frac{2246}{749}\,(100)\,=\,299.87$$

The winery can now see that it is shipping almost three times as many cases in the current period as it did in the base period of January, 1975. Since the base period is now over nine years old, the winery might consider updating the base period to a more recent month; this would be especially true if the winery was in its early stages of development in January, 1975.

CHANGING THE BASE PERIOD

The government may someday wish to update the Consumer Price Index by moving the base period forward. Choosing a new base period would involve a great deal of thought, but once that decision is made, how would the index be recalculated?

Consider a company's cost-of-living index as shown in Table 13–1. Suppose the company wished to update its index by moving the base period forward from May, 1978 to January, 1979. The company's analyst decides that the choice of May, 1978 was a hasty one, based on a desire to begin the index at that time. In retrospect, the analyst believes that January, 1979 is a more normal period and wishes to

TABLE 13–4

Updating the base period

Month	Old Cost-of-Living Index	New Cost-of-Living Index
May, 1978	100.0	100.0 / 103.7 : 96.4
June	100.7	100.7 / 103.7 : 97.1
July	101.9	101.9 / 103.7 : 98.3
August	101.4	101.4 / 103.7 : 97.8
September	102.1	102.1 / 103.7 : 98.5
October	102.1	102.1 / 103.7 : 98.5
November	103.0	103.0 / 103.7 : 99.3
December	104.2	104.2 / 103.7 : 100.5
January, 1979	103.7	103.7 / 103.7 : 100.0
February	103.7	103.7 / 103.7 : 100.0
March	104.6	104.6 / 103.7 : 100.9
April	104.6	104.6 / 103.7 : 100.9
May	105.3	105.3 / 103.7 : 101.5
June	106.5	106.5 / 103.7 : 102.7
July	106.0	106.0 / 103.7 : 102.2
August	106.9	106.9 / 103.7 : 103.1

compare subsequent cost-of-living measurements against that base period.

Table 13–4 shows the cost-of-living indices, which were derived from Table 13–1, along with the updated index using January, 1979 as the base period. Notice that each new index is computed by dividing the old index by 103.7, which is the old index in the newly chosen base period. This, of course, results in an index of 100 for January, 1979, reflecting the index value for the new base month (the decimal is again moved two places to the right to form a percentage).

The company notes that although August, 1979 had an index of 106.9 using a base period of May, 1978, it now has an index of 103.1 when the new base, January, 1979, is used. The company will continue to monitor the cost of living in its community using the newly chosen base period.

CASE STUDY: THE CHENEY ELECTRONICS COMPANY

The Cheney Electronics Company assembles electronic test equipment and sells its products to many manufacturers around the country that need precision testing devices. Al Cameron, the vice-president of manufacturing, has been studying the cost trends of various materials and subcomponents purchased from suppliers and is concerned about the rising cost of one particular component, the cathode ray tubes used in Cheney's oscilloscopes.

Al notes that the average cost of these tubes was $128 in 1981, $137 in 1982, and $155 in mid-1983. He calls the vice-president of the supplying company to complain about this increase and is told

TABLE 13–5
Wholesale price index: producer prices, all commodities. 1967 = 100

1981: 293.4			1982: 299.3		
1982	June	299.3	1983	Jan	299.9
	July	300.4		Feb	300.9
	Aug	300.2		Mar	300.6
	Sept	299.3		Apr	300.8
	Oct	299.8		May	301.7
	Nov	300.3		June	302.5
	Dec	300.7		July	303.2

SOURCE: *Survey of Current Business*, August, 1983

that, "inflation has been killing us over here—the price increases are not out of line."

Since inflating costs are a problem at Cheney as well, Al concedes the point but decides to investigate the amount of inflation to determine whether the price increase for the cathode ray tubes is in line with national trends. He finds the Producer Price indices in a recent copy of the *Survey of Current Business* and records the data shown in Table 13-5.

Al decides that the 1981 and 1982 indices can be used to deflate the tube prices for those years so that the prices in constant dollars can be determined. He also decides that the July, 1983 index (303.2) can be used as the index to deflate the current price he is paying for the tubes. Al thinks that after he has deflated the prices of the tubes, he will have a strong case to argue for a price reduction if the trend of the tube prices in constant dollars is rising.

Questions
1. What are the deflated prices (prices in constant dollars) for the cathode ray tubes?
2. How appropriate is the use of the national producer price index in the deflating process?
3. If you were the supplier of the cathode ray tubes, what would be your best argument against Al Cameron's position regarding prices?

EXERCISES

1. Locate a recent copy of the *Survey of Current Business* in your library. Determine the current value of the two consumer price indices and the current value of the producer price index.

2. Locate the most recent copy of the *Statistical Abstract of the United States* in your library. Find two or three time series measured in dollars that you would like to analyze relative to a business area you are interested in. Indicate the general type of index number that would be useful in deflating these time series and indicate the advantages of doing so.

3. Indicate the circumstances under which each of the following statements could be true:
   a. "It would be best to deflate this dollar time-series before analyzing it further."
   b. "This time series should not be deflated. Let's analyze it using the original values."

4. The Ajax Company has recorded the following annual dollar volume over several years (in millions).

1977	14.8
1978	15.3
1979	13.7
1980	15.9
1981	17.4
1982	19.4

Prepare a series of index numbers to show the movement of its sales dollars. Use 1977 as the base year.

5. Refer to Exercise 4. In early 1983 Ajax management decides that using 1977 as the base period was a mistake because of the economic conditions affecting its business in that year. The company's analyst decides that 1979 would make a better base year. Recalculate the annual dollar sales index for Ajax using 1979 as the base year.

6. The following is the annual number of units sold for a manufacturer of rocket engines involved with the space program. Prepare a series of index numbers that can be used to monitor sales volume during this period. Use 1975 as the base period and then prepare the index numbers using 1983 as the base period.

1975	5
1976	8
1977	12
1978	20
1979	18
1980	25
1981	36
1982	30
1983	42

7. A company is preparing to enter into negotiations with a union representing its hourly workers. The company's analyst has assembled data on the average hourly wage paid per month over the past four-year period, as well as the consumer price index for each of these months. The company wishes to have an analysis of both the raw data and the deflated hourly wages in preparation for the negotiations. Explain why this would be a good idea.

8. Locate a recent copy of the *Survey of Current Business*. Find a time series, either annual or monthly, that is measured in dollars and is related to an area of interest. Now find an annual or monthly index number that would be appropriate in deflating your time series. Prepare a table showing both the raw data and the deflated data. Based on your understanding of the national economy during the period of measurement, choose an appropriate base period.

14

Time-Series Analysis

Where You Have Been   Regression analysis is perhaps the most commonly used quantitative technique in business, economics, and government. This technique involves the study of a variable of interest, called the dependent variable, by examining the related behavior of predictor, or independent, variables. In addition, you have studied the construction of index numbers, which are often used in the study of time series.

Where You Are Going   We now turn to another very popular technique that also examines the movements of a numerical variable of interest. In this case, the focus will be on measuring the periodic movements of this variable rather than seeking additional explanatory variables. Also, the variable being examined is measured over several successive time periods such as weeks, months, quarters, or years. Since the variable of interest is measured over time, the technique studied in this chapter is known as *time-series analysis*.

> Time-series analysis involves the study of a single numerical variable that is measured over several successive time periods.

TIME-SERIES DATA

Variables such as people's ages, company's accounts receivable, state's acreage, and company's current employee overtime hours are not appropriate for time-series analysis if they are measured at a single point in time. In contrast, a company's monthly sales volume, quarterly cash account balance, weekly overtime hours, and order backlog, or a state's monthly unemployment rate, annual budget deficit, or quarterly welfare payments are examples of variables that could be analyzed using

TABLE 14–1
Time-series
data format

Period Number	Variable (Y)
1	—
2	—
3	—
4	—
5	—
6	—
7	—
.	.
.	.
.	.

the techniques in this chapter because these variables are all measured each time period over many such periods.

In general, whenever a time-series analysis is undertaken, the data being analyzed will follow the format shown in Table 14-1.

DEFLATION AND RATES

Before analyzing a variable measured over time, two modifications in the data might be considered. First, whenever data are measured in dollars over time, the possibility of distortion due to inflation exists. For example, suppose a company wished to examine its monthly sales volume over several years; during this period of time, inflation has eroded the value of the dollar. Therefore, some of the increase in dollar volume that the company enjoyed would not have taken place if there had been no inflation. If the company fails to deflate its sales volume before the time-series analysis takes place, a misleading picture of the company's performance may result.

Dollar values can be deflated by dividing them by some appropriate index of inflation. The company might decide to use the national Consumer Price Index as a reasonable measure of the extent to which sales volume has been inflated; Chapter 13 discussed the make-up and use of this important index. By measuring this index for each month of sales-volume data and dividing these values into the sales figures, a time series free of inflation results. The analysis performed on these data may then present a better picture of the company's performance over the measured period of time.

The national Consumer Price Index (CPI), as well as other indices, are given a value of 100 in the base period. Then, each subsequent time period relates the dollar value of the same market basket of goods to this base of 100. For example, if a particular cost index had a base period of January, 1978 and is currently at a level of 153, the goods that were priced out in January of 1978 would now cost 153% of what they cost in that period. In other words, there has been an inflationary increase of 53% since the base period.

Suppose that instead of using the CPI to deflate the time series, the company decides to use a regional price index because its operations are confined solely to that region. This regional index has a base period of June, 1975; values of this index in the months of interest are shown in Table 14-2. Also appearing in Table 14-2 are the company's monthly sales levels along with the deflated sales volumes. These latter values were found by dividing each actual dollar value by the monthly cost index, after moving the decimal point two places to the left.

TABLE 14–2
Deflating dollar
values

Month	Sales Volume (in Thousands of Dollars)	Cost-of-Living Index	Deflated Sales Volume
Jan	348	203	171.4*
Feb	373	212	175.9
Mar	403	215	187.4
Apr	397	220	180.5
May	458	222	206.3
Jun	425	230	184.8
Jul	347	231	150.2
Aug	450	231	194.8
Sep	475	235	202.1
Oct	390	239	163.2
Nov	475	240	197.9
Dec	526	242	217.4

$$\frac{*348}{2.03} = 171.4$$

A second modification in a time-series analysis should be considered whenever the series is strongly tied to a national or regional population level. For example, since the population of the United States constantly increases, there are more cars, dishwashers, houses, and clothes being sold; there are more marriages, divorces, and children; there are more pizzas, hamburgers, and gallons of milk consumed; there are more employed people and more unemployed people.

Since the absolute values of almost all population-based time series are increasing, it is often of greater interest to examine the changes in a variable relative to the population base. In other words, the original time-series values should be divided by the population size in hundreds, thousands, or millions before the data are analyzed. This is commonly done for many time-series analyses. We almost always hear about the unemployment rate rather than the number of unemployed persons. The birth rate, divorce rate, and average number of children per family are also monitored by various groups rather than monitoring the absolute numbers for these important variables.

For example, suppose a small rural county is interested in studying the number of marriage applications issued in the county over the past several years. The data shown in the second column of Table 14–3 are collected. However, county officials realize that the county has experienced some growth over the ten years of the study, and they decide to measure the county population as well. By dividing the number of marriage licenses each year by the average population for

TABLE 14–3
Hypothetical marriage
rate calculations

Year	Number of Marriage Licenses	Population of County	Marriages per Hundred Population
1	129	5223	24.7*
2	135	5305	25.4
3	110	5429	20.3
4	143	5435	26.3
5	128	5673	22.6
6	135	5785	23.3
7	153	6825	22.4
8	142	7153	19.9
9	175	7240	24.2
10	201	8519	23.6

$$*\frac{129}{5.223} = 24.7$$

that year, the marriage rate per hundred residents is determined; these values are shown in the last column of Table 14–3. County officials will subject this column to a time-series analysis.

In summary, two factors should be considered before any time-series data are analyzed. First, a time series that is in dollars might first be deflated so that the analysis is conducted in constant dollars. Second, a time series that is population based may be converted to a rate so that a clearer picture of the movement of the variable can be examined.

DECOMPOSITION

After adjustments have been made to the time-series data, the next step is to *decompose* the series into its individual components. Depending on the time period measurements of the data (annual, quarterly, monthly, and so forth), there can be as many as four major components of the series that can be isolated and analyzed.

> The decomposition of a time series consists of isolating the individual components of the series.

For a time series measured on an annual basis, two types of components are usually analyzed: *trend* and *cyclical*. If the time series is measured on smaller time intervals such as quarters or months, two additional types of components can be isolated: *seasonal* and *irregular*. The following sections discuss these four components.

Trend

The basic long-term movement of a time series is known as the *trend* of that series. The trend may either be a straight line, called a linear trend, or a curved line. In this chapter the linear case is considered because it is the most commonly used form of trend line.

> The trend of a time series is the long-term movement of the series during the time of measurement.

To examine the trend component of a time series, consider the time-series data on automobile sales shown in Table 14–4. These data are obviously measured on an annual basis; thus, the decomposition of this series will reveal two components, trend and cyclical.

The trend component is analyzed by computing the equation of the straight line that best fits the data points. The method of least squares is used for this purpose, which is the same procedure that was used to compute a regression equation. For the data presented in Table 14–4, the dependent variable will be the actual time-series values shown in the table, and the independent (or predictor) variable will be the period number. Thus, for 1968, the period number is 1, for 1969 it is 2, and for 1980 it is 13. A scatter diagram of these data points using the year number as the X variable appears in Figure 14–1.

Based on the scatter diagram shown in Figure 14-1, it can be reasonably assumed that a linear trend line is appropriate for the historical data. If this had not been the case, more advanced procedures involving curved trend lines would be used. The method of least squares is now used to produce values for both the Y-intercept and the equation slope. The following equations, the same ones used in an earlier chapter, are used:

TABLE 14–4
Passenger car retail sales (1000s) total (domestic + imports)

1968	9656	1975	8640
1969	9583	1976	10,110
1970	8405	1977	11,185
1971	10,250	1978	11,312
1972	10,950	1979	10,671
1973	11,439	1980	8979
1974	8867		

SOURCE: *Statistical Abstract of the United States, 1981.*

FIGURE 14–1
Scatter diagram: pas-
senger car retail sales

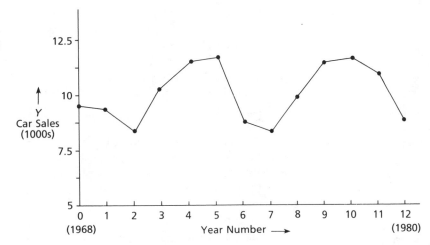

$$b = \frac{n\Sigma XY - \Sigma X \Sigma Y}{n\Sigma X^2 - (\Sigma X)^2} \qquad \textbf{(14–1)}$$

$$a = \frac{\Sigma Y - b\Sigma X}{n} \qquad \textbf{(14–2)}$$

Since the calculation of the slope and intercept using Equations 14–1 and 14–2 involves a considerable amount of arithmetic, these values are almost always calculated using a prewritten time-series computer program. Computer programs are usually used when the sample size is large and when the seasonal and irregular components are analyzed, as they are for monthly and quarterly data.

A time-series computer program that uses the least-squares procedure can compute the best-fit trend equation for the data shown in Table 14–4. Equation 14–3 is the result.

$$Y = 9630 + 62.3\,X \qquad \textbf{(14–3)}$$

The trend equation shown in Equation 14–3 is generally used for two purposes. First, the slope almost always has a useful interpretation. As is true for any equation of a straight line, the slope represents the average amount by which Y changes when X increases by one. For a time series, a unit increase in X represents the passage of one time period. For the data summarized by Equation 14–3, a unit increase in X means one year has passed. Thus, the following statement can be made, if the slope of the trend equation is 62.3: On the average, the time series is increasing at the rate of 62.3 units per year. Since Y is measured in thousands of cars, this means an average annual increase of 62,300 cars.

Such a statement summarizes the long-term movement of the time series over the time span of measurement and may help management to understand the time series better. The same interpretation of slope will be made later in this chapter when the time series being examined is a monthly time series. In that case, the slope of the trend equation is the average amount by which the series changes with each passing month.

The second common use of the trend equation is for trend-forecasting purposes. A total of 13 annual periods were used as original data. Now, if higher values of X are placed into the trend equation, the trend-line values for these future periods can be calculated. The computer program used to analyze the data presented in Table 14–3 was programmed to make such calculations for ten additional periods. The result is the computer printout shown in Table 14–5.

The trend-line values forecasted by the computer program were calculated by placing increasing values of X into the trend equation (note that the trend equation is printed by the computer program at

TABLE 14–5
Time-series computer
output—annual data

```
       PROGRAM TIMSER FOR ANNUAL DATA TIME SERIES

   TREND ANALYSIS AND CYCLICAL RESULTS(1)
          ----CURRENT AND FORECAST----

   PERIOD                DATA        REGRESSION      CYCLICAL
   1968               9656.00         9630.03         100.27
   1969               9583.00         9692.30          98.87
   1970               8405.00         9754.56          86.16
   1971              10250.00         9816.83         104.41
   1972              10950.00         9879.09         110.84
   1973              11439.00         9941.35         115.06
   1974               8867.00        10003.62          88.64
   1975               8640.00        10065.88          85.83
   1976              10110.00        10128.14          99.82
   1977              11185.00        10190.41         109.76
   1978              11312.00        10252.67         110.33
   1979              10671.00        10314.94         103.45
   1980               8979.00        10377.20          86.53
   1981                              10439.46
   1982                              10501.73
   1983                              10563.99
   1984                              10626.25
   1985                              10688.52
   1986                              10750.78
   1987                              10813.04
   1988                              10875.31
   1989                              10937.57
   1990                              10999.84

   TREND FORECAST = 9630.034180 + 62.263737 * X PERIOD
```

the end of the output shown in Table 14–5). The last forecasted value, for instance, was calculated as follows:

$$Y = 9630 + 62.3X$$

$$Y = 9630 + 62.3 \ (22)$$

$$Y = 11,000 \ (\text{approximately, due to rounding errors})$$

Note that for 1990, X = 22 because this program numbers the first period 0, not 1.

Cyclical

Notice from Table 14–5 that another column is calculated and printed by the time-series computer program. This column contains the cyclical indicators and indicates the extent to which the time series is affected by the upward and downward swings of the economy.

> The cyclical component in a time series indicates the extent to which the series responds to the upward and downward movements of the economy.

The cyclical indicators shown in the last column of Table 14–5 were calculated by dividing each original data point (Y value) by the computed trend-line value for the time period. Thus, the first cyclical value in Table 14–5 was computed as follows:

$$\frac{Y}{T} = \frac{9656}{9630.03} = 1.0027 \longrightarrow 100.27$$

(decimal moved
to obtain a
percent)

Because of the way the cyclical indicators are calculated, they measure the extent to which each data point is either above or below the trend line. In effect, the trend factor has been removed so that the movement around the trend line can be examined.

When the cyclical indictor column is examined, the following two basic questions arise:

1. To what extent does this time series follow a cyclical pattern? Some time series are not responsive to the ups and downs of the economy; an example might be the annual sales of milk. In general, when times are good people do not buy more milk and when times are bad they do not cut down on milk consumption. However, the sales of jewelry products is probably very sen-

sitive to the state of the economy. In good times such luxury products sell rather well whereas in poor economic times such products tend to be eliminated from people's budgets.

2. If there is a cyclical effect, how does it align with the national business cycle? This question can be answered by observing the peaks and valleys of the time series under study and by comparing these results with the peaks and valleys of several indicators of the national economy. The time series under study might align rather well with the economy, or it might lead or lag the economic condition of the nation or region. Table 14–6 lists a number of leading, coincident, and lagging economic indicators that are generally accepted by economists. These can be used to determine the position of the studied time series, relative to the swings of the United States economy.

The extent to which the time series analyzed in Table 14–5 follows a cyclical pattern can now be determined. Do the values shown in the last column of Table 14–5 indicate a cycle? It appears that the answer is yes: the sales of automobiles in this country generally seem to follow a three-year cycle during the period 1968 to 1980. The swings are pronounced but not dramatic. During the late 1960s sales were somewhat down; during the early 1970s they were up, followed in the mid-1970s by a somewhat depressed car market; in the late 1970s sales were again above the long-term trend line; finally, the cycle indicator for 1980 indicates that sales are again on the downturn.

Based upon this cycle history, 1981 and 1982 might be expected to be rather poor years for automobiles, followed by a three-year period of prosperity. Such a forecast, of course, assumes that the future will behave exactly like the past. Although this will probably not be precisely true, an educated guess based on a study of past trend and cyclical factors will almost always produce a forecast that is more accurate than a forecast based on no detailed analysis of the past.

Now that a moderate but definite cycle has been observed in the time series, the next step is to determine whether the observed cycle aligns with the national business cycle. The coincident indicators presented in Table 14–6 would be used for this purpose. If several of these indicators moved in approximately the same fashion as the cycle indicators shown in Table 14–5, it could be concluded that automobile sales are moderately sensitive to the ups and downs of the national economy.

It is now possible to make a forecast of automobile sales using both the trend and cyclical factors. What is the forecast for sales in 1982 based on the time-series data that have been analyzed? First, the trend line is estimated for that year. This can be done manually by placing the correct X value (year number) into the trend equation, or

TABLE 14–6
Economic indicators

Leading Indicators:
Average hourly workweek, production workers, manufacturing
Average weekly initial claims, state unemployment insurance
Index of net business formation
New orders, durable goods industries
Contracts and orders, plant and equipment
Index of new building permits, private housing units
Change in book value, manufacturing and trade inventories
Index of industrial materials prices
Index of stock prices, 500 common stocks
Corporate profits after taxes (quarterly)
Index: ratio, price to unit labor cost, manufacturing
Change in consumer installment debt

Roughly Coincident Indicators:
GNP in current dollars
GNP in 1958 dollars
Index of industrial production
Personal income
Manufacturing and trade sales
Sales of retail stores
Employees on nonagricultural payrolls
Unemployment rate, total

Lagging Indicators:
Unemployment rate, persons unemployed 15 weeks or over
Business expenditures, new plant and equipment
Book value, manufacturing and trade inventories
Index of labor cost per unit of output in manufacturing
Commercial and industrial loans outstanding in large commercial banks
Bank rates on short-term business loans

SOURCE: U.S. Department of Commerce.

the computer can be instructed to make the calculation. The regression column in Table 14–5 shows the result of ten such calculations. The trend-line forecast for 1982 is 10,501.73.

The cycle indicator for 1982 must now be estimated. If the patterns of history are followed in the future, 1982 will be the low point in the three-year down portion of the cycle. In 1975, the last low point, the cycle indicator was 85.83 so a 1982 cycle value of 85 might be estimated. This value is, of course, a judgement; other analysts might come up with different values or might modify the estimate based on the computer printout with knowledge of current economic conditions and expert projections. But using a cycle indicator of 85, the final annual forecast for 1982 is as follows:

$$Y = 10,501.73 \ (.85) = 8926.47 \text{ thousand cars}$$

$$Y = 8,926,470 \text{ cars}$$

Note that the decimal point should be moved two places to the left before the cyclical indicator is used.

Seasonal

When data are measured on an annual basis, only two types of time-series components are isolated and examined during the decomposition process: trend and cyclical. However, when the series is measured in shorter time periods such as quarters or months, seasonal and irregular components can be isolated and examined as well. Fluctuations that occur during certain periods of a year on a recurring basis are known as the *seasonal* effect.

> The seasonal component of a time series measures variation that regularly occurs each time period of the year.

TABLE 14–7
Total production of passenger cars, trucks, and buses (factory sales) in thousands

	1976	1977	1978	1979	1980	1981
Jan	856	935	898	1049	678	579
Feb	914	937	943	1006	795	610
Mar	1110	1288	1250	1237	818	786
Apr	1057	1104	189	1032	701	806
May	1042	1158	1256	1250	627	829
Jun	1141	1268	241	1110	647	892
Jul	820	944	861	806	538	639
Aug	768	780	808	600	382	431
Sep	883	1044	1043	828	662	655
Oct	899	1194	1260	1037	860	685
Nov	1009	1045	1173	837	715	548
Dec	976	942	949	660	638	497

SOURCE: *Standard and Poor's Trade and Securities Statistics*

To examine the seasonal effect for actual time-series data, consider the date shown in Table 14–7; notice that automobile sales have been measured for each month during a six-year period.

The task is to decompose this time series and examine all four components. First, a least-squares trend line will be fitted to the data so that the trend during the six-year period can be examined. As was the case with annual data, the slope of this trend line represents the average amount by which car sales change with each passing month. Table 14–8 presents the entire computer output for the data shown in Table 14–7; the last line printed gives the following trend equation:

$$Y = 1085.5 - 6.14X$$

The trend equation for the monthly data suggests that during the period for which data have been gathered, car sales went down on the average of 6140 units per month (since the trend-line slope is -6.14 in thousands of cars). This trend line should not be used as a long-term projection of automobile sales many years into the future because such a forecast would depend on too little historical data. If a long-term forecast is desired, several years of annual data should be gathered and used to forecast the future as was done in the previous chapter section. However, before the short-term trend equation is used to forecast the time series on a short-term basis, the other components of the monthly time series should be analyzed.

Next, the computer's analysis of the seasonal component in the time series is examined. The computer analysis in Table 14–8 shows the seasonal indices in the last column. Since these values add up to 1200, the average value in this column is 100, or 100%. Thus, these seasonal indices give each month's position relative to an average month for the measured period. For example, based on the monthly data collected, January tends to be 92.1% of the average month, February is 95.8% of the average month, and so forth. The lowest month for car sales is August (71.5) and the highest is October (120.8), followed by May (116.4).

The seasonal indices thus present useful information to management regarding the time-series variable of interest since these indices show the month-by-month variations in the series that tend to occur each year. This information is used in a variety of ways by management; for example, management might wish to smooth out the seasonal effects by offering major sales during slow months, increasing the staff with temporary help during busy months, and so forth.

In computing the seasonal indices shown in Table 14–8, a series of twelve-month averages of the time series values is first computed and centered on each time series value. Each monthly value is then

TABLE 14-8
Time-series analysis of monthly data—car sales

MONTH	1976	1977	1978	1979	1980	1981	1982	MO. MEAN	MEAN *0.977189
JAN		92.67	100.86	98.73	91.42	83.23		94.27	92.1
FEB		92.35	106.18	95.67	110.20	86.91		98.07	95.8
MAR		126.05	140.57	119.64	115.96	111.71		120.55	117.8
APR		106.07	21.19	101.60	101.43	115.80		103.04	100.7
MAY		109.81	139.56	125.96	92.39	121.59		119.12	116.4
JUN		120.23	26.61	114.86	96.18	133.34		110.42	107.9
JUL	85.46	89.76	94.39	85.85	80.58			87.02	85.0
AUG	79.69	74.26	87.72	65.60	58.25			73.18	71.5
SEP	90.83	99.52	112.98	93.20	102.36			98.36	96.1
OCT	91.59	118.29	131.55	120.99	132.35			123.61	120.8
NOV	102.09	107.14	118.17	102.40	107.91			105.82	103.4
DEC	97.75	100.57	92.26	85.48	93.66			94.56	92.4
								1228.01	1200.0

TIME SERIES ANALYSIS--TREND, SEASONAL, CYCLICAL, AND IRREGULAR
----CURRENT AND FORECAST----

PERIOD	DATA Y	REGRESSION T	SEAS. ADJ. TCI	CI	C	I
1976 JAN	856.00	1085.52	929.21	85.60	88.90	98.76
FEB	914.00	1079.38	953.77	88.36	91.83	107.13
MAR	1110.00	1073.24	942.27	87.80	92.55	91.17
APR	1057.00	1067.09	1049.81	98.38	95.59	104.87
MAY	1042.00	1060.95	895.19	84.38	93.65	98.19
JUN	1141.00	1054.81	1057.40	100.25	91.22	112.93
JUL	820.00	1048.66	964.30	91.95	90.23	98.24
AUG	768.00	1042.52	1073.95	103.02	92.59	78.02
SEP	883.00	1036.38	918.69	88.64	92.05	103.51
OCT	899.00	1030.23	744.27	72.24	93.77	110.67
NOV	1009.00	1024.09	975.78	95.28		
DEC	976.00	1017.95	1056.29	103.77		

1977

Month						
1977 JAN	99.13	101.20	100.31	1014.97	1011.80	935.00
FEB	93.29	104.22	97.23	977.77	1005.66	937.00
MAR	105.57	103.62	109.39	1093.38	999.52	1288.00
APR	102.67	107.51	110.38	1096.49	993.37	1104.00
MAY	90.92	110.84	100.77	994.84	987.23	1158.00
JUN	107.45	111.48	119.78	1175.10	981.08	1268.00
JUL	101.70	111.97	113.86	1110.12	974.94	944.00
AUG	100.09	112.48	112.59	1090.73	968.90	780.00
SEP	102.77	109.79	112.83	1086.19	962.65	1044.00
OCT	95.15	108.61	103.34	988.49	956.51	1194.00
NOV	99.49	106.88	106.34	1010.59	950.37	1045.00
DEC	102.41	105.43	107.97	1019.49	944.22	942.00

1978

Month						
1978 JAN	96.50	107.69	103.91	974.80	938.08	898.00
FEB	116.67	90.50	105.59	984.03	931.94	943.00
MAR	123.87	92.53	114.62	1061.12	925.79	1250.00
APR	26.62	76.67	20.41	187.71	919.65	189.00
MAY	151.39	78.02	118.12	1079.03	913.51	1256.00
JUN	30.64	80.35	24.61	223.34	907.36	
JUL	111.59	100.68	112.35	1012.51	901.22	861.00
AUG	125.37	100.69	126.23	1129.89	895.08	808.00
SEP	100.35	121.64	122.07	1085.15	888.93	1043.00
OCT	96.25	122.77	118.16	1043.13	882.79	1260.00
NOV	104.46	123.87	129.40	1134.38	876.65	1173.00
DEC	95.21	123.92	117.99	1027.07	870.50	949.00

1979

Month						
1979 JAN	105.45	124.94	131.74	1138.72	864.36	1049.00
FEB	99.21	123.29	122.32	1049.77	858.22	1006.00
MAR	98.38	125.27	123.24	1050.08	852.07	1237.00
APR	98.03	123.60	127.17	1073.88	845.93	1032.00
MAY	104.78	122.04	123.40	1028.67	839.79	1110.00
JUN	104.73	117.83	114.54	947.83	833.64	806.00
JUL	99.84	114.73	102.15	839.03	827.50	600.00
AUG	92.55	110.37	105.67	861.46	821.35	828.00
SEP	99.83	105.86	106.81	858.51	815.21	1037.00
OCT	105.19	105.88	100.81	809.44	809.07	837.00
NOV	101.76	100.88	89.65	714.30	802.92	660.00
DEC	90.48	99.08			796.78	

TABLE 14-8, *continued*

PERIOD	DATA Y	REGRESSION T	SEAS. ADJ. TCI	CI	C	I
1980 JAN	678.00	790.64	735.99	93.09	95.70	97.27
FEB	795.00	784.49	829.59	105.75	93.57	113.01
MAR	818.00	778.35	694.40	89.21	89.71	99.45
APR	701.00	772.21	696.23	90.16	86.87	103.79
MAY	627.00	766.06	538.66	70.31	82.51	85.22
JUN	647.00	759.92	599.60	78.90	78.95	99.94
JUL	538.00	753.78	632.67	83.93	79.50	105.58
AUG	382.00	747.63	534.18	71.45	79.80	84.26
SEP	662.00	741.49	688.75	92.89	84.80	105.57
OCT	860.00	735.35	711.98	96.82	87.98	107.23
NOV	715.00	729.20	691.46	94.82	90.30	101.37
DEC	638.00	723.06	690.49	95.49	93.54	102.82
1981 JAN	579.00	716.92	628.52	87.67	92.45	94.83
FEB	610.00	710.77	636.54	89.56	96.40	92.90
MAR	786.00	704.63	667.23	94.69	97.88	96.74
APR	806.00	698.49	800.52	114.61	104.44	109.74
MAY	829.00	692.34	712.20	102.87	108.63	94.70
JUN	892.00	686.20	826.65	120.47	107.57	111.99
JUL	639.00	680.06	751.44	110.50	105.06	105.17
AUG	431.00	673.91	602.70	89.43	101.63	105.17
SEP	655.00	667.77	681.47	102.05	93.71	108.90
OCT	685.00	661.62	567.10	85.71	88.18	97.21
NOV	548.00	655.48	529.96	80.85		
DEC	497.00	649.34	537.89	82.84		
1982 JAN		643.19				
FEB		637.05				
MAR		630.91				
APR		624.76				
MAY		618.62				
JUN		612.48				
JUL		606.33				
AUG		600.19				
SEP		594.05				
OCT		587.90				
NOV		581.76				
DEC		575.62				

TREND FORECAST = 1085.523560 + -6.143460 * X PERIOD

300

compared with the twelve-month average for the year that is centered on it. By dividing each monthly time-series value by its annual average, the position of that month relative to its annual average is computed. These are the values that appear in the body of the seasonal table of Table 14–8.

Table 14–9 is an example of seasonal index calculations and shows the first thirteen Y values in the time series. The first twelve data values are added, giving a sum of 11,475. This total is then divided by 12 to produce a twelve-month average of 956.25. Unfortunately, since there are an even number of data periods (12), this average is centered at the end of a month rather than in the middle of a month. Since there are six whole months on each side of the center of the Y values that have been averaged, the average of 956.25 is actually centered on the end of June/beginning of July. Since it is desirable to compare each month with an average centered in the middle of the month, a solution to this minor problem must be found.

If the next value in the twelve-month moving average is found, these two values can be averaged to yield an average that is centered in the middle of July, 1976. Table 14–9 shows that a second twelve-month average is found by dropping January, 1976 and picking up January, 1977. The total of these twelve new months is 11,554, as shown. Dividing this sum by 12 produces a new average of 962.83. Now there are two average values of Y—one is centered on the first of July and the other is centered on the end of July. If these two values are

TABLE 14–9
Monthly moving averages

Year	Month	Y	12-month Sum	12-month Average	Average of Two Indices	Seasonal Index
1976	JAN	856				
	FEB	914				
	MAR	1110				
	APR	1057				
	MAY	1042				
	JUN	1141 ⟶	11,475 ⟶	956.25 ⎫	959.54	$\dfrac{820}{959.54}(100) = 85.46$
	JUL	820 ⟶	11,554 ⟶	962.83 ⎭		
	AUG	768				
	SEP	883				
	OCT	899				
	NOV	1009				
	DEC	976				
1977	JAN	935				

averaged, the resulting average value of Y will be centered in the middle of July. This is the desired result; as shown in Table 14–9, this average value is 959.54.

The actual value of Y for July can now be compared with the average value of Y during the twelve-month period centered on that month. This is shown in the last column of Table 14–9. July's Y value (820) is divided by the average for the twelve-month period centered on July (959.54), producing a July, 1976 seasonal index of 85.46 (because the decimal was moved two places to the right). Table 14–8 shows this index opposite July for the year 1976.

This same procedure is used for the remaining July data values. The resulting five July seasonal indicators are averaged after removing the highest and lowest indices (to prevent distortions). Therefore, the modified monthly mean is equal to 87.02 for July. The same procedure is then followed for each of the other eleven months. Finally, since the sum of the twelve indices does not equal precisely 1200, each index is reduced slightly (multiplied by 1200/1228.01 = .977189) so that the total is exactly 1200. These values appear in the last column of Table 14–8 and constitute the monthly seasonal indices.

Some time series measured on a monthly basis show a moderate seasonal effect such as the car sales data. Other time series, such as coffee sales, would probably show very little seasonal effect. That is, people probably consume about the same amount of coffee every month of the year with the possible exception of the warm summer months. A time series that probably shows a most dramatic seasonal effect is sales of ski equipment. This series may drop to almost 0 in the summer months and soar to a seasonal index of 200 or more during the winter months.

The second portion of the computer printout shown in Table 14–8 is considered next. The first column of this printout shows the original data, the Y values, and the second column shows the trend-line values for each. The latter values were computed by placing ever increasing values of X (the month number) into the trend equation and solving for Y. Notice that these values are printed for twelve months beyond the end of the actual data points. This was done by instructing the computer to continue solving for Y using twelve more values for X, each incremented by one.

The next column of Table 14–8 is called seasonally adjusted data. These represent the values for Y had there been no seasonal effect in the data. Each value is computed by dividing the actual Y value for that month by the seasonal index (after the decimal point has been moved two places to the left). For example, the first seasonally adjusted data value is computed as follows:

$$\cdot \ \frac{856}{.921} = 929$$

Notice that the seasonally adjusted data column is also headed *TCI*. This implies that although the trend, cycle, and irregular effects still remain, the seasonal effect has been removed. In fact, since each month's data value is divided by the monthly index for that month, low data values are raised and high values are reduced. Thus, the data points would have appeared as shown in the TCI column if no seasonal effect occurred.

Next, each seasonally adjusted data value is divided by the trend-line value for that month. This removes the trend from the data because each data point is shown relative to the trend line; the slope of the trend line is, thus, no longer apparent. For the first January, this value is computed as follows:

$$\frac{929.21}{1085.52} = .856 \quad \text{(or 85.6\%)}$$

In Table 14–8, the column headed *CI* implies that both the seasonal and trend effects have been removed; however, the times series may show a cyclical or irregular pattern. The *CI* column should be scanned to determine whether the time series is cycling. Since these values represent the seasonally adjusted monthly data values relative to the trend line, a cycle will be evident if the data tend to fall above the trend for many successive months and then below the trend for many successive months. However, as this column suggests, the data values in the *CI* column are bumpy; that is, the extent of the cyclical pattern in the data is obscured by the irregular effect.

The irregularities can be smoothed out by averaging the *CI* values: a five-month moving average is chosen for this purpose. The choice of five months for the averaging process is arbitrary although it provides the desired smoothing effect and is used by many computer programs; a three-month moving average is also sometimes used. The following first five *CI* values are averaged, producing a smoothed value of 88.90 in the *C* column:

$$\left.\begin{array}{l} 85.60 \\ 88.36 \\ 87.80 \\ 98.38 \\ 84.38 \end{array}\right\} \quad 88.90$$

Notice that the value 88.90 is opposite March, 1976, not January. This is because March is the first month for which a five-month average can be computed; in January it was not possible to go back two months for the averaging process. Since the irregularities have been smoothed from the *CI* values by this averaging process, the column heading *C* suggests that only the presence of a cyclical effect remains in the data values.

Just as with the annual data examined earlier, it is now possible to determine whether the monthly data values are sensitive to the business cycle. Table 14–8 suggests that car sales do follow a cycle that begins at a low point in early 1976, cycles several times, and ends at a low point near the end of 1981.

Irregular

The final factor to be analyzed in a monthly or quarterly time series is its *irregular* effect. This is the component that remains in the series when the other three (trend, cyclical, and seasonal) are removed.

The irregular component of a time series is a series of movements exhibited by the data values that is not due to trend, cyclical, or seasonal factors.

The computer program that was used to analyze monthly automobile sales evaluates the irregular component as shown in the *I* column of Table 14–8. These values are computed by dividing each month's *CI* value by its *C* value. For example, the first value in the *I* column is calculated as follows:

$$\frac{87.80}{88.90} = .9876 \quad (\text{or } 98.76\%)$$

The reasoning for this arithmetic follows. For the first month, March, 1976, the average value during the five-month period centered on that month is 88.90, the *C* value. How does the month of March compare with this five-month average? The March *CI* value is 87.80, which is slightly below the average of the five-month period it is in. In fact, it is 98.76% of the five-month average. Since this slightly below average value is not due to trend (which has been removed), to the seasonal effect (which has also been removed), or to the cyclical effect (since that month's *CI* value is being compared to the five-month average of *CI* values), it must be due to other factors. Other factors that cause a time series to vary after *T*, *C*, and *S* have been removed are known as the irregular component of the series.

There are generally two uses for the *I* column. First, the following question can be addressed: how irregular is this time series? In the case of the data analyzed in Table 14–8, it might be concluded that car sales are irregular from month to month. Although many months are steady (that is, the *I* values are close to 100), some disruptive factors in the economy cause irregularly high or low sales levels during other months.

Some time series will exhibit *I* values that are all close to 100 and are very dependable because once the trend, cyclical, and seasonal factors have been identified and analyzed, very little variability in the series remains. Other series show extreme irregularities and are only partially understood after the three major components *(T, C,* and *S)* have been analyzed.

The second possible use of the *I* column is to find explanations for strong irregular indices. For example, April of 1978 shows an extremely low *I* value (26.62). This low value in the *I* column was not due to any of the other three major components of the series *(T, C,* or *S)* because those factors have all been removed. Rather, some other factor caused the apparent low factory sales of cars in that month. Depending on the purpose of analyzing these data, it may be worthwhile to examine the factors that occurred in that month to determine if an explanation for the low *I* value is possible. If so, this kind of analysis may offer insights to management regarding future conditions that will cause unusually low sales levels.

Summary of Computer-Analyzed Time-Series Analysis

The computer program used in this chapter to demonstrate the decomposition of time series is typical of prewritten time-series analysis programs for various computer installations. The output format may differ from program to program, but the analysis is basically the same for all such programs. Because of the very large amount of arithmetic necessary in a time-series analysis even if the number of time periods is small, a computer program is a necessity for an analysis. Time-series programs are commonly available on most computer systems or can easily be written.

Such programs can be summarized by reviewing the specific steps taken by the computer program used in this chapter for a time-series analysis of car sales. When the time-series data are measured on an annual basis, the following calculations are performed:

1. A least-squares trend line is fitted to the data points. The slope of this line indicates the average amount by which the series

changes with each passing year. Extensions of this trend line into the future provide long-term trend forecasts for the series.

2. Each annual Y value is divided by the computed trend-line value for that year. The result shows the position of each year relative to the trend line; such values are called cyclical relatives and enable the researcher to look for a cycle through the data.

When the time series is measured on a quarterly or monthly basis the following analysis takes place:

1. A least-squares trend line is fitted to the data. The slope of this line shows the average quarterly or monthly change in the series; by extending this line into the future, short-term trend forecasts can be made.

2. Seasonal indices are computed for each quarter or month. For monthly data, a twelve-month average of the series is computed around each month of the data, and the actual data value is compared with this average. This is done for each January, each February, and so forth. The highest and lowest seasonal indices for January are removed, and the remaining values are averaged. The same is done for each of the other eleven months. These seasonal indices are then increased or decreased slightly by multiplying each by the ratio of 1200 over their sum. This adjusts the indices so their total is exactly 1200. If quarterly data are analyzed, the process is the same except that four periods are used in the averaging process instead of twelve.

3. Each data value is divided by its seasonal index. The result is known as seasonally adjusted data.

4. Each seasonally adjusted data value is divided by the computed trend value for that time period. The result is data values from which both the seasonal and trend components have been removed.

5. These CI values are smoothed by computing five-month moving averages. Since this smoothing process tends to remove the irregular effect, the result is called the cyclical effect. The extent and timing of the cycle, if any, can then be observed and compared with the national or a regional business cycle.

6. Each period's CI value is divided by its C value. This measures the extent to which each particular month is different from the average of the five-month period around it. These values indicate the extent of the series' irregular effect; investigating

specific high and low points may provide insights into the series.

FORECASTING

Long-term Forecasting

Long-term trend forecasts are made by extending the annual time-series trend line into the future; these values are calculated by placing larger and larger X values into the trend equation. For forecasts of five or more years into the future, such trend-line extensions constitute the entire forecast because it would be difficult to anticipate business cycle effects more than a few years into the future.

For somewhat shorter long-term forecasts, up to five years, it may also be possible to predict the cyclical effect. Examination of the cyclical indicators provided by the computer output along with any current economic forecasts by experts help companies to form judgements about the state of the economy during the forecast period. Earlier in this chapter such a judgement was made, resulting in a 1982 car forecast of approximately 8,926,000 cars. This forecast combined both the trend component observed in the historical data and a prediction of the cyclical effect for that year.

Short-term Forecasting

Short-term forecasts are made using the same process that was used for long-term forecasts except that all four components are used in the process and the forecast is based on either quarterly or monthly data. Suppose, for example, an analyst wished to forecast car sales for May of 1982 based on the monthly time-series analysis shown in Table 14–8. First, the trend line through these data is extended five periods into the future. The result is a trend projection of 618.62 as shown near the end of Table 14–8.

Next, this value is adjusted upward because the value for May is high and the seasonal index is 116.4, as shown in Table 14–8. The result is a forecast made from trend and seasonal time-series components.

$$Y = (618.62)(1.164) = 720.07$$

Next, the position of the business cycle in the forecast period is determined by observing the C column of the computer output. This is a matter of judgement and may involve not only the computer output but also expert opinions about the future path of the economy. From

Table 14–8 it appears that a downturn in the economy is beginning near the end of 1981 so the analyst might predict a cyclical relative of 80 for May of 1982. The forecast for May can now be computed as follows:

$$Y = (618.62)(1.164)(.80) = 576.06$$

Finally, the irregular effect is predicted. If unusual occurrences are anticipated for May, 1982, the forecast will be adjusted based on the analyst's opinion regarding the anticipated effect. Suppose that no irregular occurrence can be foreseen; an irregular multiplier of 1.00 is, therefore, used. The final short-term forecast for May, 1982 then becomes

$$Y = (618.62)\,(1.164)\,(.80)\,(1.00) = 576.06$$

Sales of approximately 576,000 cars are forecasted for May, 1982.

In a similar fashion, forecasts for each month of 1982 can be made. Since such short-term forecasts are based on data collected for only six years, it would not be wise to forecast more than two or three years into the future using this method. Therefore, the further into the future a forecast is made, the less reliance can be placed upon it. It is reasonable to predict twelve months in advance based on six years of data as the above example illustrates. It would be foolish to use such data to make a twenty-year forecast.

CASE STUDY: TIME-SERIES ANALYSIS OF STUDENT CREDIT HOURS

The registrar at a medium-sized university wished to investigate the total number of student credit hours. Since the institution is on the quarter system, there are four credit-hour totals per year; thus, all four time-series components could be investigated.

Student credit hours for each quarter of the year were collected for seven years, 1976 through 1982. Winter Quarter, which was the first quarter of the calendar year, was designated Quarter 1, Spring became Quarter 2, Summer became Quarter 3, and Fall became Quarter 4. The following seasonal analysis emerged from the time-series computer program:

Quarter	Seasonal Index
1 (Winter)	122.0
2 (Spring)	114.2
3 (Summer)	40.8
4 (Fall)	123.0

Table 14–10 shows the rest of the analysis generated by the time-series computer program.

The registrar next turned to those questions she wished to address based on the completed analysis. The primary need in her office involved forecasting student credit hours for the next several quarters. In particular, a forecast was needed immediately for the four quarters of 1983. She noted the apparent forecast in the second column of Table 14–10 and was prepared to use the first four figures in this column as predictions for 1983 when she noticed they were all very close to each other. This did not make sense to her because she knew that summer quarter was substantially below the other quarters of the year.

By referring to the seasonal indices, she was able to modify the credit-hour predictions and generated forecasts as follows:

Winter, 1983	85,288.8 (1.22) = 104,052
Spring, 1983	85,608.3 (1.142) = 97,765
Summer, 1983	85,927.8 (.408) = 35,059
Fall, 1983	86,247.3 (1.23) = 106,084

After thinking about the computer output and rechecking her figures, the registrar was convinced she had forecasts that reflected both the seven-year trend and the seasonal factors in student credit hours. She then began to think about the cyclical effect in credit hours and began studying the C column of the computer printout. She noticed a moderate cyclical effect was apparent in the data, though the last two quarters were disrupted by low C values. She also noticed that the time series showed a very steady irregular effect until these last two quarters.

Although she had learned a lot from the analysis and was able to make better predictions because of it, she was still uncertain about how to make a forecast for 1983 based on the cyclical and irregular effects. She had a meeting in one hour with the Vice-President of Finance and the Provost of the university and, therefore, did not have time for any additional research on the question. In one hour she had to have student credit hour predictions for the next year.

TABLE 14-10
Quarterly time-series analysis

SEASONAL VARIATION
CALCULATION OF SEASONAL INDEXES USING PERCENT OF FOUR-QUARTER MOVING AVERAGE

QUARTER	1976	1977	1978	1979	1980	1981	1982	MODIFIED QTR. MEAN	ADJUSTED SEASONAL INDEX MEAN *0.999072
1		123.11	121.93	121.65	120.48	122.68	122.68	122.23	122.0
2		114.51	114.76	114.14	114.37	110.34	120.68	114.44	114.2
3	38.92	41.24	42.00	39.55	40.68	44.16		40.87	40.8
4	122.97	121.59	121.58	124.46	125.91	123.90		123.23	123.0
								400.77	400.0

PERIOD		DATA Y	REGRESSION T	SEAS. ADJ. TCI	CI	C	I
1976	1	95647.00	76342.70	78400.93	102.70		
	2	86738.00	76662.20	75937.59	99.05	98.85	100.21
	3	29763.00	76981.71	72970.29	94.79	97.62	97.10
	4	94149.00	77301.21	76548.79	99.03	97.98	101.07
1977	1	94799.00	77620.72	77705.84	100.11	99.45	100.66
	2	88327.00	77940.22	77328.73	99.22	99.55	99.66
	3	31706.00	78259.73	77733.97	99.33	98.36	100.99
	4	93290.00	78579.23	75850.37	96.53	97.71	98.79
1978	1	93631.00	78898.73	76748.44	97.27	97.11	100.17
	2	88239.00	79218.23	77251.69	97.52	98.11	99.39
	3	32295.00	79537.73	79178.02	99.55	97.42	102.18
	4	93506.00	79857.24	76025.99	95.20	96.76	98.39
1979	1	93443.00	80176.74	76594.34	95.53	95.67	99.86
	2	88521.00	80496.25	77498.58	96.28	95.57	100.74
	3	31282.00	80815.75	76694.44	94.90	97.27	97.56
	4	100435.00	81135.25	81659.68	100.65	98.35	102.33

Year	Quarter					
1980	1	98886.00	81454.76	99.51	100.92	98.61
	2	95824.00	81774.26	102.59	102.27	100.31
	3	35066.00	82093.77	104.72	105.38	99.38
	4	110297.00	82413.27	108.82	106.95	101.74
1981	1	108309.00	82732.77	107.31	106.35	100.90
	2	97645.00	83052.27	102.93	108.05	95.26
	3	38740.00	83371.77	113.92	107.35	106.12
	4	108279.00	83691.28	105.19	106.90	98.41
1982	1	104106.00	84010.78	101.58	103.27	98.36
	2	99267.00	84330.29	103.05	84.48	121.99
	3	16851.00	84649.79	48.81	85.49	57.09
	4	109327.00	84969.30	104.61		
1983	1		85288.80			
	2		85608.30			
	3		85927.80			
	4		86247.30			
1984	1		86566.81			
	2		86886.31			
	3		87205.82			
	4		87525.32			
1985	1		87844.82			
	2		88164.33			
	3		88483.83			
	4		88803.34			

TREND FORECAST = 76342.703125 + 319.503326 * X PERIOD

Questions

1. How should the registrar deal with the cyclical effect in preparing forecasts for 1983?
2. How should the irregular effect be handled for the 1983 forecasts?
3. How much confidence would you place in the forecasts made by the registrar?

EXERCISES

1. When examining a time series measured on an annual basis, why is the seasonal effect not isolated?

2. In a time series measured in dollars, explain why it might be desirable to examine the series both in original dollars and in constant (devalued) dollars.

3. A company has data on the number of tires sold in the United States annually for the last several years. Describe a modification that might be made in the data before their time-series components are analyzed, and explain why this change might be useful.

4. Explain the types and levels of management in an organization that might be interested in forecasting company sales using the following data:
   a. Annual sales for the entire company measured over the last 15 years.
   b. Quarterly sales volume over the last five years.
   c. Monthly sales volume over the last four years.

5. How is the least-squares procedure used in time-series analysis?

6. In a time-series trend equation, what does the X variable represent?

7. How does Table 14–8 enable the analyst to examine the following time-series components?
   a. Cyclical
   b. Seasonal
   c. Irregular

8. Describe a time series that might exhibit each of the following seasonal patterns:

	a	b	c
JAN	99.3	201.4	75.0
FEB	98.2	194.7	81.4
MAR	100.4	154.7	94.2
APR	99.4	110.3	99.3
MAY	101.7	90.3	103.7
JUN	98.9	51.4	109.2
JUL	102.6	15.4	120.5
AUG	100.8	02.1	125.7
SEP	97.8	05.2	109.3
OCT	103.2	55.8	98.7
NOV	99.3	125.7	90.2
DEC	98.4	193.0	92.8

9. Suppose an annual time series is analyzed and yields the following trend equation:

$$Y = 983 + 14X$$

Suppose also that the analysis, which was based on the years 1970 through 1980, produced a string of cyclical relatives that ended as follows:

1975	110.3
1976	105.4
1977	102.3
1978	100.1
1979	98.3
1980	96.2

Forecast the value of the time series for the year 1983. Use both the trend equation and an extension of the cyclical relative for that year.

10. Five years of monthly data points were subjected to a time-series analysis, producing the seasonal indices shown in Exercise 8c. The analysis also produced the following trend equation:

$$Y = 1252 - 5.4X$$

The historical data points began with January, 1978 and ended with December, 1982. The last few cyclical relatives from this analysis were as follows:

1982	JUL	80.3
	AUG	85.4
	SEP	86.4
	OCT	91.2
	NOV	95.9
	DEC	97.8

Assuming that no unusual events are anticipated for June of 1983, forecast the time-series value for that month.

11. What is wrong with the following statement? "We have collected five years of monthly sales data and subjected them to a computerized time-series analysis. Based on the results of this analysis, we project that the level of our company sales in the year 2000 will be $756,449 per month."

12. What is wrong with the following statement? "Our annual sales volume for the last 25 years has been subjected to a computerized time-series analysis. Based on this analysis, we foresee certain problem areas emerging next June."

REFERENCES

Brillinger, D. R. *Time Series*. New York: Holt, Rinehart & Winston, 1975.

Dauten, C. A., and L. M. Valentine. *Business Cycles and Forecasting*. Cincinnati: South-Western Publishing Co., 1974.

Ferber, Robert, ed. *Readings in Survey Research*. Chicago: American Marketing Association, 1978.

Groebner, D., and P. Shannon. *Business Statistics*. Columbus, OH: Charles E. Merrill, 1981.

Hanke, J. E., and A. G. Reitsch. *Business Forecasting*. Boston: Allyn & Bacon, 1981.

Hoel, P. G., and R. J. Jessen. *Basic Statistics for Business and Economics*. 3d ed. New York: John Wiley & Sons, 1982.

McClave, J. T., and P. G. Benson. *Statistics for Business and Economics*. 2d ed. San Francisco: Dellen Publishing Co., 1982.

Makridakis, S., and S. Wheelwright. *Forecasting Methods and Applications*. Santa Barbara: John Wiley & Sons, 1978.

Mendenhall, W., and J. Reinmuth. *Statistics for Management and Economics*. 3d ed. North Scituate, MA: Duxbury Press, 1978.

Montgomery, D. C., and L. A. Johnson. *Forecasting and Time Series Analysis*. New York: McGraw-Hill Book Co., 1976.

Nelson, C. R. *Applied Time Series Analysis*. San Francisco: Holden Day, 1973.

Pfaffenberger, R. C., and J. H. Patterson. *Statistical Methods for Business and Economics*. rev. ed. Homewood, IL: Richard D. Irwin, 1981.

Plane, D. R., and E. B. Oppermann. *Business and Economic Statistics.* rev. ed. Plano, TX: Business Publications, 1981.

Sincich. T. *Business Statistics by Example.* San Francisco: Dellen Publishing Co., 1982.

Tull, D. S., and G. S. Albaum. *Survey Research.* New York: Intext Educational Publishers, 1973.

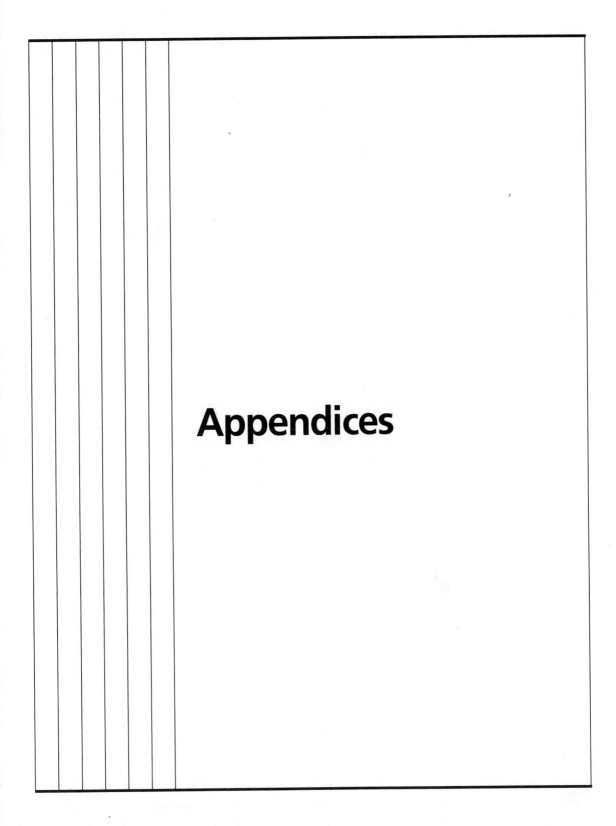

Appendices

List of Appendices

π

n	X	.05	.10	.15	.20	.25	.30	.35	.40	.45	.50	.55	.60	.65	.70	.75	.80	.85	.90	.95
1	0	.9500	.9000	.8500	.8000	.7500	.7000	.6500	.6000	.5500	.5000	.4500	.4000	.3500	.3000	.2500	.2000	.1500	.1000	.0500
	1	.0500	.1000	.1500	.2000	.2500	.3000	.3500	.4000	.4500	.5000	.5500	.6000	.6500	.7000	.7500	.8000	.8500	.9000	.9500
2	0	.9025	.8100	.7225	.6400	.5625	.4900	.4225	.3600	.3025	.2500	.2025	.1600	.1225	.0900	.0625	.0400	.0225	.0100	.0025
	1	.0950	.1800	.2550	.3200	.3750	.4200	.4550	.4800	.4950	.5000	.4950	.4800	.4550	.4200	.3750	.3200	.2550	.1800	.0950
	2	.0025	.0100	.0225	.0400	.0625	.0900	.1225	.1600	.2025	.2500	.3025	.3600	.4225	.4900	.5625	.6400	.7225	.8100	.9025
3	0	.8574	.7290	.6141	.5120	.4219	.3430	.2746	.2160	.1664	.1250	.0911	.0640	.0429	.0270	.0156	.0080	.0034	.0010	.0001
	1	.1354	.2430	.3251	.3840	.4219	.4410	.4436	.4320	.4084	.3750	.3341	.2880	.2389	.1890	.1406	.0960	.0574	.0270	.0071
	2	.0071	.0270	.0574	.0960	.1406	.1890	.2389	.2880	.3341	.3750	.4084	.4320	.4436	.4410	.4219	.3840	.3251	.2430	.1354
	3	.0001	.0010	.0034	.0080	.0156	.0270	.0429	.0640	.0911	.1250	.1664	.2160	.2746	.3430	.4219	.5120	.6141	.7290	.8574
4	0	.8145	.6561	.5220	.4096	.3164	.2401	.1785	.1296	.0915	.0625	.0410	.0256	.0150	.0081	.0039	.0016	.0005	.0001	.0000
	1	.1715	.2916	.3685	.4096	.4219	.4116	.3845	.3456	.2995	.2500	.2005	.1536	.1115	.0756	.0469	.0256	.0115	.0036	.0005
	2	.0135	.0486	.0975	.1536	.2109	.2646	.3105	.3456	.3675	.3750	.3675	.3456	.3105	.2646	.2109	.1536	.0975	.0486	.0135
	3	.0005	.0036	.0115	.0256	.0469	.0756	.1115	.1536	.2005	.2500	.2995	.3456	.3845	.4116	.4219	.4096	.3685	.2916	.1715
	4	.0000	.0001	.0005	.0016	.0039	.0081	.0150	.0256	.0410	.0625	.0915	.1296	.1785	.2401	.3164	.4096	.5220	.6561	.8145
5	0	.7738	.5905	.4437	.3277	.2373	.1681	.1160	.0778	.0503	.0313	.0185	.0102	.0053	.0024	.0010	.0003	.0001	.0000	.0000
	1	.2036	.3281	.3915	.4096	.3955	.3602	.3124	.2592	.2059	.1563	.1128	.0768	.0488	.0284	.0146	.0064	.0022	.0004	.0000
	2	.0214	.0729	.1382	.2048	.2637	.3087	.3364	.3456	.3369	.3125	.2757	.2304	.1811	.1323	.0879	.0512	.0244	.0081	.0011
	3	.0011	.0081	.0244	.0512	.0879	.1323	.1811	.2304	.2757	.3125	.3369	.3456	.3364	.3087	.2637	.2048	.1382	.0729	.0214
	4	.0000	.0004	.0022	.0064	.0146	.0283	.0488	.0768	.1128	.1562	.2059	.2592	.3124	.3601	.3955	.4096	.3915	.3281	.2036
	5	.0000	.0000	.0001	.0003	.0010	.0024	.0053	.0102	.0185	.0312	.0503	.0778	.1160	.1681	.2373	.3277	.4437	.5905	.7738
6	0	.7351	.5314	.3771	.2621	.1780	.1176	.0754	.0467	.0277	.0156	.0083	.0041	.0018	.0007	.0002	.0001	.0000	.0000	.0000
	1	.2321	.3543	.3993	.3932	.3560	.3025	.2437	.1866	.1359	.0938	.0609	.0369	.0205	.0102	.0044	.0015	.0004	.0001	.0000
	2	.0305	.0984	.1762	.2458	.2966	.3241	.3280	.3110	.2780	.2344	.1861	.1382	.0951	.0595	.0330	.0154	.0055	.0012	.0001
	3	.0021	.0146	.0415	.0819	.1318	.1852	.2355	.2765	.3032	.3125	.3032	.2765	.2355	.1852	.1318	.0819	.0415	.0146	.0021
	4	.0001	.0012	.0055	.0154	.0330	.0595	.0951	.1382	.1861	.2344	.2780	.3110	.3280	.3241	.2966	.2458	.1762	.0984	.0305
	5	.0000	.0001	.0004	.0015	.0044	.0102	.0205	.0369	.0609	.0937	.1359	.1866	.2437	.3025	.3560	.3932	.3993	.3543	.2321
	6	.0000	.0000	.0000	.0001	.0002	.0007	.0018	.0041	.0083	.0156	.0277	.0467	.0754	.1176	.1780	.2621	.3771	.5314	.7351
7	0	.6983	.4783	.3206	.2097	.1335	.0824	.0490	.0280	.0152	.0078	.0037	.0016	.0006	.0002	.0001	.0000	.0000	.0000	.0000
	1	.2573	.3720	.3960	.3670	.3115	.2471	.1848	.1306	.0872	.0547	.0320	.0172	.0084	.0036	.0013	.0004	.0001	.0000	.0000
	2	.0406	.1240	.2097	.2753	.3115	.3177	.2985	.2613	.2140	.1641	.1172	.0774	.0466	.0250	.0115	.0043	.0012	.0002	.0000

APPENDIX A, continued

π

n	X	.05	.10	.15	.20	.25	.30	.35	.40	.45	.50	.55	.60	.65	.70	.75	.80	.85	.90	.95
	3	.0036	.0230	.0617	.1147	.1730	.2269	.2679	.2903	.2918	.2734	.2388	.1935	.1442	.0972	.0577	.0287	.0109	.0026	.0002
	4	.0002	.0026	.0109	.0287	.0577	.0972	.1442	.1935	.2388	.2734	.2918	.2903	.2679	.2269	.1730	.1147	.0617	.0230	.0036
	5	.0000	.0002	.0012	.0043	.0115	.0250	.0466	.0774	.1172	.1641	.2140	.2613	.2985	.3177	.3115	.2753	.2097	.1240	.0406
	6	.0000	.0000	.0001	.0004	.0013	.0036	.0084	.0172	.0320	.0547	.0872	.1306	.1848	.2471	.3115	.3670	.3960	.3720	.2573
	7	.0000	.0000	.0000	.0000	.0001	.0002	.0006	.0016	.0037	.0078	.0152	.0280	.0490	.0824	.1335	.2097	.3206	.4783	.6983
8	0	.6634	.4305	.2725	.1678	.1001	.0576	.0319	.0168	.0084	.0039	.0017	.0007	.0002	.0001	.0000	.0000	.0000	.0000	.0000
	1	.2793	.3826	.3847	.3355	.2670	.1977	.1373	.0896	.0548	.0313	.0164	.0079	.0033	.0012	.0004	.0001	.0000	.0000	.0000
	2	.0515	.1488	.2376	.2936	.3115	.2965	.2587	.2090	.1569	.1094	.0703	.0413	.0217	.0100	.0038	.0011	.0002	.0000	.0000
	3	.0054	.0331	.0839	.1468	.2076	.2541	.2786	.2787	.2568	.2188	.1719	.1239	.0808	.0467	.0231	.0092	.0026	.0004	.0000
	4	.0004	.0046	.0185	.0459	.0865	.1361	.1875	.2322	.2627	.2734	.2627	.2322	.1875	.1361	.0865	.0459	.0185	.0046	.0004
	5	.0000	.0004	.0026	.0092	.0231	.0467	.0808	.1239	.1719	.2188	.2568	.2787	.2786	.2541	.2076	.1468	.0839	.0331	.0054
	6	.0000	.0000	.0002	.0011	.0038	.0100	.0217	.0413	.0703	.1094	.1569	.2090	.2587	.2965	.3115	.2936	.2376	.1488	.0515
	7	.0000	.0000	.0000	.0001	.0004	.0012	.0033	.0079	.0164	.0312	.0548	.0896	.1373	.1977	.2670	.3355	.3847	.3826	.2793
	8	.0000	.0000	.0000	.0000	.0000	.0001	.0002	.0007	.0017	.0039	.0084	.0168	.0319	.0576	.1001	.1678	.2725	.4305	.6634
9	0	.6302	.3874	.2316	.1342	.0751	.0404	.0207	.0101	.0046	.0020	.0008	.0003	.0001	.0000	.0000	.0000	.0000	.0000	.0000
	1	.2986	.3874	.3679	.3020	.2253	.1556	.1004	.0605	.0339	.0176	.0083	.0035	.0013	.0004	.0001	.0000	.0000	.0000	.0000
	2	.0629	.1722	.2597	.3020	.3003	.2668	.2162	.1612	.1110	.0703	.0407	.0212	.0098	.0039	.0012	.0003	.0000	.0000	.0000
	3	.0077	.0446	.1069	.1762	.2336	.2668	.2716	.2508	.2119	.1641	.1160	.0743	.0424	.0210	.0087	.0028	.0006	.0001	.0000
	4	.0006	.0074	.0283	.0661	.1168	.1715	.2194	.2508	.2600	.2461	.2128	.1672	.1181	.0735	.0389	.0165	.0050	.0008	.0000
	5	.0000	.0008	.0050	.0165	.0389	.0735	.1181	.1672	.2128	.2461	.2600	.2508	.2194	.1715	.1168	.0661	.0283	.0074	.0006
	6	.0000	.0001	.0006	.0028	.0087	.0210	.0424	.0743	.1160	.1641	.2119	.2508	.2716	.2668	.2336	.1762	.1069	.0446	.0077
	7	.0000	.0000	.0000	.0003	.0012	.0039	.0098	.0212	.0407	.0703	.1110	.1612	.2162	.2668	.3003	.3020	.2597	.1722	.0629
	8	.0000	.0000	.0000	.0000	.0001	.0004	.0013	.0035	.0083	.0176	.0339	.0605	.1004	.1556	.2253	.3020	.3679	.3874	.2986
	9	.0000	.0000	.0000	.0000	.0000	.0000	.0001	.0003	.0008	.0020	.0046	.0101	.0207	.0404	.0751	.1342	.2316	.3874	.6302
10	0	.5987	.3487	.1969	.1074	.0563	.0282	.0135	.0060	.0025	.0010	.0003	.0001	.0000	.0000	.0000	.0000	.0000	.0000	.0000
	1	.3151	.3874	.3474	.2684	.1877	.1211	.0725	.0403	.0207	.0098	.0042	.0016	.0005	.0001	.0000	.0000	.0000	.0000	.0000
	2	.0746	.1937	.2759	.3020	.2816	.2335	.1757	.1209	.0763	.0439	.0229	.0106	.0043	.0014	.0004	.0001	.0000	.0000	.0000
	3	.0105	.0574	.1298	.2013	.2503	.2668	.2522	.2150	.1665	.1172	.0746	.0425	.0212	.0090	.0031	.0008	.0001	.0000	.0000
	4	.0010	.0112	.0401	.0881	.1460	.2001	.2377	.2508	.2384	.2051	.1596	.1115	.0689	.0368	.0162	.0055	.0012	.0001	.0000
	5	.0001	.0015	.0085	.0264	.0584	.1029	.1536	.2007	.2340	.2461	.2340	.2007	.1536	.1029	.0584	.0264	.0085	.0015	.0001
	6	.0000	.0001	.0012	.0055	.0162	.0368	.0689	.1115	.1596	.2051	.2384	.2508	.2377	.2001	.1460	.0881	.0401	.0112	.0010
	7	.0000	.0000	.0001	.0008	.0031	.0090	.0212	.0425	.0746	.1172	.1665	.2150	.2522	.2668	.2503	.2013	.1298	.0574	.0105
	8	.0000	.0000	.0000	.0001	.0004	.0014	.0043	.0106	.0229	.0439	.0763	.1209	.1757	.2335	.2816	.3020	.2759	.1937	.0746
	9	.0000	.0000	.0000	.0000	.0000	.0001	.0005	.0016	.0042	.0098	.0207	.0403	.0725	.1211	.1877	.2684	.3474	.3874	.3151
	10	.0000	.0000	.0000	.0000	.0000	.0000	.0000	.0001	.0003	.0010	.0025	.0060	.0135	.0282	.0563	.1074	.1969	.3487	.5987

APPENDIX A, *continued*

π

n	X	.05	.10	.15	.20	.25	.30	.35	.40	.45	.50	.55	.60	.65	.70	.75	.80	.85	.90	.95
11	0	.5688	.3138	.1673	.0859	.0422	.0198	.0088	.0036	.0014	.0005	.0002	.0000	.0000	.0000	.0000	.0000	.0000	.0000	.0000
	1	.3293	.3835	.3248	.2362	.1549	.0932	.0518	.0266	.0125	.0054	.0021	.0007	.0002	.0000	.0000	.0000	.0000	.0000	.0000
	2	.0867	.2131	.2866	.2953	.2581	.1998	.1395	.0887	.0513	.0269	.0126	.0052	.0018	.0005	.0001	.0000	.0000	.0000	.0000
	3	.0137	.0710	.1517	.2215	.2581	.2568	.2254	.1774	.1259	.0806	.0462	.0234	.0102	.0037	.0011	.0002	.0000	.0000	.0000
	4	.0014	.0158	.0536	.1107	.1721	.2201	.2428	.2365	.2060	.1611	.1128	.0701	.0379	.0173	.0064	.0017	.0003	.0000	.0000
	5	.0001	.0025	.0132	.0388	.0803	.1321	.1830	.2207	.2360	.2256	.1931	.1471	.0985	.0566	.0268	.0097	.0023	.0003	.0000
	6	.0000	.0003	.0023	.0097	.0268	.0566	.0985	.1471	.1931	.2256	.2360	.2207	.1830	.1321	.0803	.0388	.0132	.0025	.0001
	7	.0000	.0000	.0003	.0017	.0064	.0173	.0379	.0701	.1128	.1611	.2060	.2365	.2428	.2201	.1721	.1107	.0536	.0158	.0014
	8	.0000	.0000	.0000	.0002	.0011	.0037	.0102	.0234	.0462	.0806	.1259	.1774	.2254	.2568	.2581	.2215	.1517	.0710	.0137
	9	.0000	.0000	.0000	.0000	.0001	.0005	.0018	.0052	.0126	.0269	.0513	.0887	.1395	.1998	.2581	.2953	.2866	.2131	.0867
	10	.0000	.0000	.0000	.0000	.0000	.0000	.0002	.0007	.0021	.0054	.0125	.0266	.0518	.0932	.1549	.2362	.3248	.3835	.3293
	11	.0000	.0000	.0000	.0000	.0000	.0000	.0000	.0000	.0002	.0005	.0014	.0036	.0088	.0198	.0422	.0859	.1673	.3138	.5688
12	0	.5404	.2824	.1422	.0687	.0317	.0138	.0057	.0022	.0008	.0002	.0001	.0000	.0000	.0000	.0000	.0000	.0000	.0000	.0000
	1	.3413	.3766	.3012	.2062	.1267	.0712	.0368	.0174	.0075	.0029	.0010	.0003	.0001	.0000	.0000	.0000	.0000	.0000	.0000
	2	.0988	.2301	.2924	.2835	.2323	.1678	.1088	.0639	.0339	.0161	.0068	.0025	.0008	.0002	.0000	.0000	.0000	.0000	.0000
	3	.0173	.0852	.1720	.2362	.2581	.2397	.1954	.1419	.0923	.0537	.0277	.0125	.0048	.0015	.0004	.0001	.0000	.0000	.0000
	4	.0021	.0213	.0683	.1329	.1936	.2311	.2367	.2128	.1700	.1208	.0762	.0420	.0199	.0078	.0024	.0005	.0001	.0000	.0000
	5	.0002	.0038	.0193	.0532	.1032	.1585	.2039	.2270	.2225	.1934	.1489	.1009	.0591	.0291	.0115	.0033	.0006	.0000	.0000
	6	.0000	.0005	.0040	.0155	.0401	.0792	.1281	.1766	.2124	.2256	.2124	.1766	.1281	.0792	.0401	.0155	.0040	.0005	.0000
	7	.0000	.0000	.0006	.0033	.0115	.0291	.0591	.1009	.1489	.1934	.2225	.2270	.2039	.1585	.1032	.0532	.0193	.0038	.0002
	8	.0000	.0000	.0001	.0005	.0024	.0078	.0199	.0420	.0762	.1208	.1700	.2128	.2367	.2311	.1936	.1329	.0683	.0213	.0021
	9	.0000	.0000	.0000	.0001	.0004	.0015	.0048	.0125	.0277	.0537	.0923	.1419	.1954	.2397	.2581	.2362	.1720	.0852	.0173
	10	.0000	.0000	.0000	.0000	.0000	.0002	.0008	.0025	.0068	.0161	.0339	.0639	.1088	.1678	.2323	.2835	.2924	.2301	.0988
	11	.0000	.0000	.0000	.0000	.0000	.0000	.0001	.0003	.0010	.0029	.0075	.0174	.0368	.0712	.1267	.2062	.3012	.3766	.3413
	12	.0000	.0000	.0000	.0000	.0000	.0000	.0000	.0000	.0001	.0002	.0008	.0022	.0057	.0138	.0317	.0687	.1422	.2824	.5404

SOURCE: From William J. Stevenson, *Business Statistics: Concepts and Applications*, 2d ed. (New York: Harper & Row, 1985), 584–586. Reproduced by permission of the publisher.

APPENDIX B
Table of Cumulative Binomial Probabilities

π

n	X	.05	.10	.15	.20	.25	.30	.35	.40	.45	.50	.55	.60	.65	.70	.75	.80	.85	.90	.95
1	0	.9500	.9000	.8500	.8000	.7500	.7000	.6500	.6000	.5500	.5000	.4500	.4000	.3500	.3000	.2500	.2000	.1500	.1000	.0500
	1	1.0000	1.0000	1.0000	1.0000	1.0000	1.0000	1.0000	1.0000	1.0000	1.0000	1.0000	1.0000	1.0000	1.0000	1.0000	1.0000	1.0000	1.0000	1.0000
2	0	.9025	.8100	.7225	.6400	.5625	.4900	.4225	.3600	.3025	.2500	.2025	.1600	.1225	.0900	.0625	.0400	.0225	.0100	.0025
	1	.9975	.9900	.9775	.9600	.9375	.9100	.8775	.8400	.7975	.7500	.6975	.6400	.5775	.5100	.4375	.3600	.2775	.1900	.0975
	2	1.0000	1.0000	1.0000	1.0000	1.0000	1.0000	1.0000	1.0000	1.0000	1.0000	1.0000	1.0000	1.0000	1.0000	1.0000	1.0000	1.0000	1.0000	1.0000
3	0	.8574	.7290	.6141	.5120	.4219	.3430	.2746	.2160	.1664	.1250	.0911	.0640	.0429	.0270	.0156	.0080	.0034	.0010	.0001
	1	.9928	.9720	.9393	.8960	.8438	.7840	.7183	.6480	.5748	.5000	.4253	.3520	.2818	.2160	.1563	.1040	.0608	.0280	.0073
	2	.9999	.9990	.9966	.9920	.9844	.9730	.9571	.9360	.9089	.8750	.8336	.7840	.7254	.6570	.5781	.4880	.3859	.2710	.1426
	3	1.0000	1.0000	1.0000	1.0000	1.0000	1.0000	1.0000	1.0000	1.0000	1.0000	1.0000	1.0000	1.0000	1.0000	1.0000	1.0000	1.0000	1.0000	1.0000
4	0	.8145	.6561	.5220	.4096	.3164	.2401	.1785	.1296	.0915	.0625	.0410	.0256	.0150	.0081	.0039	.0016	.0005	.0000	.0000
	1	.9860	.9477	.8905	.8192	.7383	.6517	.5630	.4752	.3910	.3125	.2415	.1792	.1265	.0837	.0508	.0272	.0120	.0037	.0005
	2	.9995	.9963	.9880	.9728	.9492	.9163	.8735	.8208	.7585	.6875	.6090	.5248	.4370	.3483	.2617	.1808	.1095	.0523	.0140
	3	1.0000	.9999	.9995	.9984	.9961	.9919	.9850	.9744	.9590	.9375	.9085	.8704	.8215	.7599	.6836	.5904	.4780	.3439	.1855
	4	1.0000	1.0000	1.0000	1.0000	1.0000	1.0000	1.0000	1.0000	1.0000	1.0000	1.0000	1.0000	1.0000	1.0000	1.0000	1.0000	1.0000	1.0000	1.0000
5	0	.7738	.5905	.4437	.3277	.2373	.1681	.1160	.0778	.0503	.0313	.0185	.0102	.0053	.0024	.0010	.0003	.0001	.0000	.0000
	1	.9974	.9185	.8352	.7373	.6328	.5282	.4284	.3370	.2562	.1875	.1312	.0870	.0540	.0308	.0156	.0067	.0022	.0005	.0000
	2	.9988	.9914	.9734	.9421	.8965	.8369	.7648	.6826	.5931	.5000	.4069	.3174	.2352	.1631	.1035	.0579	.0266	.0086	.0012
	3	1.0000	.9995	.9978	.9933	.9844	.9692	.9460	.9130	.8688	.8125	.7438	.6630	.5716	.4718	.3672	.2627	.1648	.0815	.0226
	4	1.0000	1.0000	.9999	.9997	.9990	.9976	.9947	.9898	.9815	.9688	.9497	.9222	.8840	.8319	.7627	.6723	.5563	.4095	.2262
	5	1.0000	1.0000	1.0000	1.0000	1.0000	1.0000	1.0000	1.0000	1.0000	1.0000	1.0000	1.0000	1.0000	1.0000	1.0000	1.0000	1.0000	1.0000	1.0000
6	0	.7351	.5314	.3771	.2621	.1780	.1176	.0754	.0467	.0277	.0156	.0083	.0041	.0018	.0007	.0002	.0001	.0000	.0000	.0000
	1	.9672	.8857	.7765	.6554	.5339	.4202	.3191	.2333	.1636	.1094	.0692	.0410	.0223	.0109	.0046	.0016	.0004	.0000	.0000
	2	.9978	.9842	.9527	.9011	.8306	.7443	.6471	.5443	.4415	.3438	.2553	.1792	.1174	.0705	.0376	.0170	.0059	.0013	.0001
	3	.9999	.9987	.9941	.9830	.9624	.9295	.8826	.8208	.7447	.6563	.5585	.4557	.3529	.2557	.1694	.0989	.0473	.0159	.0022
	4	1.0000	.9999	.9996	.9984	.9954	.9891	.9777	.9590	.9308	.8906	.8364	.7667	.6809	.5798	.4661	.3446	.2235	.1143	.0328
	5	1.0000	1.0000	1.0000	.9999	.9998	.9993	.9982	.9959	.9917	.9844	.9723	.9533	.9246	.8824	.8220	.7379	.6229	.4686	.2649
	6	1.0000	1.0000	1.0000	1.0000	1.0000	1.0000	1.0000	1.0000	1.0000	1.0000	1.0000	1.0000	1.0000	1.0000	1.0000	1.0000	1.0000	1.0000	1.0000
7	0	.6983	.4783	.3206	.2097	.1335	.0824	.0490	.0280	.0152	.0078	.0037	.0016	.0006	.0002	.0001	.0000	.0000	.0000	.0000
	1	.9556	.8503	.7166	.5767	.4449	.3294	.2338	.1586	.1024	.0625	.0357	.0188	.0090	.0038	.0013	.0004	.0001	.0000	.0000
	2	.9962	.9743	.9262	.8520	.7564	.6471	.5323	.4199	.3164	.2266	.1529	.0963	.0556	.0288	.0129	.0047	.0012	.0002	.0000

π

n	X	.05	.10	.15	.20	.25	.30	.35	.40	.45	.50	.55	.60	.65	.70	.75	.80	.85	.90	.95
7	3	.9998	.9973	.9879	.9667	.9294	.8740	.8002	.7102	.6083	.5000	.3917	.2898	.1998	.1260	.0706	.0333	.0121	.0027	.0002
	4	1.0000	.9998	.9988	.9953	.9871	.9712	.9444	.9037	.8471	.7734	.6836	.5801	.4677	.3529	.2436	.1480	.0738	.0257	.0038
	5	1.0000	1.0000	.9999	.9996	.9987	.9962	.9910	.9812	.9643	.9375	.8976	.8414	.7662	.6706	.5551	.4233	.2834	.1497	.0444
	6	1.0000	1.0000	1.0000	1.0000	.9999	.9998	.9994	.9984	.9963	.9922	.9848	.9720	.9510	.9176	.8665	.7903	.6794	.5217	.3017
	7	1.0000	1.0000	1.0000	1.0000	1.0000	1.0000	1.0000	1.0000	1.0000	1.0000	1.0000	1.0000	1.0000	1.0000	1.0000	1.0000	1.0000	1.0000	1.0000
8	0	.6634	.4305	.2725	.1678	.1001	.0576	.0319	.0168	.0084	.0039	.0017	.0007	.0002	.0001	.0000	.0000	.0000	.0000	.0000
	1	.9428	.8131	.6572	.5033	.3671	.2553	.1691	.1064	.0632	.0352	.0181	.0085	.0036	.0013	.0004	.0001	.0000	.0000	.0000
	2	.9942	.9619	.8948	.7969	.6785	.5518	.4278	.3154	.2201	.1445	.0885	.0498	.0253	.0113	.0042	.0012	.0002	.0000	.0000
	3	.9996	.9950	.9786	.9437	.8862	.8059	.7064	.5941	.4470	.3633	.2604	.1737	.1061	.0580	.0273	.0104	.0029	.0004	.0000
	4	1.0000	.9996	.9971	.9896	.9727	.9420	.8939	.8263	.7396	.6367	.5230	.4059	.2936	.1941	.1138	.0563	.0214	.0050	.0004
	5	1.0000	1.0000	.9998	.9988	.9958	.9887	.9747	.9502	.9115	.8555	.7799	.6846	.5722	.4482	.3215	.2031	.1052	.0381	.0058
	6	1.0000	1.0000	1.0000	.9999	.9996	.9987	.9964	.9915	.9819	.9648	.9368	.8936	.8309	.7447	.6329	.4967	.3428	.1869	.0572
	7	1.0000	1.0000	1.0000	1.0000	1.0000	.9999	.9998	.9993	.9983	.9961	.9916	.9832	.9681	.9424	.8999	.8322	.7275	.5695	.3366
	8	1.0000	1.0000	1.0000	1.0000	1.0000	1.0000	1.0000	1.0000	1.0000	1.0000	1.0000	1.0000	1.0000	1.0000	1.0000	1.0000	1.0000	1.0000	1.0000
9	0	.6302	.3874	.2316	.1342	.0751	.0404	.0207	.0101	.0046	.0020	.0008	.0003	.0001	.0000	.0000	.0000	.0000	.0000	.0000
	1	.9288	.7748	.5995	.4362	.3003	.1960	.1211	.0705	.0385	.0195	.0091	.0038	.0014	.0004	.0001	.0000	.0000	.0000	.0000
	2	.9916	.9470	.8591	.7382	.6007	.4628	.3373	.2318	.1495	.0898	.0498	.0250	.0112	.0043	.0013	.0003	.0000	.0000	.0000
	3	.9994	.9917	.9661	.9144	.8343	.7297	.6089	.4826	.3614	.2539	.1658	.0994	.0536	.0253	.0100	.0031	.0006	.0001	.0000
	4	1.0000	.9991	.9944	.9804	.9511	.9012	.8283	.7334	.6214	.5000	.3786	.2666	.1717	.0988	.0489	.0196	.0056	.0009	.0000
	5	1.0000	.9999	.9994	.9969	.9900	.9747	.9464	.9006	.8342	.7461	.6386	.5174	.3911	.2703	.1657	.0856	.0339	.0083	.0006
	6	1.0000	1.0000	1.0000	.9997	.9987	.9957	.9888	.9750	.9502	.9102	.8505	.7682	.6627	.5372	.3993	.2618	.1409	.0530	.0084
	7	1.0000	1.0000	1.0000	1.0000	.9999	.9996	.9986	.9962	.9909	.9805	.9615	.9295	.8789	.8040	.6997	.5638	.4005	.2252	.0712
	8	1.0000	1.0000	1.0000	1.0000	1.0000	1.0000	.9999	.9997	.9992	.9980	.9954	.9899	.9793	.9596	.9249	.8658	.7684	.6126	.3698
	9	1.0000	1.0000	1.0000	1.0000	1.0000	1.0000	1.0000	1.0000	1.0000	1.0000	1.0000	1.0000	1.0000	1.0000	1.0000	1.0000	1.0000	1.0000	1.0000
10	0	.5987	.3487	.1969	.1074	.0563	.0282	.0135	.0060	.0025	.0010	.0003	.0001	.0000	.0000	.0000	.0000	.0000	.0000	.0000
	1	.9139	.7361	.5443	.3758	.2440	.1493	.0860	.0464	.0233	.0107	.0045	.0017	.0005	.0001	.0000	.0000	.0000	.0000	.0000
	2	.9885	.9298	.8202	.6778	.5256	.3828	.2616	.1673	.0996	.0547	.0274	.0123	.0048	.0016	.0004	.0001	.0000	.0000	.0000
	3	.9990	.9872	.9500	.8791	.7759	.6496	.5138	.3823	.2660	.1719	.1020	.0548	.0260	.0106	.0035	.0009	.0001	.0000	.0000
	4	.9999	.9984	.9901	.9672	.9219	.8497	.7515	.6331	.5044	.3770	.2616	.1662	.0949	.0473	.0197	.0064	.0014	.0001	.0000
	5	1.0000	.9999	.9986	.9936	.9803	.9527	.9051	.8338	.7384	.6230	.4956	.3669	.2485	.1503	.0781	.0328	.0099	.0016	.0001
	6	1.0000	1.0000	.9999	.9991	.9965	.9894	.9740	.9452	.8980	.8281	.7340	.6177	.4862	.3504	.2241	.1209	.0500	.0128	.0010
	7	1.0000	1.0000	1.0000	.9999	.9996	.9984	.9952	.9877	.9726	.9453	.9004	.8327	.7384	.6172	.4744	.3222	.1798	.0702	.0115

π

n	X	.05	.10	.15	.20	.25	.30	.35	.40	.45	.50	.55	.60	.65	.70	.75	.80	.85	.90	.95
	8	1.0000	1.0000	1.0000	1.0000	1.0000	.9999	.9995	.9983	.9955	.9893	.9767	.9536	.9140	.8507	.7560	.6242	.4557	.2639	.0861
	9	1.0000	1.0000	1.0000	1.0000	1.0000	1.0000	1.0000	.9999	.9997	.9990	.9975	.9940	.9865	.9718	.9437	.8926	.8031	.6513	.4013
	10	1.0000	1.0000	1.0000	1.0000	1.0000	1.0000	1.0000	1.0000	1.0000	1.0000	1.0000	1.0000	1.0000	1.0000	1.0000	1.0000	1.0000	1.0000	1.0000
11	0	.5688	.3138	.1673	.0859	.0422	.0198	.0088	.0036	.0014	.0005	.0002	.0000	.0000	.0000	.0000	.0000	.0000	.0000	.0000
	1	.8981	.6974	.4922	.3221	.1971	.1130	.0606	.0302	.0139	.0059	.0022	.0007	.0002	.0000	.0000	.0000	.0000	.0000	.0000
	2	.9848	.9104	.7788	.6174	.4552	.3127	.2001	.1189	.0652	.0327	.0148	.0059	.0020	.0006	.0001	.0000	.0000	.0000	.0000
	3	.9984	.9815	.9306	.8389	.7133	.5696	.4256	.2963	.1911	.1133	.0610	.0293	.0122	.0043	.0012	.0002	.0000	.0000	.0000
	4	.9999	.9972	.9841	.9496	.8854	.7897	.6683	.5328	.3971	.2744	.1738	.0994	.0501	.0216	.0076	.0020	.0003	.0000	.0000
	5	1.0000	.9997	.9973	.9883	.9657	.9218	.8513	.7535	.6331	.5000	.3669	.2465	.1487	.0782	.0343	.0117	.0027	.0003	.0000
	6	1.0000	1.0000	.9997	.9980	.9924	.9784	.9499	.9006	.8262	.7256	.6029	.4672	.3317	.2103	.1146	.0504	.0159	.0028	.0001
	7	1.0000	1.0000	1.0000	.9998	.9988	.9957	.9878	.9707	.9390	.8867	.8089	.7037	.5744	.4304	.2867	.1611	.0694	.0185	.0016
	8	1.0000	1.0000	1.0000	1.0000	.9999	.9994	.9980	.9941	.9852	.9673	.9348	.8811	.7999	.6873	.5448	.3826	.2212	.0896	.0152
	9	1.0000	1.0000	1.0000	1.0000	1.0000	1.0000	.9998	.9993	.9978	.9941	.9861	.9698	.9394	.8870	.8029	.6779	.5078	.3026	.1019
	10	1.0000	1.0000	1.0000	1.0000	1.0000	1.0000	1.0000	1.0000	.9998	.9995	.9986	.9964	.9912	.9802	.9578	.9141	.8327	.6862	.4312
	11	1.0000	1.0000	1.0000	1.0000	1.0000	1.0000	1.0000	1.0000	1.0000	1.0000	1.0000	1.0000	1.0000	1.0000	1.0000	1.0000	1.0000	1.0000	1.0000
12	0	.5404	.2824	.1422	.0687	.0317	.0138	.0057	.0022	.0008	.0002	.0001	.0000	.0000	.0000	.0000	.0000	.0000	.0000	.0000
	1	.8816	.6590	.4435	.2749	.1584	.0850	.0424	.0196	.0083	.0032	.0011	.0003	.0001	.0000	.0000	.0000	.0000	.0000	.0000
	2	.9804	.8891	.7358	.5583	.3907	.2528	.1513	.0834	.0421	.0193	.0079	.0028	.0008	.0002	.0000	.0000	.0000	.0000	.0000
	3	.9978	.9744	.9078	.7946	.6488	.4925	.3467	.2253	.1345	.0730	.0356	.0153	.0056	.0017	.0004	.0001	.0000	.0000	.0000
	4	.9998	.9957	.9761	.9274	.8424	.7237	.5833	.4382	.3044	.1938	.1117	.0573	.0255	.0095	.0028	.0006	.0001	.0000	.0000
	5	1.0000	.9995	.9954	.9806	.9456	.8822	.7873	.6652	.5269	.3872	.2607	.1582	.0846	.0386	.0143	.0039	.0007	.0001	.0000
	6	1.0000	.9999	.9993	.9961	.9857	.9614	.9154	.8418	.7393	.6128	.4731	.3348	.2127	.1178	.0544	.0194	.0046	.0005	.0000
	7	1.0000	1.0000	.9999	.9994	.9972	.9905	.9745	.9427	.8883	.8062	.6956	.5618	.4167	.2763	.1576	.0726	.0239	.0043	.0002
	8	1.0000	1.0000	1.0000	.9999	.9996	.9983	.9944	.9847	.9644	.9270	.8655	.7747	.6533	.5075	.3512	.2054	.0922	.0256	.0022
	9	1.0000	1.0000	1.0000	1.0000	1.0000	.9998	.9992	.9972	.9921	.9807	.9579	.9166	.8487	.7472	.6093	.4417	.2642	.1109	.0196
	10	1.0000	1.0000	1.0000	1.0000	1.0000	1.0000	.9999	.9997	.9989	.9968	.9917	.9804	.9576	.9150	.8416	.7251	.5565	.3410	.1184
	11	1.0000	1.0000	1.0000	1.0000	1.0000	1.0000	1.0000	1.0000	.9999	.9998	.9992	.9978	.9943	.9862	.9683	.9313	.8578	.7176	.4596
	12	1.0000	1.0000	1.0000	1.0000	1.0000	1.0000	1.0000	1.0000	1.0000	1.0000	1.0000	1.0000	1.0000	1.0000	1.0000	1.0000	1.0000	1.0000	1.0000
13	0	.5133	.2542	.1209	.0550	.0238	.0097	.0037	.0013	.0004	.0001	.0000	.0000	.0000	.0000	.0000	.0000	.0000	.0000	.0000
	1	.8646	.6213	.3983	.2336	.1267	.0637	.0296	.0126	.0049	.0017	.0005	.0001	.0000	.0000	.0000	.0000	.0000	.0000	.0000
	2	.9755	.8661	.6920	.5017	.3326	.2025	.1132	.0579	.0269	.0112	.0041	.0013	.0003	.0001	.0000	.0000	.0000	.0000	.0000
	3	.9969	.9658	.8820	.7473	.5843	.4206	.2783	.1686	.0929	.0461	.0203	.0078	.0025	.0007	.0001	.0000	.0000	.0000	.0000
	4	.9997	.9935	.9658	.9009	.7940	.6543	.5005	.3530	.2279	.1334	.0698	.0321	.0126	.0040	.0010	.0002	.0000	.0000	.0000
	5	1.0000	.9991	.9925	.9700	.9198	.8346	.7159	.5744	.4268	.2905	.1788	.0977	.0462	.0182	.0056	.0012	.0002	.0000	.0000
	6	1.0000	.9999	.9987	.9930	.9757	.9376	.8705	.7712	.6437	.5000	.3563	.2288	.1295	.0624	.0243	.0070	.0013	.0001	.0000

π

n	X	.05	.10	.15	.20	.25	.30	.35	.40	.45	.50	.55	.60	.65	.70	.75	.80	.85	.90	.95
	7	1.0000	1.0000	.9998	.9988	.9944	.9818	.9538	.9023	.8212	.7095	.5732	.4256	.2841	.1654	.0802	.0300	.0075	.0009	.0000
	8	1.0000	1.0000	1.0000	.9998	.9990	.9960	.9874	.9679	.9302	.8666	.7721	.6470	.4995	.3457	.2060	.0991	.0342	.0065	.0003
	9	1.0000	1.0000	1.0000	1.0000	.9999	.9993	.9975	.9922	.9797	.9539	.9071	.8314	.7217	.5794	.4157	.2527	.1180	.0342	.0031
	10	1.0000	1.0000	1.0000	1.0000	1.0000	.9999	.9997	.9987	.9959	.9888	.9731	.9421	.8868	.7975	.6674	.4983	.3080	.1339	.0245
	11	1.0000	1.0000	1.0000	1.0000	1.0000	1.0000	1.0000	.9999	.9995	.9983	.9951	.9874	.9704	.9363	.8733	.7664	.6017	.3787	.1354
	12	1.0000	1.0000	1.0000	1.0000	1.0000	1.0000	1.0000	1.0000	1.0000	.9999	.9996	.9987	.9963	.9903	.9762	.9450	.8791	.7458	.4867
	13	1.0000	1.0000	1.0000	1.0000	1.0000	1.0000	1.0000	1.0000	1.0000	1.0000	1.0000	1.0000	1.0000	1.0000	1.0000	1.0000	1.0000	1.0000	1.0000
14	0	.4877	.2288	.1028	.0440	.0178	.0068	.0024	.0008	.0002	.0001	.0000	.0000	.0000	.0000	.0000	.0000	.0000	.0000	.0000
	1	.8470	.5846	.3567	.1979	.1010	.0475	.0205	.0081	.0029	.0009	.0003	.0001	.0000	.0000	.0000	.0000	.0000	.0000	.0000
	2	.9699	.8416	.6479	.4481	.2811	.1608	.0839	.0398	.0170	.0065	.0022	.0006	.0001	.0000	.0000	.0000	.0000	.0000	.0000
	3	.9958	.9559	.8535	.6982	.5213	.3552	.2205	.1243	.0632	.0287	.0114	.0039	.0011	.0002	.0000	.0000	.0000	.0000	.0000
	4	.9996	.9908	.9533	.8702	.7415	.5842	.4227	.2793	.1672	.0898	.0426	.0175	.0060	.0017	.0003	.0000	.0000	.0000	.0000
	5	1.0000	.9985	.9885	.9561	.8883	.7805	.6405	.4859	.3373	.2120	.1189	.0583	.0243	.0083	.0022	.0004	.0000	.0000	.0000
	6	1.0000	.9998	.9978	.9884	.9617	.9067	.8164	.6925	.5461	.3953	.2586	.1501	.0753	.0315	.0103	.0024	.0003	.0000	.0000
	7	1.0000	1.0000	.9997	.9976	.9897	.9685	.9247	.8499	.7414	.6047	.4539	.3075	.1836	.0933	.0383	.0116	.0022	.0002	.0000
	8	1.0000	1.0000	1.0000	.9996	.9978	.9917	.9757	.9417	.8811	.7880	.6627	.5141	.3595	.2195	.1117	.0439	.0115	.0015	.0000
	9	1.0000	1.0000	1.0000	1.0000	.9997	.9983	.9940	.9825	.9574	.9102	.8328	.7207	.5773	.4158	.2585	.1298	.0467	.0092	.0004
	10	1.0000	1.0000	1.0000	1.0000	1.0000	.9998	.9989	.9961	.9886	.9713	.9368	.8757	.7795	.6448	.4787	.3018	.1465	.0441	.0042
	11	1.0000	1.0000	1.0000	1.0000	1.0000	1.0000	.9999	.9994	.9978	.9935	.9830	.9602	.9161	.8392	.7189	.5519	.3521	.1584	.0301
	12	1.0000	1.0000	1.0000	1.0000	1.0000	1.0000	1.0000	.9999	.9997	.9991	.9971	.9919	.9795	.9525	.8990	.8021	.6433	.4154	.1530
	13	1.0000	1.0000	1.0000	1.0000	1.0000	1.0000	1.0000	1.0000	1.0000	.9999	.9998	.9992	.9976	.9932	.9822	.9560	.8972	.7712	.5123
	14	1.0000	1.0000	1.0000	1.0000	1.0000	1.0000	1.0000	1.0000	1.0000	1.0000	1.0000	1.0000	1.0000	1.0000	1.0000	1.0000	1.0000	1.0000	1.0000
15	0	.4633	.2059	.0874	.0352	.0134	.0047	.0016	.0005	.0001	.0000	.0000	.0000	.0000	.0000	.0000	.0000	.0000	.0000	.0000
	1	.8290	.5490	.3186	.1671	.0802	.0353	.0142	.0052	.0017	.0005	.0001	.0000	.0000	.0000	.0000	.0000	.0000	.0000	.0000
	2	.9638	.8159	.6042	.3980	.2361	.1268	.0617	.0271	.0107	.0037	.0011	.0003	.0001	.0000	.0000	.0000	.0000	.0000	.0000
	3	.9945	.9444	.8227	.6482	.4613	.2969	.1727	.0905	.0424	.0176	.0063	.0019	.0005	.0001	.0001	.0000	.0000	.0000	.0000
	4	.9994	.9873	.9383	.8358	.6865	.5155	.3519	.2173	.1204	.0592	.0255	.0093	.0028	.0007	.0001	.0000	.0000	.0000	.0000
	5	.9999	.9978	.9832	.9389	.8516	.7216	.5643	.4032	.2608	.1509	.0769	.0338	.0124	.0037	.0008	.0001	.0000	.0000	.0000
	6	1.0000	.9997	.9964	.9819	.9434	.8689	.7548	.6098	.4522	.3036	.1818	.0950	.0422	.0152	.0042	.0008	.0001	.0000	.0000
	7	1.0000	1.0000	.9994	.9958	.9827	.9500	.8868	.7869	.6535	.5000	.3465	.2131	.1132	.0500	.0173	.0042	.0006	.0000	.0000
	8	1.0000	1.0000	.9999	.9992	.9958	.9848	.9578	.9050	.8182	.6964	.5478	.3902	.2452	.1311	.0566	.0181	.0036	.0003	.0001
	9	1.0000	1.0000	1.0000	.9999	.9992	.9963	.9876	.9662	.9231	.8491	.7392	.5968	.4357	.2784	.1484	.0611	.0168	.0022	.0001
	10	1.0000	1.0000	1.0000	1.0000	.9999	.9993	.9972	.9907	.9745	.9408	.8796	.7827	.6481	.4845	.3135	.1642	.0617	.0127	.0006

π

n	X	.05	.10	.15	.20	.25	.30	.35	.40	.45	.50	.55	.60	.65	.70	.75	.80	.85	.90	.95
	11	1.0000	1.0000	1.0000	1.0000	1.0000	.9999	.9995	.9981	.9937	.9824	.9576	.9095	.8273	.7031	.5387	.3518	.1773	.0556	.0055
	12	1.0000	1.0000	1.0000	1.0000	1.0000	1.0000	.9999	.9997	.9989	.9963	.9893	.9729	.9383	.8732	.7639	.6020	.3958	.1841	.0362
	13	1.0000	1.0000	1.0000	1.0000	1.0000	1.0000	1.0000	1.0000	.9999	.9995	.9983	.9948	.9858	.9647	.9198	.8329	.6814	.4510	.1710
	14	1.0000	1.0000	1.0000	1.0000	1.0000	1.0000	1.0000	1.0000	1.0000	1.0000	.9999	.9995	.9984	.9953	.9866	.9648	.9126	.7941	.5367
	15	1.0000	1.0000	1.0000	1.0000	1.0000	1.0000	1.0000	1.0000	1.0000	1.0000	1.0000	1.0000	1.0000	1.0000	1.0000	1.0000	1.0000	1.0000	1.0000
16	0	.4401	.1853	.0743	.0281	.0100	.0033	.0010	.0003	.0001	.0000	.0000	.0000	.0000	.0000	.0000	.0000	.0000	.0000	.0000
	1	.8108	.5147	.2839	.1407	.0635	.0261	.0098	.0033	.0010	.0003	.0001	.0000	.0000	.0000	.0000	.0000	.0000	.0000	.0000
	2	.9571	.7892	.5614	.3518	.1971	.0994	.0451	.0183	.0066	.0021	.0006	.0001	.0000	.0000	.0000	.0000	.0000	.0000	.0000
	3	.9930	.9316	.7899	.5981	.4050	.2459	.1339	.0651	.0281	.0106	.0035	.0009	.0002	.0000	.0000	.0000	.0000	.0000	.0000
	4	.9991	.9830	.9209	.7982	.6302	.4499	.2892	.1666	.0853	.0384	.0149	.0049	.0013	.0003	.0000	.0000	.0000	.0000	.0000
	5	.9999	.9967	.9765	.9183	.8103	.6598	.4900	.3288	.1976	.1051	.0486	.0191	.0062	.0016	.0003	.0000	.0000	.0000	.0000
	6	1.0000	.9995	.9944	.9733	.9204	.8247	.6881	.5272	.3660	.2272	.1241	.0583	.0229	.0071	.0016	.0002	.0000	.0000	.0000
	7	1.0000	.9999	.9989	.9930	.9729	.9256	.8406	.7161	.5629	.4018	.2559	.1423	.0671	.0257	.0075	.0015	.0002	.0000	.0000
	8	1.0000	1.0000	.9998	.9985	.9925	.9743	.9329	.8577	.7441	.5982	.4371	.2839	.1594	.0744	.0271	.0070	.0011	.0001	.0000
	9	1.0000	1.0000	1.0000	.9998	.9984	.9929	.9771	.9417	.8759	.7728	.6340	.4728	.3119	.1753	.0796	.0267	.0056	.0005	.0000
	10	1.0000	1.0000	1.0000	1.0000	.9997	.9984	.9938	.9809	.9514	.8949	.8024	.6712	.5100	.3402	.1897	.0817	.0235	.0033	.0001
	11	1.0000	1.0000	1.0000	1.0000	1.0000	.9997	.9987	.9951	.9851	.9616	.9147	.8334	.7108	.5501	.3698	.2018	.0791	.0170	.0009
	12	1.0000	1.0000	1.0000	1.0000	1.0000	1.0000	.9998	.9991	.9965	.9894	.9719	.9349	.8661	.7541	.5950	.4019	.2101	.0684	.0070
	13	1.0000	1.0000	1.0000	1.0000	1.0000	1.0000	1.0000	.9999	.9994	.9979	.9934	.9817	.9549	.9006	.8029	.6482	.4386	.2108	.0429
	14	1.0000	1.0000	1.0000	1.0000	1.0000	1.0000	1.0000	1.0000	.9999	.9997	.9990	.9967	.9902	.9739	.9365	.8593	.7161	.4853	.1892
	15	1.0000	1.0000	1.0000	1.0000	1.0000	1.0000	1.0000	1.0000	1.0000	1.0000	.9999	.9997	.9990	.9967	.9900	.9719	.9257	.8147	.5599
	16	1.0000	1.0000	1.0000	1.0000	1.0000	1.0000	1.0000	1.0000	1.0000	1.0000	1.0000	1.0000	1.0000	1.0000	1.0000	1.0000	1.0000	1.0000	1.0000
17	0	.4181	.1668	.0631	.0225	.0075	.0023	.0007	.0002	.0000	.0000	.0000	.0000	.0000	.0000	.0000	.0000	.0000	.0000	.0000
	1	.7922	.4818	.2525	.1182	.0501	.0193	.0067	.0021	.0006	.0001	.0000	.0000	.0000	.0000	.0000	.0000	.0000	.0000	.0000
	2	.9497	.7618	.5198	.3096	.1637	.0774	.0327	.0123	.0041	.0012	.0003	.0001	.0000	.0000	.0000	.0000	.0000	.0000	.0000
	3	.9912	.9174	.7556	.5489	.3530	.2019	.1028	.0464	.0184	.0064	.0019	.0005	.0001	.0000	.0000	.0000	.0000	.0000	.0000
	4	.9988	.9779	.9013	.7582	.5739	.3887	.2348	.1260	.0596	.0245	.0086	.0025	.0006	.0001	.0000	.0000	.0000	.0000	.0000
	5	.9999	.9953	.9681	.8943	.7653	.5968	.4197	.2639	.1471	.0717	.0301	.0106	.0030	.0007	.0001	.0000	.0000	.0000	.0000
	6	1.0000	.9992	.9917	.9623	.8929	.7752	.6188	.4478	.2902	.1662	.0826	.0348	.0120	.0032	.0006	.0001	.0000	.0000	.0000
	7	1.0000	.9999	.9983	.9891	.9598	.8954	.7872	.6405	.4743	.3145	.1834	.0919	.0383	.0127	.0031	.0005	.0000	.0000	.0000
	8	1.0000	1.0000	.9997	.9974	.9876	.9597	.9006	.8011	.6626	.5000	.3374	.1989	.0994	.0403	.0124	.0026	.0003	.0000	.0000
	9	1.0000	1.0000	1.0000	.9995	.9969	.9873	.9617	.9081	.8166	.6855	.5257	.3595	.2128	.1046	.0402	.0109	.0017	.0001	.0000
	10	1.0000	1.0000	1.0000	.9999	.9994	.9968	.9880	.9652	.9174	.8338	.7098	.5522	.3812	.2248	.1071	.0377	.0083	.0008	.0000
	11	1.0000	1.0000	1.0000	1.0000	.9999	.9993	.9970	.9894	.9699	.9283	.8529	.7361	.5803	.4032	.2347	.1057	.0319	.0047	.0001
	12	1.0000	1.0000	1.0000	1.0000	1.0000	.9999	.9994	.9975	.9914	.9755	.9404	.8740	.7652	.6113	.4261	.2418	.0987	.0221	.0012

		π																	
n	X	.05	.10	.15	.20	.25	.30	.35	.40	.45	.50	.55	.60	.65	.70	.75	.80	.85	.90	.95
	13	1.0000	1.0000	1.0000	1.0000	1.0000	1.0000	.9999	.9995	.9981	.9936	.9816	.9536	.8972	.7981	.6470	.4511	.2444	.0826	.0088
	14	1.0000	1.0000	1.0000	1.0000	1.0000	1.0000	1.0000	.9999	.9997	.9988	.9959	.9877	.9673	.9226	.8363	.6904	.4802	.2382	.0503
	15	1.0000	1.0000	1.0000	1.0000	1.0000	1.0000	1.0000	1.0000	1.0000	.9999	.9994	.9979	.9933	.9807	.9499	.8818	.7475	.5182	.2078
	16	1.0000	1.0000	1.0000	1.0000	1.0000	1.0000	1.0000	1.0000	1.0000	1.0000	1.0000	.9998	.9993	.9977	.9925	.9775	.9369	.8332	.5819
	17	1.0000	1.0000	1.0000	1.0000	1.0000	1.0000	1.0000	1.0000	1.0000	1.0000	1.0000	1.0000	1.0000	1.0000	1.0000	1.0000	1.0000	1.0000	1.0000
18	0	.3972	.1501	.0536	.0180	.0056	.0016	.0004	.0001	.0000	.0000	.0000	.0000	.0000	.0000	.0000	.0000	.0000	.0000	.0000
	1	.7735	.4503	.2241	.0991	.0395	.0142	.0046	.0013	.0003	.0001	.0000	.0000	.0000	.0000	.0000	.0000	.0000	.0000	.0000
	2	.9419	.7338	.4797	.2713	.1353	.0600	.0236	.0082	.0025	.0007	.0001	.0000	.0000	.0000	.0000	.0000	.0000	.0000	.0000
	3	.9891	.9018	.7202	.5010	.3057	.1646	.0783	.0328	.0120	.0038	.0010	.0002	.0000	.0000	.0000	.0000	.0000	.0000	.0000
	4	.9985	.9718	.8794	.7164	.5187	.3327	.1886	.0942	.0411	.0154	.0049	.0013	.0003	.0000	.0000	.0000	.0000	.0000	.0000
	5	.9998	.9936	.9581	.8671	.7175	.5344	.3550	.2088	.1077	.0481	.0183	.0058	.0014	.0003	.0000	.0000	.0000	.0000	.0000
	6	1.0000	.9988	.9882	.9487	.8610	.7217	.5491	.3743	.2258	.1189	.0537	.0203	.0062	.0014	.0002	.0000	.0000	.0000	.0000
	7	1.0000	.9998	.9973	.9837	.9431	.8593	.7283	.5634	.3915	.2403	.1280	.0576	.0212	.0061	.0012	.0002	.0000	.0000	.0000
	8	1.0000	1.0000	.9995	.9957	.9807	.9404	.8609	.7368	.5778	.4073	.2527	.1347	.0597	.0210	.0054	.0009	.0001	.0000	.0000
	9	1.0000	1.0000	.9999	.9991	.9946	.9790	.9403	.8653	.7473	.5927	.4222	.2632	.1391	.0596	.0193	.0043	.0005	.0000	.0000
	10	1.0000	1.0000	1.0000	.9998	.9988	.9939	.9788	.9424	.8720	.7597	.6085	.4366	.2717	.1407	.0569	.0163	.0027	.0002	.0000
	11	1.0000	1.0000	1.0000	1.0000	.9998	.9986	.9938	.9797	.9463	.8811	.7742	.6257	.4509	.2783	.1390	.0513	.0118	.0012	.0000
	12	1.0000	1.0000	1.0000	1.0000	1.0000	.9997	.9986	.9942	.9817	.9519	.8923	.7912	.6450	.4656	.2825	.1329	.0419	.0064	.0002
	13	1.0000	1.0000	1.0000	1.0000	1.0000	1.0000	.9997	.9987	.9951	.9846	.9589	.9058	.8114	.6673	.4813	.2836	.1206	.0282	.0015
	14	1.0000	1.0000	1.0000	1.0000	1.0000	1.0000	1.0000	.9998	.9990	.9962	.9880	.9672	.9217	.8354	.6943	.4990	.2798	.0982	.0109
	15	1.0000	1.0000	1.0000	1.0000	1.0000	1.0000	1.0000	1.0000	.9999	.9993	.9975	.9918	.9764	.9400	.8647	.7287	.5203	.2662	.0581
	16	1.0000	1.0000	1.0000	1.0000	1.0000	1.0000	1.0000	1.0000	1.0000	.9999	.9997	.9987	.9954	.9858	.9605	.9009	.7759	.5497	.2265
	17	1.0000	1.0000	1.0000	1.0000	1.0000	1.0000	1.0000	1.0000	1.0000	1.0000	1.0000	.9999	.9996	.9984	.9944	.9820	.9464	.8499	.6028
	18	1.0000	1.0000	1.0000	1.0000	1.0000	1.0000	1.0000	1.0000	1.0000	1.0000	1.0000	1.0000	1.0000	1.0000	1.0000	1.0000	1.0000	1.0000	1.0000
19	0	.3774	.1351	.0456	.0144	.0042	.0011	.0003	.0001	.0000	.0000	.0000	.0000	.0000	.0000	.0000	.0000	.0000	.0000	.0000
	1	.7547	.4203	.1985	.0829	.0310	.0104	.0031	.0008	.0002	.0000	.0000	.0000	.0000	.0000	.0000	.0000	.0000	.0000	.0000
	2	.9335	.7054	.4413	.2369	.1113	.0462	.0170	.0055	.0015	.0004	.0001	.0000	.0000	.0000	.0000	.0000	.0000	.0000	.0000
	3	.9868	.8850	.6841	.4551	.2631	.1332	.0591	.0230	.0077	.0022	.0005	.0001	.0000	.0000	.0000	.0000	.0000	.0000	.0000
	4	.9980	.9648	.8556	.6733	.4654	.2822	.1500	.0696	.0280	.0096	.0028	.0006	.0001	.0000	.0000	.0000	.0000	.0000	.0000
	5	.9998	.9914	.9463	.8369	.6678	.4739	.2968	.1629	.0777	.0318	.0109	.0031	.0007	.0001	.0000	.0000	.0000	.0000	.0000
	6	1.0000	.9983	.9837	.9324	.8251	.6655	.4812	.3081	.1727	.0835	.0342	.0116	.0031	.0006	.0001	.0000	.0000	.0000	.0000
	7	1.0000	.9997	.9959	.9767	.9225	.8180	.6656	.4878	.3169	.1796	.0871	.0352	.0114	.0028	.0005	.0000	.0000	.0000	.0000
	8	1.0000	1.0000	.9992	.9933	.9713	.9161	.8145	.6675	.4940	.3238	.1841	.0885	.0347	.0105	.0023	.0003	.0000	.0000	.0000

APPENDIX B, continued

n	X										π									
		.05	.10	.15	.20	.25	.30	.35	.40	.45	.50	.55	.60	.65	.70	.75	.80	.85	.90	.95
	9	1.0000	1.0000	.9999	.9984	.9911	.9674	.9125	.8139	.6710	.5000	.3290	.1861	.0875	.0326	.0089	.0016	.0001	.0000	.0000
	10	1.0000	1.0000	1.0000	.9997	.9977	.9895	.9653	.9115	.8159	.6762	.5060	.3325	.1855	.0839	.0287	.0067	.0008	.0000	.0000
	11	1.0000	1.0000	1.0000	1.0000	.9995	.9972	.9886	.9648	.9129	.8204	.6831	.5122	.3344	.1820	.0775	.0233	.0041	.0003	.0000
	12	1.0000	1.0000	1.0000	1.0000	.9999	.9994	.9969	.9884	.9658	.9165	.8273	.6919	.5188	.3345	.1749	.0676	.0163	.0017	.0000
	13	1.0000	1.0000	1.0000	1.0000	1.0000	.9999	.9993	.9969	.9891	.9682	.9223	.8371	.7032	.5261	.3322	.1631	.0537	.0086	.0002
	14	1.0000	1.0000	1.0000	1.0000	1.0000	1.0000	.9999	.9994	.9972	.9904	.9720	.9304	.8500	.7178	.5346	.3267	.1444	.0352	.0020
	15	1.0000	1.0000	1.0000	1.0000	1.0000	1.0000	1.0000	.9999	.9995	.9978	.9923	.9770	.9409	.8668	.7369	.5449	.3159	.1150	.0132
	16	1.0000	1.0000	1.0000	1.0000	1.0000	1.0000	1.0000	1.0000	.9999	.9996	.9985	.9945	.9830	.9538	.8887	.7631	.5587	.2946	.0665
	17	1.0000	1.0000	1.0000	1.0000	1.0000	1.0000	1.0000	1.0000	1.0000	1.0000	.9998	.9992	.9969	.9896	.9690	.9171	.8015	.5797	.2453
	18	1.0000	1.0000	1.0000	1.0000	1.0000	1.0000	1.0000	1.0000	1.0000	1.0000	1.0000	.9999	.9997	.9989	.9958	.9856	.9544	.8649	.6226
	19	1.0000	1.0000	1.0000	1.0000	1.0000	1.0000	1.0000	1.0000	1.0000	1.0000	1.0000	1.0000	1.0000	1.0000	1.0000	1.0000	1.0000	1.0000	1.0000
20	0	.3585	.1216	.0388	.0115	.0032	.0008	.0002	.0000	.0000	.0000	.0000	.0000	.0000	.0000	.0000	.0000	.0000	.0000	.0000
	1	.7358	.3917	.1756	.0692	.0243	.0076	.0021	.0005	.0001	.0000	.0000	.0000	.0000	.0000	.0000	.0000	.0000	.0000	.0000
	2	.9245	.6769	.4049	.2061	.0913	.0355	.0121	.0036	.0009	.0002	.0000	.0000	.0000	.0000	.0000	.0000	.0000	.0000	.0000
	3	.9841	.8670	.6477	.4114	.2252	.1071	.0444	.0160	.0049	.0013	.0003	.0000	.0000	.0000	.0000	.0000	.0000	.0000	.0000
	4	.9974	.9568	.8298	.6296	.4148	.2375	.1182	.0510	.0189	.0059	.0015	.0003	.0000	.0000	.0000	.0000	.0000	.0000	.0000
	5	.9997	.9887	.9327	.8042	.6172	.4164	.2454	.1256	.0553	.0207	.0064	.0016	.0003	.0000	.0000	.0000	.0000	.0000	.0000
	6	1.0000	.9976	.9781	.9133	.7858	.6080	.4166	.2500	.1299	.0577	.0214	.0065	.0015	.0003	.0000	.0000	.0000	.0000	.0000
	7	1.0000	.9996	.9941	.9679	.8982	.7723	.6010	.4159	.2520	.1316	.0580	.0210	.0060	.0013	.0002	.0000	.0000	.0000	.0000
	8	1.0000	.9999	.9987	.9900	.9591	.8867	.7624	.5956	.4143	.2517	.1308	.0565	.0196	.0051	.0009	.0001	.0000	.0000	.0000
	9	1.0000	1.0000	.9998	.9974	.9861	.9520	.8782	.7553	.5914	.4119	.2493	.1275	.0532	.0171	.0039	.0006	.0000	.0000	.0000
	10	1.0000	1.0000	1.0000	.9994	.9961	.9829	.9468	.8725	.7507	.5881	.4086	.2447	.1218	.0480	.0139	.0026	.0002	.0000	.0000
	11	1.0000	1.0000	1.0000	.9999	.9991	.9949	.9804	.9435	.8692	.7483	.5857	.4044	.2376	.1133	.0409	.0100	.0013	.0001	.0000
	12	1.0000	1.0000	1.0000	1.0000	.9998	.9987	.9940	.9790	.9420	.8684	.7480	.5841	.3990	.2277	.1018	.0321	.0059	.0004	.0000
	13	1.0000	1.0000	1.0000	1.0000	1.0000	.9997	.9985	.9935	.9786	.9423	.8701	.7500	.5834	.3920	.2142	.0867	.0219	.0024	.0000
	14	1.0000	1.0000	1.0000	1.0000	1.0000	1.0000	.9997	.9984	.9936	.9793	.9447	.8744	.7546	.5836	.3828	.1958	.0673	.0113	.0003
	15	1.0000	1.0000	1.0000	1.0000	1.0000	1.0000	1.0000	.9997	.9985	.9941	.9811	.9490	.8818	.7625	.5852	.3704	.1702	.0432	.0026
	16	1.0000	1.0000	1.0000	1.0000	1.0000	1.0000	1.0000	1.0000	.9997	.9987	.9951	.9840	.9556	.8929	.7748	.5886	.3523	.1330	.0159
	17	1.0000	1.0000	1.0000	1.0000	1.0000	1.0000	1.0000	1.0000	1.0000	.9998	.9991	.9964	.9879	.9645	.9087	.7939	.5951	.3231	.0755
	18	1.0000	1.0000	1.0000	1.0000	1.0000	1.0000	1.0000	1.0000	1.0000	1.0000	.9999	.9995	.9979	.9924	.9757	.9308	.8244	.6083	.2642
	19	1.0000	1.0000	1.0000	1.0000	1.0000	1.0000	1.0000	1.0000	1.0000	1.0000	1.0000	1.0000	.9998	.9992	.9968	.9885	.9612	.8784	.6415
	20	1.0000	1.0000	1.0000	1.0000	1.0000	1.0000	1.0000	1.0000	1.0000	1.0000	1.0000	1.0000	1.0000	1.0000	1.0000	1.0000	1.0000	1.0000	1.0000

SOURCE: From William J. Stevenson, Business Statistics: Concepts and Applications, 2d ed. (New York: Harper & Row, 1985), 587–593. Reproduced by permission of the publisher.

APPENDIX C
Individual Terms of the Poisson Distribution

X	μ 0.005	0.01	0.02	0.03	0.04	0.05	0.06	0.07	0.08	0.09
0	0.9950	0.9900	0.9802	0.9704	0.9608	0.9512	0.9418	0.9324	0.9231	0.9139
1	0.0050	0.0099	0.0192	0.0291	0.0384	0.0476	0.0565	0.0653	0.0738	0.0823
2	0.0000	0.0000	0.0002	0.0004	0.0008	0.0012	0.0017	0.0023	0.0030	0.0037
3	0.0000	0.0000	0.0000	0.0000	0.0000	0.0000	0.0000	0.0001	0.0001	0.0001

X	μ 0.1	0.2	0.3	0.4	0.5	0.6	0.7	0.8	0.9	1.0
0	0.9048	0.8187	0.7408	0.6703	0.6065	0.5488	0.4966	0.4493	0.4066	0.3679
1	0.0905	0.1637	0.2222	0.2681	0.3033	0.3293	0.3476	0.3595	0.3659	0.3679
2	0.0045	0.0164	0.0333	0.0536	0.0758	0.0988	0.1217	0.1438	0.1647	0.1839
3	0.0002	0.0011	0.0033	0.0072	0.0126	0.0198	0.0284	0.0383	0.0494	0.0613
4	0.0000	0.0001	0.0002	0.0007	0.0016	0.0030	0.0050	0.0077	0.0111	0.0153
5	0.0000	0.0000	0.0000	0.0001	0.0002	0.0004	0.0007	0.0012	0.0020	0.0031
6	0.0000	0.0000	0.0000	0.0000	0.0000	0.0000	0.0001	0.0002	0.0003	0.0005
7	0.0000	0.0000	0.0000	0.0000	0.0000	0.0000	0.0000	0.0000	0.0000	0.0001

X	μ 1.1	1.2	1.3	1.4	1.5	1.6	1.7	1.8	1.9	2.0
0	0.3329	0.3012	0.2725	0.2466	0.2231	0.2019	0.1827	0.1653	0.1496	0.1353
1	0.3662	0.3614	0.3543	0.3452	0.3347	0.3230	0.3106	0.2975	0.2842	0.2707
2	0.2014	0.2169	0.2303	0.2417	0.2510	0.2584	0.2640	0.2678	0.2700	0.2707
3	0.0738	0.0867	0.0998	0.1128	0.1255	0.1378	0.1496	0.1607	0.1710	0.1804
4	0.0203	0.0260	0.0324	0.0395	0.0471	0.0551	0.0636	0.0723	0.0812	0.0902
5	0.0045	0.0062	0.0084	0.0111	0.0141	0.0176	0.0216	0.0260	0.0309	0.0361
6	0.0008	0.0012	0.0018	0.0026	0.0035	0.0047	0.0061	0.0078	0.0098	0.0120
7	0.0001	0.0002	0.0003	0.0005	0.0008	0.0011	0.0015	0.0020	0.0027	0.0034
8	0.0000	0.0000	0.0001	0.0001	0.0001	0.0002	0.0003	0.0005	0.0006	0.0009
9	0.0000	0.0000	0.0000	0.0000	0.0000	0.0000	0.0001	0.0001	0.0001	0.0002

X	μ 2.1	2.2	2.3	2.4	2.5	2.6	2.7	2.8	2.9	3.0
0	0.1225	0.1108	0.1003	0.0907	0.0821	0.0743	0.0672	0.0608	0.0550	0.0498
1	0.2572	0.2438	0.2306	0.2177	0.2052	0.1931	0.1815	0.1703	0.1596	0.1494
2	0.2700	0.2681	0.2652	0.2613	0.2565	0.2510	0.2450	0.2384	0.2314	0.2240
3	0.1890	0.1966	0.2033	0.2090	0.2138	0.2176	0.2205	0.2225	0.2237	0.2240
4	0.0992	0.1082	0.1169	0.1254	0.1336	0.1414	0.1488	0.1557	0.1622	0.1680
5	0.0417	0.0476	0.0538	0.0602	0.0668	0.0735	0.0804	0.0872	0.0940	0.1008
6	0.0146	0.0174	0.0206	0.0241	0.0278	0.0319	0.0362	0.0407	0.0455	0.0504
7	0.0044	0.0055	0.0068	0.0083	0.0099	0.0118	0.0139	0.0163	0.0188	0.0216
8	0.0011	0.0015	0.0019	0.0025	0.0031	0.0038	0.0047	0.0057	0.0068	0.0081
9	0.0003	0.0004	0.0005	0.0007	0.0009	0.0011	0.0014	0.0018	0.0022	0.0027
10	0.0001	0.0001	0.0001	0.0002	0.0002	0.0003	0.0004	0.0005	0.0006	0.0008
11	0.0000	0.0000	0.0000	0.0000	0.0000	0.0001	0.0001	0.0001	0.0002	0.0002
12	0.0000	0.0000	0.0000	0.0000	0.0000	0.0000	0.0000	0.0000	0.0000	0.0001

APPENDIX C, *continued*

μ

X	3.1	3.2	3.3	3.4	3.5	3.6	3.7	3.8	3.9	4.0
0	0.0450	0.0408	0.0369	0.0334	0.0302	0.0273	0.0247	0.0224	0.0202	0.0183
1	0.1397	0.1304	0.1217	0.1135	0.1057	0.0984	0.0915	0.0850	0.0789	0.0733
2	0.2165	0.2087	0.2008	0.1929	0.1850	0.1771	0.1692	0.1615	0.1539	0.1465
3	0.2237	0.2226	0.2209	0.2186	0.2158	0.2125	0.2087	0.2046	0.2001	0.1954
4	0.1734	0.1781	0.1823	0.1858	0.1888	0.1912	0.1931	0.1944	0.1951	0.1954
5	0.1075	0.1140	0.1203	0.1264	0.1322	0.1377	0.1429	0.1477	0.1522	0.1563
6	0.0555	0.0608	0.0662	0.0716	0.0771	0.0826	0.0881	0.0936	0.0989	0.1042
7	0.0246	0.0278	0.0312	0.0348	0.0385	0.0425	0.0466	0.0508	0.0551	0.0595
8	0.0095	0.0111	0.0129	0.0148	0.0169	0.0191	0.0215	0.0241	0.0269	0.0298
9	0.0033	0.0040	0.0047	0.0056	0.0066	0.0076	0.0089	0.0102	0.0116	0.0132
10	0.0010	0.0013	0.0016	0.0019	0.0023	0.0028	0.0033	0.0039	0.0045	0.0053
11	0.0003	0.0004	0.0005	0.0006	0.0007	0.0009	0.0011	0.0013	0.0016	0.0019
12	0.0001	0.0001	0.0001	0.0002	0.0002	0.0003	0.0003	0.0004	0.0005	0.0006
13	0.0000	0.0000	0.0000	0.0000	0.0001	0.0001	0.0001	0.0001	0.0002	0.0002
14	0.0000	0.0000	0.0000	0.0000	0.0000	0.0000	0.0000	0.0000	0.0000	0.0001

μ

X	4.1	4.2	4.3	4.4	4.5	4.6	4.7	4.8	4.9	5.0
0	0.0166	0.0150	0.0136	0.0123	0.0111	0.0101	0.0091	0.0082	0.0074	0.0067
1	0.0679	0.0630	0.0583	0.0540	0.0500	0.0462	0.0427	0.0395	0.0365	0.0337
2	0.1393	0.1323	0.1254	0.1188	0.1125	0.1063	0.1005	0.0948	0.0894	0.0842
3	0.1904	0.1852	0.1798	0.1743	0.1687	0.1631	0.1574	0.1517	0.1460	0.1404
4	0.1951	0.1944	0.1933	0.1917	0.1898	0.1875	0.1849	0.1820	0.1789	0.1755
5	0.1600	0.1633	0.1662	0.1687	0.1708	0.1725	0.1738	0.1747	0.1753	0.1755
6	0.1093	0.1143	0.1191	0.1237	0.1281	0.1323	0.1362	0.1398	0.1432	0.1462
7	0.0640	0.0686	0.0732	0.0778	0.0824	0.0869	0.0914	0.0959	0.1002	0.1044
8	0.0328	0.0360	0.0393	0.0428	0.0463	0.0500	0.0537	0.0575	0.0614	0.0653
9	0.0150	0.0168	0.0188	0.0209	0.0232	0.0255	0.0280	0.0307	0.0334	0.0363
10	0.0061	0.0071	0.0081	0.0092	0.0104	0.0118	0.0132	0.0147	0.0164	0.0181
11	0.0023	0.0027	0.0032	0.0037	0.0043	0.0049	0.0056	0.0064	0.0073	0.0082
12	0.0008	0.0009	0.0011	0.0014	0.0016	0.0019	0.0022	0.0026	0.0030	0.0034
13	0.0002	0.0003	0.0004	0.0005	0.0006	0.0007	0.0008	0.0009	0.0011	0.0013
14	0.0001	0.0001	0.0001	0.0001	0.0002	0.0002	0.0003	0.0003	0.0004	0.0005
15	0.0000	0.0000	0.0000	0.0000	0.0001	0.0001	0.0001	0.0001	0.0001	0.0002

μ

X	5.1	5.2	5.3	5.4	5.5	5.6	5.7	5.8	5.9	6.0
0	0.0061	0.0055	0.0050	0.0045	0.0041	0.0037	0.0033	0.0030	0.0027	0.0025
1	0.0311	0.0287	0.0265	0.0244	0.0225	0.0207	0.0191	0.0176	0.0162	0.0149
2	0.0793	0.0746	0.0701	0.0659	0.0618	0.0580	0.0544	0.0509	0.0477	0.0446
3	0.1348	0.1293	0.1239	0.1185	0.1133	0.1082	0.1033	0.0985	0.0938	0.0892
4	0.1719	0.1681	0.1641	0.1600	0.1558	0.1515	0.1472	0.1428	0.1383	0.1339

APPENDIX C, *continued*

X	5.1	5.2	5.3	5.4	5.5	5.6	5.7	5.8	5.9	6.0
5	0.1753	0.1748	0.1740	0.1728	0.1714	0.1697	0.1678	0.1656	0.1632	0.1606
6	0.1490	0.1515	0.1537	0.1555	0.1571	0.1584	0.1594	0.1601	0.1605	0.1606
7	0.1086	0.1125	0.1163	0.1200	0.1234	0.1267	0.1298	0.1326	0.1353	0.1377
8	0.0692	0.0731	0.0771	0.0810	0.0849	0.0887	0.0925	0.0962	0.0998	0.1033
9	0.0392	0.0423	0.0454	0.0486	0.0519	0.0552	0.0586	0.0620	0.0654	0.0688
10	0.0200	0.0220	0.0241	0.0262	0.0285	0.0309	0.0334	0.0359	0.0386	0.0413
11	0.0093	0.0104	0.0116	0.0129	0.0143	0.0157	0.0173	0.0190	0.0207	0.0225
12	0.0039	0.0045	0.0051	0.0058	0.0065	0.0073	0.0082	0.0092	0.0102	0.0113
13	0.0015	0.0018	0.0021	0.0024	0.0028	0.0032	0.0036	0.0041	0.0046	0.0052
14	0.0006	0.0007	0.0008	0.0009	0.0011	0.0013	0.0015	0.0017	0.0019	0.0022
15	0.0002	0.0002	0.0003	0.0003	0.0004	0.0005	0.0006	0.0007	0.0008	0.0009
16	0.0001	0.0001	0.0001	0.0001	0.0001	0.0002	0.0002	0.0002	0.0003	0.0003
17	0.0000	0.0000	0.0000	0.0000	0.0000	0.0001	0.0001	0.0001	0.0001	0.0001

μ

X	6.1	6.2	6.3	6.4	6.5	6.6	6.7	6.8	6.9	7.0
0	0.0022	0.0020	0.0018	0.0017	0.0015	0.0014	0.0012	0.0011	0.0010	0.0009
1	0.0137	0.0126	0.0116	0.0106	0.0098	0.0090	0.0082	0.0076	0.0070	0.0064
2	0.0417	0.0390	0.0364	0.0340	0.0318	0.0296	0.0276	0.0258	0.0240	0.0223
3	0.0848	0.0806	0.0765	0.0726	0.0688	0.0652	0.0617	0.0584	0.0552	0.0521
4	0.1294	0.1249	0.1205	0.1162	0.1118	0.1076	0.1034	0.0992	0.0952	0.0912
5	0.1579	0.1549	0.1519	0.1487	0.1454	0.1420	0.1385	0.1349	0.1314	0.1277
6	0.1605	0.1601	0.1595	0.1586	0.1575	0.1562	0.1546	0.1529	0.1511	0.1490
7	0.1399	0.1418	0.1435	0.1450	0.1462	0.1472	0.1480	0.1486	0.1489	0.1490
8	0.1066	0.1099	0.1130	0.1160	0.1188	0.1215	0.1240	0.1263	0.1284	0.1304
9	0.0723	0.0757	0.0791	0.0825	0.0858	0.0891	0.0923	0.0954	0.0985	0.1014
10	0.0441	0.0469	0.0498	0.0528	0.0558	0.0588	0.0618	0.0649	0.0679	0.0710
11	0.0245	0.0265	0.0285	0.0307	0.0330	0.0353	0.0377	0.0401	0.0426	0.0452
12	0.0124	0.0137	0.0150	0.0164	0.0179	0.0194	0.0210	0.0227	0.0245	0.0264
13	0.0058	0.0065	0.0073	0.0081	0.0089	0.0098	0.0108	0.0119	0.0130	0.0142
14	0.0025	0.0029	0.0033	0.0037	0.0041	0.0046	0.0052	0.0058	0.0064	0.0071
15	0.0010	0.0012	0.0014	0.0016	0.0018	0.0020	0.0023	0.0026	0.0029	0.0033
16	0.0004	0.0005	0.0005	0.0006	0.0007	0.0008	0.0010	0.0011	0.0013	0.0014
17	0.0001	0.0002	0.0002	0.0002	0.0003	0.0003	0.0004	0.0004	0.0005	0.0006
18	0.0000	0.0001	0.0001	0.0001	0.0001	0.0001	0.0001	0.0002	0.0002	0.0002
19	0.0000	0.0000	0.0000	0.0000	0.0000	0.0000	0.0000	0.0001	0.0001	0.0001

μ

X	7.1	7.2	7.3	7.4	7.5	7.6	7.7	7.8	7.9	8.0
0	0.0008	0.0007	0.0007	0.0006	0.0006	0.0005	0.0005	0.0004	0.0004	0.0003
1	0.0059	0.0054	0.0049	0.0045	0.0041	0.0038	0.0035	0.0032	0.0029	0.0027
2	0.0208	0.0194	0.0180	0.0167	0.0156	0.0145	0.0134	0.0125	0.0116	0.0107
3	0.0492	0.0464	0.0438	0.0413	0.0389	0.0366	0.0345	0.0324	0.0305	0.0286
4	0.0874	0.0836	0.0799	0.0764	0.0729	0.0696	0.0663	0.0632	0.0602	0.0573

FUNDAMENTALS OF BUSINESS STATISTICS

APPENDIX C, *continued*

	μ									
X	7.1	7.2	7.3	7.4	7.5	7.6	7.7	7.8	7.9	8.0
5	0.1241	0.1204	0.1167	0.1130	0.1094	0.1057	0.1021	0.0986	0.0951	0.0916
6	0.1468	0.1445	0.1420	0.1394	0.1367	0.1339	0.1311	0.1282	0.1252	0.1221
7	0.1489	0.1486	0.1481	0.1474	0.1465	0.1454	0.1442	0.1428	0.1413	0.1396
8	0.1321	0.1337	0.1351	0.1363	0.1373	0.1382	0.1388	0.1392	0.1395	0.1396
9	0.1042	0.1070	0.1096	0.1121	0.1144	0.1167	0.1187	0.1207	0.1224	0.1241
10	0.0740	0.0770	0.0800	0.0829	0.0858	0.0887	0.0914	0.0941	0.0967	0.0993
11	0.0478	0.0504	0.0531	0.0558	0.0585	0.0613	0.0640	0.0667	0.0695	0.0722
12	0.0283	0.0303	0.0323	0.0344	0.0366	0.0388	0.0411	0.0434	0.0457	0.0481
13	0.0154	0.0168	0.0181	0.0196	0.0211	0.0227	0.0243	0.0260	0.0278	0.0296
14	0.0078	0.0086	0.0095	0.0104	0.0113	0.0123	0.0134	0.0145	0.0157	0.0169
15	0.0037	0.0041	0.0046	0.0051	0.0057	0.0062	0.0069	0.0075	0.0083	0.0090
16	0.0016	0.0019	0.0021	0.0024	0.0026	0.0030	0.0033	0.0037	0.0041	0.0045
17	0.0007	0.0008	0.0009	0.0010	0.0012	0.0013	0.0015	0.0017	0.0019	0.0021
18	0.0003	0.0003	0.0004	0.0004	0.0005	0.0006	0.0006	0.0007	0.0008	0.0009
19	0.0001	0.0001	0.0001	0.0002	0.0002	0.0002	0.0003	0.0003	0.0003	0.0004
20	0.0000	0.0000	0.0001	0.0001	0.0001	0.0001	0.0001	0.0001	0.0001	0.0002
21	0.0000	0.0000	0.0000	0.0000	0.0000	0.0000	0.0000	0.0000	0.0001	0.0001

	μ									
X	8.1	8.2	8.3	8.4	8.5	8.6	8.7	8.8	8.9	9.0
0	0.0003	0.0003	0.0002	0.0002	0.0002	0.0002	0.0002	0.0002	0.0001	0.0001
1	0.0025	0.0023	0.0021	0.0019	0.0017	0.0016	0.0014	0.0013	0.0012	0.0011
2	0.0100	0.0092	0.0086	0.0079	0.0074	0.0068	0.0063	0.0058	0.0054	0.0050
3	0.0269	0.0252	0.0237	0.0222	0.0208	0.0195	0.0183	0.0171	0.0160	0.0150
4	0.0544	0.0517	0.0491	0.0466	0.0443	0.0420	0.0398	0.0377	0.0357	0.0337
5	0.0882	0.0849	0.0816	0.0784	0.0752	0.0722	0.0692	0.0663	0.0635	0.0607
6	0.1191	0.1160	0.1128	0.1097	0.1066	0.1034	0.1003	0.0972	0.0941	0.0911
7	0.1378	0.1358	0.1338	0.1317	0.1294	0.1271	0.1247	0.1222	0.1197	0.1171
8	0.1395	0.1392	0.1388	0.1382	0.1375	0.1366	0.1356	0.1344	0.1332	0.1318
9	0.1256	0.1269	0.1280	0.1290	0.1299	0.1306	0.1311	0.1315	0.1317	0.1318
10	0.1017	0.1040	0.1063	0.1084	0.1104	0.1123	0.1140	0.1157	0.1172	0.1186
11	0.0749	0.0776	0.0802	0.0828	0.0853	0.0878	0.0902	0.0925	0.0948	0.0970
12	0.0505	0.0530	0.0555	0.0579	0.0604	0.0629	0.0654	0.0679	0.0703	0.0728
13	0.0315	0.0334	0.0354	0.0374	0.0395	0.0416	0.0438	0.0459	0.0481	0.0504
14	0.0182	0.0196	0.0210	0.0225	0.0240	0.0256	0.0272	0.0289	0.0306	0.0324
15	0.0098	0.0107	0.0116	0.0126	0.0136	0.0147	0.0158	0.0169	0.0182	0.0194
16	0.0050	0.0055	0.0060	0.0066	0.0072	0.0079	0.0086	0.0093	0.0101	0.0109
17	0.0024	0.0026	0.0029	0.0033	0.0036	0.0040	0.0044	0.0048	0.0053	0.0058
18	0.0011	0.0012	0.0014	0.0015	0.0017	0.0019	0.0021	0.0024	0.0026	0.0029
19	0.0005	0.0005	0.0006	0.0007	0.0008	0.0009	0.0010	0.0011	0.0012	0.0014
20	0.0002	0.0002	0.0002	0.0003	0.0003	0.0004	0.0004	0.0005	0.0005	0.0006
21	0.0001	0.0001	0.0001	0.0001	0.0001	0.0002	0.0002	0.0002	0.0002	0.0003
22	0.0000	0.0000	0.0000	0.0000	0.0001	0.0001	0.0001	0.0001	0.0001	0.0001

APPENDIX C, *continued*

	μ									
X	9.1	9.2	9.3	9.4	9.5	9.6	9.7	9.8	9.9	10.0
0	0.0001	0.0001	0.0001	0.0001	0.0001	0.0001	0.0001	0.0001	0.0001	0.0000
1	0.0010	0.0009	0.0009	0.0008	0.0007	0.0007	0.0006	0.0005	0.0005	0.0005
2	0.0046	0.0043	0.0040	0.0037	0.0034	0.0031	0.0029	0.0027	0.0025	0.0023
3	0.0140	0.0131	0.0123	0.0115	0.0107	0.0100	0.0093	0.0087	0.0081	0.0076
4	0.0319	0.0302	0.0285	0.0269	0.0254	0.0240	0.0226	0.0213	0.0201	0.0189
5	0.0581	0.0555	0.0530	0.0506	0.0483	0.0460	0.0439	0.0418	0.0398	0.0378
6	0.0881	0.0851	0.0822	0.0793	0.0764	0.0736	0.0709	0.0682	0.0656	0.0631
7	0.1145	0.1118	0.1091	0.1064	0.1037	0.1010	0.0982	0.0955	0.0928	0.0901
8	0.1302	0.1286	0.1269	0.1251	0.1232	0.1212	0.1191	0.1170	0.1148	0.1126
9	0.1317	0.1315	0.1311	0.1306	0.1300	0.1293	0.1284	0.1274	0.1263	0.1251
10	0.1198	0.1210	0.1219	0.1228	0.1235	0.1241	0.1245	0.1249	0.1250	0.1251
11	0.0991	0.1012	0.1031	0.1049	0.1067	0.1083	0.1098	0.1112	0.1125	0.1137
12	0.0752	0.0776	0.0799	0.0822	0.0844	0.0866	0.0888	0.0908	0.0928	0.0948
13	0.0526	0.0549	0.0572	0.0594	0.0617	0.0640	0.0662	0.0685	0.0707	0.0729
14	0.0342	0.0361	0.0380	0.0399	0.0419	0.0439	0.0459	0.0479	0.0500	0.0521
15	0.0208	0.0221	0.0235	0.0250	0.0265	0.0281	0.0297	0.0313	0.0330	0.0347
16	0.0118	0.0127	0.0137	0.0147	0.0157	0.0168	0.0180	0.0192	0.0204	0.0217
17	0.0063	0.0069	0.0075	0.0081	0.0088	0.0095	0.0103	0.0111	0.0119	0.0128
18	0.0032	0.0035	0.0039	0.0042	0.0046	0.0051	0.0055	0.0060	0.0065	0.0071
19	0.0015	0.0017	0.0019	0.0021	0.0023	0.0026	0.0028	0.0031	0.0034	0.0037
20	0.0007	0.0008	0.0009	0.0010	0.0011	0.0012	0.0014	0.0015	0.0017	0.0019
21	0.0003	0.0003	0.0004	0.0004	0.0005	0.0006	0.0006	0.0007	0.0008	0.0009
22	0.0001	0.0001	0.0002	0.0002	0.0002	0.0002	0.0003	0.0003	0.0004	0.0004
23	0.0000	0.0001	0.0001	0.0001	0.0001	0.0001	0.0001	0.0001	0.0002	0.0002
24	0.0000	0.0000	0.0000	0.0000	0.0000	0.0000	0.0000	0.0001	0.0001	0.0001

SOURCE: From William J. Stevenson, *Business Statistics: Concepts and Applications*, 2d ed. (New York: Harper & Row, 1985), 594–598. Reproduced by permission of the publisher.

APPENDIX D
Table of Cumulative Poisson Probabilities

X	.005	.01	.02	.03	.04	.05	.06	.07	.08	.09
0	.9950	.9900	.9802	.9704	.9608	.9512	.9418	.9324	.9231	.9139
1	1.0000	1.0000	.9998	.9996	.9992	.9988	.9983	.9977	.9970	.9962
2	1.0000	1.0000	1.0000	1.0000	1.0000	1.0000	1.0000	.9999	.9999	.9999

X	.10	.11	.12	.13	.14	.15	.16	.17	.18	.19
0	.9048	.8958	.8869	.8781	.8694	.8607	.8521	.8437	.8353	.8870
1	.9953	.9944	.9934	.9922	.9911	.9898	.9885	.9871	.9856	.9841
2	.9998	.9998	.9997	.9997	.9996	.9995	.9994	.9993	.9992	.9990
3	1.0000	1.0000	1.0000	1.0000	1.0000	1.0000	1.0000	1.0000	1.0000	1.0000

X	.20	.21	.22	.23	.24	.25	.26	.27	.28	.29
0	.8187	.8106	.8025	.7945	.7866	.7788	.7711	.7634	.7558	.7483
1	.9825	.9808	.9791	.9773	.9754	.9735	.9715	.9695	.9674	.9653
2	.9989	.9987	.9985	.9983	.9981	.9978	.9976	.9973	.9970	.9967
3	.9999	.9999	.9999	.9999	.9999	.9999	.9998	.9998	.9998	.9998
4	1.0000	1.0000	1.0000	1.0000	1.0000	1.0000	1.0000	1.0000	1.0000	1.0000

X	.30	.32	.34	.36	.38	.40	.42	.44	.46	.48
0	.7408	.7261	.7118	.6977	.6839	.6703	.6570	.6440	.6313	.6188
1	.9631	.9585	.9538	.9488	.9437	.9384	.9330	.9274	.9217	.9158
2	.9964	.9957	.9949	.9940	.9931	.9921	.9910	.9898	.9885	.9871
3	.9997	.9997	.9996	.9995	.9994	.9992	.9991	.9989	.9987	.9985
4	1.0000	1.0000	1.0000	1.0000	1.0000	.9999	.9999	.9999	.9999	.9999

X	.50	.55	.60	.65	.70	.75	.80	.85	.90	.95
0	.6065	.5769	.5488	.5220	.4966	.4724	.4493	.4274	.4066	.3867
1	.9098	.8943	.8781	.8614	.8442	.8266	.8088	.7907	.7725	.7541
2	.9856	.9815	.9769	.9717	.9659	.9595	.9526	.9451	.9371	.9287
3	.9982	.9975	.9966	.9956	.9942	.9927	.9909	.9889	.9865	.9839
4	.9998	.9997	.9996	.9994	.9992	.9989	.9986	.9982	.9977	.9971
5	1.0000	1.0000	1.0000	.9999	.9999	.9999	.9998	.9997	.9997	.9995
6	1.0000	1.0000	1.0000	1.0000	1.0000	1.0000	1.0000	1.0000	1.0000	.9999

APPENDIX D, *continued*

μ

X	1.0	1.1	1.2	1.3	1.4	1.5	1.6	1.7	1.8	1.9
0	.3679	.3329	.3012	.2725	.2466	.2231	.2019	.1827	.1653	.1496
1	.7358	.6990	.6626	.6268	.5918	.5578	.5249	.4932	.4628	.4337
2	.9197	.9004	.8795	.8571	.8335	.8088	.7834	.7572	.7306	.7037
3	.9810	.9743	.9662	.9569	.9463	.9344	.9212	.9068	.8913	.8747
4	.9963	.9946	.9923	.9893	.9857	.9814	.9763	.9704	.9636	.9559
5	.9994	.9990	.9985	.9978	.9968	.9955	.9940	.9920	.9896	.9868
6	.9999	.9999	.9997	.9996	.9994	.9991	.9987	.9981	.9974	.9966
7	1.0000	1.0000	1.0000	.9999	.9999	.9998	.9997	.9996	.9994	.9992
8	1.0000	1.0000	1.0000	1.0000	1.0000	1.0000	1.0000	.9999	.9999	.9998
9	1.0000	1.0000	1.0000	1.0000	1.0000	1.0000	1.0000	1.0000	1.0000	1.0000

μ

X	2.0	2.1	2.2	2.3	2.4	2.5	2.6	2.7	2.8	2.9
0	.1353	.1225	.1108	.1003	.0907	.0821	.0743	.0672	.0608	.0550
1	.4060	.3796	.3546	.3309	.3084	.2873	.2674	.2487	.2311	.2146
2	.6767	.6496	.6227	.5960	.5697	.5438	.5184	.4936	.4695	.4460
3	.8571	.8386	.8194	.7993	.7787	.7576	.7360	.7141	.6919	.6696
4	.9473	.9379	.9275	.9162	.9041	.8912	.8774	.8629	.8477	.8318
5	.9834	.9796	.9751	.9700	.9643	.9580	.9510	.9433	.9349	.9258
6	.9955	.9941	.9925	.9906	.9884	.9858	.9828	.9794	.9756	.9713
7	.9989	.9985	.9980	.9974	.9967	.9958	.9947	.9934	.9919	.9901
8	.9998	.9997	.9995	.9994	.9991	.9989	.9985	.9981	.9976	.9969
9	1.0000	.9999	.9999	.9999	.9998	.9997	.9996	.9995	.9993	.9991
10	1.0000	1.0000	1.0000	1.0000	1.0000	.9999	.9999	.9999	.9998	.9998
11	1.0000	1.0000	1.0000	1.0000	1.0000	1.0000	1.0000	1.0000	1.0000	.9999
12	1.0000	1.0000	1.0000	1.0000	1.0000	1.0000	1.0000	1.0000	1.0000	1.0000

μ

X	3.0	3.1	3.2	3.3	3.4	3.5	3.6	3.7	3.8	3.9
0	.0498	.0450	.0408	.0369	.0334	.0302	.0273	.0247	.0224	.0202
1	.1991	.1847	.1712	.1586	.1468	.1359	.1257	.1162	.1074	.0992
2	.4232	.4012	.3799	.3594	.3397	.3208	.3027	.2854	.2689	.2531
3	.6472	.6248	.6025	.5803	.5584	.5366	.5152	.4942	.4735	.4532
4	.8153	.7982	.7806	.7626	.7442	.7254	.7064	.6872	.6678	.6484
5	.9161	.9057	.8946	.8829	.8705	.8576	.8441	.8301	.8156	.8006
6	.9665	.9612	.9554	.9490	.9421	.9347	.9267	.9182	.9091	.8995
7	.9881	.9858	.9832	.9802	.9769	.9733	.9692	.9648	.9599	.9546
8	.9962	.9953	.9943	.9931	.9917	.9901	.9883	.9863	.9840	.9815
9	.9989	.9986	.9982	.9978	.9973	.9967	.9960	.9952	.9942	.9931
10	.9997	.9996	.9995	.9994	.9992	.9990	.9987	.9984	.9981	.9977
11	.9999	.9999	.9999	.9998	.9998	.9997	.9996	.9995	.9994	.9993
12	1.0000	1.0000	1.0000	1.0000	.9999	.9999	.9999	.9999	.9998	.9998
13	1.0000	1.0000	1.0000	1.0000	1.0000	1.0000	1.0000	1.0000	1.0000	.9999
14	1.0000	1.0000	1.0000	1.0000	1.0000	1.0000	1.0000	1.0000	1.0000	1.0000

APPENDIX D, *continued*

						μ				
X	4.0	4.2	4.4	4.6	4.8	5.0	5.2	5.4	5.6	5.8
0	.0183	.0150	.0123	.0101	.0082	.0067	.0055	.0045	.0037	.0030
1	.0916	.0780	.0663	.0563	.0477	.0404	.0342	.0289	.0244	.0206
2	.2381	.2102	.1851	.1626	.1425	.1247	.1088	.0948	.0824	.0715
3	.4335	.3954	.3594	.3257	.2942	.2650	.2381	.2133	.1906	.1700
4	.6288	.5898	.5512	.5132	.4763	.4405	.4061	.3733	.3421	.3127
5	.7851	.7531	.7199	.6858	.6510	.6160	.5809	.5461	.5119	.4783
6	.8893	.8675	.8436	.8180	.7908	.7622	.7324	.7017	.6703	.6384
7	.9489	.9361	.9214	.9049	.8867	.8666	.8449	.8217	.7970	.7710
8	.9786	.9721	.9642	.9549	.9442	.9319	.9181	.9026	.8857	.8672
9	.9919	.9889	.9851	.9805	.9749	.9682	.9603	.9512	.9409	.9292
10	.9972	.9959	.9943	.9922	.9896	.9863	.9823	.9775	.9718	.9651
11	.9991	.9986	.9980	.9971	.9960	.9945	.9927	.9904	.9875	.9840
12	.9997	.9996	.9993	.9990	.9986	.9980	.9972	.9962	.9949	.9932
13	.9999	.9999	.9998	.9997	.9995	.9993	.9990	.9986	.9980	.9973
14	1.0000	1.0000	.9999	.9999	.9999	.9998	.9997	.9995	.9993	.9990
15	1.0000	1.0000	1.0000	1.0000	1.0000	.9999	.9999	.9998	.9998	.9996
16	1.0000	1.0000	1.0000	1.0000	1.0000	1.0000	1.0000	.9999	.9999	.9999
17	1.0000	1.0000	1.0000	1.0000	1.0000	1.0000	1.0000	1.0000	1.0000	1.0000

						μ				
X	6.0	6.2	6.4	6.6	6.8	7.0	7.2	7.4	7.6	7.8
0	.0025	.0020	.0017	.0014	.0011	.0009	.0007	.0006	.0005	.0004
1	.0174	.0146	.0123	.0103	.0087	.0073	.0061	.0051	.0043	.0036
2	.0620	.0536	.0463	.0400	.0344	.0296	.0255	.0219	.0188	.0161
3	.1512	.1342	.1189	.1052	.0928	.0818	.0719	.0632	.0554	.0485
4	.2851	.2592	.2351	.2127	.1920	.1730	.1555	.1395	.1249	.1117
5	.4457	.4141	.3837	.3547	.3270	.3007	.2759	.2526	.2307	.2103
6	.6063	.5742	.5423	.5108	.4799	.4497	.4204	.3920	.3646	.3384
7	.7440	.7160	.6873	.6581	.6285	.5987	.5689	.5393	.5100	.4812
8	.8472	.8259	.8033	.7796	.7548	.7291	.7027	.6757	.6482	.6204
9	.9161	.9016	.8858	.8686	.8502	.8305	.8096	.7877	.7649	.7411
10	.9574	.9486	.9386	.9274	.9151	.9015	.8867	.8707	.8535	.8352
11	.9799	.9750	.9693	.9627	.9552	.9466	.9371	.9265	.9148	.9020
12	.9912	.9887	.9857	.9821	.9779	.9730	.9673	.9609	.9536	.9454
13	.9964	.9952	.9937	.9920	.9898	.9872	.9841	.9805	.9762	.9714
14	.9986	.9981	.9974	.9966	.9956	.9943	.9927	.9908	.9886	.9859
15	.9995	.9993	.9990	.9986	.9982	.9976	.9969	.9959	.9948	.9934
16	.9998	.9997	.9996	.9995	.9993	.9990	.9987	.9983	.9978	.9971
17	.9999	.9999	.9999	.9998	.9997	.9996	.9995	.9993	.9991	.9988
18	1.0000	1.0000	1.0000	.9999	.9999	.9999	.9998	.9997	.9996	.9995
19	1.0000	1.0000	1.0000	1.0000	1.0000	1.0000	.9999	.9999	.9999	.9998
20	1.0000	1.0000	1.0000	1.0000	1.0000	1.0000	1.0000	1.0000	1.0000	.9999
21	1.0000	1.0000	1.0000	1.0000	1.0000	1.0000	1.0000	1.0000	1.0000	1.0000

APPENDIX D, *continued*

X	8.0	8.5	9.0	9.5	10.0	10.5	11.0	11.5	12.0	12.5
0	.0003	.0002	.0001	.0001	.0000	.0000	.0000	.0000	.0000	.0000
1	.0030	.0019	.0012	.0008	.0005	.0003	.0002	.0001	.0001	.0001
2	.0138	.0093	.0062	.0042	.0028	.0018	.0012	.0008	.0005	.0003
3	.0424	.0301	.0212	.0149	.0103	.0071	.0049	.0034	.0023	.0016
4	.0996	.0744	.0550	.0403	.0293	.0211	.0151	.0107	.0076	.0053
5	.1912	.1496	.1157	.0885	.0671	.0504	.0375	.0277	.0203	.0148
6	.3134	.2562	.2068	.1649	.1301	.1016	.0786	.0603	.0458	.0346
7	.4530	.3856	.3239	.2687	.2202	.1785	.1432	.1137	.0895	.0698
8	.5925	.5231	.4557	.3918	.3328	.2794	.2320	.1906	.1550	.1249
9	.7166	.6530	.5874	.5218	.4579	.3971	.3405	.2888	.2424	.2014
10	.8159	.7634	.7060	.6453	.5830	.5207	.4599	.4017	.3472	.2971
11	.8881	.8487	.8030	.7520	.6968	.6387	.5793	.5198	.4616	.4058
12	.9362	.9091	.8758	.8364	.7916	.7420	.6887	.6329	.5760	.5190
13	.9658	.9486	.9261	.8981	.8645	.8253	.7813	.7330	.6815	.6278
14	.9827	.9726	.9585	.9400	.9165	.8879	.8540	.8153	.7720	.7250
15	.9918	.9862	.9780	.9665	.9513	.9317	.9074	.8783	.8444	.8060
16	.9963	.9934	.9889	.9823	.9730	.9604	.9441	.9236	.8987	.8693
17	.9984	.9970	.9947	.9911	.9857	.9781	.9678	.9542	.9370	.9158
18	.9993	.9987	.9976	.9957	.9928	.9885	.9823	.9738	.9626	.9481
19	.9997	.9995	.9989	.9980	.9965	.9942	.9907	.9857	.9787	.9694
20	.9999	.9998	.9996	.9991	.9984	.9972	.9953	.9925	.9884	.9827
21	1.0000	.9999	.9998	.9996	.9993	.9987	.9977	.9962	.9939	.9906
22	1.0000	1.0000	.9999	.9999	.9997	.9994	.9990	.9982	.9970	.9951
23	1.0000	1.0000	1.0000	.9999	.9999	.9998	.9995	.9992	.9985	.9975
24	1.0000	1.0000	1.0000	1.0000	1.0000	.9999	.9998	.9996	.9993	.9988
25	1.0000	1.0000	1.0000	1.0000	1.0000	1.0000	.9999	.9998	.9997	.9994
26	1.0000	1.0000	1.0000	1.0000	1.0000	1.0000	1.0000	.9999	.9999	.9997
27	1.0000	1.0000	1.0000	1.0000	1.0000	1.0000	1.0000	1.0000	.9999	.9999

SOURCE: From William J. Stevenson, *Business Statistics: Concepts and Applications,* 2d ed. (New York: Harper & Row, 1985), 599–602. Reproduced by permission of the publisher.

APPENDIX E
Table of Areas for Standard Normal Probability Distribution

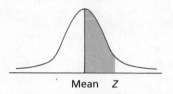

Mean Z

Z	.00	.01	.02	.03	.04	.05	.06	.07	.08	.09
0.0	.0000	.0040	.0080	.0120	.0160	.0199	.0239	.0279	.0319	.0359
0.1	.0398	.0438	.0478	.0517	.0557	.0596	.0636	.0675	.0714	.0753
0.2	.0793	.0832	.0871	.0910	.0948	.0987	.1026	.1064	.1103	.1141
0.3	.1179	.1217	.1255	.1293	.1331	.1368	.1406	.1443	.1480	.1517
0.4	.1554	.1591	.1628	.1664	.1700	.1736	.1772	.1808	.1844	.1879
0.5	.1915	.1950	.1985	.2019	.2054	.2088	.2123	.2157	.2190	.2224
0.6	.2257	.2291	.2324	.2357	.2389	.2422	.2454	.2486	.2518	.2549
0.7	.2580	.2612	.2642	.2673	.2704	.2734	.2764	.2794	.2823	.2852
0.8	.2881	.2910	.2939	.2967	.2995	.3023	.3051	.3078	.3106	.3133
0.9	.3159	.3186	.3212	.3238	.3264	.3289	.3315	.3340	.3365	.3389
1.0	.3413	.3438	.3461	.3485	.3508	.3531	.3554	.3577	.3599	.3621
1.1	.3643	.3665	.3686	.3708	.3729	.3749	.3770	.3790	.3810	.3830
1.2	.3849	.3869	.3888	.3907	.3925	.3944	.3962	.3980	.3997	.4015
1.3	.4032	.4049	.4066	.4082	.4099	.4115	.4131	.4147	.4162	.4177
1.4	.4192	.4207	.4222	.4236	.4251	.4265	.4279	.4292	.4306	.4319
1.5	.4332	.4345	.4357	.4370	.4382	.4394	.4406	.4418	.4429	.4441
1.6	.4452	.4463	.4474	.4484	.4495	.4505	.4515	.4525	.4535	.4545
1.7	.4554	.4564	.4573	.4582	.4591	.4599	.4608	.4616	.4625	.4633
1.8	.4641	.4649	.4656	.4664	.4671	.4678	.4686	.4693	.4699	.4706
1.9	.4713	.4719	.4726	.4732	.4738	.4744	.4750	.4756	.4761	.4767
2.0	.4772	.4778	.4783	.4788	.4793	.4798	.4803	.4808	.4812	.4817
2.1	.4821	.4826	.4830	.4834	.4838	.4842	.4846	.4850	.4854	.4857
2.2	.4861	.4864	.4868	.4871	.4875	.4878	.4881	.4884	.4887	.4890
2.3	.4893	.4896	.4898	.4901	.4904	.4906	.4909	.4911	.4913	.4916
2.4	.4918	.4920	.4922	.4925	.4927	.4929	.4931	.4932	.4934	.4936
2.5	.4938	.4940	.4941	.4943	.4945	.4946	.4948	.4949	.4951	.4952
2.6	.4953	.4955	.4956	.4957	.4959	.4960	.4961	.4962	.4963	.4964
2.7	.4965	.4966	.4967	.4968	.4969	.4970	.4971	.4972	.4973	.4974
2.8	.4974	.4975	.4976	.4977	.4977	.4978	.4979	.4979	.4980	.4981
2.9	.4981	.4982	.4982	.4983	.4984	.4984	.4985	.4985	.4986	.4986
3.0	.49865	.4987	.4987	.4988	.4988	.4989	.4989	.4989	.4990	.4990
4.0	.4999683									

APPENDIX F
Table of Random Numbers

76308	81870	56194	82145	39689	80578	48867
17997	27746	31485	79338	77699	79670	12200
90287	29825	58111	63618	23423	98122	27622
88984	34258	58900	92055	40430	13600	67650
38701	87958	31291	11272	79154	78990	52820
47594	57030	83622	98042	26654	32747	92271
88219	66670	96521	13841	16472	21518	18070
18577	85216	17117	89525	12537	50977	84862
63879	30223	60923	57563	82732	32901	35310
26921	90580	30554	22126	49030	82172	33360
24668	75119	86944	65054	84632	46567	59500
13617	53676	75913	57961	86015	54912	68556
18301	88651	91713	22680	86506	80540	45397
78448	93827	77334	67953	90160	29820	62810
71651	45391	92475	82123	71032	96058	63060
27946	68955	74802	22111	84623	83809	92754
61811	57299	35745	45807	86015	43299	44635
39398	37002	73568	52667	86506	19379	50338
94352	25816	69410	72125	90160	29331	13543
43088	42206	10505	27219	71032	13114	63620
85970	35632	91891	40086	67987	31452	40268
18622	31872	78624	61129	31537	77570	74969
34310	23464	33479	63127	87371	50490	65142
90890	87484	30126	24071	38398	15690	11968
50160	44927	35804	82877	80339	15339	64524
40883	21335	75567	98697	63236	61795	43600
99820	92176	89820	67985	58831	40853	67442
96730	35287	30587	23483	36926	49890	99544
19978	78167	14482	15185	70612	79080	53630
14479	63629	10070	40778	40058	44187	14311
79187	43934	11340	59790	85236	55515	40443
73070	57700	60689	68662	82114	82956	76694
54561	56872	56377	79550	49077	54597	44393
33135	11746	33060	65098	16590	66045	33398
38249	94511	42467	79657	20130	78280	86382

APPENDIX F, *continued*

85847	22486	93569	91855	63420	67450	32927
94823	45000	47532	57770	28336	11827	39218
34677	36354	68300	43098	44018	95132	67820
20160	43755	51769	79654	84181	38781	41299
40391	24426	34676	42714	41123	89129	22943
22810	27731	66268	75303	58947	10870	77806
62500	11834	79387	33201	48820	39683	97818
14810	76572	83121	77336	88499	96208	20498
59143	85115	97518	67371	86488	57727	93840
50284	24698	18669	84687	66983	10982	83282
81839	83131	51176	81291	53270	34995	63202
79862	59870	31550	30349	38695	99783	36850
43772	76622	54767	14020	66505	18015	47131
10798	75300	53779	16087	86884	30376	34790
29607	14022	62895	72195	10148	44963	98559
32376	35302	50560	70384	25261	53792	64261
87319	97405	90436	90122	18160	81797	70490
94144	91416	34230	51659	86225	44073	97091
92396	37832	35125	44163	89450	95350	64717
63434	54675	40670	55393	65289	73590	46554
45774	92679	46103	62513	61409	52832	43294
81730	81854	35625	35256	17855	19168	33707
33969	29131	90398	96752	89230	32763	24154
49972	50153	19246	83810	55928	40872	23485
74296	48171	39177	86010	39249	18252	91050
76290	35390	16527	27358	52412	95019	96172
89826	84318	24379	42745	11686	12499	35247
25520	94710	84209	59980	73065	41722	26321
16290	95205	47511	23316	74951	56038	33059
37403	38221	76241	66151	14644	51314	58313
33558	40785	49615	96305	83815	55106	67906
84867	10575	95189	93267	76148	51478	56886
91123	51351	18536	61509	10680	98766	73630
92745	26116	93578	70688	21976	98236	32551
44668	39331	10269	64547	21089	30293	71185

APPENDIX G
Table of the *t* Distribution

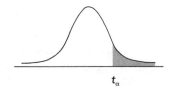

t_α

df	$t_{.100}$	$t_{.050}$	$t_{.025}$	$t_{.010}$	$t_{.005}$
1	3.078	6.314	12.706	31.821	63.657
2	1.886	2.920	4.303	6.965	9.925
3	1.638	2.353	3.182	4.541	5.841
4	1.533	2.132	2.776	3.747	4.604
5	1.476	2.015	2.571	3.365	4.032
6	1.440	1.943	2.447	3.143	3.707
7	1.415	1.895	2.365	2.998	3.499
8	1.397	1.860	2.306	2.896	3.355
9	1.383	1.833	2.262	2.821	3.250
10	1.372	1.812	2.228	2.764	3.169
11	1.363	1.796	2.201	2.718	3.106
12	1.356	1.782	2.179	2.681	3.055
13	1.350	1.771	2.160	2.650	3.012
14	1.345	1.761	2.145	2.624	2.977
15	1.341	1.753	2.131	2.602	2.947
16	1.337	1.746	2.120	2.583	2.921
17	1.333	1.740	2.110	2.567	2.898
18	1.330	1.734	2.101	2.552	2.878
19	1.328	1.729	2.093	2.539	2.861
20	1.325	1.725	2.086	2.528	2.845
21	1.323	1.721	2.080	2.518	2.831
22	1.321	1.717	2.074	2.508	2.819
23	1.319	1.714	2.069	2.500	2.807
24	1.318	1.711	2.064	2.492	2.797
25	1.316	1.708	2.060	2.485	2.787
26	1.315	1.706	2.056	2.479	2.779
27	1.314	1.703	2.052	2.473	2.771
28	1.313	1.701	2.048	2.467	2.763
29	1.311	1.699	2.045	2.462	2.756
inf.	1.282	1.645	1.960	2.326	2.576

SOURCE: From "Table of Percentage Points of the *t*-Distribution." Computed by Maxine Merrington, *Biometrika*, Vol. 32 (1941), p. 300. Reproduced by permission of the trustees of *Biometrika*.

APPENDIX H
Table of Chi-square Distribution

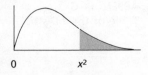

0   x^2

df	$\chi^2 0.995$	$\chi^2 0.990$	$\chi^2 0.975$	$\chi^2 0.950$	$\chi^2 0.900$
1	0.0000393	0.0001571	0.0009821	0.0039321	0.0157908
2	0.0100251	0.0201007	0.0506356	0.102587	0.210720
3	0.0717212	0.114832	0.215795	0.351846	0.584375
4	0.206990	0.297110	0.484419	0.710721	1.063623
5	0.411740	0.554300	0.831211	1.145476	1.61031
6	0.675727	0.872085	1.237347	1.63539	2.20413
7	0.989265	1.239043	1.68987	2.16735	2.83311
8	1.344419	1.646482	2.17973	2.73264	3.48954
9	1.734926	2.087912	2.70039	3.32511	4.168216
10	2.15585	2.55821	3.24697	3.94030	4.86518
11	2.60321	3.05347	3.81575	4.57481	5.57779
12	3.07382	3.57056	4.40379	5.22603	6.30380
13	3.56503	4.10691	5.00874	5.89186	7.04150
14	4.07468	4.66043	5.62872	6.57063	7.78953
15	4.60094	5.22935	6.26214	7.26094	8.54675
16	5.14224	5.81221	6.90766	7.96164	9.31223
17	5.69724	6.40776	7.56418	8.67176	10.0852
18	6.26481	7.01491	8.23075	9.39046	10.8649
19	6.84398	7.63273	8.90655	10.1170	11.6509
20	7.43386	8.26040	9.59083	10.8508	12.4426
21	8.03366	8.89720	10.28293	11.5913	13.2396
22	8.64272	9.54249	10.9823	12.3380	14.0415
23	9.26042	10.19567	11.6885	13.0905	14.8479
24	9.88623	10.8564	12.4011	13.8484	15.6587
25	10.5197	11.5240	13.1197	14.6114	16.4734
26	11.1603	12.1981	13.8439	15.3791	17.2919
27	11.8076	12.8786	14.5733	16.1513	18.1138
28	12.4613	13.5648	15.3079	16.9279	18.9302
29	13.1211	14.2565	16.0471	17.7083	19.7677
30	13.7867	14.9535	16.7908	18.4926	20.5992
40	20.7065	22.1643	24.4331	26.5093	29.0505
50	27.9907	29.7067	32.3574	34.7642	37.6886
60	35.5347	37.4848	40.4817	43..1879	46.4589
70	43.2752	45.4418	48.7576	51.7393	55.3290
80	51.1720	53.5400	57.1532	60.3915	64.2778
90	59.1963	61.7541	65.6466	69.1260	73.2912
100	67.3276	70.0648	74.2219	77.9295	82.3581

APPENDIX H, *continued*

df	$\chi^2 0.100$	$\chi^2 0.050$	$\chi^2 0.025$	$\chi^2 0.010$	$\chi^2 0.005$
1	2.70554	3.84146	5.02389	6.63490	7.87944
2	4.60517	5.99147	7.37776	9.21034	10.5966
3	6.25139	7.81473	9.34840	11.3449	12.8381
4	7.77944	9.48773	11.1433	13.2767	14.8602
5	9.23635	11.0705	12.8325	15.0863	16.7496
6	10.6446	12.5916	14.4494	16.8119	18.5476
7	12.0170	14.0671	16.0128	18.4753	20.2777
8	13.3616	15.5073	17.5346	20.0902	21.9550
9	14.6837	16.9190	19.0228	21.6660	23.5893
10	15.9871	18.3070	20.4831	23.2093	25.1882
11	17.2750	19.6751	21.9200	24.7250	26.7569
12	18.5494	21.0261	23.3367	26.2170	28.2995
13	19.8119	22.3621	24.7356	27.6883	29.8194
14	21.0642	23.6848	26.1190	29.1413	31.3193
15	22.3072	24.9958	27.4884	30.5779	32.8013
16	23.5418	26.2962	28.8454	31.9999	34.2672
17	24.7690	27.5871	30.1910	33.4087	35.7185
18	25.9894	28.8693	31.5264	34.8053	37.1564
19	27.2036	30.1435	32.8523	36.1908	38.5822
20	28.4120	31.4104	34.1696	37.5662	39.9968
21	29.6151	32.6705	35.4789	38.9321	41.4010
22	30.8133	33.9244	36.7807	40.2894	42.7956
23	32.0069	35.1725	38.0757	41.6384	44.1813
24	33.1963	36.4151	39.3641	42.9798	45.5585
25	34.3816	37.6525	40.6465	44.3141	46.9278
26	35.5631	38.8852	41.9232	45.6417	48.2899
27	36.7412	40.1133	43.1944	46.9630	49.6449
28	37.9159	41.3372	44.4607	48.2782	50.9933
29	39.0875	42.5569	45.7222	49.5879	52.3356
30	40.2560	43.7729	46.9792	50.8922	53.6720
40	51.8050	55.7585	59.3417	63.6907	66.7659
50	63.1671	67.5048	71.4202	76.1539	79.4900
60	74.3970	79.0819	83.2976	88.3794	91.9517
70	85.5271	90.5312	95.0231	100.425	104.215
80	96.5782	101.879	106.629	112.329	116.321
90	107.565	113.145	118.136	124.116	128.299
100	118.498	124.342	129.561	135.807	140.169

SOURCE: From "Tables of the Percentage Points of the χ^2-Distribution,: *Biometrika*, Vol. 32 (1941), pp. 188–189, by Catherine M. Thompson. Reproduced by permission of the trustees of *Biometrika*.

APPENDIX I

Data Base

The following data base contains nine variables measured on N = 200 fictitious company employees. Each row represents the values of the nine variables for a single employee. The number in the first column (1–200) is the employee number. Each subsequent column represents the values of one variable for all 200 employees.

The nine variables are defined as follows:

$X1$ = number of years with the company

$X2$ = number of overtime hours during the last six months

$X3$ = sex: 1 = male; 2 = female

$X4$ = number of company courses completed

$X5$ = number of sick days taken during the last six months

$X6$ = score on company aptitude test

$X7$ = college credit standing: 0 = 0–89 credits; 1 = 90–179 credits; 2 = 180+ credits

$X8$ = annual salary

$X9$ = employee age

APPENDIX I

n	X1	X2	X3	X4	X5	X6	X7	X8	X9
1	9	100	1	3	8	97.51	1	18450	35
2	19	180	2	1	3	91.36	1	21750	40
3	14	92	2	3	4	107.29	1	27900	39
4	7	94	1	2	0	91.16	1	18950	43
5	12	24	1	2	3	121.13	1	26840	53
6	6	46	2	1	4	101.42	1	23700	48
7	5	130	1	2	3	103.07	1	20500	28
8	3	74	1	1	1	124.67	1	21400	30
9	18	174	1	2	5	106.79	1	19850	35
10	18	166	2	4	2	105.77	1	26800	42
11	15	174	2	2	4	98.77	1	33400	61
12	21	78	2	2	3	102.07	1	25600	53
13	4	56	1	2	5	94.89	1	26800	48
14	12	194	1	3	6	100.91	1	29800	32
15	22	138	1	4	4	100.91	1	24600	40
16	22	194	2	1	3	79.74	0	32950	58
17	21	104	1	1	5	90.11	1	36700	63
18	14	104	1	5	8	95.53	1	32900	56
19	6	30	1	5	9	106.10	1	27600	43
20	12	170	1	2	4	109.91	1	25600	34

APPENDIX I, *continued*

n	X1	X2	X3	X4	X5	X6	X7	X8	X9
21	11	82	1	0	6	85.73	0	28350	42
22	8	164	2	4	6	85.69	0	35900	57
23	19	196	1	3	1	102.12	1	38600	65
24	1	116	1	0	9	95.25	1	18300	28
25	6	54	2	0	7	102.17	1	34800	53
26	17	156	1	4	3	115.23	1	31700	46
27	20	154	1	3	5	107.69	1	33500	45
28	7	144	1	3	4	109.81	1	26000	29
29	20	42	2	2	6	107.03	1	32950	56
30	25	146	2	2	5	104.73	1	37000	65
31	22	108	2	0	4	104.73	1	40100	62
32	12	152	2	5	5	102.45	1	29700	35
33	12	110	1	3	9	110.88	1	26400	30
34	4	24	2	4	4	85.25	0	25000	25
35	18	101	1	3	5	90.64	1	37800	41
36	2	4	2	1	5	84.74	0	23800	27
37	13	154	1	4	9	106.61	1	28700	35
38	18	12	2	3	0	93.49	1	39400	58
39	10	134	2	1	5	94.71	1	29400	34
40	17	60	2	1	6	87.96	1	36700	41
41	3	6	1	3	9	99.84	1	18300	22
42	16	12	1	1	6	98.66	1	26500	33
43	16	104	2	0	3	108.02	1	27000	38
44	22	66	1	3	7	88.99	0	37400	59
45	5	26	2	1	3	99.93	1	36000	50
46	1	20	2	5	4	103.67	1	27000	31
47	7	42	1	3	3	84.68	0	26000	32
48	5	112	1	4	2	122.43	1	29700	40
49	21	76	1	5	4	79.74	0	40500	61
50	16	150	2	3	5	90.11	1	36700	53
51	20	0	2	1	4	95.53	1	38400	58
52	25	102	1	3	6	106.01	1	42900	63
53	14	94	2	2	1	109.91	1	27800	36
54	22	196	2	0	7	86.68	0	23800	41
55	14	46	2	3	6	87.22	0	25400	36
56	2	154	1	1	9	107.64	1	14200	25
57	16	84	1	1	3	74.95	0	21500	39
58	6	120	1	3	6	90.16	1	38100	44
59	7	44	2	1	6	97.43	1	35400	51
60	10	182	1	4	9	88.27	0	39700	64

APPENDIX I, *continued*

n	X1	X2	X3	X4	X5	X6	X7	X8	X9
61	9	136	1	4	4	84.02	0	28600	36
62	9	72	2	0	5	91.96	1	22400	37
63	7	44	2	1	7	85.38	0	23850	34
64	14	184	2	1	7	94.05	1	33840	52
65	8	68	2	1	3	94.45	1	21000	28
66	21	68	1	5	4	100.23	1	36700	62
67	22	126	1	5	4	94.19	1	38600	58
68	20	60	2	3	3	99.19	1	34800	60
69	6	62	2	2	5	79.62	0	35900	52
70	3	168	2	1	6	87.46	0	28600	27
71	15	112	1	1	4	92.50	1	29700	36
72	4	96	1	3	6	100.08	1	30100	43
73	11	0	1	5	7	95.32	1	32600	47
74	21	48	2	3	4	85.38	0	42850	56
75	12	110	1	4	7	94.05	1	37800	42
76	10	82	1	5	2	94.45	1	37000	39
77	4	28	1	0	3	100.23	1	26150	27
78	3	48	1	3	1	94.71	1	32000	32
79	8	72	1	0	9	99.98	1	35000	41
80	11	124	1	5	4	102.89	1	38000	50
81	3	154	1	2	3	107.69	1	21450	26
82	15	64	1	2	7	114.86	1	38200	42
83	21	24	1	2	6	98.59	1	39250	49
84	2	170	1	3	4	110.42	1	22850	27
85	17	180	1	2	5	96.81	1	33900	39
86	3	156	1	2	8	92.86	1	22800	25
87	7	120	1	5	6	100.74	1	25650	29
88	23	192	1	2	8	96.71	1	42750	62
89	2	102	2	2	1	93.05	1	36800	40
90	16	108	1	1	3	89.20	0	36750	41
91	20	186	1	3	2	88.02	0	38950	47
92	6	22	1	0	3	90.94	1	25000	28
93	25	10	2	2	3	102.43	1	41000	60
94	13	176	2	3	4	110.88	1	38600	52
95	11	90	2	3	7	85.25	0	38100	45
96	22	68	1	0	6	90.64	1	41250	62
97	12	56	2	1	3	84.74	0	31400	36
98	12	88	1	2	1	106.61	1	32800	35
99	10	126	1	3	6	94.06	1	25400	31
100	4	14	1	2	1	96.71	1	22300	26

APPENDIX I, *continued*

n	X1	X2	X3	X4	X5	X6	X7	X8	X9
101	3	12	1	0	7	93.05	1	24700	24
102	11	136	1	2	3	89.20	0	29800	35
103	11	144	1	2	5	111.16	1	32600	42
104	18	190	2	3	5	112.40	1	38000	48
105	11	164	1	0	4	122.30	1	37800	50
106	4	182	2	2	3	91.70	1	29400	29
107	5	166	1	1	6	112.81	1	31700	32
108	21	54	1	4	5	99.21	1	43600	60
109	9	26	2	3	7	93.02	1	21450	29
110	22	102	1	1	4	108.69	1	31700	43
111	19	154	2	1	4	102.77	1	32000	45
112	18	110	1	2	0	94.30	1	31800	42
113	13	26	2	2	7	94.45	1	30000	38
114	3	100	2	3	7	100.23	1	27800	35
115	3	120	1	4	1	84.71	1	25100	24
116	8	22	1	0	8	99.19	1	27200	33
117	14	146	2	4	7	79.62	1	33800	38
118	17	40	2	5	5	87.46	1	32900	47
119	7	72	1	2	7	81.56	1	29100	31
120	10	170	1	4	0	98.77	1	32000	45
121	5	98	2	0	8	102.87	1	22400	26
122	17	166	2	5	7	94.89	1	32800	42
123	11	44	2	4	3	101.24	1	25600	32
124	2	198	2	2	0	111.89	1	31400	29
125	24	152	2	2	8	90.64	1	41250	61
126	24	30	2	3	2	84.74	0	37800	57
127	10	20	1	1	6	96.61	1	35900	43
128	10	40	1	3	4	93.49	1	34200	40
129	0	74	1	3	7	94.71	1	30850	29
130	7	112	2	0	2	97.71	1	31200	29
131	18	12	2	5	3	108.30	1	34800	37
132	5	172	1	4	0	84.02	0	35850	40
133	24	54	1	0	6	91.96	1	38900	53
134	1	134	1	2	5	85.38	0	24100	26
135	8	44	1	3	7	71.15	0	26350	32
136	3	64	1	1	2	89.08	0	24950	26
137	3	180	2	1	9	90.94	1	22800	23
138	13	176	2	1	3	109.59	1	29100	35
139	10	70	2	0	3	109.94	1	34300	41
140	20	114	1	4	5	114.50	1	40000	51

APPENDIX I, *continued*

n	X1	X2	X3	X4	X5	X6	X7	X8	X9
141	11	146	2	1	5	91.58	1	34300	40
142	16	26	1	0	3	95.53	1	34250	39
143	19	36	1	5	2	112.16	1	39950	57
144	10	140	2	0	1	108.67	1	39800	40
145	13	118	2	1	9	106.01	1	34700	37
146	20	186	1	2	7	108.81	1	36800	45
147	2	82	2	5	6	94.06	1	21200	23
148	13	34	1	4	3	96.71	1	28750	32
149	5	158	1	2	4	100.16	1	31200	32
150	18	6	2	2	4	95.47	1	36800	46
151	20	76	1	1	9	90.93	1	35700	48
152	24	114	2	1	8	122.93	1	39850	53
153	8	154	1	5	4	79.90	0	28750	31
154	15	50	1	4	3	93.76	1	35800	38
155	23	198	1	2	7	102.32	1	42900	61
156	7	18	2	1	1	99.19	1	25600	30
157	21	158	1	0	3	79.62	0	42650	58
158	7	158	1	4	4	84.46	0	26450	26
159	15	96	2	2	5	81.58	0	35800	38
160	2	10	2	1	7	98.77	1	21100	23
161	20	48	1	1	9	102.87	1	37850	42
162	12	94	1	0	5	94.88	1	32600	37
163	18	130	1	1	4	100.91	1	33950	38
164	7	112	1	4	2	100.91	1	28700	31
165	4	104	2	1	9	79.74	0	24850	26
166	22	34	2	5	4	90.11	1	42850	59
167	10	90	1	2	7	117.02	1	39700	50
168	8	90	1	2	6	98.05	1	36400	38
169	9	180	1	5	3	82.06	0	37400	40
170	20	138	2	1	3	111.51	1	37950	45
171	23	124	1	0	4	84.85	0	39800	48
172	13	0	1	4	2	104.97	1	32400	35
173	17	16	1	3	7	114.18	1	36150	41
174	8	94	1	0	8	83.98	0	26800	28
175	20	14	2	3	3	90.25	1	37400	40
176	8	96	1	0	3	93.49	1	30000	32
177	12	118	2	5	4	94.71	1	34800	35
178	25	152	1	0	7	97.96	1	.41900	63
179	25	108	1	0	7	108.30	1	40000	60
180	3	190	1	5	3	84.02	0	21450	20

APPENDIX I, *continued*

n	X1	X2	X3	X4	X5	X6	X7	X8	X9
181	2	114	1	4	4	91.96	1	22600	27
182	21	20	2	2	5	83.05	1	41000	57
183	9	138	2	1	5	89.20	0	39850	48
184	14	10	1	4	2	88.02	0	36400	43
185	16	36	1	4	1	80.94	1	39800	53
186	5	176	1	0	5	102.43	1	32100	32
187	24	198	1	2	5	110.88	1	42300	63
188	25	172	2	3	6	95.00	1	41700	64
189	11	190	1	2	3	106.80	1	28600	31
190	1	64	1	5	4	87.62	0	20000	21
191	3	48	1	1	6	97.57	1	24800	27
192	0	126	1	0	4	110.33	1	18250	20
193	15	32	1	3	4	85.48	0	31700	43
194	3	8	2	1	3	117.39	1	38000	37
195	5	158	1	2	7	111.04	1	26400	27
196	1	10	1	1	4	85.33	0	27450	28
197	7	118	1	3	6	94.69	1	31300	32
198	2	148	2	3	3	98.05	1	21400	23
199	2	94	1	1	1	92.44	1	20000	24
200	5	68	1	3	6	100.91	1	30000	31

APPENDIX J

Derivations

CORRELATION DERIVATION

$$r = \frac{\sum Z_X Z_Y}{N} = \sum \frac{\left(\dfrac{X - \mu_X}{\sigma_X}\right)\left(\dfrac{Y - \mu_X}{\sigma_Y}\right)}{N}$$

$$r = \frac{\sum (X - \mu_X)(Y - \mu_Y)}{\dfrac{\sqrt{\dfrac{\sum X^2}{N} - \left(\dfrac{\sum X}{N}\right)^2}\ \sqrt{\dfrac{\sum Y^2}{N} - \left(\dfrac{\sum Y}{N}\right)^2}}{N}}$$

$$r = \frac{\sum (X - \mu_X)(Y - \mu_Y)}{\dfrac{\sqrt{\dfrac{N\sum X^2 - (\sum X)^2}{N^2}}\ \sqrt{\dfrac{N\sum Y^2 - (\sum Y)^2}{N^2}}}{N}}$$

$$\frac{N\sum (X - \mu_X)(Y - \mu_Y)}{\sqrt{N\sum X^2 - (\sum X)^2}\ \sqrt{N\sum Y^2 - (\sum Y)^2}}$$

$$r = \frac{N \sum (XY - Y\mu_X - X\mu_Y + \mu_X\mu_Y)}{\sqrt{N\sum X^2 - (\sum X)^2}\ \sqrt{N\sum Y^2 - (\sum Y)^2}}$$

$$r = \frac{N\left[\sum XY - \dfrac{\sum X \sum Y}{N} - \dfrac{\sum X \sum Y}{N} + N\left(\dfrac{\sum X}{N}\dfrac{\sum Y}{N}\right)\right]}{\sqrt{N\sum X^2 - (\sum X)^2}\ \sqrt{N\sum Y^2 - (\sum Y)^2}}$$

$$r = \frac{N\left(\sum XY - \dfrac{\sum X\sum Y}{N} - \dfrac{\sum X\sum Y}{N} + \dfrac{\sum X\sum Y}{N}\right)}{\sqrt{N \sum X^2 - (\sum X)^2}\ \sqrt{N\sum Y^2 - (\sum Y)^2}}$$

$$r = \frac{N\left(\Sigma XY - \frac{\Sigma X \Sigma Y}{N}\right)}{\sqrt{N\Sigma X^2 - (\Sigma X)^2}\ \sqrt{N\Sigma Y^2 - (\Sigma Y)^2}}$$

$$r = \frac{N\Sigma XY - \Sigma X \Sigma Y}{\sqrt{N\Sigma X^2 - (\Sigma X)^2}\ \sqrt{N\Sigma Y^2 - (\Sigma Y)^2}}$$

LEAST-SQUARES DERIVATION

$$d = y - y_r$$
$$d = y - (a + bx)$$
$$d^2 = [y - (a + bx)]^2$$
$$\Sigma d^2 = \Sigma [y - (a + bx)]^2$$
$$\Sigma d^2 = \Sigma (y - a - bx)^2$$

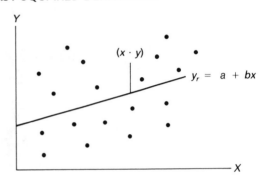

PARTIAL DERIVATIVES

$$\frac{\delta \Sigma}{\delta b} = 2\Sigma(y - bx - a)(-x) \qquad \frac{\delta \Sigma}{\delta a} = 2\Sigma(y - bx - a)(-1)$$

$$= 2\Sigma(-xy + bx^2 + ax) \qquad\qquad = 2\Sigma(-y + bx + a)$$

TO OBTAIN MINIMUMS SET PARTIALS = 0

$$\frac{\delta \Sigma}{\delta b} = 0: \ 2\Sigma(-xy + bx^2 + ax) = 0$$

$$\Sigma(-xy + bx^2 + ax) = 0$$
$$-\Sigma xy + a\Sigma x + b\Sigma x^2 = 0$$

$$\frac{\delta \Sigma}{\delta a} = 0: \ 2\Sigma(-y + bx + a) = 0$$

$$\Sigma(-y + bx + a) = 0$$
$$-\Sigma y + Na + b\Sigma x = 0$$

FIND AN *a* AND *b* SUCH THAT Σd^2 IS A MINIMUM

$$a\Sigma x + b\Sigma x^2 = \Sigma xy \qquad *(N)$$
$$Na + b\Sigma x = \Sigma y \qquad *(\Sigma x)$$

$$Na\Sigma x + Nb\Sigma x^2 = N\Sigma xy$$
$$Na\Sigma x + b(\Sigma x)^2 = \Sigma x \Sigma y$$

$$Nb\Sigma x2 - b(\Sigma x)^2 = N\Sigma xy - \Sigma x \Sigma y$$
$$b(N\Sigma x^2 - (\Sigma x)^2) = N\Sigma xy - \Sigma x \Sigma y \qquad \text{Slope Formula}$$
$$b = \frac{N\Sigma xy - \Sigma x \Sigma y}{N\Sigma x^2 - (\Sigma x)^2}$$

$$Na + b\Sigma x = \Sigma y$$
$$Na = \Sigma y - b\Sigma x$$
$$a = \frac{\Sigma y}{N} \frac{b\Sigma x}{N} \qquad \text{Y-Intercept Formula}$$
$$a = \bar{y} - b\bar{x}$$

Answers to
Even-numbered
Exercises

CHAPTER 1

2. A statistic is a numerical measurement of a sample; a parameter is a numerical measurement of a population.

4. Descriptive statistics involves providing brief summaries of data collections to aid the decision-making process. Inferential statistics is concerned with determining attributes of items sampled from a population and inferring that the population has these same attributes.

6. Data are large volumes of numerical measurements; information consists of summaries of such data collections and can be used in the decision-making process.

8. a. *Misleading:* a sample of five was taken. *Useful:* a random sample of 500 employees was surveyed using an unbiased question.

    b. *Misleading:* the statement is the opinion of a manager who does not have direct contact with the factory. *Useful:* the defective rate has been measured by company quality control people during the past three months.

    c. *Misleading:* union steward's comment at a tavern after work. *Useful:* overtime data have been collected for the past month and compared with overtime data for the same period a year ago.

CHAPTER 2

2. Usually between four and ten classes are used. The objective is to choose the number of categories so that the maximum amount of information is conveyed.

4.

X4	f
0	3
1	5
2	8
3	4
4	3
5	2
Total	25

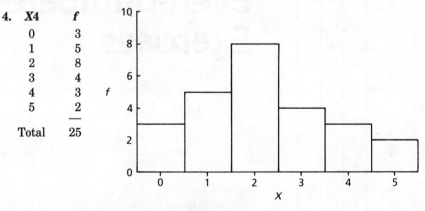

6. Frequency distribution:

Classes	f
below $20,000	5
20,000 to 29,999	26
30,000 to 39,999	17
40,000 and over	2
	50

Less-than-or-equal-to frequency distribution:		Greater-than-or-equal-to frequency distribution:	
X	**f**	**X**	**f**
19,999	5	20,000	45
29,999	31	30,000	19
39,999	48	40,000	2

8. Too few: detail of original data collection is lost.
   Too many: data collection is not adequately summarized.

10.

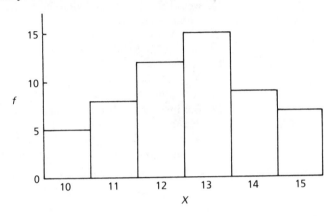

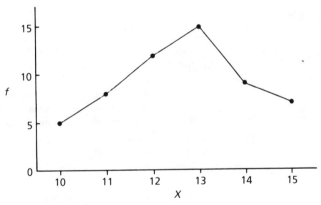

12. Greater-than-or-equal-to
   frequency distribution:

X	**f**
25	2648
36	1934
46	987
56	468

14. The middle class is too large: detail of data collection is lost.

CHAPTER 3

2. The mean is distorted if unusually large or small values are contained in the data collection.

4. The average checking account balances of the two branches are about the same. However, the accounts of Branch 2 are considerably more variable than those of Branch 1.

6. For either a sample or a population, the values are added and divided by the number of them to compute the mean. But for standard deviation, you would need to know whether to divide by N (population size) or $n - 1$ (sample size minus one).

8. $\sigma = \sqrt{9} = 3$
   $cv = 3/55 = .05$

10. $\sum X = 34$ $\sum X^2 = 90$
    $\overline{X} = 34/15 = 2.27$
    $cv = .96/2.27 = .42$ $s = \sqrt{\dfrac{90 - \dfrac{34^2}{15}}{14}} = .96$

12. Because on such exams there are often a few low scores which would distort the mean downward.

14. **a.** mean $= 75.8$ **b.** mean $= 70.5$
    median $= 77.5$ median $= 77.5$

CHAPTER 4

2. Objective probability is determined through experimentation and is more precise than subjective probability. Objective probability is only an estimate and should be applied only to situations that are similar to the one under which the data were acquired.

4. Events are mutually exclusive if they cannot occur at the same time.

6. Two events are independent if the occurrence of one is unrelated to the occurrence of the other.

8. When events are not mutually exclusive, they are simply added together. For mutually exclusive events, the items that are in both events are subtracted.

10. To revise probability estimates on the basis of sample data.

12. **a.** not a ten   **b.** not a face card   **c.** a black card
    d. a heart, diamond, or spade   **e.** not a four of hearts

14. **a.** yes   **b.** yes   **c.** no

16. $3/(3 + 2) = .6$ or 60%

18. **a.** $(19/100) + (18/100) = 37/100 = .37$ **b.** $1 - (45/100) = .55$
    c. $(10/100)(10/100) = .01$

20. **a.** 1.35% **b.** $(.09 + .05) - .0135 = .1265$ **c.** $1 - .14 = .86$

22. **a.** $80/1000 = .08$ or 8% **b.** $120/1000 = .12$ or 12%
    c. $20/1000 = .02$ or 2% **d.** $120/1000 = .12$ or 12% **e.** yes

24.

Tires

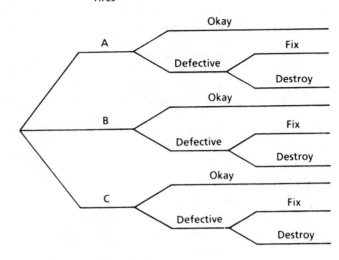

26. a. (.7 × .5) + (.3 × .25) = .425
   b. The probability that one will buy is .5. The probability that neither will buy is .25. The probability that both will buy is .25.
   c. 1 − .25 = .75
28. a. P(C|D) = P(C and D)/P(D) = .0425/.1025 = .4146
   b. P(2 GOOD PARTS|C) = (.85 × .95 × .95) = .767
       P(2 GOOD PARTS|I) = (.15 × .6 × .6)   = .054
                                              ⎯⎯⎯⎯
                                              .821

   c. P(D|C) = (.85 × .05) = .0425
       P(D|I) = (.15 × .60) = .0900
                              ⎯⎯⎯⎯
                              .1325
   d. I would need at least 2 good parts which would revise the probability of the machine being set up correctly to .767/.821 = .934.

CHAPTER 5

2. a. continuous   **b.** discrete
   c. continuous   **d.** discrete
   e. discrete   **f.** continuous
   g. discrete   **h.** continuous
4. expected value = average = 1.60
6. Use the Poisson approximation of the binomial.
   μ = (.01)(300) = 3
   P(X = 0) = .0498
   P(X ≤ 2) = .0498 + .1494 + .2240 = .4232

8. X: bad fill   **a.** $P(X = 0) = .2621$
     $\pi = .20$ **b.** $P(X \le 1) = .2621 + .3932 = .6553$
     $n = 6$ **c.** $P(X \ge 1) = 1 - P(X = 0) = 1 - .2621 = .7379$
10. $\mu = 120/\text{hour} = 2/\text{minute}$ $P(X = 0) = .1353$
12. a. binomial table   **b.** Poisson approximation
     c. binomial table   **d.** Poisson approximation
     e. normal curve approximation
14. $\mu = 96/8 \text{ hours} = 12/\text{hour} = .20/\text{minute}$
     $P(X = 0) = .8187$
     $P(X \ge 1) = 1 - P(X = 0) = 1 - .8187 = .1813$
16. So that insights into the real situation can be discovered by manipulating the model.

CHAPTER 6

2. Discrete random variables can assume only certain specified values, while continuous random variables may assume any value within some specified range.
4. A probability distribution is continuous when the random variable may assume any value within some specified range.
6. Because the normal curve is symmetrical around its mean.
8. a. $Z = 0.00$ **b.** $Z = 0.43$ **c.** $Z = -0.67$
10. $Z = (250 - 200)/30 = 1.67$ $P = (.5 - .4525) = .0475$
     $Z = (275 - 200)/30 = 2.50$ $P = (.5 - .4938) = .0062$
12. a. $Z = (75,000 - 100,000)/10,000 = -2.5$ $P = (.5 - .4938) = .0062$
     b. $Z = (110,000 - 100,000)/10,000 = 1.0$ $P = (.5 - .3413) = .1587$
     c. $Z = (95,000 - 100,000)/10,000 = -0.5$ $P = .1915 + .5000 = .6915$
     d. $Z = (120,000 - 100,000)/10,000 = 2.0$ $P = .4772 + .5000 = .9772$
     e. $Z = (85,000 - 100,000)/10,000 = -1.5$ $P = .4332$
     $Z = (90,000 - 100,000)/10,000 = -1.0$ $P = .3413$
     $\overline{}$
     $.0919$
     f. $0.67 = (X - 100,000)/10,000 = \$106,700$
     g. $-1.04 = (X - 100,000)/10,000 = \$89,600$
14. a. $Z = (4.1 - 5)/.5 = -1.8$ $P = (.5 - .4641) = .0359$
     b. $Z = (4.8 - 5)/.5 = -0.4$ $P = .1554$
     $Z = (5.3 - 5)/.5 = 0.6$ $P = .2257$
     $\overline{}$
     $.3811$
     c. $Z = (4.0 - 5)/.5 = -2.0$ $P = (.5 - .4772) = 0.0228$
     $(0.0228)(0.0228) = .00052$
     d. $-0.52 = (X - 5)/.5 = 4.74$ million
16. a. $Z = (1,525 - 1,500)/20 = 1.25$ $P = .3944$
     b. $Z = (1,475 - 1,500)/20 = -1.25$ $P = .3944$
     $Z = (1,490 - 1,500)/20 = -0.50$ $P = .1915$
     $\overline{}$
     $.2029$
     c. $1.645 = (X - 1,500)/20 = 1,532.9$ hours
     d. $-1.28 = (X - 1,500)/20 = 1,474.4$ hours

e. $Z = (1,499.5 - 1,500)/20 = -0.025 \quad P = .0100$
$Z = (1,500.5 - 1,500)/20 = 0.025 \quad P = .0100$

$.0200$

18. $\mu = 500(.08) = 40 \quad \sigma = \sqrt{500(.08)(.92)} = 6.066$
  a. $Z = (49.5 - 40)/6.066 = 1.57 \quad P = (.5 - .4418) = .0582$
  b. $Z = (39.5 - 40)/6.066 = -0.08 \quad P = (.5 - .0319) = .4681$
  c. $Z = (45.5 - 40)/6.066 = .91 \quad P = .3186$
      $Z = (44.5 - 40)/6.066 = .74 \quad P = .2704$

$.0482$

20. a. $Z = (.11 - .06)/.02 = 2.5 \quad P = .4938$
      $Z = (.09 - .06)/.02 = 1.5 \quad P = .4332$

$.0606$

  b. $Z = (.12 - .06)/.02 = 3.0 \quad P = (.5 - .49865) = .00135$
  c. $Z = (.03 - .06)/.02 = -1.5 \quad P = (.5 - .4332) = .0668$
  d. $-0.84 = (X - .06)/.02 = .0432$ or 4.32%
22. $-1.75 = (X - 500)/50 = 412.5$ hours
24. This answer will vary with each class.

CHAPTER 7

2. No listing of the population exists.
6. A smaller sample size can be used because each strata is represented by design rather than through the random selection of many items.
8. Because sampled items are concentrated, thus saving driving or walking time.
14. The term infinite population refers to a very large population. Simple random samples cannot be used because no population listing exists. Stratified, cluster, systematic, and judgement samples can all be used.

CHAPTER 8

2. A sampling distribution includes every possible sample statistic of a certain sample size that can be drawn from a distribution.
4. Because the central limit theorem allows statisticians to assume that the sampling distribution of sample statistics can be approximated by a normal probability distribution whenever the sample size is large.
6. Increases the variability.
8. When the sample comprises a large part of the population and is selected without replacement.
10. a. $\mu = 2 \quad \sigma = .7$
    b.

A,C,D = 3,1,2	$X = 2.00$	$X^2 = 4.00$
A,C,D = 3,2,2	$X = 2.33$	$X^2 = 5.43$
A,B,D = 3,1,2	$X = 2.00$	$X^2 = 4.00$
B,C,D = 1,2,2	$X = 1.67$	$X^2 = 2.79$
	8.00	16.22

c. $\mu = 8/4 = 2$ $\quad \sigma = \sqrt{[16.22 - (8^2/4)]/4} = .23$
d. $\mu = 2$ $\quad \sigma_{\bar{x}} = .7/\sqrt{3}\,[\sqrt{(4-3)/(4-1)}] = .23$
e. $\pi = 2/4 = .5$ $\quad \sigma_p = \sqrt{.5(.5)/2} = .35$
f.

A,A = Y,Y	$p = 1.0$	$p^2 = 1.00$	
A,B = Y,N	$p = .5$	$p^2 = .25$	
A,C = Y,Y	$p = 1.0$	$p^2 = 1.00$	
A,D = Y,N	$p = .5$	$p^2 = .25$	
B,A = N,Y	$p = .5$	$p^2 = .25$	
B,B = N,N	$p = 0.0$	$p^2 = 0.00$	
B,C = N,Y	$p = .5$	$p^2 = .25$	
B,D = N,N	$p = 0.0$	$p^2 = 0.00$	
C,A = Y,Y	$p = 1.0$	$p^2 = 1.00$	
C,B = Y,N	$p = .5$	$p^2 = .25$	
C,C = Y,Y	$p = 1.0$	$p^2 = 1.00$	
C,D = Y,N	$p = .5$	$p^2 = .25$	
D,A = N,Y	$p = .5$	$p^2 = .25$	
D,B = N,N	$p = 0.0$	$p^2 = 0.00$	
D,C = N,Y	$p = .5$	$p^2 = .25$	
D,D = N,N	$p = 0.0$	$p^2 = 0.00$	
	8.0	6.00	

g. $\pi = 8/16 = .5$ $\quad \sigma = \sqrt{[6 - (8^2/16)]/16} = .35$
h. $\pi = 2/4 = .5$ $\quad \sigma_p = \sqrt{.5(.5)/2} = .35$
i. .25

12. Greater variations. A larger sample size provides a smaller standard error.

14. $\pi = .5$ $\quad \sigma_p = \sqrt{.5(.5)/100}\,\sqrt{[(500 - 100)/(500 - 1)]} = .045$
$Z = (.54 - .50)/.045 = .89$ $\quad P = (.5 - .3133) = .1867$
$Z = (.46 - .50)/.045 = .89$ $\quad P = (.5 - .3133) = .1867$

$\qquad\qquad\qquad\qquad\qquad\qquad\qquad\qquad .3734$

16. a. Yes
b. $\sigma_p = \sqrt{.1(.9)/100} = .03$
$\sigma_p = \sqrt{.1(.9)/100}\,\sqrt{[(1{,}000 - 100)/(1{,}000 - 1)]} = .028$
c. It measures the proportion of the population not included in the sample, and it always reduces the standard error.

18. $\sigma_{\bar{x}} = \sigma/\sqrt{n} = .50/\sqrt{49} = .07$ $\quad .52 = (X - 7.50)/.07$ $\quad X = \$7.54$

20. $\pi = .08$ $\quad \sigma_p = \sqrt{.08(.92)/121}\,\sqrt{[(500 - 121)/(500 - 1)]} = .0215$
$Z = (.10 - .08)/.0215 = .93$ $\quad P = .3238 + .3238 = .6476$

CHAPTER 9

2. A point estimate does not provide information about how close the estimate is to the population parameter.
4. It increases the interval estimate.
6. When the sample standard deviation is used to estimate the population standard deviation, and the sample size is less than 30.
8. Both distributions are symmetrical and bell-shaped. The t distribution is less peaked at the mean and has more area in the tails than the normal

distribution. The normal curve is defined through knowledge of its mean and standard deviation. There is a family of t distributions based on the number of degrees of freedom.

10. When the population is finite and the sample size is larger than 5 percent of the population.

12. Sample size is a practical matter which is different for each unique situation. Cost and availability are important. The amount of error that can be tolerated and the desired confidence are also important.

14. If the variable can be assumed to be normally distributed, the t distribution should be used.

16. $\bar{X} \pm Z\sigma_{\bar{x}}$
    $12.8 \pm 2.33 \, (2.5)/\sqrt{25}$
    $12.8 \pm 2.33 \, (.5)$
    12.8 ± 1.165
    11.635 to 13.965 gallons

18. $\bar{X} \pm Z\sigma_{\bar{x}}$
    $23{,}400 \pm 1.645 \, (7{,}000/\sqrt{22})$
    $23{,}400 \pm 1.645 \, (1{,}492.5)$
    $23{,}400 \pm 2{,}455$
    \$20,945 to \$25,855

20. $p \pm Z\sigma_p$
    $.90 \pm 2.58\sqrt{.9(.1)/200}$
    $.90 \pm 2.58 \, (.0212)$
    $.90 \pm .055$
    .845 to .955, or 84.5% to 95.5% of the accounts receivable

22. $n = (Z\sigma/e)^2$
    $n = [1.96(3{,}000)/400]^2$
    $n = 216$

24. $p \pm Z\sigma_p$
    $.3125 \pm 1.96\sqrt{.3125(.6875)/384}$
    $.3125 \pm 1.96 \, (.02364)$
    $.3125 \pm .046$
    .2665 to .3585, or 26.7% to 35.9%

26. No! The probability of running out is approximately 50%.
    $1.88 = (p - .20)/\sqrt{.2(.8)/200}$
    $1.88 = (p - .20)/.028 = .25264$
    $(.25264)(1{,}000) = 253$ desserts

28. $p \pm Z\sigma_p$
    $.356 \pm 1.645\sqrt{.356(.644)/90}$
    $.356 \pm 1.645(.05)$
    $.356 \pm .082$
    .274 to .438, or 27.4% to 43.8%

CHAPTER 10

2. Hypothesis testing involves testing a claim about a population, whereas estimation involves estimating a population parameter.

4. Correct decision or an error.
6. It depends on the ramification of making each type of error in a particular situation. Usually, it is more important to control for Type I errors.
8. When the result of accepting the null hypothesis when it is false is not damaging or expensive.
10. Decreased.
12. Type II error.
14. $H_0: \pi = .20$ $\qquad$ $H_1: \pi > .20$
16. $H_0: \pi = .20$ $\qquad$ $c = .20 + 2.05 \sqrt{.20(.80)/100}$
    $H_1: \pi > .20$ $\qquad$ $c = .20 + 2.05(.04)$
    $\qquad\qquad\qquad\qquad c = .20 + .082$
    $\qquad\qquad\qquad\qquad c = .282$

Decision Rule: Reject H_0 if $p > .282$

18. $H_0: \mu = 24$ $\qquad$ $c = 24 \pm 1.96(.4/\sqrt{36})$
    $H_1: \mu \neq 24$ $\qquad$ $c = 24 \pm 1.96(.067)$
    $\qquad\qquad\qquad\qquad c = 24 \pm .13$
    $\qquad\qquad\qquad\qquad c = 23.87$ and 24.13

Decision Rule: Reject H_0 if $\overline{X} < 23.87$ or if $\overline{X} > 24.13$

20. $H_0: \mu = 300$ $\qquad$ $c = 300 - 1.28(50/\sqrt{49})$
    $H_1: \mu < 300$ $\qquad$ $c = 300 - 1.28(7.14)$
    $\qquad\qquad\qquad\qquad c = 300 - 9.14$
    $\qquad\qquad\qquad\qquad c = 290.86$

Decision Rule: Reject H_0 if $\overline{X} < \$290.86$

22. $H_0: \mu = 3$ $\qquad$ $c = 3 + 2.33(.3/\sqrt{64})$
    $H_1: \mu > 3$ $\qquad$ $c = 3 + 2.33(.0375)$
    $\qquad\qquad\qquad\qquad c = 3 + .087$
    $\qquad\qquad\qquad\qquad c = 3.087$

Decision Rule: Reject H_0 if $\overline{X} > 3$ minutes 5 seconds

24. $H_0: \mu = 40$ $\qquad$ $c = 40 - 1.645(4/\sqrt{35})$
    $H_1: \mu < 40$ $\qquad$ $c = 40 - 1.645(.676)$
    $\qquad\qquad\qquad\qquad c = 40 - 1.11$
    $\qquad\qquad\qquad\qquad c = 38.89$

Decision Rule: Reject H_0 if $\overline{X} > 38.89$ miles per gallon

26. $Z = (38.89 - 41)/.676 = 3.12$ $\qquad$ $P = (.5 - .4990) = .001$

CHAPTER 11

2. They have different sampling distributions which have different standard errors.
4. If the null hypothesis is true, the probability of rejecting it (making a Type I error) is .01.
6. **a.** Sampling distribution of sample means.
   b. Sampling distribution of sample proportions.
   c. Sampling distribution of differences between sample means.
   d. Sampling distribution of differences between sample proportions.
8. No! Hypothesis testing does not disprove the null hypothesis. There is always the possibility of a Type I error.

10. When the population standard deviation is unknown and the sample size is less than 30.

12. The binomial distribution.

14. No! Because the normal curve is a good approximation of the binomial distribution.

16. H_0: $\mu = 9$ $c = \mu - Zs_{\bar{x}}$
 H_1: $\mu < 9$ $c = 9 - 2.05(2/\sqrt{64})$
       $c = 9 - 2.05(.25)$
       $c = 9 - .51$
       $c = 8.49$

Decision Rule: Reject H_0 if $\overline{X} < 8.49$ years.
    Since the sample mean, 8.5, is not less than the critical value, 8.49, the null hypothesis is accepted. The employees' union claim of at least 9 years has not been rejected.

18. H_0: $\pi = .08$ $c = \pi + Z\sigma_p$
 H_1: $\pi > .08$ $c = .08 + 1.645 \sqrt{.08(.92)/200}$
       $c = .08 + 1.645(.019)$
       $c = .08 + .031$
       $c = .111$

Decision Rule: Reject H_0 if $p > .111$.
    Since the sample proportion, $20/200 = .10$, is not greater than the critical value, .111, the null hypothesis is accepted. The company should not revise its guidelines for granting mortgages.

20. H_0: $\pi_1 = \pi_2$ $c = 0 \pm 2.58\sqrt{[.654(.346)(1/300 + 1/400)]}$
 H_1: $\pi_1 \neq \pi_2$ $c = 0 \pm 2.58(.036)$
       $c = 0 \pm .0929$
       $c = .093$

Decision Rule: Reject H_0 if $(p_1 - p_2) < -.093$ or if $(p_1 - p_2) > .093$
    Since the difference in sample proportions, $(p_1 - p_2) = -.06$, is not less than the critical value, $-.093$, the null hypothesis is accepted. The marketing strategy should be used in both regions.

22. H_0: $\mu = 1.6$ $c = \mu \pm Zs_{\bar{x}}$
 H_1: $\mu \neq 1.6$ $c = 1.6 \pm 1.96(.07/\sqrt{15})$
       $c = 1.6 \pm 1.96(.018)$
       $c = 1.6 \pm .0354$

Decision Rule: Reject H_0 if $\overline{X} < 1.5646$ or if $\overline{X} > 1.6354$
    Since the sample mean, 1.5, is less than the critical value, 1.5646, the null hypothesis is rejected. The production process is producing faucets with an average diameter of 1.6 inches.

24. H_0: $\pi_1 = \pi_2$ $c = 0 \pm 2.58\sqrt{[.38(.62)(1/50 + 1/75)]}$
 H_1: $\pi_1 \neq \pi_2$ $c = 0 \pm 2.58(.089)$
       $c = 0 \pm .23$
       $c = .23$

Decision Rule: Reject H_0 if $(p_1 - p_2) < -.23$ or if $(p_1 - p_2) > .23$
    Since the difference in sample proportions, $(p_1 - p_2) = -.05$, is not less than the critical value, $-.23$, the null hypothesis is accepted. There is no difference in the proportion of men and women who would purchase the blade.

26. $H_0: \mu_1 = \mu_2$ $c = 0 - 1.645\sqrt{[(312)^2/50] + [(322)^2/50]}$

$H_1: \mu_1 < \mu_2$ $c = 0 - 1.645(63.4)$

                        $c = 0 - 104.3$

                        $c = -104.3$

Decision Rule: Reject H_0 if $(\overline{X}_1 - \overline{X}_2) < -104.3$

     Since the difference in sample means, $(\overline{X}_1 - \overline{X}_2) = -66$, is not less than the critical value, -104.3, the null hypothesis is accepted. There is no difference between the mean residential electricity usage per household last December and this December.

28. $H_0: \mu_1 = \mu_2$

$H_1: \mu_1 \neq \mu_2$

$c = 0 \pm 2.492\sqrt{[(5)^2(9-1) + (4)^2(17-1)]/(9 + 17 - 2)}\sqrt{(1/9) + (1/17)}$

$c = 0 \pm 2.492\sqrt{(19)(.17)}$

$c = 0 \pm 2.492(1.8)$

$c = 0 \pm 4.5$

Decision Rule: Reject H_0 if $(\overline{X}_1 - \overline{X}_2) < -4.5$ or if $(\overline{X}_1 - \overline{X}_2) > 4.5$

     Since the difference in sample means, $(\overline{X}_1 - \overline{X}_2) = 3$, is not less than the critical value, 4.5, the null hypothesis is accepted. There is no difference between the two training programs.

30. H_0: The payment status is independent of the proximity of debtor.

H_1: The payment status is dependent on the proximity of debtor.

$df = (c - 1)(r - 1) = (2 - 1)(3 - 1) = 2$

Decision Rule: Reject H_0 if $\chi^2 > 4.6$

$f_o - f_e$	$f_o - f_e$	$(f_o - f_e)^2$	$(f_o - f_e)^2/f_e$
$(25 - 41)$	-16	256	6.24
$(73 - 57)$	16	256	4.49
$(19 - 43)$	-24	576	13.39
$(84 - 60)$	24	576	14.40
$(85 - 45)$	40	1600	35.56
$(22 - 62)$	-40	1600	25.81
			99.89

     Since the calculated χ^2, 99.89, is greater than the critical value χ^2, 4.6, the null hypothesis is rejected. The payment status is dependent on the proximity of debtor.

32. H_0: Smoking is independent of age.

H_1: Smoking is dependent on age.

$df = (c - 1)(r - 1) = (3 - 1)(2 - 1) = 2$

Tested at the .05 significance level:

Decision Rule: Reject H_0 if $\chi^2 > 5.99$

$f_o - f_e$	$f_o - f_e$	$(f_o - f_e)^2$	$(f_o - f_e)^2/f_e$
$(10 - 24.5)$	-14.5	210.25	8.58
$(15 - 14.4)$	0.6	0.36	0.03
$(38 - 24.1)$	13.9	193.21	8.02
$(53 - 38.5)$	14.5	210.25	5.46
$(22 - 22.6)$	-0.6	0.36	0.02
$(24 - 37.9)$	-13.9	193.21	5.10
			27.21

Since the calculated χ^2, 27.21, is greater than the critical value χ^2, 5.99, the null hypothesis is rejected. Smoking is dependent on age.

CHAPTER 12

2. A scatter diagram allows an analyst to determine whether a relationship exists between two variables and to describe the kind and the degree of this relationship.
4. That no linear relationship exists between two variables.
6. Price.
8. 0.
10. No! $s_{Y.X}$ can be equal to s_Y when the mean of Y is used to predict Y.
12. H_0: $\rho = 0$
H_1: $\rho \neq 0$
Decision Rule: Reject H_0 if $t < -2.045$ or if $t > 2.045$
$t = r \sqrt{(n - 2)/(1 - r^2)}$
$t = .3\sqrt{(1000 - 2)/(1 - .3^2)}$
$t = .3(5.75)$
$t = 1.73$

Since the calculated t, 1.73, is less than the critical t, 2.045, the null hypothesis is accepted. The population coefficient is not significantly different from zero.
14. A good explanatory variable is related to the dependent variable and not highly related to any other independent variable.

16. **a.**

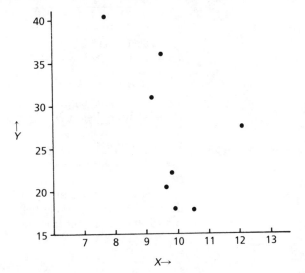

b. $r = -.52$
c. H_0: $\rho = 0$
H_1: $\rho \neq 0$
Decision Rule: Reject H_0 if $t < -3.7$ or if $t > 3.7$

$t = r\sqrt{(n - 2)/(1 - r^2)}$

$t = -.52\sqrt{(8 - 2)/(1 - (-.52)^2)}$

$t = -.52(2.87)$

$t = -1.49$

    Since the calculated t, -1.49, is not less than the critical t, -3.7, the null hypothesis is accepted. The population coefficient is not significantly different from zero.

d. $r = (-.52)^2 = .27$

18. a. $Y_R = -0.5574 + 0.0023X$

b. H_0: $\beta = 0$

H_1: $\beta \neq 0$

Tested at the .05 significance level.

Decision Rule: Reject H_0 if $t < -2.365$ or if $t > 2.365$

$t = b\sqrt{(X - \overline{X})^2}/s_{Y.X}$

$t = .0023\sqrt{108,578}/.09$

$t = .0023(329.5)/.09$

$t = 8.42$

    Since the calculated t, 8.42, is greater than the critical t, 2.365, the null hypothesis is rejected. The population regression coefficient is significantly different from zero.

c. $Y_R = -0.5574 + 0.0023(1000)$

$Y_R = -0.5574 + 2.3$

$Y_R = 1.743$

$s_F = s_{Y.X}\sqrt{1 + 1/n + (X - \overline{X})^2/\Sigma(X - \overline{X})^2}$

$s_F = .09\sqrt{1 + 1/9 + (1000 - 1092.5)^2/108,578}$

$s_F = .09\sqrt{1 + .111 + .079}$ $Y_R \pm ts_F$

$s_F = .09\sqrt{1.19}$ $1.743 \pm 1.895(.098)$

$s_F = .09(1.091)$ $1.743 \pm .186$

$s_F = .098$ \$1.56 to \$1.93

20. a. H_0: $\beta = 0$

H_1: $\beta \neq 0$

Tested at the .05 significance level.

Decision Rule: Reject H_0 if $t < -2.228$ or if $t > 2.228$

$t = b\sqrt{(X - \overline{X})^2}/s_{Y.X}$

$t = 1.731\sqrt{1718.75}/8.678$

$t = 1.731(41.46)/8.678$

$t = 8.27$

    Since the calculated t, 8.27, is greater than the critical t, 2.228, the null hypothesis is rejected. The population regression coefficient is significantly different from zero.

b. $Y_R = 8.871 + 1.731X$

c. $s_{Y.X} = 8.678$

d. $s_F = s_{Y.X}\sqrt{1 + 1/n + (X - \overline{X})^2/\Sigma(X - \overline{X})^2}$

$s_F = 8.678\sqrt{1 + 1/12 + (40 - 32.333)^2/1718.75}$

$s_F = 8.678\sqrt{1 + .083 + .034}$

$s_F = 8.678\sqrt{1.117}$

$s_F = 8.678(1.057)$

$s_F = 9.173$

    e. $Y_R \pm ts_F$
       78.111 ± 2.764(9.173)
       78.111 ± 25.353
       $52,758 to $103,464

22. a. $Y_R = -6.491 + 0.731X$
   b. $r = .896$
      There is a high positive linear relationship between advance ticket sales and the number of hot dogs purchased.
   c. $H_0: \beta = 0$ or $\rho = 0$
      $H_1: \beta \neq 0$ or $\rho \neq 0$
      Tested at the .05 significance level
      Decision Rule: Reject H_0 if $t < -2.447$ or if $t > 2.447$

$$t = b\sqrt{(X - \bar{X})^2}/s_{Y.X} \qquad \text{or} \qquad t = r\sqrt{(n-2)/(1-r^2)}$$

$$t = 0.731\sqrt{554.47}/3.488 \qquad\qquad t = .896\sqrt{(8-2)/(1-.803)}$$
$$t = 0.731(23.55)/3.488 \qquad\qquad\quad t = .896(5.52)$$
$$t = 4.94 \qquad\qquad\qquad\qquad\qquad t = 4.94$$

      Since the calculated t, 4.94, is greater than the critical t, 2.447, the null hypothesis is rejected. The population regression coefficient is significantly different from zero, or the population correlation coefficient is significantly different from zero.
   d. Hot dog sales increase on an average of 731.

   e. $s_F = s_{Y.X}\sqrt{1 + 1/n + (X - \bar{X})^2/\Sigma(X - \bar{X})^2}$
      $s_F = 3.488\sqrt{1 + 1/8 + (40 - 43.212)^2/554.75}$
      $s_F = 3.488\sqrt{1 + .125 + .0186}$ $Y_R \pm ts_F$
      $s_F = 3.488\sqrt{1.1436}$ 22.749 ± 1.943(3.729)
      $s_F = 3.488(1.069)$ 22.749 ± 7.245
      $s_F = 3.729$ 15,504 to 29,994 hot dogs

24. a. Because each variable on the primary diagonal is related to itself.
   b. Because the bottom half of a correlation matrix is the same as the top half.
   c. Variable 5 (.81) and variable 6 (.69).
   d. The $r = -.49$ shows a negative or inverse relationship.
   e. There is no relationship ($r = .19$).
   f. Models that include variables 4 and 6 or variables 2 and 5 should be best. The predictor variables in these two models are related to the dependent variable and not too highly related to each other.

CHAPTER 13

4.	1977	14.8/14.8:	100.00
	1978	15.3/14.8:	103.38
	1979	13.7/14.8:	92.57
	1980	15.9/14.8:	107.43
	1981	17.4/14.8:	117.57
	1982	19.4/14.8:	131.08

              Base year: 1977

6.

	Index, 1975 Base	Index, 1983 Base
1975	100	11.9
1976	160	19.0
1977	240	28.6
1978	400	47.6
1979	360	42.9
1980	500	59.5
1981	720	85.7
1982	600	71.4
1983	840	100.0

CHAPTER 14

2. So that the movements of the series could be examined both in measured dollars and deflated dollars; different insights into the series could result.

4. **a.** top management
   b. mid-level management
   c. first-line management

6. the period number

8. **a.** almost no seasonal effect: sales of milk or coffee
   b. sales of ski equipment
   c. soft drink sales

10. Forecast Y = TSCI

    T = 1252 − 5.4(65) assuming the historical data points were numbered 0 to 59, making June month number 65.

    T = 901

    Forecast Y = (901)(1.092)(1.02)(1.00) = 1004

    Cyclical component assumed to continue rising to level of 102 by June; irregular component assumed to be one.

12. Several years of annual data cannot be used to make short-term forecasts.

INDEX